Comic Books Incorporated

The publisher and the University of California Press
Foundation gratefully acknowledge the generous support
of the Ahmanson Foundation Endowment Fund in Humanities.

Comic Books Incorporated

How the Business of Comics
Became the Business of Hollywood

Shawna Kidman

UNIVERSITY OF CALIFORNIA PRESS

University of California Press, one of the most distinguished university presses in the United States, enriches
lives around the world by advancing scholarship in the
humanities, social sciences, and natural sciences. Its
activities are supported by the UC Press Foundation and
by philanthropic contributions from individuals and
institutions. For more information, visit www.ucpress.edu.

University of California Press
Oakland, California

Library of Congress Cataloging-in-Publication Data

Names: Kidman, Shawna, 1981– author.
Title: Comic books incorporated : how the business of
    comics became the business of Hollywood / Shawna
    Kidman.
Description: Oakland, California : University of
    California Press, [2019] | Includes bibliographical
    references and index. |
Identifiers: LCCN 2018049380 (print) | LCCN 2018052913
    (ebook) | ISBN 9780520969865 (Ebook) |
    ISBN 9780520297555 (cloth : alk. paper) |
    ISBN 9780520297562 (pbk. : alk. paper)
Subjects: LCSH: Motion pictures and comic books—
    United States—History—20th century. | Comic books,
    strips, etc.—United States—History—20th century.
Classification: LCC PN1997.85 (ebook) | LCC PN1997.85.
    K46 2019 (print) | DDC 741.5/973—dc23
LC record available at https://lccn.loc.gov/2018049380

Manufactured in the United States of America

27 26 25 24 23 22 21 20 19
10 9 8 7 6 5 4 3 2 1

For Tim

Contents

Illustrations

Acknowledgments

The research for this book would have been untenable had it not been for the high quality and comprehensive work of a dedicated community of comic book fans, critics, and historians, both amateur and professional. I have unending appreciation and gratitude for their time and energy, and for their dedication to and love for this medium. I owe special thanks to Kenneth Quattro, John Jackson Miller, and Jamie Coville for their insightful analysis and generous willingness to share and curate their discoveries of primary documents online. Open access to these materials drove much of the early research and conceptualization that went into this book. I would also like to thank Kenneth Quattro, Patrick Rosenkranz, the estate of Clay Geerdes, and Gary Groth and his team at Fantagraphics for agreeing to let me reprint their original archival research and photography in the pages of this book. Additionally, I am genuinely grateful to Paul Levitz and Gregory Noveck, my wonderful bosses at DC Comics, in what seems like a lifetime ago. Their kindness, leadership, and wisdom provided me a wonderful introduction to the world of comic books. The spark they lit started me on this path and I am so thankful it did.

I began this project in earnest nearly a decade ago as a graduate student at the University of Southern California. Early on, my thinking was deeply influenced by Tara McPherson, David James, and Sarah Banet-Weiser; clear traces of their keen wisdom and guidance are still visible to me throughout this text. My fellow graduate students Stephanie Yeung,

Kate Fortmueller, Patty Ahn, Taylor Nygaard, and Brett Service offered generous feedback and valuable critiques on early chapter drafts, and I remain grateful for their friendship and support. I benefited immensely from the straightforward advice and detailed editing of Steve Ross, who encouraged my passion for writing and helped cultivate and develop my interest in storytelling. I was also fortunate to work under the guidance of Henry Jenkins, whose fast and thorough feedback and enthusiasm in engaging thoughtfully and deeply with my arguments made me a better scholar and vastly improved the quality of this book. In his humble mentorship and genuine love of discourse and scholarship, Henry is a consummate academic and an amazing role model. Most importantly, I owe a special debt of gratitude to Ellen Seiter, from whom I got the unfaltering support that every graduate student hopes for, but few receive. She not only taught me everything I needed to know to become an academic, but showed me that it was possible to succeed in this profession as a woman and a mother, giving me the unyielding encouragement I needed to make it through my most difficult moments. In no uncertain terms, I owe my career to her mentorship.

Through their wisdom and an interminable well of excellent advice, Nitin Govil, Julia Himberg, and Tom Kemper helped make the transition from dissertation to book, and from graduate student to faculty member, as seamless and predictable as anyone could hope. Eric Hoyt also proved a tremendous help during this time. I have so appreciated and relied on his close reads of this manuscript, as well as his detailed notes, words of encouragement, advice, and friendship. The friendship and unconditional support of Cara Takakjian were also essential as I navigated the challenges of this book and of academia more generally. I am additionally very grateful to Derek Kompare and Jennifer Holt for their enthusiastic and constructive feedback on later drafts of this book. Jennifer has been giving me instrumental and sage advice since before I started graduate school, and her notes on this manuscript prompted a major breakthrough, for which I owe a special thanks.

Three years ago, I was truly blessed in finding a wonderful home at UC San Diego, where I have met incredible institutional support. I am grateful to all of my colleagues in the Department of Communication for their ongoing encouragement, and for creating an intellectual environment conducive to the kind of research and writing I love doing. I want to specifically acknowledge Stefan Tanaka, for helping me work through some of the book's historical challenges. I am also grateful to Patrick Anderson, Dan Hallin, Robert Horwitz, and Val Hartouni for their help navigating this new institution in a way that allowed me to create the space I needed to complete this project on my terms. At UC Press, I have been lucky in teaming up with Raina Polivka, a wonderful and supportive editor who has walked me through this process with kindness, understanding, and efficiency, helping me to produce my best possible work. Thanks are also due to Yi Hong Sim, graduate researcher extraordinaire, whose assistance in preparing and acquiring the tables and art for publication was professional, efficient, and incredibly helpful.

In a book about the often invisible human infrastructures that support cultural production, I want to make a special point of acknowledging the network of family members and caretakers whose labor and support have been as instrumental and indispensable to me as my academic community. In addition to the many child care facilities I used both long and short term, I relied enormously on the help of several wonderful nannies and healthcare professionals, most notably Tatyanna, Katelyn, Barbara, Brenda, and Laura; their love for and dedication to my children made my writing time far more bearable and productive. I am also grateful for the support of my family, including my mother Marla, and my in-laws Joan and, especially, Bruce, who spent weeks on end in California to help out, particularly during the early stages of this project. If it were not for this wonderful and generous group of people, I could never have completed this manuscript while raising my two amazing children.

And were it not for my two amazing children I would never have had the will, or motivation to see this project through. My sweet Cora puts so much hard work into everything she does, and inspires me daily with her focus and determination. In defiance of my innate cynicism and seriousness, she wears a smile every day and finds beauty, love, and laughter in everyone and everything she encounters. My little Wylie is proving to be just as silly, sweet, and strong-minded. His curiosity, ceaseless movement, and independence have been a source of great levity and joy this last year and a half. Both kiddos have had to share me with this book for the entirety of their lives thus far, and for that, I will remain continually grateful. Most of all, though, I am grateful to my husband, and my partner in everything, Tim. He supported me throughout this process in every way one person can support another. He believed in me, even when I did not, and has sacrificed as much as I have, if not more, so that I could pursue a career that fulfills me and a project I believe in. I could not and would not have finished this book without him. Tim, I am so thankful to you for this gift and I love you with all my heart.

Lastly, I want to acknowledge my father, Bart Feldmar, who passed away as I was completing this manuscript. My dad was a learned Jew—a true and dedicated scholar of his faith. For more than thirty years, he woke up every morning at 5 am to read, study, and debate Jewish philosophy and law. And each night and weekend he retired to a room lined from floor to ceiling with hundreds of books, each one containing his meticulous and beautifully penned margin notes. It is from him that I acquired my love of learning and my lifelong drive to seek out the kinds of answers that can help us live better lives. Finishing this book without him has been bittersweet, since I know how very proud he would have been. Dad, I wish you could be here with me to see this in print.

Introduction

An Unruly Medium

Comic books used to be one of the most popular media in America. In 1954, publishers issued one billion of them, around ninety million copies each month.[1] This meant that for every one book published in this country, there were two comic books. And each issue passed on to an average of three readers. Even more impressive than the sheer volume of units moved was the remarkable breadth of their reach. Market surveys conducted in the 1940s reported that 93 percent of kids consumed at least a dozen every month. Nearly half of adults under age thirty read them, with more female readers than male, and as many as one-third of adults over thirty read them too.[2] All told, the medium boasted seventy million fans, half of the entire U.S. population.[3] Before television irreversibly altered popular culture, Americans of all educational backgrounds, men and women alike, were reading comic books—a lot of them.

And then, the comic book market crashed. In 1955, sales plummeted by more than half, to just thirty-five million copies each month. Over the next several years, twenty-four out of twenty-nine active publishers closed their doors.[4] Just like that, comic books went from being one of the most popular forms of entertainment in America to a medium struggling for its survival. It would continue to struggle for decades, with sales steadily and persistently declining decade after decade. In 2017, sixty years after their peak popularity, fewer than eight million comic books were sold each month.[5] More concerning than sales, however, is the size of the audience. Fifty percent of all Americans used to read comic books. Industry insiders estimate that today, that audience likely stands at fewer than two million people, or one-half of one percent of the U.S. population. That readership has also been infamous for its lack of diversity—specifically, the scarcity of women, children, and people of color.[6] Comic books began as a mass medium. Today, they attract but a tiny niche audience, a demographic so narrow that the health of comic book publishing has been under sustained and significant threat.[7]

And yet, comic books are more respected today than at any time in their history and *seem* about as popular as ever. Comic book stories and characters dominate the summer box office, they fill up the fall television schedule, they pervade streaming platforms, and they consume entire aisles of the toy store. Comic properties account for five of the ten most profitable film franchises of all time, including the top slot, for the Marvel Cinematic Universe. It has earned more than $15 billion at the box office in just the last decade.[8] In 2017–2018, television networks aired more than a dozen ongoing live-action series based on comic books, with another nine appearing exclusively on major streaming services.[9] These higher-profile programs join a full roster of original animated and interactive projects, including superhero-based series for Cartoon Network and Disney XD, direct-to-video films, and hundreds of comic-book-based video, mobile, and computer games. Appealing to many different age groups and demographics, these products reach a wide swath of the population, creating a broad and lucrative market for licensed merchandise of all kinds, from action figures to T-shirts to iPhone cases. The abundance of cross-media comic book adaptations and licensed goods has strengthened the properties' trademarks, making the logos of characters like Superman some of the world's most recognizable icons.

These two sides of comic book culture—the popular and the esoteric, the mass and the niche—originate in the interdependence between publishing and licensing that has long defined this particularly American art form. Adaptations between various media (e.g., from books to films, or films to video games) are ubiquitous today, and have in fact been common throughout recorded history (e.g., from poetry to pottery, or the Bible to painting). But the aggressive, consistent, and particular way in which comic books extend into other media texts and cultural goods is unique, and perhaps the medium's most distinctive characteristic. Comic book adaptations and merchandising are never incidental, and they are rarely an afterthought. The future potential of these derivative products and their historical existence have long shaped comic books' production, distribution, consumption, interpretation, and recirculation.

Producers have so frequently adapted comic books to other media that comics are really only "books" in a very narrow sense; this cultural form has expanded beyond its physical limits to influence a wide range of consumer products and media texts. This phenomenon has created a bifurcation in comic book culture. As Henry Jenkins notes, "comics are increasingly a fringe (even an avant-garde) form of entertainment, one that appeals predominantly to college students or college-educated professionals. While few read comics, their content flows fluidly across media platforms, finding wide audiences in film, television, and computer games."[10] A fundamental tendency to spread across media has allowed comic books to be at once one thing and simultaneously its opposite. This is a structuring paradox that defines the medium.

For individuals involved in the comic book industry, this paradox creates a number of complications. Creators must produce content that will retain their most loyal fans and simultaneously appeal to the uninitiated mainstream, and while editors and employees work to navigate corporate environments, they also push on both ends of this spectrum.[11] Scholars have been similarly vexed, and comic book studies have wrestled with finding the right approach to the field. Some have used the popularity of comic book adaptations and the medium's broad diffusion through American culture as a justification for more research; intellectuals write volumes on comic books and movies, comic books and philosophy, or comic books and religion. Others reject this approach, arguing against the study of any and all "comics-related phenomena" in other media, preferring instead to treat the medium as a discrete form with firm artistic and narrative boundaries.[12] Both methods unfortunately allow an unacknowledged slippage between the immense popularity and cultural relevance of comic book *properties* and the rather limited reach of the *comic books* themselves. To focus on comic books without considering their extensions into other media is to ignore the actual context in which comics are produced, circulated, and consumed. Conversely, to treat comic book adaptations as interchangeable with comic "books" is to gloss over the complex dynamics that make comic book culture so appealing in the first place.

So what happens when the symbiotic tension between publishing and licensing and the paradox it creates moves instead to the center of our focus—not an inconvenient reality best overlooked, but the actual nucleus of comics books' power? A different picture of the medium emerges, one rooted in a complex history rife with contradiction. This book tells *that* story. It is a seventy-year saga in which comic books maneuvered a path not just between publishing and licensing, but between autonomy and dependence, and between the fringe and the mass.

While there are ups and downs and a few unexpected turns, by and large, this evolution has been relatively coherent and predictable, its historic arc bent in a particular direction: the medium's development was characterized by a gradual structural containment. Like many other new media, comic books began as a disorganized, lowbrow, and brash mass medium, reviled perhaps even more than it was loved. Over time, it transformed into a heavily exploited, corporate-financed, well-branded, and highly esteemed niche art form. In short, the entertainment industry brought an unruly medium into the fold. Examining the material details and everyday practices that bore witness to that process, this book explains how and why it happened—and how and why comics declined in popularity so profoundly while mass media took them up so aggressively.

The transformation was incremental and slow, but it helped set the stage for the relatively sudden explosion of large-scale, multimedia comic book adaptations that constitute the new core of mainstream film and television production in the twenty-first century. At the heart of this history was a process whereby multimedia producers incorporated comic book properties *and* comic book strategies into their business models. This approach, which spanned the second half of the twentieth century, was the entertainment industry's logical response to a dynamic set of political, economic, and social shifts.

This evolution toward multimedia did not occur at a distinct moment in time. Comic books moved fluidly across media from the very start, and their ability to do so was foundational to both the art form and the industry that produced it. Furthermore, at no point in history did comics develop in isolation; they were both deeply informed by and deeply impactful on the culture industries writ large. More specifically, conglomerates emerging in the middle of the twentieth century gradually adopted the operating logic employed by the comic book industry, transforming that much smaller business in the process.

It can be tempting to ascribe many emerging trends in film, television, and social media (including transmedia storytelling, niche targeting, the cultivation of fans, and the diversification of distribution channels) solely to new technologies and evolving cultural norms. Tracing the history of these strategies back through comic books, however, reveals that there was a clear industrial precedent for many contemporary strategies in entertainment. Mass media's embrace of comic books and comic book culture has been structural both to comic books and to convergence-era Hollywood. It is thus hard to imagine either comic books without contemporary multimedia production or contemporary multimedia production without comic books.

COMIC BOOKS ACROSS MEDIA

Comic book culture is probably unique in the extent to which it incorporated other forms—its strength was its ability to nimbly navigate a path forward in the shadows of other media. But popular culture's tendency to flourish and expand in margins and in-between spaces has long been a feature of the American media landscape. Since at least the 1960s, interindustry relations and business practices—galvanized by mergers and acquisitions, new technologies, changing markets, and eventually deregulation—have consistently produced the most significant forces of change in U.S. cultural production. Political economists Graham Murdock and Peter Golding noted the growth of these interconnections back in 1977, describing them as "indicative of a basic shift in the structure of the communications industry, away from the relatively simple situation of sector specific monopolies and towards something altogether more complex and far reaching." Unfortunately, they observed, communication research, academic as well as governmental, was often fragmentary; most work focused on a particular sector, a piecemeal approach that "necessarily devalues the centrality and importance of the emerging relations between sectors."[13]

Forty years later, studies that look across these sectors to examine the relationships and production apparatuses that arise *between* these media industries are more important than ever. The structural convergence that was only just becoming visible back then has continued to intensify through today. As a result, a complex web of legal, financial, and human associations across communication sectors has become a permanent fixture of the landscape. Research that works across media is thus not only historically accurate, but continues to provide important insight into contemporary culture. As industry scholar Jennifer Holt has argued, such an approach can also create "a foundation for more explicitly politicized avenues of research," particularly when questions about law and policy enter into the analysis. She and other scholars have argued that any examination of industry therefore "must view film, cable and broadcast history as integral pieces of the same puzzle, and parts of the same whole."[14] Attending to this entire puzzle can be challenging. Media histories typically seek out specificity located in the particular in addition to a broader context. If the goal is to examine film, cable, *and* broadcast, this toggling becomes virtually impossible.

Comic books are, of course, not included on Holt's short list, and they are rarely included on any other. The comic book business has always been (and remains today) small in size relative to other media industries. Low overall sales volume and an undersized workforce make it easy to overlook, despite the integral role the medium has played in shaping other contemporary mass media industries.[15] Its small size, however, makes it an ideal site for research, offering both considerable detail and an opportunity to weave in and out of a broader structural account to which it is integral.

This history works to take advantage of this unique position. First, it provides a close analysis of the everyday material relations that have constituted the medium's production, distribution, and consumption, and argues that these details are in themselves an important site of study. Second, it allows for a macro perspective by theorizing and tracking movement and change through and in between the media industries. In this respect, transmedia, which in most media literature refers to a mode of storytelling that moves across media, here refers not just to content, but to methodology as well. This book analyzes *an industry which itself traverses sectors,* offering insight into the marginal spaces between media businesses. Finally, this book takes up Jennifer Holt's call to ask the kinds of questions that facilitate more politically engaged media research and advocacy. The comic book industry offers a wonderful vantage point from which to consider important issues like media regulation, media consolidation, intellectual property law, labor struggles, distribution structures, and financial engineering, all of which are considered here.

INFRASTRUCTURE AND THE CULTURAL NARRATIVE

Despite this well-situated standpoint, a history of comic books necessarily defies easy answers and can prove as unruly as its subject. The paradox arising from the medium's fundamental split between licensing and publishing is more perplexing and multifaceted the closer you look. There is the fact that comic books are both mass and niche, popular and fringe, autonomous and dependent. But there are others binaries too—a whole laundry list of them. While many reproach comic books for their conservative themes and lack of diversity, fans have long celebrated their subversive roots and daring creativity.[16] They point to virtuoso artists like Jack Kirby, inspired writers like Alan Moore, and other creators whose distinctive voices and visions have made comic books one of the great American art forms. Critics, meanwhile, have for many decades disparaged the medium for being essentially authorless, the product of nothing more than merchandising strategy and corporate branding.[17]

Its success in that corporate sphere and its reputation as a go-to source for big-budget Hollywood projects have made the medium mainstream, a kind of playground for big shots with money to burn. And yet defenders diligently guard its outsider status, pointing to its infamous reputation as the detritus of the lives of geeks, nerds, and other outcasts. Even that which seems undeniable today—that comic books are a kind of safe investment, a reliable and permanent feature of American mass culture—has until very recently been quite uncertain. Throughout most of their history, cultural gatekeepers viewed comics as a source of risk, a volatile form with limited appeal. Depending on the context, then, comic books have brought with them wildly different connotations and associations. They have, as a result, become quite good at being, or at least seeming to be, many things at once.

While I argue that the mass/niche paradox I began with is at this medium's core, I believe that many of that paradox's derivatives, the contradictions noted here, actually represent a kind of narrative problem. Like many other beloved media, comic books bring with them a fabled past, rich with lore and intrigue. Stories have been told and retold, dramatized and sensationalized, in bedrooms and basements, in the pages of fanzines, in convention halls, on shop floors, and more recently online—in blogs, comments, and discussion boards. The panoply of voices here and the variety of narratives offered speak to the ecstatic plurality of the current moment in popular culture, when so many people have the means to express so many different views, and so many choose to write about popular culture. But along the way, moments in the medium's history have taken on epic proportions and myth-like qualities.

Much of this storytelling is very insightful, and many voices from across this vast spectrum appear in the pages of this book. In this competitive environment, however, certain narratives tend to rise to the top and gather momentum, snowballing, while competing versions fade away. And more often than not, it is the cultural story that sustains. There are brave heroes and evil villains, battles decisively won and tragically lost, and cathartic instances of retribution and reward. But most notably, within comic book culture, there tends to be a particular and familiar narrative thrust, in which the embattled but worthy comic book, with the help of fans and creators, stands up to those who would destroy it. Just like superheroes, they restore justice and order and all that is right with the world. In this version of the story, comic books are fundamentally subversive, subcultural, and resistant.

There is a different version of the story, though, one less pervasive and a little less sexy. It sees comic books as fundamentally corporate, a dominant form in a culture built to support its growth. It is a story about regulation and competition, law and labor struggles, demographics and financing. It is about distribution and the networked circulation of comics between sectors, the guidelines that determine how and for whom and for what benefits employees will work, and the flow of balance sheets that give order and meaning to everyday business decisions. These are the infrastructures of comic book culture, and by and large, they belong to and are controlled by the comic book industry.

This book is about these infrastructures. It works to recover their narratives, which sometimes get lost amidst the excitement and noise of a competing discourse. Borrowing from Brian Larkin's anthropological definition, I use the term infrastructure broadly to refer to "built networks that facilitate the flow of goods, people, or ideas and allow for their exchange over space. . . . They comprise the architecture for circulation, literally providing the undergirding of modern societies."[18] In the context of media generally, and comic books specifically, these architectures of circulation take many different forms. They can have a physical component, as does the distribution system that moves comic books back and forth across the country. They can be conceptual, as are the legal frameworks that dictate the nature of business relationships and the material working conditions those relations produce. And they can be routine based, as are the standardized, taken-for-granted practices and protocols that give shape to workplaces on an everyday, almost mechanical, basis.

It is immediately clear that these are not infrastructures in the traditional sense. They are not sewers, bridges, power grids, or underground cable networks, nor any other clearly tangible structure, since they often lack a physical presence. But raw materiality is not a requirement of infrastructure, and media is a product unlike any other. As cultural artifacts, they tend to lack physicality themselves. Even before digital technology relegated our media to the cloud, the tangible circular record album and the thirty-two-page floppy comic were rarely as important as the immaterial content they contained (nostalgic collectors may argue otherwise, but the general rule holds true). The value of media is cultural and social, not utilitarian or physical, so it makes sense that the infrastructures that support its production tend to be less material and more human. There are, of course, still factory lines and radio towers and the like, but more impactful are the ways in which everyday relationships between individuals take on particular patterns, abide by established protocols, and adhere to predetermined networks of communication.

So while research on tubes and pipes has advantages, many other less concrete systems contribute to the circulation of goods and ideas. As media scholars Lisa Parks and Nicole Starosielski note, "our current mediascapes would not exist without our current media infrastructures," wherever and in whatever form they exist.[19] Furthermore, according to information scholars Susan Leigh Star and Karen Ruhleder, it can be more useful to "ask *when*—not *what*—is an infrastructure." So an analysis of a distribution system or a legal framework may ultimately be less significant and informative when we imagine these structures simply as *things,* "stripped of use," than when we understand them as built on and through networks of actual use.[20] They exist relationally, coming into common use through their adoption by communities of practice (people who learn conventions of use as part of their membership in a group), and subsequently, they sink into the backdrop of everyday life and work.[21] They are human infrastructures, and their strength relies on human activity as well as human consent.

Unfortunately, the study of infrastructure has its downsides. Star and Geoffrey Bowker wryly note that "delving into someone else's infrastructure has about the entertainment value of reading the yellow pages of the phone book. One does not encounter the dramatic stories of battle and victory, of mystery and discovery that make for a good read."[22] This feels particularly true with regards to comic book culture, which has so many and such good dramatic stories. But there can be intrigue in infrastructure too, particularly those in focus here (or so I hope)! Of particular interest are four systems that have profoundly impacted the shape and nature of the medium.

First are the distribution networks that have historically moved comic books between publishers and consumers. They include a physical component consisting of trucks, warehouses, delivery routes, and newsstands. But my primary interest is the network of relationships among printers, distributors, wholesalers, and retailers and the standards and practices they developed over time. Second, I consider the legal frameworks that have created the conditions of creation, labor, exchange, and reception, which not only impact the medium but actually help make it legible and meaningful to those who produce and consume it.

Third comes a reader-centered system of exchange and communication dispersed across zines, message boards, conventions, and shop floors. First generated through encounters between fans, publishers, and creators, this community network was later taken up and exploited by multimedia producers building new demographics. And finally, I look at the innovative financial structures that have come to dictate corporate media in the twenty-first century. Basic changes in the way entertainment companies account for and fund their projects brought major shifts to the decision-making process in Hollywood, and that has impacted the ways producers conceive, create, and sell cultural products.

(IN)VISIBILITY AND INTENTION

A focus on these distribution, legal, corporate, and financial infrastructures ultimately generates a very different narrative about what comic books are, how they came to be, and why they are meaningful in contemporary culture. By emphasizing these elements, then, this history offers a structural revision—a reframing of the prevailing historical account of comic books that reveals a political and economic dimension often lost in the conversation. The impulse here is not to seek out the true story. It is rather to understand how truth or consensus forms in history-telling to begin with. *Why have certain narratives prevailed over others? Why do cultural forces tend to overshadow industrial ones? And why do infrastructures so often become invisible?* This last question has been particularly salient within critical media, technology, and infrastructure studies, and scholars have noted that invisibility turns out to be a fundamental and defining characteristic of infrastructure.[23] Media historian Lisa Gitelman argues that the success of a new medium in fact depends on users' inattention or blindness to its infrastructure. A process of adoption, which ends in imperceptibility, in fact defines most media: each form is really a mixture of technological structures and the social protocols that develop around them.[24]

And yet, our everyday experience with infrastructure is marked by arresting visibility as well, most conspicuously when systems neglect a particular use or population (e.g., a stairway for the person who uses a wheelchair) or break down entirely (e.g., the collapse of a bridge).[25] As Larkin has observed, there are other instances of visibility too, specifically when infrastructures are "deployed in particular circulatory regimes to establish sets of effects." This occurs when an infrastructure—perhaps a new technology or a project that comes out of a political win—remains visible to certain populations for its distinct symbolic value (e.g., the Panama Canal or the Hoover Dam). Considering this, Larkin proposes, "the point is not to assert [visibility or invisibility] as an inherent condition of infrastructures but to examine how (in)visibility is mobilized and why."

Along these lines, we can observe in the American media landscape a seemingly pervasive erasure of infrastructure that attributes the architecture of communication systems to individual human actors or cultural forces. These influences perhaps seem more benevolent or appealing than things like distribution networks, legal requirements, and organizational bureaucracy. As such, these latter systems tend to disappear and often remain invisible—until, that is, they become useful as *visible* infrastructures. Take, for example, CBS's decision in 2017 to briefly black out its programming to Dish TV subscribers; the move intentionally angered audiences by denying them an important football game on Thanksgiving. It was an attempt to put pressure on the satellite service during a tough negotiation.[26] Viewers generally do not care about television distribution or the carriage fees that make it possible. Moreover, the media industries have no interest in asking them to care, except of course when public pressure might benefit their bottom line, as it did then. So to the list of questions posed here, I add these: *Why, in particular moments and in particular forms, do some media infrastructures suddenly materialize? And in general, how is the (in)visibility of media infrastructures mobilized, and why?*

These questions are not rhetorical. The general erasure of infrastructure within comic book culture, as well as its occasional reappearance, served a particular goal. It helped generally to obscure and, when necessary, bolster sources of power, namely big players in the media industries. So while we may know that there is no cabal of executives conspiring in a boardroom to decide what culture will look like, we can understand that those with the most power (via financial capital, political influence, and social standing) have the greatest ability to push a medium toward their own interests. Reflecting on the development of the internet, Christian Sandvig has observed the extent to which the web was "willfully bent" to reflect particular (corporate) visions of the technology's noblest purpose and best use. As a result, he argues, media infrastructures like the internet usually "do not have the essential characteristics that are often attributed to them." Rather, these systems form gradually, shaped by the "purposeful decisions" of individuals and organizations with particular intentions and particular "ideas about what content and which audiences are valuable and indeed how culture ought to work."[27]

In other words, the intentions and interests of powerful players become embedded within the architecture or infrastructure of most media and communication systems, comic books included. In obscuring or ignoring those infrastructures, we thus obscure and ignore the powers that shape them. Raymond Williams once wrote that "society has a specific organization, a specific structure, and that the principles of this organization and structure can be seen as directly related to certain social intentions, intentions by which we define the society."[28] In this, he reminds us not only to examine, carefully and closely, these specific structures and organizations, and to understand the logic by which they operate, but also to remember that they exist and come into being, not simply by chance, but by intention. In this historical analysis of the infrastructures that support comic book culture, the intentions that shaped them gradually come into focus, and the everyday workings of the industry and the medium's course of development become more clear and predictable. We can see what the essential characteristics of the medium became and how they reflected the interests and purpose of certain powerful players.

There were, nonetheless, constraints on that process. Industry does not function in a vacuum, nor does infrastructure act upon itself. As many have noted, including Raymond Williams, infrastructural relations of production may set limits and exert pressures, but "they neither wholly control nor wholly predict the outcome of complex activity within or at these limits, and under or against these pressures."[29] For this reason, creators, workers, fans, and the general public remain an important part of this story.

Their presence, however, was not in the end potent enough to make comic books a particularly subversive medium. The introduction of corporate control in both publishing and licensing situated the industry at the intersections between film, television, and consumer goods. Once there, it benefited from favorable regulatory and legal regimes, strong financial backing, and also, for wholly unrelated reasons, the support of readers who happened to occupy high social positions. These conditions imbued the comic book industry with power, and as it grew, that power had an increasingly constraining influence. Over time, it marginalized and/or moderated the medium's more rebellious impulses, reemphasizing a conservative core. To the extent that comic book culture maintained independent or subversive elements, these remnants and outgrowths, more often than not, helped to bolster the medium's most powerful players. This last tendency—of the medium's resistant side to shore up its dominant side—contributes further to comic books' paradoxical nature; the complex cultural negotiations this dynamic entails make up much of the historical analysis that follows.

FROM NEWSSTANDS TO MULTIPLEXES

Focusing on industrial infrastructure and intersections with other media, this book moves through four critical moments in the history of comic books, ordered roughly chronologically. Taken together, these four case studies portray the evolution of the medium as driven largely by intentional—although not always conscious—strategic thinking by corporate actors. The first of these historical turning points begins with public controversy in the late 1940s and the market crash of the 1950s, events that ultimately strengthened publishing just before the commencement of mass media conglomeration. The story continues through the rise of comic book auteurism and fandom in the 1960s, developments that shaped corporate approaches to the management of intellectual properties. Next comes the reorganization of distribution networks in the 1970s and 1980s, a strategy that modeled niche targeting techniques and enabled the resurrection of comics in quality media of the 1990s. And the history ends in the mid-2000s, when new financial practices opened the door to an explosion of comic book adaptations in mainstream media.

While the historical accounts of these four moments comprise a unified narrative about the comic book industry over the course of eighty years, they also function as four separate case studies. Each revolves around a different topic and takes as its focus a different structural element: respectively, distribution, copyright law, human networks, and financing. Effectively addressing these elements—each of which has both a history that precedes its role in the comic book industry and a story that continues through today—requires a little bit of jumping around. So whenever possible, I include subject headings that distinguish between the different timeframes.

Offering periodizations is always a tricky matter. Events do not generally occur in annual increments, and the patterns, tendencies, and phenomena that constitute this or that period do not shift abruptly, but rather gradually decline as new ones gradually phase in. As such, the eras I define throughout this history should be understood as inherently porous. Along these lines, the dates speckled throughout the book do not purport to constitute a detailed timeline of events. Rather, they are meant to provide context and to locate the reader within a complex and somewhat irregular chronology.

To provide additional clarification around timelines, chapter 1 gives a brief historical overview, intended to situate the larger narrative within its proper time and place. It is therefore best read before the four case studies that follow. Quick histories of this sort open many books about comics (as well as film, television, and other media). This one is different in a few notable ways. It offers (1) a reperiodization of comic book history, calibrated around licensing instead of publishing; (2) a focus on industry; and (3) an insistence on the form's transmedial nature. Of interest throughout is the process by which the comic book industry gradually enmeshed itself into multimedia production practices, offering up its core elements as drivers of strategic growth throughout the entertainment industry. Pointing to strength of copyright, ease of licensing, and corporate synergistic appeal, it explains why this particular medium was so disposed to emerging trends and how it laid the foundation for media in the digital era. This synopsis works to provide a particular kind of historical context (more political-economic than social-cultural) and a unique historical perspective both for readers who know nothing about comic books and for fans who know everything about them.

From this distinctive vantage point, the first major upheaval in the medium's history takes on a decidedly new significance. In 1954, a morality crusade against comic books (claiming that they posed a threat to the nation's youth) created a public relations crisis for the medium. The industry responded swiftly and decisively, creating a strict code of censorship. But a year later, the comic book market crashed anyway; sales declined rapidly, significantly, and permanently. Most histories attribute the latter incident, an industrial failure, to the former, a social crisis. The assumption is that negative attention from the controversy, followed by misguided changes in content, devalued the medium. Examining the political and economic context of the 1950s, chapter 2 shows that the industry was facing many serious challenges that had nothing to do with content or censorship. Furthermore, self-regulation, implemented for the ostensible purpose of self-censorship, actually helped the industry reorganize and stabilize. Distribution turns out to have been the lynchpin in this transformation. It was the deterioration of distribution networks that had put the industry's overall health at risk, and it was the re-disciplining of these networks that put the business back on firm footing. Through this self-regulation, major publishers gained a competitive edge that they carried into the next era of history, an era they now had the ability to dictate.

With a focus on the 1960s and 1970s, chapter 3 looks at the evolution of the business after the fallout of the 1954 crisis. In order to thrive in tough times, the comic book industry embraced a new business model. Major publishers came under the purview of emerging media conglomerates, and publishing became subservient to licensing. The same era saw the burgeoning of a fan community and the closely related growth of comic book auteurism. At the heart of these simultaneous shifts lay an increasingly troubling paradox. While the rise of fandom afforded more respect to pop culture and its creators, licensing—in relying on corporate-owned intellectual properties and the laws that protected them—tended to exploit these same creators. This uncomfortable tension played out dramatically in the legal struggle of Jerry Siegel and Joe Shuster to win back the rights to Superman, a character they had invented. With a focus on their complicated tale, this chapter examines the public discourse that praised authors alongside the internal business practices that rewarded owners. Despite ostensible contradictions, both forces were rooted in our deeply entrenched copyright regime. And they both served to bolster corporate interests as the business embarked on its next internal reorganization and push toward multimedia.

In the 1970s and 1980s, the medium's readership narrowed significantly, as comic books moved off of newsstands and into specialty retail stores. Educated adult male fans flocked to these comic shops, forming a loyal and discerning fan community. Chapter 4 considers how this rather distinct demographic transformed into a highly valuable subculture that brought both cultural legitimation and new licensing opportunities to the medium. Structural changes in the media industries resulting from deregulation had intensified the need for quality niche audiences and quality niche media that might appeal to them. A well-educated, culturally savvy, male cadre of industry insiders took this opportunity to exploit comic books, for which they had personal affinities, for a wider audience of consumers. This was especially evident in the success of HBO's 1989 horror anthology series *Tales from the Crypt,* based on a title from the once-scorned publisher EC Comics. The network was able to leverage the show's cult audience and the community network that supported it to rebrand itself as a home for quality television. In the process, it helped transform EC from an emblem of offensiveness into a marker of good taste in less than a generation. Even though the comic book audience had shrunk, its outsized influence helped reopen the door to a wider cultural embrace; the medium was poised for an expansion into products with more mass appeal, most notably the tentpole franchise film.

It took quite a bit longer, though, for mainstream film to turn to comic books as a reliable source of material. For another decade, industry insiders remained reluctant to put major comic book films into production. They associated the genre with a new paradigm in Hollywood that favored large-scale, conglomerate-friendly, multimedia production, and they resisted its encroachment. They also believed that comic book films were not worth the risk their big budgets entailed. Chapter 5 examines how the material conditions of the business in the 1990s helped validate this negative narrative, holding up the development of comic book films, until a new economic paradigm emerged, around 2001, and rather swiftly reversed it. This evolution in Hollywood's financial structure began with speculative buying on the fringes of the film business, and comic book properties were deeply entangled in it from the start. Ultimately, an influx of private capital in film financing, in conjunction with other changes in the business, fundamentally changed the economics of the comic book film. The genre transformed from a highly risky investment into one of the business's safest bets. This shift helped Marvel establish itself as a mini film studio in 2005 and permanently changed the industry narrative about what kinds of projects executives and producers should pursue. The comic book film proceeded to take over franchise film production all over Hollywood and has dominated the cinematic landscape ever since, shoring up comic book publishing in the process.

Notably, a focus on the United States limits the scope of this history. For almost all of the seven decades covered in these pages, the American comic book industry was a primarily domestic business. While publishers did distribute some comics to foreign countries, international sales remained a minor consideration. A number of factors are responsible for this restraint on the industry's international growth, including periodic restrictions around the world on imported comic books from the United States and, more importantly, the vibrancy of regional comic book cultures, particularly in east Asia (where manga was a much larger cultural force than comics were in the U.S.) and in Europe (where *bande dessinée* in France and Belgium and comic books in England largely satisfied local demand). While a comparative or genuinely transnational analysis of global comic book industries would be of great value, such an investigation is outside the scope of this book.

The trends this book does cover, however, are increasingly global in nature. As multimedia production transforms into a transnational affair conducted back-and-forth across various borders (of nations and currencies, of media and industries) by multinational corporations, the local infrastructures that support these operations expand, overlap, and sometimes collide. Progressing into the future of media industry research, it will be ever more incumbent upon scholars to seriously consider these intersections and to understand what happens in the margins between these corporations, industries, and nations. This kind of agenda will make understanding media infrastructure more important, not less, since it is these often hidden or obscured networks, frameworks, and organizational structures that make these transmedial, transindustrial, and transnational relations possible.

1

Incorporating Comics

A Brief Transmedia History of the
U.S. Comic Book Industry

There are many histories of the American comic book in print. They tell
both truth and lore, often detailing the backstories of fans' favorite characters and creators. This is not one of those histories, in three important
ways. First, it offers a reperiodization. Most popular accounts look to
the Golden, Silver, and Bronze Ages to break down the development of
the comic book. Each of these eras refers to a stage in the evolution
of the superhero, many of which were conceived and developed during
the Golden Age of the 1940s. They were resurrected and reconceived for
a more established readership during the Silver Age of the late 1950s and
1960s. And they were reimagined as more sophisticated and relevant
during the Bronze Age of the 1970s and early 1980s. While this framework allows for flexibility, as well as the addition of new ages (critics
have proposed Iron, Dark, and Modern Ages too), its underlying emphasis on superheroes sidelines the medium's many other notable genres and
formats.[1]

Moreover, its preoccupation with comic book *content* sometimes
comes at the expense of good history. This tends to happen when an
event that was important to readers, workers, or publishers failed to
directly impact the evolution of the superhero and, as such, gets relegated as a footnote of this framework (e.g., the 1954 market crash, the
1967 purchase of DC Comics, or the 1978 release of the *Superman*
movie). To remedy this, historians have offered a number of alternative

periodizations,[2] but none has caught on quite yet. So I offer one more here, in the hope that it may be more relevant in the current moment, when the comic book adaptation is generally outshining the comic book itself. Pegged to the development of licensing instead of publishing, this framework also consists of three major periods: an establishing era (1933–1954), a phase of crisis and experimentation (1955–1988), and an age of institutionalization (1989–2010). In deemphasizing comic book content and its creative evolution, this periodization has the benefit of an unencumbered look at other facets of comic book development.

That brings us to a second distinguishing feature: this brief history takes *industry* as its focus. In so doing, it deemphasizes questions about aesthetics, narratives, and creators, which are already the focus of many excellent books about comics.[3] These cultural histories excel at showing how readers interpreted meanings, appropriated texts, and navigated this mass medium in ways that have enriched their lives and enhanced the social and cultural impact of the comic books themselves. They also, unfortunately, often minimize the importance of industry actions, by either ignoring the business of comic books entirely or giving it only a minor role. This history shifts the comic book industry from the margins of the narrative to its center. It thus offers a different perspective, one motivated by questions of power and rooted in institutional, economic, and political context. These concerns come from a long tradition of media and communication scholarship that has made the culture industries a critical focus of study. A substantial body of work ranging from critical theorists like Theodor Adorno to political economists like Herb Schiller reminds us of the tremendous influence media-makers can have on all facets of life, from presidential elections to American ideological values to basic social patterns. When we restrict ourselves to examining only the end use of media (point of consumption, audience experience, the text itself) and not development, production, and distribution, this power can fade from view. With that in mind, this history examines the comic book industry—including the workers, the companies, the everyday business practices, the organizational rules, etc.—as a determining influence on both the comic books themselves and the society that consumes them.

Finally, this account positions comic books as being, fundamentally and quintessentially, a transmedial form. Henry Jenkins has defined a *transmedia* story as any that "unfolds across multiple media platforms, with each new text making a distinctive and valuable contribution to the whole."[4] Comic book stories tend to fit this category exceedingly well, to which anyone who has been to a movie theater or turned on a television in the last twenty years can easily attest. Characters born in comics often leap off the page to appear in not only film and television but video games, toys, novels, and even fine art. There can be no doubt, then, that comic books adapt well across media. Conventional wisdom, however, largely identifies this adaptability across media platforms as a relatively new phenomenon. And many fans assume that comic book characters used to live primarily in the pages of the comic books themselves. Nothing could be further from the truth: comic books and comic book characters have been groomed for adaptation almost from their inception.

Despite this, some fans and scholars have historically been (perhaps overly) invested in the boundaries that define comic books as comic books; whether big movie studios choose to adapt them or not, the thesis goes, the medium-specific qualities of the form are paramount.[5] *Medium specificity* is a condition in which artwork is essentially constituted by the characteristic qualities of the raw material of its form. This idea dictates that any text in any form should, ideally, respond to the specific physical elements of that form and fulfill that medium's representational potential. Under this guiding principle, a character or story created to shine in a comic book—embodied by both the flatness of the page and the brightness of the color, by the borders of the panels and the limitations of the physical pages—could hardly be the best subject of a film, which boasts a vastly different (though not necessarily superior) set of affordances.

Instead of critiquing the nature of transmedial adaptations, this history celebrates them and acknowledges their significance. More specifically, it highlights the extent to which comic books have always functioned as a springboard for transmedia. Never bound by its printed form, this medium and the stories it has generated have long lived between and across other media. Far from limiting their development, this itinerant existence has been the core of comic books' power and creativity. (For a complete list of comic book adaptations in film and television, from 1940 to 2010, see Appendix A.)

COPYRIGHTABILITY

Before beginning this industrial transmedia history, it is important to establish exactly *how* and *why* the media industries at large have considered comic book stories so ripe for transmedia exploitation. Scholars have offered a variety of explanations, particularly as adaptations become ever more common in the digital era. Jared Gardener, for example, points to the development of home video and digital viewing technologies that allow film audiences to consume texts in the same way comic book fans read comics. That is, they go at their own speed and stop, rewind, start over, zoom in, and freeze frame as they please, analyzing the story in a far more layered and complex fashion. As a result, Gardner argues, the two media have moved closer together, pursuing similar visual and story elements (like the Easter egg) that celebrate these shared possibilities.[6] While Gardner's observation here, among explanations from many other scholars,[7] is insightful, the long history of comic books' transmediality and the extent to which it was so often driven by industrial as opposed to creative needs points in a different direction. The medium's regulatory, legal, and financial history offers an abundance of reasons as to why corporate multimedia producers have been adapting comic books for so many decades.

One factor in particular has played a determining role in comic books' tendency to cross between media: copyrightability. Comic book characters are among the easiest properties to copyright and trademark, a characteristic that makes them attractive to licensors as well as corporations interested in exploiting synergies. As legal scholar Leslie Kurtz has explained, this is largely due to their pictorial nature, which makes them less abstract and, accordingly, easier to protect against copyright infringement than most literary characters; visuality makes the ideas behind comic books seem more concrete and well-defined. This becomes especially clear in the context of the courtroom, where images have often been the subject of seemingly more objective side-by-side comparisons. A similarity in appearance between two images has on many occasions been enough, all on its own, to constitute infringement (for an early and very formative example of this principle in action, see figures 1 and 2); written descriptions are far less effective in this regard. That cartoon and comic book characters can often be perceived in their entirety through a single vivid mental image only furthers this legal protection, since courts can look to an isolated text, or a single page even, to completely define a distinguishable look, personality, and manner of movement.[8]

This inherent legal strength only improved over time. Case law in the 1950s established that characters who were flatter, consistent, memorable, and easily removed from the story or context in which they were created ultimately received more protection than more complex and fully human characters.[9] Many of today's most beloved comic book characters are of course profoundly human and their stories deeply complex. In the 1930s

EXHIBIT I

ACTION COMICS

WONDER COMICS

November 1938, page 8

May 1939, page 4

A.

June 1938, page 1

May 1939, page 1

B.

May 1939, page 1

March 1939, page 12

May 1939, page 13

C.

December 1938, page 5

May 1939, page 9

D.

FIGURES 1 AND 2. Exhibit submitted with the affidavit of Jack Liebowitz in *Detective Comics v. Bruns Publications* (1939). These illustrations provided very compelling visual evidence that Bruns's *Wonder Comics* had infringed on Detective Comics' *Action Comics*. Detective Comics ultimately prevailed in the lawsuit, and Superman, the star of *Action Comics*, went on to be one of the most successful and best-protected characters in history. Images Courtesy of Wayne Smith and Ken Quattro.

January 1939, page 9   May 1939, page 8

E.

July 1938, page 2   May 1939, page 13

F.

June 1938, page 1   May 1939, page 9

G.

December 1938, page 1   May 1939, page 1

H.

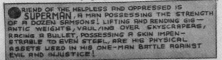

and 1940s, however, publishers were motivated largely by the need to find visually striking and communicative cover art that would attract returning child-age readers. Unpredictable distribution channels, irregular publishing schedules, and too much competition on overcrowded newsstands meant that customers were not expected to follow titles on a regular basis. But a bright cover with a recognizable protagonist, even in the absence of a strong story within the pages of the comic, could hope to build an audience anyway. The result of this strategy in comic books—and it was similar in other media targeted at kids—was characters defined by simple and vibrant visuality. Strong story and character were an afterthought. These forms reached their young audience through consistent and memorable images that could be caught by just a glance, simple stories that did not rely on a continuing or sequential narrative, and characters who could cross over into multiple titles (or media) should they prove popular.

The resulting fixedness of comic book heroes like Superman has long been remarked upon. Back in 1962, Umberto Eco wrote the now infamous essay "The Myth of Superman," in which he describes the character as archetypal and immutable, "aesthetically and commercially deprived of the possibility of development."[10] Not only did this flatness, typical of so many comic book characters, give the medium strong copyright protection, but their intensely visual nature also gave them strong trademark protection.[11] That these characters could often be roughly attributed to individual, living, breathing creators additionally satisfied the rhetorical needs of copyright law and thus further strengthened their protections in court. Chapter 3 explores this particular requirement of the law, as well as its substantial impact on the industry's creative laborers. In short, by the distinctiveness of copyright and trademark law, the complementary pressures of early retail sales at newsstands, and their fundamental visuality, comic books became a medium that naturally produced very reliable intellectual properties. This essential characteristic of the form would go on to shape the entirety of its future by pushing comic books toward licensing opportunities from the very start.

GILDED AGE (1933–1955):
THE ESTABLISHING ERA OF LICENSING

In 1933, a print salesman named Max C. Gaines issued the first modern comic book to newsstands. It was titled *Famous Funnies,* and, like most of the comic books that followed over the next few years, it consisted entirely of reprints from newspaper comic strips. At only ten cents a copy, these early comic books sold well to children, who were still just emerging as a distinct demographic to producers of mass media and consumer goods. The Great Depression was at its height, times were tough, comic books were affordable, and unlike radio and film, they constituted a possession—one that could be traded, reread, and cherished. Still, since reprints were popular enough, it took until the late 1930s for publishers to actively seek out original content. Among the first who did were Harry Donenfeld and Jack Liebowitz, who ran the publishing house National Allied Publications (later known as National Comics, and then DC Comics, after one of its first titles, *Detective Comics*) along with a distribution operation called Independent News Company. In 1938, they released *Action Comics* #1, and on the cover was a character called Superman (see figure 3). Like most other comics at the time, the issue was thirty-two pages long and consisted of a number of different stories featuring different characters. The Superman piece was just thirteen pages, but boosted by the cover image—vivid, dynamic, and in its clarity and simplicity already somehow iconic—it became a smash with kids, who began requesting follow-ups immediately. Word of the character's popularity and demands for more copies worked their way up through the distribution chain, from newsstand retailers, to wholesalers, and eventually to publishers, who learned of it at some point that summer.[12]

The phenomenal and quite immediate success of Superman had three dramatic and very significant results. First, it helped establish the industry as an industry. A few publishers had been active in this budding medium in the mid-thirties, most notably National, Dell, and Eastern Color. All three companies had grown out of other businesses, and none ever worked exclusively in comic book publishing. The composition of the industry changed quickly after Superman. The success of *Action Comics* turned comic books from an experimental form, of interest to companies with established ventures in printing or distribution, into a financially viable medium that could stand on its own. New publishers, most of which dealt exclusively in publishing and used original content (if not always the most original characters and stories), started popping up almost immediately. Archie, Fox, Harvey, Timely (later Atlas, then Marvel), and Quality all opened their doors in 1939.[13]

Second, Superman's rise in popularity triggered a pattern of genre fads that would dictate the creative development of the medium for the next thirty years. As the first modern American superhero, the character launched a genre that seemed to capture the zeitgeist of a nation on the verge of World War II. Courageous, noble, and aggressively patriotic,

FIGURE 3. Although the comic book is dated June 1938, *Action Comics #1* debuted earlier that spring. The center of a long and costly legal battle, this eye-catching cover helped turn Superman into National's biggest star. Interestingly, the character continued to share *Action Comics* with other heroes like Pep Morgan and Tex Thompson for several years and did not get his own title, *Superman*, until June of 1939. Photo from the Hulton Archive.

superheroes like Wonder Woman, Captain Marvel, and Captain America fought crime on the home front and axis forces overseas, promising an Allied victory that, for years, remained elusive.[14] So it comes as little surprise that as the war came to an end, so did superheroes. There were at least forty superhero titles in print in 1944, but that number started dropping as soon as peace came in 1945, and there were only three remaining—Batman, Superman, and Wonder Woman—by 1952.[15]

The end of this particular genre, however, was only the beginning of a long procession of replacement genres. First to come, in 1946, were teen comics, popularized by Archie, and funny animals, propelled by the medium's youngest readers.[16] Next were the more mature genres, beginning with crime in 1948, followed by romance in 1949, and horror in 1951.[17] The pattern was almost always the same: a handful of comics in the new genre would appear, sell extraordinarily well, and inspire a flood of imitators, creating a glut in the market and thus triggering a gradual decline. The first genre to rise and fall, superheroes enjoyed a relatively long period of popularity, but ultimately fell even harder, disappearing from newsstands more completely than other failed genres would after it. These characters nonetheless maintain a strong hold on the popular imagination, and decades later, we still strongly associate this time with classic superheroes. Their legacy, however, and Superman's in particular, was less about dominating the entire era than it was about establishing comic books as a fad-based medium. Content in the 1940s and 1950s was amazingly diverse, and characterized primarily by the ebb and flow of various genres.

The third result of Superman's immediate popularity, and perhaps the most important for this history, was the way the character set off a licensing bonanza. After his debut in comic books in 1938, Superman appeared almost immediately in a syndicated newspaper strip (which ran from 1939 to 1966) and, soon after, a nationally broadcast radio series (1940–1951). The superhero also sparked a bidding war between film studios and soon became the star of an Oscar-nominated series of Max Fleischer cartoons (1941–1942), and later the subject of two film serials for Columbia Pictures, one in 1948 and one in 1950; by some accounts, the former was the most profitable film serial of all time.[18] There were also countless licensed products, and a high-profile nationally syndicated television series (1952–1958). Notably, behind these many adaptations and licensed products were the roots of a network of relationships between Hollywood and comic book publishing. This little industry was quietly and strategically embedding itself within a still-forming mass media logic that was just beginning to emerge out of budding mass media organizations.

Comic books were not the only old medium seeking a home in this new ecosystem, which by the mid-1950s revolved around the new medium of television. Licensing had played an important role on TV from its start in the late 1940s, as characters that originated in film, radio, comic books, and pulps quickly migrated over to satisfy content-hungry advertisers and networks. Among the many property owners to carve out space within this burgeoning industry was Robert Maxwell, who, like other early licensors, was able to exercise considerable control over the series he produced.[19] Maxwell had gotten his start in New York in the 1940s, when National Comics put him in charge of merchandising Superman. He was responsible for producing the character's very popular radio series, and he started a company, Superman Inc., to organize his licensing activities. In 1951, Maxwell came to Hollywood for *The Adventures of Superman* television series; he wrote the pilot episode himself and eventually handed the reins to Whitney Ellsworth, a former editorial director at National who had also turned into a Hollywood producer.[20] In prompting and supporting these efforts, Superman was helping lay the groundwork of a budding licensing empire.

Although no other character would undergo quite his level of exploitation, many popular characters of the 1940s did follow in Superman's footsteps. The decade saw nearly a dozen get their own radio programs or film serials, the latter produced largely by Columbia and Republic, and exhibited as matinees targeting kids. Among these characters were superheroes like Batman and Captain Marvel, but as other comic book genres grew in popularity, like westerns and jungle adventures, studios licensed those stories as well. For the most part, these early adaptations have failed to occupy a significant space in American cultural memory, perhaps because they screened to a pre-baby-boomer audience, or perhaps because they simply failed to make an impression.

There can be no doubt, though, that *industrially* these early licensing opportunities had a lasting impact, and reinforced the crucial role that intellectual property law was already playing in the medium's formation. Almost as soon as National began selling Superman as a media property, the publisher began protecting its copyright in court. The company brought its first infringement suit in 1939, and won, a victory that forced Bruns Publications to cancel its title *Wonder Comics*, starring the rather derivative Wonder Man (see figure 1 and figure 2).[21] The immediate objective of cases like this was to prevent other publishers, like Bruns and later Fawcett, from creating copycat superheroes that bore too strong a resemblance to Superman, thereby giving National a monopoly on the popular genre. The long-term and perhaps more significant effect, however, was to shore up the character's copyright and trademark claims, strengthening its legal protections for years to come. Since popularity and uniqueness within the market bolster intellectual property claims, early wins like this tend to beget bigger ones later on. So while Superman and other early characters like him represented important and lasting cultural contributions, they were always industrial products as well, shaped dramatically by publishers' attempts to achieve enduring commercial viability.

The logic of comic book licensing and character protection was at play in other spaces as well. One of National's biggest competitors was Dell, which built its business around exclusive licenses to publish comics based on a variety of copyrighted characters from film and other media. The company negotiated a deal with Disney first, in 1940, but soon also secured the rights to titles from Warner Bros. and MGM, and eventually got sole access to popular characters like Popeye and the Lone Ranger.[22] By the early 1950s, Dell was publishing seventy different comic book titles at a combined circulation of more than two hundred forty million copies a year.[23] Issues of particularly popular ones such as *Walt Disney Comics* could often sell three million per issue, with lesser performing comics regularly selling over one million.[24]

Though Dell proved to be the market champion through much of the 1940s and 1950s, it was not alone in achieving staggering sales numbers. Between 1946 and 1949, the market exploded, making comic book publishing an enormously attractive business for young entrepreneurs, who found extremely low financial and infrastructural barriers to entry. The actual creative work for an entire comic, including the artwork and the copyright to all characters, cost less than $1,000. Print runs started at three hundred thousand issues and, at less than two cents a copy, would have cost $6,000. A comic could thus be considered a success if it eventually sold only half of its issues. With publishers earning five to six cents on each comic sold (coming out to around $8,000), the issue broke even, with any advertising fees collected considered an added bonus.[25]

This was not a high sales bar, and not all of this money had to be paid up front. Once a publisher got a deal with one of fourteen national distributors, that firm would subsidize a portion of the money in advance. Distributors also arranged the shipment of comics from the printers to the wholesalers (of which there were typically two to three per American town), tracked sales, and took care of all returns. They also provided promotional materials and sent representatives to individual towns to teach delivery men how to sell to newsstand retailers and how to display items properly. [26] In short, distributors not only provided access to physical infrastructure (trucks, warehouses, newsstands, etc.), but took care of the procedural know-how the business required—the nuts and bolts. Taking responsibility for these kinds of activities was common practice throughout media distribution. This sector managed physical circulation through human operations—relationship-building, deal-making, and on-site-training, for instance, convincing a retailer to feature a specific product prominently and showing him how to do so most effectively.[27] Accordingly, entrepreneurial individuals who lacked experience but nonetheless had access to writers and artists could quickly assemble a book, make a deal with a distributor, and turn a profit in less than a few months. And the commonness of new genre fads meant that new publishers could introduce a new title in a new genre and have a chance at a genuine hit.

Unfortunately, the benefits of easy distribution turned out to be short-lived. The fast growth this system spurred in the late 1940s caught up with the industry by the early 1950s and began causing serious problems. Most notably, the rise of television between 1949 and 1954 was corroding the audience for comic books, while simultaneously, struggles in the supply chain (between publishers, distributors, and retailers) were creating a surplus of product. Then, in the spring of 1954, a public relations crisis brought more distress. It was the crest of a third wave of public outcry over the medium's allegedly lurid content and its potential threat to young readers. On its own, this comic book scare would have been unlikely to leave a lasting impression on the medium. But the timing—it coincided with the McCarthy hearings in the U.S. Senate—turned the controversy into a lightning rod, and the struggle would later be seen as representative of cultural struggles in Cold War America. More importantly, it put additional pressure on distributors and wholesalers and intensified the existing discrepancy between decreasing demand and increasing supply. The result was a crash in the market. Chapter 2 provides an in-depth analysis of this era and of the causes and consequences of both the public controversy and the market crash. Comics' Gilded Age ultimately came to an end with plummeting sales, waning audience interest, and a dramatic decline in public support. Companies like Dell, National, and Archie had built up strength and were well positioned to face these challenges, but their competitors, by and large, were not so lucky.

CRISIS AND EXPERIMENTATION (1956–1988): THE ERA OF LOWBROW ADAPTATIONS

In order to survive beyond this moment, the industry had to undergo a dramatic restructuring, transforming into a fundamentally different kind of business. The first major and visible shift was a narrowing of the field, as more than half of the industry's existing publishers and distributors closed their doors. Most of the failed shops were smaller operations that had spent the 1940s and early 1950s focusing solely on publishing. Their content was shaped less by licensing than by the genre fads that dominated that era. Left standing were the larger companies, like DC and Dell, which had interests beyond publishing. Moving forward, these leaders of industry increasingly dictated the actions of everyone else in the market. As a result, they had the ability to shape the medium on their own terms, and in general they were determined to conduct business in ways that would support licensing.

Even in the mid-1950s, when smaller publishers were still fighting for survival (and largely losing the battle), the prosperity of licensed titles at Dell continued to rise.[28] By 1957, the company accounted for a third of all comic book sales and had become enough of a powerhouse to start its own distribution business and toy company; Dell's business, on the back of these exclusive licenses, remained strong into the early 1970s.[29] Successful licensing was also responsible for the longevity of Harvey Comics, which acquired a number of characters from Paramount in the early fifties, including Casper the Friendly Ghost. As a result, Harvey too, despite its smaller size and poor distribution, managed to survive the turbulence of the mid-1950s, publishing comic books into the 1990s.[30] Pursuing a slightly different strategy, DC and Charlton took advantage of the 1955 downturn in publishing by buying up the titles of defunct companies. These publishers began amassing vast catalogs of stories and characters that they could exploit in the near or distant future (many of the properties remained dormant for decades, and many remain untouched even today).[31]

In short, parts of the comic book industry continued to make the maintenance and exploitation of strong intellectual properties a priority. This dedication is particularly notable given that comic books had entered a decade-long media blackout. This near total absence of comic book adaptations in film and television from 1956 to 1966 was a rather undesirable byproduct of the comic book scare and crash. The continuation of the Superman television series through 1958 was the only exception. Given the lack of opportunity in film and television, along with all of the industry's other problems, companies had to begin experimenting on a variety of fronts, looking for new strategies to achieve viability, growth, and durability. Some of these attempts proved more successful than others.

A new approach to content was perhaps the most visible of these efforts, if not the most successful. It was spearheaded, not surprisingly, by the most powerful publishing companies remaining in the market, those that had control of the industry's regulation and distribution systems. DC Comics had the first breakthrough. In 1956, the publisher revived the superhero genre, a decision that gave rise to what fans refer to as the Silver Age of Comics. As the genre that had first helped establish DC as an industry leader, and a character type that boasted a number of well-protected intellectual properties, superheroes promised to put DC back in a position of market dominance. The return of this genre found enough success that the other remaining publishers felt inspired to follow DC's lead and introduce superheroes of their own. Among these imitators was Marvel Comics, an outgrowth of Atlas Comics (officially Magazine Management Co.), which had endured the market crash through good distribution. Its creative staff, which included Jack Kirby and Stan Lee, spent the early sixties introducing a stable of characters like the Fantastic Four (1961), the Hulk (1962) and the X-Men (1963); their collective value as intellectual properties would eventually grow so strong it created an entire framework for the industry's expansion.

Their ultimate potency can be largely attributed to the fan base that Silver Age superheroes helped generate. This emerging community was constituted in part by boyhood fans of the Golden Age of superheroes and in part by new, younger lovers of superheroes. Marvel in particular, through a more sophisticated approach to the genre, was able to reach a male college-age readership that had weakened during the 1950s, as the more rebellious generation of baby boomers began to come of age. This fandom was, from its beginnings in 1960,[32] closely intertwined with industry forces; these readers supported the medium through tough times, and eventually conferred on it tremendous value. By galvanizing a particular kind of fan, superheroes helped shape what was becoming not merely the industry's target demographic, but its sole audience: young educated men. Even after superheroes declined in popularity toward the end of the 1960s, and sales (which had briefly plateaued) began to fall off again, publishers continued to pursue this same audience. They tried out more genre fads, both old and new, and worked to make comics more socially relevant. But experimentations with content during the 1970s fell flat and barely staved off perpetually declining sales, which persisted through the early 1980s.

Ultimately, then, it was innovations in other areas of the business—licensing, ownership, and distribution—that finally helped reverse a two-decade downward trend. Structural shifts in these areas began to transform the industry into a business that would not only survive but thrive in the evolving, increasingly corporate and conglomerated media landscape. The return of comic book adaptations to other media in the late 1960s was the first visible sign that this transformation was succeeding. But the wheels had been turning in this direction ever since Robert Maxwell first formed Superman Inc. back in the early 1940s.[33] The relationships he and other comic book executives and editors developed, and the synergistic strategies that supported them, served as the foundation of a new multimedia conglomerate landscape into which comics were always and already integrated.

In the 1960s, the television industry started bringing more of their licensing activity in-house, but DC Comics and parent company National Periodical Publications (NPP) maintained its foothold in the business. Superman Inc. shrewdly transformed into the Licensing Corporation of America (LCA) and was headed by Jay Emmett, a former publicist for *Adventures of Superman* and the nephew of comic book industry titan Jack Liebowitz.[34] Representing dozens of properties, from Bugs Bunny to James Bond, Emmett's LCA aimed to be an adaptable and accommodating partner to media producers. And as media scholar Avi Santo has shown through archival research, the efforts paid off. By 1966, when NPP officially acquired LCA (although the company had never operated very far outside National's orbit), it represented more than thirty properties from which it was generating an annual gross of an estimated $100 million; as *Time* noted, the merger was an "all-in-the-family transaction." Liebowitz saw aggressive licensing as a way to further integrate NPP's existing intellectual properties into a media landscape that was increasingly boosted by merchandise and was also networked across platforms. His approach to cross-divisional collaboration and multi-modal media exploitation would soon spread across the media industries, as increasingly complex networks of ownership found new and ever multiplying ways to merchandise popular culture. Liebowitz explained to shareholders at the time that DC's characters could be and soon would be "molded and merchandised to suit every taste—as television performers, as illustrations for magazine advertising and point-of-sale displays, as promotional products for the ice-cream, dairy, soft-drink, baking and confectionary industries, as syndicated comic strips, and as hundreds of different toy and apparel products for children and teenagers."[35] Conspicuously missing from this list of possible ventures was film, or really any highbrow or legitimized art form. For Liebowitz, the key was not prestige but widespread exploitation of the properties, the type that could bring in the kind of cash flow the struggling publishing business needed to survive. Product visibility on this level would also help to further shore up DC's trademark claims by making their characters, logos, and images more recognizable. Liebowitz's vision for the company's future was quickly borne out.

In 1965, ABC asked producer William Dozier to turn Batman into a television series (1965–1967). Not having been a comic book fan himself, he thought the relatively outlandish superhero premise would only work if it did not take itself too seriously. So he created a tongue-in-cheek version of the character, with bright visuals and deadpan humor. The network promoted this camp aesthetic as having roots in New York's Pop Art scene, and the series proved an instant hit.[36] Its upbeat approach enabled the show to appeal to kids as well, and opened the door to merchandising opportunities which Jay Emmett helped integrate seamlessly and relentlessly into the show.[37] His embrace of a still innovative synergistic approach to production paid off, and in the series' first year, LCA sold five hundred merchandise licenses for $80 million worth of Batman products.[38] The series was an instant hit and the buzz from the show not only doubled sales of Batman comic books, but temporarily boosted the entire comic book publishing industry. It was perfect timing for NPP, which went public on the New York Stock Exchange that very year.[39] But not everyone was pleased with the series. Comic book fans hoping for something more sophisticated disliked *Batman*'s tone—a sentiment that only intensified in later years as increasingly serious versions of the character emerged.

Such concerns did not appear to trouble rising media mogul Steve Ross. The CEO of a cleaning and parking corporation, Kinney National Services, Ross was looking to shift the emphasis of his entire business, and Batmania—as it was known at the time—caught his eye. In 1967, he purchased NPP and its holdings, including LCA and DC Comics. The acquisition gave Kinney a well-placed foothold in the entertainment and leisure industry. Sharing a vision with Jack Liebowitz—who would remain a board member of the corporation until he was ninety-one years old—Ross saw a great deal of potential in both managing and owning licensable properties. These businesses would serve as the foundation for Warner Communications Inc. (WCI), a multimedia empire borne out of Kinney's 1969 purchase of Warner Bros. Seven Arts.[40] Just a year earlier, Perfect Film and Chemical (later Cadence Industries) had purchased Marvel Comics, with similar aspirations, although far less impressive results.

The long-established licensability of comic books had helped this small industry incorporate itself into the ground floor of corporate networks. This shift in ownership and organizational structure would have a deep impact on the medium's future. That DC and Marvel, both corporate owned and licensing focused, were the only major comic book publishing companies to weather the continued storm of declining sales allowed them to wield disproportionate influence on the medium as a whole. Under Cadence and WCI, a new era of comic book adaptations began, one driven by the exposure and merchandising opportunities promulgated by Liebowitz, Ross, and the emerging conglomerate model. Unfortunately, the Batman craze was relatively short-lived, perhaps due to its escapist nature in a time of social upheaval and political conflict. But there were plenty of other comic book adaptations to take its place.

First came a wave of Saturday morning cartoons arriving in the late 1960s, with programs based on DC, Marvel, and Archie characters.[41] A second wave came in the early 1980s, with Marvel producing more aggressively against DC's most notable offering, *Super Friends* (its run started on ABC in 1973 and continued in various iterations through the mid-1980s). Upholding the tradition of the serial matinees, these licensed media products were lowbrow affairs—produced largely by the low-budget animation house Filmation—that were inexpensive and for kids' eyes only. They also took a cue from the successful *Batman* series on ABC and approached their source material playfully. Comic book cartoons nonetheless had a tremendous impact by introducing a generation of children to characters that they were less and less likely to ever encounter on the physical page. Comic book sales had been in decline for some time, and the child-age audience for the medium had dramatically shrunk. Animated series thus took on the burden of maintaining character recognition and shoring up publishers' future copyright and trademark claims.

They were soon joined by live-action television series, with three notable productions airing in the late 1970s, all on CBS: *Wonder Woman* (1975–1979), *The Incredible Hulk* (1977–1982), and *The Amazing Spider-Man* (1977–1979). These programs had a tremendous cultural influence and, unlike earlier products, have often been accepted by fans as core or canonical comic book texts. As television series, though, they were far from prestigious. The early 1970s had seen the birth of quality television with programs like *All in the Family* (1971–1979), *M*A*S*H* (1972–1983), and *The Mary Tyler Moore Show* (1970–1977), also all on CBS. Addressing contemporary political and social issues, these shows were embraced by audiences and critics for their relevance and for all the ways they differed from the ostensibly vapid television of the sixties. *Wonder Woman, The Incredible Hulk,* and *The Amazing Spider-Man* were not part of this quality trend. CBS picked up the superhero concept in a downturn, after it lost its esteemed president Fred Silverman to ABC and before its profile rose again with the success of *Dallas* (1978–1991) in the 1980s. For most of the public, then, these comic book series were yet another example of the escapist fare and "jiggle TV" that were reappearing across the networks.

The same could be said of the half-dozen comic-book-based films that hit theaters in the 1980s, the dawn of the blockbuster era. Movie adaptations like *Conan the Barbarian* (1982, Universal) and *Howard the Duck* (1986, Universal) seemed to epitomize to critics the troubling trend of ill-conceived, poorly made, big-budget films increasingly dominating summer box offices and only periodically bringing in strong financial returns.[42] When the stars of these films were female, as with *Supergirl* (1984, TriStar) and *Sheena* (1984, Columbia), critical responses were even worse. Considered some of the least tasteful films of the decade, most of these comic book adaptations were nominated for the mocking Golden Raspberry Awards ("Razzies"), and quite a few won. All in all, however, the licensing business had during this transitional period experienced extensive and unrelenting growth. Non-publishing revenues surpassed those from publishing by 1979, and by 1985 the comic books themselves generated only one-third of the industry's profits.[43]

In addition to the expansion of licensing and the closely associated changes in ownership and corporate structure, this period saw one other significant change in infrastructure worth noting here: a comprehensive reorganization of distribution. By the 1970s, the mom-and-pop newsstands that had sold hundreds of millions of comic books in the 1940s had practically disappeared, and the industry still had not found a suitable replacement. The solution ultimately came from an unexpected source, Underground Comix. Lasting from 1969 to 1973, the Underground was a creative movement that generated subversive, auteurist, and often X-rated independent comic books that relied on the ability of specialty retailers (head shops) to connect with a specialty audience (counterculture college students and hippies). Its brief success demonstrated the possibility of a direct distribution system, which debuted in 1973 and, by the mid-eighties, had spawned three thousand specialty comic book shops supporting 80 percent of comic book sales.[44]

A superior alternative to more traditional chain retail stores, these shops stabilized readership and helped foster the fan community that promised to support the medium through thick and thin. Together with the support of corporate backers and advancements in licensing, this move

FIGURE 4. *Fritz the Cat,* 1972, directed by Ralph Bakshi. Famous for its existential depiction of the 1960s and its innovative and X-rated animation style, the film was also reproached for its violence, sexism, and misogyny. One of its harshest critics was Robert Crumb, who disavowed the adaptation and killed Fritz off in the comics shortly after the film's release. Image from the Core Collection Production Photographs of the Margaret Herrick Library, Academy of Motion Picture Arts and Sciences.

helped put the comic book industry on firmer footing and gave rise to the industry's first boom since the early fifties. After decades of decline, the publishing business began to grow again in 1983, and the growth continued relatively unabated for a decade. Chapter 4 addresses this shift to the direct market in much greater detail, and explains how the new audience that emerged out of specialty shops impacted the medium long term.

This new distribution strategy had one very notable consequence: it opened the door to a different kind of licensing opportunity. Conglomerate ownership and synergy had successfully generated the lowbrow adaptations and child-centered products noted above. But not until direct distribution cultivated a more loyal fan base and supported more independent publishing was the comic book industry able to move into higher-quality adaptations, specifically, cult products for niche audiences. The first was a set of films released in the early 1970s that aligned with the Underground. Based on titles from independent and defunct publishers, these were unlike almost all the other adaptations produced from the 1960s through the 1980s in that they did not emanate from either DC or Marvel.

Most notable was *Fritz the Cat* (1972, Cinemation), a feature-length, animated adaptation of Robert Crumb's X-rated comic of the same title (see figure 4). Crumb had published the character in independent publications like *Help!* and achieved a subcultural legitimacy in the Underground that translated well to the independent circles in which the film was released. Ultimately an incredible financial success, *Fritz* showed that the right comic book material adapted the right way for the right audiences could deepen the medium's potential; it seemed to show a way forward to leaders of the New Hollywood as well, who were beginning to embrace niche audiences, and more specifically, communities of young, savvy, male consumers. The same year, Amicus Films and Metromedia released *Tales from the Crypt*, a low-budget horror film, to mediocre reviews, and enough financial success to justify a sequel the following year, *Vault of Horror*. Adapted from popular horror comics written in the 1950s, these films also represented a cultish current within comic book culture, one that would later prove very successful within Hollywood.

Despite success with more respectable niche audiences, in addition to the mass market appeal of superhero cartoons, live-action TV series, and movies like *Conan the Barbarian,* there remained limits to comic books' growth in multimedia production. Many in the industry still seemed largely unaware of the magnitude of its potential, so the institutionalization of comic book licensing remained incomplete. If there was any indication of what was to come, any suspicion or hope, it lay in one last film adaptation from this transitional era: the 1978 release of *Superman* (Warner Bros.) and, to a lesser extent, its three sequels (1980, 1983, and 1987). Written by Mario Puzo, of *Godfather* fame, directed by Richard Donner shortly after his success with *The Omen,* and featuring film legends Gene Hackman and Marlon Brando, *Superman* was a conscious attempt to produce a different kind of comic book movie, one that would be respected rather than mocked. And it succeeded, winning three Academy Awards, earning $300 million, and helping to launch a new wave of popular science-fiction cinema.

The blockbuster model it demonstrated, however, in terms of establishing the right credentials and the right tone, was not replicated in any meaningful way until 1989 with the release of the Tim Burton–directed *Batman* (Warner Bros.). It took nearly another twenty years following that before Marvel began producing similar films in any noticeable quantity. The singularity of *Superman*'s early success is attributable to two factors. First, there is the singularity of Superman himself. The character that launched the industry, that began comic book licensing and was continuously adapted across every mass medium over the course of forty years, Superman had the recognizablity as an icon and the respect as a pop-cultural institution to carry this franchise on his back. These characteristics were of course the result of decades of vigilant protection of copyright and trademark claims. Second, the entertainment industry was not yet structured to take advantage of the opportunities that franchises like Superman had to offer. That would change in the 1990s.

INSTITUTIONALIZATION (1989–2010):
THE ERA OF QUALITY TRANSMEDIA

Although media conglomeration was well underway by the 1960s, technological limitations, regulations imposed by the FCC, and the federal government's aggressive enforcement of antitrust law continued to restrain both vertical and horizontal integration into the eighties. At this point, though, a wave of deregulation supported by the rise of neoliberal ideology triggered consolidation throughout the media industries. A first wave of corporate mergers in 1985 was followed by a second beginning in 1989, and finally a third in 1995 that saw the last remaining separations between the various media industries disappear.[45] Simultaneously, advancements in satellite broadcasting, cable technologies, and computing facilitated a shift toward increased product differentiation and personalization. So whereas before, as Henry Jenkins notes, "each medium had its own distinctive functions and markets," these political and technological developments were suddenly making it more "desirable for companies to distribute content across those various channels rather than within a single media platform." In short, "digitization set the conditions for convergence; corporate conglomerates created its imperative."[46]

As core media holdings for companies like Warner Communications, comic books had for many years been a part of emerging strategies in corporate synergy. But it was not until the late 1980s, the dawn of this new era, that the form assumed such a central role in the production of mass culture across media. The growth of the franchised film was one of the first signs of this more aggressive integration of comic book culture. As Derek Johnson has noted, the term "franchise" was not even employed within cultural contexts until the eighties, when market logics from other business sectors (most recognizably, fast food) began migrating toward the media industries. The structural changes noted above had brought a greater need for what he describes as networks of production constituted across multiple industrial sites, or "multiplied cultural production." Corporations that wanted to create value across various businesses and territories over long periods of time increasingly sought to "develop brands that could be deployed across media channels." In this environment, strong content based on protectable intellectual properties became more important than ever, since companies could use them to coordinate, streamline, and control production, distribution, and consumption systems that were otherwise unwieldy.[47] Comic book characters had already been a staple of franchised production when the practice gained prominence in a newly deregulated Hollywood. This history, and the strong copyright protections it supported, made comic books ripe for intensified exploitation by producers desperate for, and largely unpracticed in, this emerging media mode.

Thus came a notable increase of comic book adaptations in television, gaming, publishing, and finally, film. In the summer of 1989, the year WCI merged with Time Inc. (parent company of HBO) to form Time Warner, the company released both the high-profile, critically acclaimed *Batman* and the very successful HBO horror anthology series *Tales from the Crypt* (1989–1996). The next few years brought a string of television series, including *Lois & Clark* (1993–1997, ABC) and a new crop of animated series for kids. The newest development, however, was the many comic-book-based films to hit the country's ever-increasing number of multiplexes. Some were for kids, like the phenomenally successful *Teenage Mutant Ninja Turtles* (1990, New Line Cinema) and also *Richie Rich* (1994, Warner Bros.), but many targeted adults, including those who were not necessarily interested in comic books or comic book characters. Unlike the action-adventure comic book movies of the 1980s, these were more respected, if not always highly prestigious films, like *The Crow* (1994, Miramax) and *Men in Black* (1997, Columbia). A handful came from traditional comic book properties like Batman, which inspired three blockbuster sequels to the 1989 film (in 1992, 1995, and 1997), but this last category, remarkably in light of the film trends of today, was the slowest to catch on. Hollywood executives hesitated, throughout most of the 1990s, to greenlight superhero franchises and other big films closely associated with the medium. Chapter 5 surveys film production practices in the 1990s to reveal the sources of that hesitation, as well as the reason for an eventual reversal of attitudes.

For a time, though, most film adaptations were coming from publishing houses other than industry stalwarts DC and Marvel, and featured characters who were not classic superheroes. This trend, at least in part, reflected a recent boom in comic book publishing that had opened the door to new companies, thereby giving Hollywood more choices. And that boom was itself another byproduct of the success of the direct distribution system and the thousands of specialty comic book shops it spawned. Unfortunately, even after a decade of growth, volatility in the publishing market had not disappeared. In 1993, after reaching an industry-wide sales peak, comic books saw yet another tremendous decline in sales, the result of two bubbles—one in speculative collecting, the other in retail outlets.[48]

In the fallout of that decline, many publishers once again were forced to close their doors, and Marvel became the center of a high-powered corporate media battle that dragged on for the better part of the 1990s. Media investor Ron Perelman had acquired the company for $82.5 million in 1989, when sales were still on the rise. But the company eventually fell into bankruptcy proceedings and was subsequently targeted for a hostile takeover by business magnate Carl Icahn. The affair finally ended when the toy company Toy Biz assumed control. Those involved were left to lament how a very small number of people allowed "a pretty decent company to fall apart."[49] One of the more unfortunate consequences of the incident was the extent to which it deterred film and television producers, who, without the uncertainty of warring legal claims, might have begun developing more Marvel properties earlier on, and perhaps generated licensing revenue to save the company from further turmoil. By this point, licensing constituted the financial backbone of the industry, and as the decade wore on, it became clear that the most profitable and enduring new crop of comic book publishers would be companies like Dark Horse that were willing to shape their catalog and business strategies to take advantage of multimedia opportunities.

There were, of course, other important developments within comic book publishing during this era, not all of which revolved entirely around licensing. Two particularly important trends had their roots in the late 1980s, but did not reap significant dividends until the first years of the new millennium. These were the very interconnected rise of manga and of the graphic novel, two categories of comic book publishing boosted enormously by another innovation in distribution, the move into chain bookstores. The increasing interest in manga seemed to stem from an influx of anime television shows targeted at kids that began airing in 1988, once again pointing to the power of film and television in shaping the fate of the publishing business. Growth came slowly at first, with Japanese and American companies establishing publishing units to translate Japanese comics for an American audience. But with the multimedia successes of *Pokémon* (1998–2003, WBTV) and *Sailor Moon* (1995, 1997–2000) in the late 1990s, and the related (and much belated) discovery that young women were fans of the medium too, manga exploded in popularity. The first two years of the new millennium brought a 300 percent increase in sales, a spike so significant it helped lift the entire comic book market.[50]

Importantly, manga was making its biggest impact not in specialty comic book shops with already established comic book fans, but with new readers in new demographics who found the product on the shelves of general-interest retail spaces like Borders and Barnes & Noble. In fact, manga titles outsold traditional American comic book publishers in this space, even as companies like DC, Marvel, and Dark Horse ramped up their production of graphic novels (also referred to as trade paperbacks, which is essentially a set of comic books bound together and sold as a single unit).[51] An important format within the medium since the 1970s, graphic novels benefited immensely from both increased critical attention (e.g., Art Spiegelman's *Maus* won the Pulitzer Prize in 1992, and Alan Moore's 1986 *Watchmen* was eventually included on *Time Magazine's* List of 100 Greatest Novels) and the benefit of being sold beside more traditional works of great literature. These two new sources of revenue for the comic book industry—manga and graphic novels—were vital after the crash of 1993 saw about half the nation's specialty shops permanently shutter.[52]

When the manga and graphic novel booms came to an end in 2007 and 2008, respectively, the importance of licensing to the survival of publishing once again came into stark view. The decline of the book-seller Borders, the migration of anime from broadcast and cable television to the web, a shrinking fan base, and an overall contracted market did not bode well for an industry about to move into the uncertain space of digital publishing.[53] By this point, though, the woes of publishing had practically become a footnote for the industry. The immensely successful 2000 release of *X-Men* (20th Century Fox) and 2002 release of *Spider-Man* (Sony) outperformed already high expectations, opening the floodgates on cinematic comic book adaptations. The first decade of the new millennium saw dozens of these films hit theaters with impressive results.

This explosion of content, along with the establishment of the Marvel Cinematic Universe—an independently financed and produced franchise based around the publishers' marquee characters—brought comic books to the center of the media industry's attention. Unconcerned about struggles in publishing, Disney purchased Marvel for $4 billion in late 2009, and Warner Bros. transformed its longtime subsidiary DC Comics into a new company, DC Entertainment, several weeks later. In the decade leading up to these deals, approaches to film financing had shifted. Increasing attention to global box office numbers, the entry of private equity, and changes in the economics of theatrical exhibition had transformed superhero movies from an unreliable genre into a fail-safe investment.[54]

While some suspected, at the time, that Disney had overpaid for Marvel, time would prove them wrong; reliance on comic book adaptations became increasingly routine in Hollywood. As expected by most comic book industry insiders, 2010 brought substantial reorganizations of both Marvel and DC (which together accounted for more than 75 percent of the industry's market share) oriented around the furtherance of in-house licensing opportunities, primarily via adaptations through sister companies.[55] Publishing alone—even when it relied on ever-adapting distribution models, a loyal fan base, and good relations with creative talent—was not, and had not been for some time, enough to sustain the comic book business. Licensing had become ever more vital, not just to the industry and its biggest companies, but to the medium at large.

Of course, comic books were becoming just as vital to multimedia producers as multimedia producers were to comic books. Increasingly, it was not just the properties themselves that had become so useful, but their underlying logic. As contemporary film and television institutions faced a new set of circumstances—the disruption of distribution channels, a fragmentation of audiences, and structural reorganizations—that pushed multimedia production into transition, they looked to the comic book business for solutions. Initially a chaotic industry built on a shaky foundation, comic book companies had spent half a century occupying a somewhat precarious position within the broader entertainment industry, often in the margins between other, more stable media. In so doing, the industry had developed responses to these challenges that, in the era of convergence, became increasingly applicable throughout multimedia.

As described above, the comic book industry had learned very early on to mobilize its characters across various media platforms simultaneously and to assimilate itself into corporate networks and infrastructures. They had also, importantly, fostered a more reciprocal exchange with audiences. In all these ways, comic book culture had been a culture of convergence for nearly half a century when the rest of the entertainment industry began moving toward this logic. A mode of culture defined by three primary elements—content flows across media, networked corporate structures, and new relationships between consumers and producers—*convergence culture* is often associated with the digital innovations of the new millennium.[56]

While advancements in technology had certainly made these characteristics more widespread, such convergences had always been possible, and have long been present within the world of comic books. Accordingly, in addition to the fundamentals that had driven comic books' incorporation into the entertainment industries in years prior (namely, copyrightability), the industry's fundamental transmediality drove a more intense integration beginning in the 1990s, as structural and technological changes intensified. As Hollywood took up the cultural logic of the medium, franchises grew more sophisticated in nature, and comic books began to blossom within mainstream mass media.

At the heart of this exchange between comics and multimedia, and of the growth of transmedia texts and practices, was a question of reception. Multimedia producers were becoming interested in finding the kinds of engaged quality audiences that the comic book industry had been cultivating so successfully for decades. A wide range of factors in the media landscape, and in the political and economic climate more broadly, drove this need for new audiences. For instance, technological, structural, and cultural shifts that were facilitating more product personalization, more tech commerce, and more ancillary possibilities had opened the door for consumers who were more media literate, more engaged, and more loyal. Simultaneously, transformations in advertising, television, and film were making young male viewers increasingly attractive to a variety of investors. All together, these changes were shaping a new ideal consumer of the twenty-first century, and he happened to bear a striking resemblance to the dedicated fans that the comic book industry had been cultivating since the early sixties—a community that consisted largely of educated, tech-savvy men in their twenties, thirties, and forties.[57]

As the new millennium approached, then, a confluence of factors had arisen to support the final stage of comic book culture's incorporation into mass media. First, a structural convergence in the entertainment industries drove media corporations to seek out new and intensified synergies that pushed comic book properties toward a new strategic center. Second, conglomerates in search of new demographics looked to comic books for help in cultivating more engaged and loyal audiences of young men. And third, changes in film financing made these products even more attractive, as they increasingly looked like risk-free investments.

These elements brought the final era of this history to a close. By 2010, the multimedia exploitation of comic book characters had become an embedded practice in television, film, video games, toy manufacturing, and comic book publishing itself. These adaptations had become so commonplace and so popular that they constituted the new mainstream of popular culture. Adults and children, men and women, people of every race, nationality, and language on the globe had become consumers of American comic books. Most members of this global audience would have only very occasionally laid eyes on an actual, physical comic book. But the intellectual properties originating in their pages, as well as the underlying cultural logic of comic books—their sprawling narratives, iconic characters, and well-honed appeal—had spread as widely and deeply as any media trend in modern history.

Where comic books go from this point forward remains to be seen. At the time of writing, a decade has passed since the Disney deal, and comic book licensing shows no signs of slowing down, despite the prognostications of critics who hope for its demise. But histories (and the historians who write them) are not in the business of predictions, nor should they attempt to historicize very recent events whose repercussions remain unclear. Accordingly, this brief industrial and transmedial history ends here. What comes in the chapters that follow is a deeper look backward. This does not mean the stories contained cannot help us understand the future. As we navigate things that seem new, understanding past responses to such novelties can help us navigate them better, perhaps differently, and at the very least, knowingly. This history also provides a clearer understanding of our present. Comic books dominate the cultural landscape, and it is worth knowing where they come from, what they mean, and who and what gave them that meaning. It can be tempting to think that creativity exists in a vacuum and that pop culture trends, particularly ones this massive and enduring, reflect audience desire. Uncovering the political and economic contexts of this evolution and the underlying architecture of its form prove far more informative than such magical thinking.

2

Comic Book Crisis

Public Relations, Regulation, and
Distribution in the 1950s

On April 22, 1954, the *New York Times* ran a page-one story that
included, verbatim, a conversation between Senator Estes Kefauver (a
Democrat from Tennessee) and an independent comic book publisher
named Bill Gaines. The exchange was about comic book cover art, an
unusual topic for such a reputable publication, but it was part of Gaines's
testimony to the Senate Subcommittee on Juvenile Delinquency. The piv-
otal moment came when Gaines was asked if there was any limit to what
he would publish in the horror and crime comics he was selling to America's youth. Foolishly, he answered, "only within the bounds of good
taste." Kefauver then showed the room the vivid and graphic cover of
the May issue of *Crime Suspense Stories* (see figure 5), and this discussion followed:

> *Senator Kefauver.* This seems to be a man with a bloody ax holding a wom-
> an's head up which has been severed from her body. Do you think that is
> in good taste?
>
> *Bill Gaines.* Yes, sir; I do, for the cover of a horror comic. A cover in bad
> taste, for example, might be defined as holding the head a little higher so
> that the neck could be seen dripping blood from it and moving the body
> over a little further so that the neck of the body could be seen to be
> bloody.
>
> *Senator Kefauver.* You have blood coming out of her mouth.
>
> *Bill Gaines.* A little.[1]

FIGURE 5. The cover of *Crime SuspenStories #22* (May 1954), a publication of EC Comics. Illustration copyright © Johnny Craig. Courtesy of Fantagraphics Books (www.fantagraphics.com).

It was the 1950s' version of a perfect sound bite, and newspapers across the country ran with it.[2] The moment marked the apex of an anti–comic book campaign that had raised anxieties about the impact of the still relatively new medium on children. Psychiatrists, church officials, PTAs, and local politicians had been trying to link comic books to juvenile delinquency, illiteracy, and moral corruption. When the government got involved in the spring of 1954 and held televised hearings on the issue, the public was far from convinced—there were bigger things to worry about at the time (e.g., nuclear war, communism, McCarthyism). But Gaines's dreadful notion of good taste was too awful to ignore.

The moment, and the attention it brought, proved to be a turning point in comic book history. The Senate hearings preceded a wave of anti–comic book legislation from local and state censors. It also prompted the major comic book publishers to create a trade organization and a code of self-censorship. Shortly after, in 1955, the comic book market crashed quite dramatically, and as a result, the medium changed in fundamental ways. Creative offerings narrowed significantly, the form stopped appealing to a diverse audience, and publishers who did not fit into a particular model of corporate management vanished from the landscape. The post-1954 terrain looked very different from the glory days that had come before it.

Sixty years later, the words spoken between Gaines and Kefauver have remained etched in the minds of comic book fans and scholars. Historical accounts often attribute the 1955 market crash to this comic book scare and its fallout.[3] The timing of these two incidents seems to support this conclusion, not just because they occurred in direct and close succession, but because the debate at the heart of the comic controversy—a disagreement about taste, value, and artistic expression—aligns so perfectly with our collective memory of Cold War cultural politics. Bill Gaines is remembered as a proud defender of comic books and of popular culture, and as an advocate of free speech.[4] His opponents meanwhile, including both Kefauver and the psychiatrist Fredric Wertham, are characterized as villains, censors who sought to stamp out subversive art and cultural heterogeneity.[5] The battle between these two sides has become a kind of lore within comic book culture; in framing comic books as a subversive medium that had to fight for survival and acceptance, the story has helped inspire writing, organize the community, and shape its identity.[6]

Historians have largely advanced a similar narrative. Both Paul Lopes and Jim Trombetta, for example, explain how the comics controversy demonstrated the establishment's eagerness to silence whatever was "genuinely and brazenly subversive."[7] David Hadju describes the affair as part of a generational culture war, one that was about "class and money and taste; about traditions and religions and biases rooted in time and place."[8] James Burkhart Gilbert also sees the comic book crusade, like many controversies over mass media, as "a struggle in which the participants were arguing over power—over who had the right and the responsibility to shape American culture."[9] This discourse typically relegates the ensuing industrial crisis to a mere side effect of the comic scare. The directness of Gaines's words and the disdain they provoked, meanwhile, seem representative of the whole anti–comic book affair, and the whole era really. But this is only part of the story.

Bill Gaines was one of twenty-five individuals who testified to the Senate subcommittee over three long days of questioning. Most of the others were representatives from the magazine and comic book industry and testified in depth on the ins and outs of their business—what the distribution chain looked like, details about standard protocols within and between sectors, how networks of relationships formed among companies and workers, and which professional practices shaped their day-to-day work lives. It was a deeply bureaucratic proceeding. And it revealed that salacious content (even if it included axe-wielding men and bloody beheaded women) was not the most significant problem facing comic books, not even in a hearing *about* said salacious content. As the senators learned, the industry's distribution infrastructure was breaking down. There was an oversupply problem with physical and financial repercussions, reports of entrenched anticompetitive practices, and souring relationships between distributors and retailers along delivery routes. Demand was also in critical decline.

Publishers developed the Comics Code to respond to public concern, but their aggressive enforcement of it ultimately helped to solve all of these other problems as well. Supported by an effective public relations campaign, self-censorship was able to squash public concern by the year's end. Then came the additional benefits. The careful implementation of self-regulation allowed the biggest publishers and distributors to eliminate smaller competitors and increase their own market share. These companies took control of the medium and went about reorganizing the business. They formed new relationships with one another and consolidated their holdings, erected new barriers to entry, and rationalized the distribution system, making it more effective, efficient, and disciplined. These accomplishments were consequential; they had a lasting and material impact on the people who worked in the industry, on the product they sold, and on those who consumed it. This is the other part of the story.

At the time, the comic book scare remained the center of public attention. The exchange between Gaines and Kefauver traveled; the debates over distribution practices did not. In the decades since, the nature of the narrative has changed; today we support Gaines's efforts and villainize his opponents, instead of vice versa. But the focus on cultural value remains the same. The established historical narrative about comic books in the 1950s offers a drama about artistic freedom and censorship and not, generally, a deep understanding of the industry's distribution infrastructure. But the one actually necessitates the other. While most accounts of censorship focus on texts and cultural contexts, the regulation of mass media inevitably involves vast and powerful infrastructures of enforcement capable of containing the inherent disorderliness of popular culture. So while scholars should continue analyzing the objects and ideologies at the center of media censorship, it is equally important to consider the material foundations that support systems of both restriction and circulation. Distribution became the primary mechanism of self-regulation, organizing the industry's basic operations, and determining who would survive and who would not. While debates over censorship and good taste may have seemed more newsworthy, there was drama in distribution too.

But distributors did not draw attention to themselves at the Senate hearings. And when comic book publishers launched a PR campaign, they kept public focus on comic book content, how images of axe-wielding men and bloody beheaded women were disappearing from newsstands across the country. They were less informative about changes in the distribution network. In the process, industry leaders not only improved the reputation of their product, but helped legitimize their business and discourage further government oversight. Unfortunately, these efforts also served to contain the medium, preventing new and independent publishers from entering the industry and limiting the creative possibilities their voices might have brought.

Examining the comic book industry's public relations efforts and distribution practices during the 1940s and 1950s, this chapter points to inconsistencies in the standard cultural explanation and recenters the narrative on infrastructure and the politics of visibility. In revising this historical account, I argue that comic book culture does not have roots in a subversive cultural tradition, but was in fact the product of an increasingly well-established industry that operated in constructive collaboration with a pro-business government. If comic book culture represented something in American culture that was genuinely fringe, that facet of it disappeared after the 1955 crash. Notably, though, this dissident strand was the victim not of fascists, or censors, or politicians, but of the market itself, and of the fully sanctioned ability of entrenched and powerful players to intervene in that market on their own behalf.

THE COMIC BOOK SCARES (1940–1954)

Public concern over comic books arose in three distinct periods. Each time, interest lasted for about a year before sharply falling off. Notably, sales of comic books suffered only after the last wave of criticism; after the first two scares, sales rose. The relatively quick closure of these early controversies was in part due to the actions of the comic book industry, which responded to public criticism swiftly and deftly. By the third wave of criticism, however, a number of factors—internal to the industry as well as external—had made such a resolution unattainable. The similarities across these three crises reveal the emergence of public relations efforts in the early days of mass media, and demonstrate their effectiveness even before corporate management made such strategies standard.

Pre-War Jitters (1940)

In May 1940, author and reporter Sterling North wrote a column about comic books titled "A National Disgrace" that accused these "lurid . . . sex-horror serials" of a "hypodermic injection of sex and murder." The article was reprinted in newspapers across the country and stirred up concern among intellectuals.[10] At this time, comic books had been a popular form of entertainment for less than two years. Their relative newness prompted librarians, psychologists, and cultural intellectuals like North to enter into a robust debate on the possible dangers as well as potential values the medium represented.[11] Leaving no time for the dust to settle, however, or any opportunity for consensus to be reached, the comic book industry sprang into action. Within months of these first rumblings, National Comics (later DC Comics) began forming an advisory board, composed of prominent psychologists and educators, to help counsel them on content and create an in-house code of ethics. Within a few years, other leading publishers, including Fawcett, would do the same.[12] By 1941, the individuals hired by these companies were publishing articles, in both scholarly journals and in the popular press, that strongly argued for comic books' many benefits.

It is in fact difficult to find writing in favor of comics during these early years that was not authored by an intellectual associated with one of the major publishers. It is not apparent whether these advocates spoke in favor of comics only after they came onto the industry payroll or if it was their favorable opinions that helped them obtain that work in the first place. Regardless, it is clear that companies like National and Fawcett were not willing to watch the debate complacently from the sidelines.

As this controversy heightened, though, the public seems to have been largely occupied by the looming threat of World War II. After the United States entered the conflict, the flamboyant patriotism of comic book superheroes and the fact that soldiers overseas were happily purchasing them in droves protected the medium from widespread criticism.[13] Certain members of the industry nonetheless maintained their vigilance in the debate. In short, publishers were actively involved in the conversation from the very start, whether visibly to consumers or not. That involvement helped shape the debate that slowly and quietly evolved throughout the forties.[14]

A Rising Threat (1948)

Their vigilance was warranted, since the issue reared its head again soon after the war ended. In taking mothers and fathers away from the home front, war had roused public concerns over juvenile delinquency.[15] Those fears were mounting in the late 1940s, when Dr. Fredric Wertham came onto the scene. Born in Germany in 1895, he had studied psychiatry and psychoanalysis in Europe before moving to the United States. After briefly directing Bellevue's mental health clinic in New York, he spent the 1940s and 1950s doing psychiatric clinical work in both Queens and Harlem. Then Wertham decided to make some of his research public, in particular, his ideas about the threat of comic books. He quickly became the object of significant, if not lasting, media fascination.[16]

His public crusade against the menace of comics began in 1948 when two articles, one about him and one by him, appeared in the popular publications *Colliers* and *Reader's Digest*. They criticized not only comic books themselves, but also the industry, which claimed that its product was harmless.[17] At the same time, reports began emerging of copycat events, in which children reenacting comic book scenes were putting themselves into mortal danger. By year's end, there had been articles, radio debates and symposiums, committees founded to evaluate and censor comics, local boycotts, and even a wave of comic book burnings.[18] There was also a wave of local and state measures proposed, almost all of which focused on curbing the dissemination of crime comics; these were generally criticized by the press and ultimately struck down.[19]

Wertham's quick success in the public arena caught the attention of Washington, and of one politician in particular, Estes Kefauver. New to the U.S. Senate, Kefauver had gained notoriety for spearheading televised hearings on organized crime, and emerged a presidential hopeful.[20] Keen to remain in the public eye, he recruited Wertham in 1950 to seek out media-effects research that could prove popular culture was a root cause of criminality.[21] After only several months, Wertham came back having found that authorities on the subject believed that if comic books had any effect at all, they were only a secondary or lesser cause of delinquency.[22]

The industry, meanwhile, had roused to action once again. After World War II, National Comics started including "public announcement" pages in its comics on topics like "how to study" and "how to do chores." According to Jack Liebowitz, who ran the company, this was not only a direct response to concerns from parents and schools but a "conscious attempt to present DC as a good citizen" when other, newer companies "didn't have any standards at all."[23] In other words, he was hoping to set his reputable company in opposition to less reputable ones, using the perceived foibles of others to highlight his virtues. These early strategies were less invested in educating the public about a new medium than they were in brand and product differentiation. Intraindustry competition was providing the backdrop on which public controversy and popular discourse played out; the commercial and social dimensions of this issue were inherently intertwined.

Publishers used other tactics of persuasion as well. In early July of 1948, they formed the Association of Comic Magazine Publishers (ACMP) and released a code of content. Only fourteen publishers joined the group, however, representing just one-third of the industry, and they were among the least reputable. The organization's creation still managed to alleviate public concern.[24] Simultaneously, academics were again publishing articles in favor of the medium, producing research that rather effectively refuted Wertham's most provocative claims.[25] Notably, many—if not all—of these researchers had for years received institutional support from an organization known as the Child Study Association of America (CSAA). Dating back to the 1880s, the group concerned itself with providing parents scientifically researched information about publications targeted at children. Many of the members had impressive scholarly and political pedigrees. However, in an obvious conflict of interest, the CSAA had for decades received contributions from the country's "most distinguished publishing houses." Among these, not surprisingly, were National

Comics and Fawcett, comic book publishers that donated thousands of dollars to the group during the 1940s.[26]

Perhaps due to the industry's many efforts, or perhaps simply because the topic grew boring, Americans largely lost interest in the debate by 1949. Amidst dwindling public attention, the ACMP deteriorated. The organization became anathema to more established companies that wanted to distance themselves from their lesser competitors, and by 1954, with only three members left, it became totally impotent.[27] In this respect, this first attempt at a comic book code suffered from some of the same problems that had plagued Hollywood's Production Code twenty years prior. Although both the ACMP and the Motion Picture Producers & Distributors of America (MPPDA) were industry organizations formed to protect their members from public calls for censorship, a lack of urgency prevented publishers and producers, respectively, from fully endorsing their nonbinding rules.[28] The state of affairs changed dramatically for Hollywood in 1934, when federal legislation seemed imminent and movie studios reluctantly agreed to give the Hays Office more compulsory power.

In 1954, a different set of industrial exigencies would give the Comics Code Administration (CCA), the successor of the ACMP, a similarly powerful hold over members. That public concern would flare up again was entirely foreseeable. Fortunately, comic book publishers had become very capable of weathering such attacks. Having significantly contributed to the academic and political discourse from the medium's start in the early 1940s, industry leaders had been learning how to shape public opinion—drawing attention to actions and opinions that helped their cause, and marginalizing everything else.

The Rise of the Lurid Comic (1948–1954)

Unfortunately, the savvy publishers were not alone in the market, and their dominance over their smaller competitors had begun to slip away. The medium as a whole was growing more lurid, violent, and sexual, instead of less. Patriotic and relatively wholesome heroes like Captain America and Superman had been popular during the war, but they were replaced by other, more mature genres, as the audience steadily expanded to include more adults and women. In 1948, Lev Gleason Publications, a minor firm with only three titles, saw its comic book *Crime Does Not Pay* reach a circulation of 1.5 million copies an issue.[29] The book jump-started a brief crime fad, which was followed by crazes for westerns, then romances, then horror, and finally war and science fiction. Faced with this encroachment, the more established comic book publishers, which had relied on tamer genres (National Comics with superheroes, Dell with licensed characters and funny animals, Archie with teens), began following some of these trends in hope of maintaining market share. This meant that almost everyone was producing comics that were more likely to stoke public concern.

Some remained shrewd about these genre experiments; others, however, were less so. Bill Gaines seems to have personified the latter tendency. Bill Gaines was the son of Max C. Gaines, a founding father of the comic book industry.[30] In 1945, after some considerable early successes, the elder Gaines swore off the industry's growing obsession with genre fads to start a new company, Educational Comics, which sought to enrich children's educational lives. Not surprisingly, this vision was not popular with readers. Educational Comics was $100,000 in debt when Max died in a boating accident in the summer of 1947. The company fell into the hands of his rebellious son Bill, who had wanted to become a chemistry teacher, was reportedly uninterested in comics, hated the business, and resented his deceased father. Soon enough, though, Bill Gaines found inspiration and replaced his father's older employees with a new, younger, more cynical, and incredibly talented staff that included Al Feldstein (future editor of EC and then *Mad Magazine*), Harvey Kurtzman, and Johnny Craig.[31]

Perhaps as a repudiation of his father's lofty aspirations, he changed the company's name to Entertaining Comics and began publishing the kind of genre books his father hated. In the spring of 1950, hoping to get out ahead of the next fad, he tried out two horror stories in one of his regularly published crime books.[32] They sold well, so EC introduced a New Trend line that capitalized on horror, crime, and war comics, all provocative genres. Before long, the new horror titles were selling up to 90 percent of their print runs. Other publishers quickly followed EC's lead until the genre exploded, accounting at one point for 150 different titles. With this success, Gaines finally climbed out of his father's debt.[33]

EC's move into horror, however, remained an exceedingly risky endeavor. Following closely in the wake of the second wave of public concern, the New Trend titles—visibly and proudly the goriest, most violent, and most disgusting comics yet—were tempting fate when government officials and critics like Wertham were still keeping an eye on the medium. The gamble served EC well in the short run, attracting eyeballs on newsstands. But building the company on a foundation of shock was hardly a long-term strategy, a reality of which more established companies were well aware. Given Gaines's happenstance entry into the comic book industry, though, and his short tenure thus far, longevity and stability may never have been his goal.

Gaines also remained a small player in what had become a very large business. By 1954, the comic book industry was issuing 90 million comics each month.[34] EC's share of this pie was minute. The company printed about 2.5 million comics a month, with individual issues reaching a circulation of only about 300,000 copies, the minimum print run for most of the industry.[35] Meanwhile, Dell, which focused on licensed kids' characters, had ninety different titles that *averaged* 800,000 copies an issue, with some regularly selling more than 3 million.[36] Gaines had a surefire win introducing horror comics, and EC's were considered the best in terms of quality. But in terms of numbers, the 1950s were by no means the age of EC Comics, as many have claimed.[37] With more than six hundred titles hitting newsstands each week, EC's eleven comic books would have been invisible to those not actively seeking them.

Small size need not have been a problem for Gaines, if only the risks that he took had been calculated. It remains unclear, however, whether or not Gaines fully comprehended that New Trend was a risk at all. Years later, he would comment that he could never anticipate what was going to offend people, since "we were always getting into trouble, and we never knew why exactly, so it couldn't be prevented."[38] It is nonetheless easy to see why Gaines has inspired so much admiration within the comic book community over the decades. Staking out a somewhat untenable position within the industry, Gaines was a rogue creative entrepreneur. He intuitively made something out of nothing (or less than nothing, considering his father's debt), he threw caution to the wind by ignoring the protocol around maintaining respectability, and he was about to refuse—boldly and boisterously—to kowtow to the more powerful figures in the industry, all while making an important and lasting artistic contribution.

THE 1954 SENATE SUBCOMMITTEE HEARINGS ON JUVENILE DELINQUENCY AND COMIC BOOKS

Public concern over the threat of comics peaked again in 1954. There was nothing this time around that, in and of itself, could account for the dramatic decline in sales about to hit. Despite popular memory, nobody was throwing comic books into bonfires anymore—either literally or metaphorically. When the Senate Judiciary Committee created the Subcommittee to Investigate Juvenile Delinquency in April of 1953, the medium was not even on the agenda. Then, at the end of 1953, two incidents occurred. First, an issue of EC's satire magazine *Panic* featured a divorced Santa Claus, which prompted the attorney general of Massachusetts to try to restrict its sale. The case was so flimsy, the judge dismissed it, but the incident caused some bad press.[39] Second, Wertham published another article in *Ladies' Home Journal* that provided a condensed version of his scathing upcoming book on the danger of comic books and the comic book industry titled *Seduction of the Innocent.* Wertham's outrage again struck a chord. The public began sending angry letters to the new subcommittee, which announced on February 20, 1954, that it would hold a special session on comics.[40]

The Intellectual Climate

Despite Wertham's role in getting comic books back on the public agenda, his ideas were not universally or even widely embraced. While some academics did read his work—a few who agreed, and a few who did not—the majority completely ignored him.[41] Public intellectuals gave him more attention, but rarely praise. The prominent critic Robert Warshow, for example, criticized Wertham for his lurid writing, sense of doom, and weak logic, while himself offering, in contrast, a rather nuanced perspective of comic books. Warshow found the medium, and material from EC Comics in particular, to display "an undisciplined imaginativeness" but also to yield too easily to immediate gratification. Though he concluded that "some kind of regulation seems necessary," he was against an official code which might make the medium seem "mechanically fabricated."[42] This perspective seems to have been in line with the mainstream; his article was picked up by major publications like the *Boston Globe,* which strongly encouraged readers to "read the entire article" and learn that the "wholesale effect of comic books" was probably not "as devastating as Dr. Wertham believes."[43]

Warshow was by no means the only critic of Wertham who reached a general audience; plenty of other intellectuals were putting forward similarly sensible and diplomatic arguments—acknowledging the potential harm of a new medium researchers knew little about without blaming it for any major social injury.[44] Even Laura Bender, Wertham's successor at the Bellevue children's ward, joined the discussion, arguing that comics were probably harmless and perhaps even educational.[45]

Like many of these supporters, she received payments from the comic book industry, but these ties were not publicized or well known.

In general, while mass culture tended to provoke controversy in the United States—particularly when a new medium like comics rose to popularity, and particularly when that medium appealed to kids—these controversies tended to fade away quickly. Members of the public were, not surprisingly, frightened by the effects of an emerging media environment more expansive and frenzied than the one they had known in the first half of the twentieth century. But most Americans were far from being convinced of pop culture's evils. And at this particular moment in history, the science of media effects had proved that such evils probably did not exist. The late 1940s and 1950s saw the rise of empirical social research that concluded mass media had very little impact on consumers—either positive or negative. Though these studies were often funded by the media industries (and were heavily criticized in later years), they gave credibility to a characteristically American live-and-let-live attitude: if kids wanted to read violent comics, why not just let them?

In addition to doubts about the genuineness of the threat of comic books, there was also a very widespread fear of censorship. Americans were growing skeptical of committees tasked with suppressing personal expression—be it a political belief or a garish piece of art or entertainment.[46] And they were certainly not likely to embrace government censorship or deny the very legitimate right of commercial producers to sell their products in a manner of their own choosing. An American fondness for capitalist enterprise would here and elsewhere serve as a barrier to cultural repression as imposed by the government. This belief in market freedom would not, however, prevent capitalism itself from imposing the kind of limitations that would be viewed as abhorrent had they been imposed by state actors.

The Political Climate

The same overall attitude was reflected by Congress's ongoing examinations of several media industries—comic books being only the first—conducted during the 1950s and 1960s. The subcommittee hearings on comic books were held on April 21, 22, and June 4, 1954, during the exact three-month span of the Army-McCarthy hearings. That latter event initiated the decline of McCarthyism in America and provoked increasing public disapproval of governmental overreach and state intrusion into private life. The Senate was sensitive to these concerns;

investigations into mass media were never about censorship but rather the pursuit of a core "belief in the regulating power of a capitalist system." Historian Shawn Selby has argued effectively that the senators only ever wanted to find a way to help industry help itself; they were in search of a laissez-faire approach to elevating culture.[47] So while the threat of censorship may have seemed real to both those involved in the proceedings and those watching from the sidelines, it was never more than a threat, and one designed to promote business solutions over government interference.

Industry had been responding slavishly to consumer demand in a kind of race to the bottom, and the senators hoped that the same competitive approach could be used to improve the product. For Senator Kefauver, the best strategy for achieving this goal was merely to expose the industry's problems to the public, who could then make more informed purchasing decisions. For other senators, it meant promoting self-regulation, and figuring out exactly where on the distribution chain—among publishers, printers, distributors, wholesalers, and retailers—it would be possible to encourage restrictions that could correct industry practices.[48]

Characterizations of these hearings as a witch hunt align with a different version of Cold War–era history, as a time when fear of communism rooted out cultural threats and forced social conformity. But another significant feature of anticommunism was aggressive support of big business and the enthusiastic embrace of a free-market model. To the extent that the Senate investigation into comic books is representative of Cold War culture, then, it is more so in this latter sense, as an example of mid-century pro-business politics. This is perhaps best illustrated by the fact that the majority of the hearings were dedicated to a lengthy discussion of business practices.

This political climate provided industry representatives with considerable leeway in presenting their case as they defined it and in defending their right to exist in the manner they saw fit. Their first priority was to avoid drawing additional negative attention to their product and their (perhaps anticompetitive) business practices; their second was to make it clear that the industry as a whole was well organized and disciplined enough to implement effective self-regulation. In short, they wanted to make visible only the conduct that was favorable to their interests. With these goals, the entire affair, with only limited television coverage, could have passed relatively unnoticed as dry administrative proceedings, but for the presence of a number of individual actors who raised the stakes for everyone else. There was Wertham, who set the release of his book for April 19, just two days before testimony began. There was Senator Kefauver, who wanted media attention. And then there was Bill Gaines.

Bill Gaines, Bad Taste, and Bad Judgment

As it happened, Gaines's problems began well before his testimony. As comic book scholar Amy Nyberg has discovered, days before the comic book hearings were even announced, Gaines was quoted by the *Hartford Courant* in an exposé about the danger the medium posed. Unhappy with his portrayal, he wrote an accusatory letter to the newspaper, prompting not a retraction, but an even more incendiary response. Gaines then ran full-page ads in his comic books that bore the headline, "Are you a red dupe?" (see figure 6).[49] In big bold letters, in the center of the ad, Gaines included the sentence, "The group most anxious to destroy comics are the communists!" The ad's fine print, positioned under a zany comic strip about censorship in Soviet Russia, included more specific accusations, even mentioning Wertham by name. An amazing piece of propaganda, this ad managed to mock the anti-comics crusade and simultaneously launch a very serious attack against the subcommittee and thousands of concerned Americans by claiming that all critics of comics were either communists or communist dupes.

Of his own volition, Gaines sent this ad to the subcommittee, apparently because he believed they "would be interested."[50] Indeed they were. Notably, it is not clear that they would have taken special notice of Bill Gaines or EC Comics had the publisher not actively brought himself to their attention, both with this ad and with a request to be heard publicly at the subcommittee hearings.[51] Even though Gaines had singled out Wertham in his ad, Wertham did not do the same to Gaines; Wertham's upcoming book, his public crusade, and his testimony focused not on horror or on EC Comics, but on crime books and the superhero stories of National Comics.

Unfortunately, when Gaines did eventually testify, he was not at his best and was easily manipulated by the rhetoric of the senators.[52] Gaines reported, years later, that he had stayed awake the previous night on uppers, specifically the diet pill Dexedrine. By the time he spoke, late in the afternoon, he had already started to crash and was left sitting there, in his own words, "like a punch-drunk fighter" getting pummeled by his opponents.[53] Gaines probably did not have a chance at a fair hearing that day. However, he did not help his own cause, or that of comics more generally, when he arrived on the national political stage—at his

ARE YOU A RED DUPE?

IN THE TOWN OF GAZOOSKY IN THE HEART OF SOVIET RUSSIA, YOUNG MELVIN BLIZUNKEN – SKOVITCHSKY PUBLISHED A *COMIC MAGAZINE*...

...SO THEY CAME AND *SMASHED* HIS FOUR-COLOR PRESS...

...AND *HUNG* POOR MELVIN THE NEXT MORNING!

- HERE IN AMERICA, WE CAN *STILL* PUBLISH COMIC MAGAZINES, NEWSPAPERS, SLICKS, BOOKS AND THE BIBLE. WE DON'T *HAVE* TO SEND THEM TO A CENSOR FIRST. NOT *YET*...
- BUT THERE ARE SOME PEOPLE IN AMERICA WHO WOULD *LIKE* TO CENSOR... WHO WOULD *LIKE* TO SUPPRESS COMICS. IT ISN'T THAT THEY DON'T LIKE COMICS FOR *THEM!* THEY DON'T LIKE THEM FOR *YOU!*
- THESE PEOPLE SAY THAT *COMIC BOOKS* AREN'T AS GOOD FOR CHILDREN AS *NO* COMIC BOOKS, OR SOMETHING LIKE THAT. SOME OF THESE PEOPLE ARE NO-GOODS. SOME ARE DO-GOODERS. SOME ARE WELL-MEANING. AND SOME ARE JUST PLAIN MEAN.
- BUT WE ARE CONCERNED WITH AN AMAZING REVELATION. AFTER MUCH SEARCHING OF NEWSPAPER FILES, WE'VE MADE AN ASTOUNDING DISCOVERY:

THE GROUP MOST ANXIOUS TO DESTROY COMICS ARE THE COMMUNISTS!

- WE'RE SERIOUS! NO KIDDIN'! *HERE!* READ THIS:

THE [COMMUNIST] "DAILY WORKER" OF JULY 13, 1953 BITTERLY ATTACKED THE ROLE OF:

"...SO-CALLED 'COMICS' IN BRUTALIZING AMERICAN YOUTH, THE BETTER TO PREPARE THEM FOR MILITARY SERVICE IN IMPLEMENTING OUR GOVERNMENT'S AIMS OF WORLD DOMINATION, AND TO ACCEPT THE ATROCITIES NOW BEING PERPETRATED BY AMERICAN SOLDIERS AND AIRMEN IN KOREA UNDER THE FLAG OF THE UNITED NATIONS."

THIS ARTICLE ALSO QUOTED GERSHON LEGMAN (WHO CLAIMS TO BE A GHOST WRITER FOR DR. FREDERICK WERTHAM, THE AUTHOR OF A RECENT SMEAR AGAINST COMICS PUBLISHED IN "THE LADIES HOME JOURNAL"). THIS SAME G. LEGMAN, IN ISSUE #3 OF "NEUROTICA", PUBLISHED IN AUTUMN 1948, WILDLY CONDEMNED COMICS, ALTHOUGH ADMITTING THAT:

"THE CHILD'S NATURAL CHARACTER... MUST BE DISTORTED TO FIT CIVILIZATION... FANTASY VIOLENCE WILL PARALYZE HIS RESISTANCE, DIVERT HIS AGGRESSION TO UNREAL ENEMIES AND FRUSTRATIONS, AND IN THIS WAY PREVENT HIM FROM REBELLING AGAINST PARENTS AND TEACHERS... THIS WILL SIPHON OFF HIS RESISTANCE AGAINST SOCIETY, AND *PREVENT REVOLUTION*."

- SO THE *NEXT* TIME SOME JOKER GETS UP AT A P.T.A. MEETING, OR STARTS JABBERING ABOUT THE "NAUGHTY COMIC BOOKS" AT YOUR LOCAL CANDY STORE, GIVE HIM THE *ONCE-OVER*. WE'RE NOT SAYING HE *IS* A COMMUNIST! HE MAY BE INNOCENT OF THE WHOLE THING! HE MAY BE A *DUPE!* HE MAY NOT EVEN *READ* THE "DAILY WORKER"! IT'S JUST THAT HE'S *SWALLOWED* THE *RED BAIT*... HOOK, LINE, AND *SINKER!*

FIGURE 6. EC Comics ran this full-page "ad" in *Haunt of Fear* #26 and several other comics released in the summer of 1954. Illustration copyright © Al Feldstein and Jack Davis. Image courtesy of Fantagraphics Books (www.fantagraphics.com).

own request—physically and mentally unprepared to meet the opponents he had actively worked to alienate in the months prior.

In short, Bill Gaines was not a particularly effective advocate for a medium he has since been praised for defending.[54] He struggled when it came to any kind of politics, even within his own industry and certainly when it came to public relations. The boisterous disruptiveness for which fans have long admired him displayed the epitome of how a media representative should *not* perform in a moment of crisis. In this may be the crux of his appeal. The comic book hearings came at a turning point in the history of mass media. A decade before the media business began to consolidate, and several years before the quiz show and payola scandals, the mid-1950s held the possibility of a more innocent and authentic version of American commercial media. Bill Gaines—dreadfully unaware of the virtues of polish, the dangers of bad publicity, and the importance of playing by the rules—was in many ways a relic of this era. He was the kind of person who became increasingly unimaginable in the decades that followed, as the media industries grew increasingly corporate and disciplined.

Regardless, it was Gaines's unintentional foibles rather than his genius that transformed him into a lightning rod for the controversy. His contemporaries within comic book publishing fully recognized his blunders and chose to distance themselves from him. They even offered him up as a straw man within their own testimonies—if not directly and by name, then often by insinuation. He was someone they could define themselves positively against, with his folly highlighting their virtue. In his ability to attract attention without ever achieving any kind of control over the discourse, he had a great deal in common with the controversy's other lightning rod, his supposed nemesis, Fredric Wertham.

Fredric Wertham and a Futile Crusade

In contrast to Bill Gaines, Wertham was able to speak at the subcommittee hearings almost without interruption.[55] The respect the senators gave him suggested that they embraced his ideas completely. And indeed, the subcommittee did accept his most basic and general claim, that comic books were *one of many* contributing factors in recent cases of juvenile delinquency,[56] to which a number of other witnesses also testified. Aside from this, however, Wertham's arguments were actually met with considerable skepticism. Foremost among these assertions was his insistence that comic books were not simply a preferred source of entertainment for youths already involved in bad behavior, but actually had the power—in combination with other factors—to drive otherwise normal children to delinquency. The only serious questions Wertham received during his testimony were on this point, and it was a subject the subcommittee returned to repeatedly in the days that followed. Ultimately, the senators decided against Wertham's way of thinking on this issue. Their final report sided with the consensus of experts that comic books could not cause delinquency in well-adjusted children and noted that Wertham had failed to offer statistical results to prove otherwise.[57]

As for Wertham's other alarmist claims and very detailed research, most of it was simply ignored. Countless studies, critiques, and histories written over the course of the last sixty years have worked to debunk Wertham's thinking.[58] Even today, his ideas and their alleged impact continue to inspire intense ire among comic book fans and lovers of popular culture.[59] But the government and most of those attuned to the issue at the time dismissed him almost immediately. Even his reasonable claim, that comic books may have been negatively influencing the "theoretical development" of children, was largely passed over.[60] In making this particular accusation, Wertham suggested that repeated overexposure to the kind of violence regularly depicted in comic books could gradually lead children to ethical or moral confusion. This was a rational argument to make (even those testifying in favor of comic books made similar statements, and similar claims are still made today), except for the evidence he used to explain it. Instead of citing the horror stories of EC Comics or some of the other, racier publishers as examples, Wertham pointed to *Tarzan,* published by Dell, and *Superman,* published by National Comics. These two titles were in fact the only ones he mentioned by name throughout his testimony, merely relating vague, often unidentifiable, plots from other publishers in works whose titles he could not recall. Wertham took a similar approach—accusing the industry's most respected and established publishers—in his book, which gave more attention to the relatively clean superhero genre than to horror and crime books.[61]

Notably, both during the hearings and in their official report, the senators chose not to highlight these superhero and jungle books, but instead drew attention to the horror comics of small publishers like Gaines (see figure 7).[62] The subcommittee was rejecting Wertham's explicit attempt to accuse the entire comic book industry, and the more established wing of it in particular, of wrongdoing. In making his argument, and in targeting the more established publishers, Wertham thus found himself in the same position as Gaines. They were both in opposi-

FIGURE 7. Senate hearings before the Subcommittee to Investigate Juvenile Delinquency, April 21, 1954. From left to right, Senator Thomas Hennings, presidential hopeful Senator Estes Kefauver, and subcommittee chairman Senator Robert Hendrickson examine the slides prepared by the subcommittee's staff director and first witness, Richard Clendenen (bottom right). Photo from the Bettmann Archive.

tion to the most powerful forces involved in this controversy, specifically, the bigger companies. Wertham was also violating a central principle of American political ideology by turning a commercial industry motivated by capitalist values into the enemy.

When the subcommittee finally released its recommendations, Wertham was incensed and insulted. Within a year, though, average Americans ceased to care about either his research or comic books in general; both the controversy and Wertham—its biggest enthusiast—faded from public view. The fears he had stoked were soon channeled elsewhere. When Kefauver took over the Senate subcommittee, he continued to pursue the crusade against mass media, redirecting it toward television, the latest source of American anxiety.[63] In later years, these concerns morphed into similar outcries around video games, the internet, and most recently, social media. But American support of free corporate enterprise has tended to dampen these controversies. At the very least, resistance to censorship and government interference has afforded industry representatives an opportunity to defend their products and shape the debate, usually by shifting attention in the right direction—by using both visibility and invisibility in their favor.

The Subtlety of Good Public Relations

Although the comic book industry would have preferred that no attention be paid to the hearings, Kefauver, Wertham, and Gaines made such an outcome impossible. They attracted considerable interest to the proceedings, in part by producing an appealing and satisfying narrative about taste and appropriateness that most Americans could agree with. Instead of fighting the tide, industry representatives by and large chose to support this perspective, refusing to challenge its fundamental assumption, namely that crude content was bad for society. Regardless, the subcommittee seems to have already been convinced that too many comic books were of exceedingly low quality and that something had to be done to rectify matters. There was no way to win on this issue. So the seventeen individuals who spoke on behalf of the magazine and comic book industry, besides Bill Gaines, shifted attention away from taste.

Instead, they testified in depth on the ins and outs of the business, speaking about shipments, bundling, returns, and credits.[64] Delivering boring testimony seems to have been the general aim. Representatives from Dell, National, and Magazine Management—publishers that together represented more than half of the industry's volume—all gave lengthy but ultimately unmemorable testimonies. While they faced what appears to have been tough questioning, unlike Wertham and Gaines, they were far more effective at downplaying potential problems that could attract additional attention. As a result, their very presence has been expunged from some histories that claim that nobody from the comic book industry but Gaines appeared to defend the medium.[65]

All were careful to explain that while there were many "bad" and potentially harmful comic books on the market, there were far more good comic books, many of which, incidentally, these companies themselves were responsible for publishing. And when the senators suggested otherwise, pointing out the crime titles in their own catalogues, these representatives were quick to explain that such books could be easily eliminated from their stock, and that some had *already* in fact been cancelled. (Others, notably, they would continue publishing without controversy for a decade to come.) That the major publishers were able to deal with these "bad" books so effectively, they argued, served as evidence that the industry was more than capable of dealing with the problem of corrupt comics all on its own.[66] On this point, the subcommittee members were in total agreement, as indicated by their stated approval of the formation of the industry body, the Comics Magazine

Association of America (CMAA), and its efforts at self-regulation through the creation of the Comics Code, overseen by the Comics Code Administration (CCA).[67]

The industry had offered a rather routine solution to what had seemed like an extraordinary cultural moment. It was a shrewd strategy, in part because it was completely in line with the desires of the senators, who wanted a way to placate public concerns without resorting to censorship. More notably, understanding that flash and brazenness had generated the most disruptive and threatening moments of the controversy, the more established players offered the opposite: the creation of a bureaucratic organization, the establishment of internal rules, and, perhaps most importantly, quiet and unobtrusive compliance. In short, they offered an infrastructural solution. It was a concrete answer to a public crisis that had created a moment of hypervisibility. But this tangible solution would fade easily into the background as soon as that moment passed, thereby allowing publishers and distributors to conduct business without interference from the state or the public. The details of what the CMAA did once it was up and running certainly mattered to those within the comic book industry, and those details could be used to satisfy the concerns of government officials, should they arise. But it was the very dull fact of the organization's creation that had the biggest impact on public opinion.

There was, however, a sticking point: distribution. The most heated and involved exchanges during the hearings (at least after Wertham and Gaines left the stage) tended to be about distribution practices and about the very specific methods that publishers, distributors, wholesalers, and retailers used to bring comic books to the public. In its current state, the system was not functioning properly, and its failures forced its inner workings out into the open; the questioning exposed parts of the business most industry leaders would have preferred remain invisible. Testimony given by publishers, wholesalers, and retailers provides a comprehensive description of how the practices and protocols that kept comic books moving back and forth across the country also helped organize, expand, and eventually discipline the medium. Distribution shaped every aspect of the business—including, notably, its imminent censorship.

HOW TO CENSOR A MASS MEDIUM (1954–1955)

The two most visible mechanisms of censorship tend to be legislation and content protocols, and both emerged here. As noted, though, legislative censorship was frowned upon and met resistance. The creation of a comics code had more success, especially as a public relations tool. But its enforcement depended on distribution, a sector of the business that grew increasingly important and impactful in the wake of the controversy.

Legislation

The senators had argued that regulation was at least partially the responsibility of citizens' and parents' groups,[68] which since 1948 had been boycotting stores and pressuring newsstands in an effort to reduce the sale of comic books to children.[69] Their hard work resulted in more than fifty cities eventually taking action, either by passing ordinances or by setting up censorship committees. According to a study conducted in 1956, however, this kind of regulation had been "spasmodic and highly localized," not to mention only "quasi-legal." It almost always relied on the "effectiveness of warning, threat, or boycott" alone since authorities almost never brought legal action to fruition within the court system.[70]

After the Senate hearings, as the CMAA was forming its code, states thus started stepping forward to do what neither the federal government nor local authorities would. Between 1954 and 1955, twelve states introduced resolutions to curb sales, most of which focused on preventing comic books featuring sex and violence from reaching minors. Even these efforts, though, faced obstacles, with governors vetoing the bills or courts striking them down as unconstitutional.[71] The only truly successful law—which made the sale of obscene comics to minors an illegal act in New York state—was not passed until May 1955,[72] three months after the Senate released its report, a full six months after the establishment of the CCA, and well after the decline in comic book sales had begun. These local acts of censorship thus had a limited impact on the comic book market, particularly in comparison to those imposed by the industry itself.

Codes of Self-Censorship

By mid-August of 1954, the same summer the hearings took place, the comic-book industry leapt into action to establish the CMAA, which drafted the Comics Code, appointed Charles Murphy as comic book czar, and created the CCA, all within a month.[73] The speed with which publishers formed these organizations may make this response seem hasty. To the contrary, the big publishers created the Code with prudence and forethought. It was no different from the careful and deliberate approach they had taken for the entirety of the fifteen years prior. And while the subcommittee may have encouraged these actions, there was no force involved, with no legislative recommendations ever made, and certainly no legislative action. It was a gentlemen's agreement, willingly entered into by all involved.

Ironically, Bill Gaines actually helped launch the CMAA, with an open invitation to other publishers in the industry to initiate a collective public relations campaign to repair the industry's image.[74] Of course, other publishers had been quietly and effectively pursuing such a campaign for years and had little to gain by joining forces with the maligned Gaines. So even though publishers responded to Gaines's invitation, the group he started quickly turned against him. By the fourth meeting, nearly the entire industry had signed on, and they elected John Goldwater of Archie Publications as CMAA chairman, with Jack Liebowitz of National Comics (later DC), Monroe Froehlich of Atlas (later Marvel), and several other major publishers elected to a Special Committee on Organization tasked with drafting a code of ethics.[75] Unhappy with the new direction the group was taking and the impending decision to limit horror and crime publications, Gaines walked out. On September 14, 1954, he wrote a statement to the press accusing the CMAA of lacking "sincerity" and using a "smoke screen to deceive the public." He claimed that in creating a code of ethics, the other publishers planned not to eradicate harmful comic books, as they publicly claimed, but merely to print deceptive covers with innocuous titles while publishing the same old material inside.[76] He was not wrong.

When it came to the actual writing of the Code, the CMAA ignored Wertham just as it had Gaines. Its general standards demanded that all comic books show crime and divorce in a negative light, portray authority figures with respect, and refrain from using profanity or depicting sex. These rules gave a superficial nod to Wertham's concerns about children's theoretical development, and their requirements demanded minor changes in content at nearly all of the publishing houses. The Code's stricter and more explicit standards, however—that comics refrain from using the words "crime," "horror," and "terror" and that they eliminate, *specifically,* the inclusion of "walking dead, torture, vampires, and vampirism, ghouls, cannibalism and werewolfism"[77]—targeted the less established players like Gaines (whom Wertham had largely ignored). Ultimately, it was these more exacting guidelines that caused the greatest

AND INSIDE THE SHIP, THE MAN REMOVED HIS SPACE HELMET AND SHOOK HIS HEAD, AND THE INSTRUMENT LIGHTS MADE THE BEADS OF PERSPIRATION ON HIS DARK SKIN TWINKLE LIKE DISTANT STARS...

THE END

FIGURE 8. The final panel of "Judgment Day," story by Bill Gaines and Al Feldstein, art by Joe Orlando. Gaines ended up printing "Judgment Day" without Code approval in the very last comic book he ever published, *Incredible Science Fiction* #33 (February 1955). Illustration copyright © Joe Orlando. Image courtesy of Fantagraphics Books (www.fantagraphics.com).

strain for publishers, small ones in particular, since they demanded that individual titles be eliminated.

One of the often-told tales about EC Comics' ensuing clash with the CCA concerns the title "Judgment Day," a story by Gaines and Al Feldstein about a futuristic astronaut (see figure 8). Charles Murphy rejected the story in January 1955, allegedly for the way it humanized its black protagonist. According to most accounts of the incident, this decision demonstrated the inherent injustice faced by a noble Gaines and the regressive and horrid nature of the Code; as a kind of parable, it speaks to the plain and certain immorality of censorship.[78] But Feldstein himself later acknowledged that Murphy's response to his story was basically "illogical," and had "nothing to do with the code." The dispute was really about business;[79] the CCA's retrogressive judgment was informed less by bad personal politics than by the complex web of relationships that informed the industry's decision-making at that moment. The CMAA was not immoral so much as it was amoral. The unintended consequences of this capitalistic stance were, not surprisingly, incredibly racist; ethical stances have little hope in moments of industrial crisis. Of singular importance to the all-white and male CMAA was shifting attention and blame to Gaines and helping more reputable publishers evade further scrutiny. In this respect, the Code was a clear continuation of the successful public relations strategy that publishers like DC, Archie, and Dell used to maintain a low profile throughout the comic book controversy. It doubled down on a familiar cultural narrative about media's effects on children, so the CMAA could turn its attention to something that mattered more to them, but was far less legible to the public: distribution.

Enforcing Self-Censorship through Distribution

Creating a code of censorship is one thing; enforcing it is quite another. Whether censorship is mandated by the federal government (which it hardly ever is) or by an industry organization with no legal power (which is generally the case), its rules are meaningless unless the monitoring body has found a way to administer them. Censorship often seems like an occurrence that is primarily value-based, politically motivated, and culturally contingent. As a result, historical accounts often fail to account for the extent to which it is fundamentally also an industrial and economic process. For this reason, distribution—which accounts for an enormous amount of the profits, workers, and actual labor within media businesses—has often additionally functioned as a lynchpin of national censorship campaigns. My use of the term *distribution* here relies on the broader definition recommended by media scholar Alisa Perren, and refers to the space in between production and consumption, the three sectors of the business commonly referred to at the time as distribution, wholesale, and retail.[80]

As Lee Grieveson notes, as early as 1912, federal legislation that tried to curb content, and could thus be interpreted as a violation of the First Amendment, usually focused instead "on the disciplining of circulation," which the government had more power to restrict through the interstate commerce clause.[81] Self-regulation from industry also relied on control over distribution. For example, no movie producer was compelled to comply with the Production Code of the 1930s, but because Hollywood was vertically integrated and the major studios controlled distribution and exhibition, they were able to lock out dissenters.[82] Acquiescence of companies to such codes in any medium is thus less about loyalty to the industry or desire to serve the public responsibly than it is about maintaining their access to the public. If there is no outside, no alternative way to reach consumers, then producers of media have to play ball with industry heavyweights, those that control distribution networks.

In the case of comic books, which had to physically traverse the country, sometimes multiple times over, access to reliable distribution networks and strong representation along those routes was of course critical; a comic book, no matter how brilliant, was valueless if it could not first reach its audience. Distribution could thus effectively function as a point of enforcement, with distributors, wholesalers, and retailers refusing to accept comics that lacked the seal of approval. In contrast to Hollywood, however, comic book publishers were only just beginning to pursue vertical integration, oligopolistic power, and stability. With the 1954 creation of the CMAA and the subsequent enforcement of the Comics Code came a restructuring of the business that moved it toward such consolidation. Distribution played a critical role as the larger publishers increased their power over the smaller ones.

As comic book historians Amy Nyberg and Jean-Paul Gabilliet have noted, one of the CCA's most important functions was to force a rather uneven "reorganization of the industry" that seemed to spare the largest publishers while allowing the smaller companies to suffer and eventually fail. Scholars have largely explained this variance through diverging approaches to content. Most acknowledge that the smaller companies tended to churn out "second rate fare" and "questionable content" while the more established publishers "easily adjusted to the Comics Code Authority's demands," which they had personally crafted through the CMAA.[83]

Reports on the comic book industry written at the time, though, indicate that editorial decisions about content played a secondary role to pure market power in what was becoming an industry-wide shakeout. Several smaller publishers told the *Wall Street Journal* in 1955 that "this is the kind of business you must be in in a big way or not at all" since "no one but the bigger fellows is making any money."[84] A closer look at the industry's structure reveals that what actually separated the "bigger fellows"—those few publishers who had the power to regulate everyone else—from the small ones was not content, or even market share, but control of distribution.

DISTRIBUTION INFRASTRUCTURE IN THE COMIC BOOK INDUSTRY

The importance of this sector of the business was nothing new. From the beginning, distribution was a primary driver of the industry's basic structure, its early successes, and eventually, its failures. More significantly, distribution practices played a tremendous role in actually *organizing* the rest of the business. And ultimately, this sector would be at least as important as the editorial division in determining the era's winners and losers.

Boom and Oversupply (1940–1954)

In the late 1940s, the comic book industry saw tremendous growth as sales increased steadily and substantially. This, together with a well-established and efficient distribution system, made comic book publishing an extremely attractive business. Young creative entrepreneurs found very few barriers to entry. Not only were the startup capital requirements relatively low, but established distribution companies generally handled the more technical aspects of the business, including financing, shipping, sales, records, and returns. In short, the infrastructure of the business was already in place—the physical retail spaces and the networks that served them, the relationships between workers in various sectors, and the everyday practices and protocols that constituted the know-how of the industry. All an aspiring new publisher had to do was make a long-term deal with a distributor, a surprisingly easy task due to consolidation in national distribution.

From the 1860s to the 1920s, American News Company (ANC) exercised nearly complete control over magazine distribution in the United States.[85] At that point, it began facing competition from the in-house circulation departments of large publishers like Hearst.[86] But in the late 1940s, American News still owned one-third of the country's twelve hundred wholesalers in addition to one thousand retailers nationwide (see figure 9), giving it a stranglehold on the business.[87] This power gave the company some logistical leeway. ANC could not keep up with its own seven hundred–plus titles, so executives would typically agree to carry a new title after inspecting just a single issue. ANC would continue carrying it for years to come (and without further review), usually guaranteeing it space at its owned and operated newsstands.[88]

This process allowed a lot of publications with minimal profits and perhaps questionable content to slip under the radar, including many low-selling comic books.[89] By 1954, ANC was in fact distributing 287 comics for thirteen different publishers, accounting for about half of the industry's volume.[90] These titles included some of the market's best sellers, but also many second-rate titles from minor publishers; these

FIGURE 9. One of about two thousand newsstands in the city of New York. The ubiquity of these retailers nationwide and their ease of access to consumers supported the comic book industry's explosive growth in the late 1930s and 1940s. Photo courtesy of the New York Public Library.

companies would enter the market with a few successful comics in a newly trending genre and, on the strength of those, quickly expand their line to include others that failed to perform.[91]

Mike Benton, a meticulous comic book historian, has stated that so many publishers entered the business between 1950 and 1955, there were simply too many to count.[92] This was partly due to the industry's fundamental impermanence; both big publishers and individuals with no history in the business could temporarily set up a company to put out one comic, and then dissolve the company and disappear if the comic was either unsuccessful or too racy.[93] The Senate's inquiry into the industry, which made a record of existing publishers, or at least those that could be traced to an address, indicated that by 1954 there were at least forty-four in the market.[94] Overall, then, the industry *seemed* to be doing enormously well. In 1954, publishers issued approximately 650 titles, bringing in an estimated revenue of $90 million, all on a product that cost just ten cents.[95]

Signs of a Bust (1953–1955)

This success, however, was precarious. In addition to public concern, there was the rising threat of television. Media historian Patrick Parsons has explained that the industry could have recovered from other problems had demand not been severely eroded by the emergence of television. He cites a 1960 study that suggested that kids were between three and ten times more likely to read comic books regularly if they lacked access to a TV set. Since the technology exploded in the United States from 1950 to 1955,[96] it follows that readership was likely already well in decline when anti-comics sentiment peaked in 1954.[97] Most observers of the 1960s also recognized that television was a primary factor in the industry's demise.[98] In most cases, however, competition from another product—no matter how great—could not cause the kind of quick, dramatic, and permanent decline in sales experienced by comics. Market economics typically solves problems like this in a more predictable and orderly fashion, as a natural decline in audience demand gradually brings about a decline in supply.

Instead, a decade and a half of low barriers to entry was doing just the opposite, propelling a persistent oversupply that would soon bring disaster. At the height of the crisis, in January 1955, industry observers pointed out that "the entire industry for more than a year has been in a severe recession," not only because of "public resistance" to the medium, but because of "overproduction, both in terms of separate titles and the number of each title printed."[99] Indeed, overproduction has long been a problem in media, since distributors tend to subsidize production and "pay producers for rights to much more product than they can ever hope to sell."[100] Within the comic book industry, which had to deal with the physical mass of the enormous volume of unsold publications, this strategy was beginning to take a toll. The ease of distribution had driven growth in the comic book market since the medium's origin in the 1930s, but a reckoning was fast approaching; what had been a boon to growth was becoming, according to trade publications, "the industry's single biggest headache."[101]

Part of the problem was that comic books could turn a profit selling through just half of their print runs. This led to a large physical surplus of books, which carried considerable transactional costs. Newsstand retailers could send the comics back up the distribution chain (to the wholesaler and then the distributor), but had to wait weeks or months to receive refunds.[102] The excess also generated a black market.

Distributors would request refunds from publishers, promising to destroy the comics, but instead put them back into circulation at discount prices, further distorting a market already glutted with product.[103] This problem would become increasingly commonplace and damaging over the next two decades.

Furthermore, there seems to have been a worsening mismatch between large national distribution networks and the mom-and-pop retail system they worked with. Even though the market was producing in excess of five hundred different comic book titles, the average newsstand had the shelf space to carry just sixty-five.[104] And given the choice, most of those retailers were reluctant to increase that number. Not only did ten-cent comic books have a lower profit margin than the average twenty-five-cent magazine,[105] but the product had a bad reputation of attracting "crowds of loitering children."[106] Some comics continued to do well, of course, like many from Dell, whose *Walt Disney* and *Warner Bros.* titles regularly sold one to two million copies per issue.[107] But an ever-increasing number of copycat titles pursuing the latest genre trends—from romance to sci-fi—were becoming a burden to newsstands that were, financially and physically, too small to handle them all.

There was also the problem of tie-ins. Retailers claimed that wholesalers would deliver large bundles that included both desirable and undesirable magazines and comics. In order to continue getting and selling the desirable publications (popular science magazines or TV and radio periodicals), they had to take material they did not want, either because it was too racy and brought unwelcome customers or because it just did not sell well. The tie-in strategy had a lot in common with Hollywood block-booking of the 1920s and 1930s, which forced theater owners to play "sex-smut" films in order to gain access to big box-office winners. Eventually, in the 1948 decision *United States v. Paramount Pictures, Inc.,* the Supreme Court outlawed block-booking as an unfair trade practice.[108] Not surprisingly, then, comic book wholesalers and distributors fervently denied the existence of tie-ins when they testified in front of the 1954 subcommittee. Regardless of their true existence, it is clear that newsstands were finding themselves stuck with far more comics than they had the ability to display and sell. And they lacked the kind of control over supply they needed to reduce those shipments.[109]

In short, problems in the comic book industry were mounting, with retailers and distributors becoming increasingly frustrated with the medium, for reasons that had nothing to do with Bill Gaines or Fredric Wertham. In the 1940s, a well-functioning distribution infrastructure had helped the comic book industry expand and find considerable success. By the 1950s, however, its network of relationships had significantly deteriorated and its established protocols had ceased to function properly; distribution was bringing the industry to its knees. Its breakdown caught the attention of the U.S. senators charged with investigating and improving the medium. Standards and practices nobody would have bothered to question when business was humming along became the source of prolonged questioning and intense debate. Failure made this complex infrastructure visible, at least to the government officials tasked with overseeing it. For everyone else, though, this part of the business remained hidden. The public's interest in comic books—stoked by Fredric Wertham and Bill Gaines—was purely cultural and social; they wanted tasteless content eliminated.

The Code and the Crash (1954–1955)

The industry-drafted code of censorship offered the perfect solution. It placated the public by making immediate and visible changes to newsstand content. It also minimized the threat of sustained public intrusion and government oversight. This was especially important since business practices were becoming increasingly monopolistic. In fact, the state was far more likely throughout the middle of the twentieth century to intervene in matters of fair trade in order to maintain free markets than in questions over content. The Code had other advantages too, many of which had nothing to do with the government. Specifically, the industry was beginning to feel the effects of all the market problems noted above: a shrinking audience, massive overproduction, and mounting problems in distributor-retailer relations. Business leaders needed to act, but this time around, small-time publishers would not hijack their efforts, as had happened with the ACMP. The CMAA intended to use self-censorship to limit the power of the industry's more minor players.

The CCA thus became an all-in-one solution to a looming crisis. *Barron's Business* noted at the time that "through the elimination of [comics] that are objectionable," the Code "expected to reduce materially the overall number of titles published." In the process, it hoped to put the business on "stronger economic footing" so that the "the industry may be restored to profitability."[110] Numerous first-hand accounts also suggest that the Code functioned as a competitive mechanism. Al Feldstein explained in a 1996 interview that "this was a very crowded, competitive field, and [EC was] a maverick publishing company that was usurping a lot of the dimes that were available for comic books. And people like Donenfeld and Liebowitz at DC and . . . the publisher of Archie, John Goldwater, wanted [them] out of business. [They] were bad boys, and [they] were giving the comic book business a bad name."[111]

Goldwater's own description is basically consistent with Feldstein's: he has noted that he and other industry leaders saw the publication of offensive comics "as a threat to everything we had worked so hard to create."[112] Although Goldwater claimed that he worked to eliminate these comics out of a "moral obligation" to his reading public, the public relations director the CMAA hired while Goldwater was at the helm remembers it differently. He explained that the Code never intended to create "obstacles to the continued publication of the same basic material" and was in fact designed to "find a way to make the smallest possible concessions necessary to end the controversy."[113] And, with the help of a big PR push, the plan worked.[114] Although comic book content continued enraging observers like Wertham, by the end of 1955, the public had moved on.[115]

Popular accounts of the comic book controversy often argue that this imposition of censorship dramatically impacted the medium's future. By shaming the entire art form and aggressively curbing content, the Comics Code supposedly limited comic books to a narrow juvenile audience, triggering a dramatic decline in sales.[116] But examination of the industry's infrastructures—at how the business was organized, how it circulated its goods, how it standardized distribution and sales practices nationally—reveals that the market's decline was less about quality of content and public reception that it was about economics. Similarly, the industry's censorious response to the Senate hearings was not rooted in the publishers' overly conservative morality as much as in overly competitive, protective, and strategic business practices.

By 1961, *Barron's* reported that "the comic book business appears to be flourishing."[117] To be sure, the medium would never be what it was in terms of popularity or volume, but the business had been able to evolve into something else. Sales in supermarkets and chain stores were on the rise as mom-and-pop corner stands began to wane, and licensing would soon supplant publishing as the industry's primary source of income.[118] There was also this uncomplicated by-product of the Code: by the 1960s, only eleven publishers were still in business—just one-quarter the number in 1954.[119] So while the overall pie was much smaller, those who remained in the market were maintaining a significantly larger chunk of it.

WINNERS AND LOSERS (1953–1958)

The role that distribution played in reining in the industry was immediately clear to publishers like EC. Within weeks of the Senate hearings—months before the CCA was even announced—they began receiving massive returns from distributors, bundles of comics that had never been opened. This problem only intensified after the Code was introduced; wholesalers refused any publication that did not bear the CCA seal, meaning that a publisher had to join in order to survive. Even then, however, a publication could still face resistance from wholesalers. So if a publisher improved or changed its content to comply with the Code—as some did several times—it still might never have the opportunity to win the public back over.[120]

Notably, though, wholesaler resistance was an obstacle that in many cases appears to have been overcome with strong distributor support. As media industry experts Amanda Lotz and Timothy Havens explain, media distributors have long practiced "differential promotion" in which they "tend to shower praise, attention, and money on only a small fraction of the products they acquire . . . [those] that they believe have the greatest potential . . . [and] largely abandon texts they see as potentially unsuccessful, releasing them to the public with little fanfare or promotional support."[121] This tendency was likely more pronounced in the mid-1950s, as the distribution sector faced an increasing number of hardships.

In the case of comic books, the ability of distributors to pick and choose winners was complicated by the industry's infrastructure, in which distributing was intricately intermingled with publishing in the move toward vertical integration. Following is a closer examination of this network of ownership, with the varying types of distributors divided into three categories: 1) the financially invested distributors, 2) the magazine distributors, and 3) American News Company (ANC). Major publishers tended to be backed by the first type, distributors (often wholly owned subsidiaries) that were invested in their product. Willing to give their titles the support they needed in the face of wholesaler and retailer resistance, public controversy, and other market challenges, they were able to push comic books past these obstacles and on to the market, where the consumers could decide.

In contrast, publishers that relied on disinterested distributors specializing in magazines suffered a quick demise. And then there were the publishers distributed by American News Company; for years shielded by the distributor's monopolistic power, they would soon be facing more trouble than anyone. Overall, the success of publishers operating in the early 1950s turns out to have been strongly correlated with which kind of distributor they used. Distributors had a determining impact on whether or not a publisher survived the turbulent years of the late 1950s to embark upon the next era of comic book history (see table 1).

Financially Invested Distributors

In the early nineteenth century, major magazine publishers began spinning their internal circulation departments off into distribution companies. Over time, these independent national distributors were joined by smaller competitors until there were thirteen nationwide. When comic books proved profitable in the forties, a number of these independent distributors invested in the medium. Independent News Co., a distributor of girlie magazines and pulps, had actually helped establish the medium by introducing Superman through its publishing division National Allied (later National Comics and then DC). By 1954, it was a vertically integrated company, a leader in both national distribution and comic book publishing, with the standing to continue pushing its product through the distribution chain despite possible resistance from wholesalers and retailers.

Even with the enormous attention given to National's comic books in Wertham's *Seduction of the Innocent* (Superman, Batman, and Wonder Woman were central targets), National kept these titles in print and on newsstands, selling 1.5 million copies of *Superman* per issue in the middle of the crisis.[122] The company gave the same support to lesser selling titles from American and Prize Comics, and continued to distribute at least three of their horror comics well into the 1960s even after all of them had been *specifically* called out by name as objectionable during the Senate hearings.[123] Unlike EC Comics, National was not receiving bundles of unopened books back from its distributor, since the same men (Harry Donenfeld and Jack Liebowitz) were in charge of both companies. They had the infrastructural power to get their product through wholesalers and to the public. From 1956 to 1960, revenues at the firm doubled.[124]

Run by Martin Goodman, Marvel Comics (officially known as Magazine Management Co.) also distributed its own comic books through a wholly owned subsidiary called Atlas Magazines. As at National, comic books were a major source of income, but in contrast, Atlas's

TABLE I   ORGANIZATION OF THE COMIC BOOK INDUSTRY IN 1954

Distributor (Total Titles)	Publishers	Final Year	No. of Titles
AMERICAN NEWS COMPANY			
American News Company (287)	**Archie**	ongoing	15
(ceased distribution operation in 1957)	**Dell**	1973	107
	Standard Comics Group	1959	16
	Preferred Comics Group / St. John Publications	1958	55
	Magazine Enterprises	1958	17
	Quality Romance Group	1956	18
	Star Publications	1955	19
	Toby	1955	16
	United Features	1955	6
	Fiction House Inc.	1954	13
FINANCIALLY INVESTED DISTRIBUTORS			
Curtis Circulation (103)	**Gilberton**	1971	103
Independent News Co. (65)	**National Comics (DC Comics)**	ongoing	40
	American Comics Group	1967	12
	Prize Comic Group	1963	10
Atlas Magazines (64)	**Magazine Management Co. (Marvel)**	ongoing	64
Leader News Co. (22)	EC Comics	1956	9
(ceased operation in 1956)	Stanhall/Ribage/Master Publications	1954	8
Capital Distributing Co. (21)	**Charlton Comics**	1986	21
MAGAZINE DISTRIBUTORS			
Publishers Distributing Co. (37)	**Harvey Comics**	1994	26
	Lev Gleason Comics	1956	9
Kable News Co. (36)	Farrell Comic Group	1958	7
	Premier Magazines	1956	6
	Stanley P. Morse	1955	8
	Joseph Wolfert	1955	5
	Allen Hardy (Comic Media)	1954	10
Hearst (ICD) (16)	Avon Periodicals	1956	16
Ace News Corp (11)	Ace Fiction	1956	11
Fawcett Publications (9)	Fawcett Publications	1953	9

SOURCES: Publisher/distributor information from *Juvenile Delinquency (Comic Books): Hearings before the Subcommittee to Investigate Juvenile Delinquency of the Committee on the Judiciary,* United States Senate (1954). Final year of operation from Mike Benton, *The Comic Book in America: An Illustrated History* (Dallas: Taylor, 1993).

NOTES: The publishers in bold text survived into the 1960s, the next era of comic book publishing and licensing. Publishers of three titles or fewer are not included in this chart, so as to eliminate the market's most impermanent and minor participants (all of which folded); accordingly, some of each distributor's total titles are not accounted for in the final column. Overall, publishers are listed in the order of their survival but organized according to their distributor. Distributors are divided into three basic categories, explained in detail in the text.

distribution business was small. This meant that Goodman was able to keep his comic books alive through the initial shakeout in 1955, but the decline in comics sales and trouble in the distribution sector eventually forced him to fold the distribution arm. After a brief time with American News Co., Goodman eventually asked his competitors at National to distribute Marvel comics through Independent News. Determined to maintain its share of the shrinking market, National shrewdly took Marvel on only after Goodman agreed to cut his output to just eight titles, limiting the company's competitive threat for years to come.[125] The power of distribution had again helped National secure its standing into the future, and also in this instance provided Marvel with a lifeline to the 1960s.

Two other publishers benefited from close ties with distributors. John Santangelo founded Charlton in 1920, eventually transforming it into a vertically integrated company boasting a paper mill and a major distributor, Capital Distributing.[126] Although he got into comic book publishing in the 1940s, Santangelo waited until after the crash to invest heavily in the business. Seeing an opportunity in licensing, he began buying up titles from failing publishers. With his own distribution business, he could profit from their discarded material, which boasted a number of crime and horror comics.[127] Never known for its high quality or tame nature, Charlton Comics managed to survive well into the 1980s.

Gilberton, who published *Classics Illustrated,* also had strong distribution. Like the executives at National and Dell, the publisher's founder, Al Kanter, had for years insisted on his books' "complete separation from the 'bad' comics."[128] He nonetheless suffered individual attacks from Wertham for the way in which his titles depicted violence and threatened to distract children from reading the real "great novels" upon which his comics were based. He also, quite notably, refused to join the CCA. For many publishers, this decision would have proved extremely problematic, but *Classics Illustrated* happened to be the only comic book client of Curtis, a major distributor known for its aggressive promotional activities with retailers.[129] With its support, Gilberton was able to survive bad press and potential wholesaler resistance and stay afloat into the 1960s, at which point competition from paperbacks finally pushed them out of the market.[130]

Finally, there was Leader News Co., which distributed EC Comics. Run by Michael Estrow, this was the smallest of the national distributors. In addition to handling eight of his own comics under various imprints

(Stanhall, Ribage, and Master), Estrow handled a few other publishers as well. Given the composition of his business, Estrow likely would have supported all of these products if only he could. But he was 69 years old in 1956, and both his distribution and his publishing businesses operated in low volumes in an increasingly tough field. Finding himself $32,000 in debt to his printer and at least $100,000 in debt to EC Comics, he decided to retire. Leader went bankrupt, and Estrow died just a few years later.[131] His demise was the last straw for Bill Gaines, who promptly wrote the following note to a friend: "EC is out of business except for MAD. Distributor went bankrupt and clipped us for $150,000." Gaines would later say this was "the best thing that could've happened to [him]" because it allowed him to get out of business with a weak distributor.[132] Like Martin Goodman, he briefly worked with American News Co. before going to National; with the latter's support, *Mad* prospered for decades.

In short, publishers with strong distribution seemed largely able to survive, and sometimes even strengthened their market position. Meanwhile, comic book companies in low standing with their distributors folded one after the next.

Magazine Distributors

By the mid-1950s, magazine distribution was no longer a very profitable business.[133] Comic books were in a particularly bad position because of low profit margins. But oversupply, declining demand, and distressed distribution chains plagued many other sectors of publishing too. For those that handled magazines, paperbacks, *and* comic books, the latter were only exacerbating matters, particularly once the Senate hearings put these companies' operations under a spotlight and threatened to bring continued government oversight. Accordingly, most independent national distributors completely stopped carrying comic books by 1956; they either dropped the titles completely or simply chose no longer to push them with wholesalers, thereby letting them fail.

The more powerful distributors had an established record of swiftly cutting off comic book publishers that became a drain. Fawcett had been a major publisher and distributor of pulps, fan magazines, and comic books. But after National Comics brought a successful copyright infringement suit against them in 1951 and sales began to decline, they decided to drop the entire line; the publisher discontinued comics in 1953, a full year before the Senate hearings.[134] Two other firms, Publisher's Distributing Co. and Hearst (which owned and operated its own distribution firm, International Circulation Division), behaved similarly. In 1955, Hearst had bought Avon, a paperback publisher that also sold comics. It was a bad year for comics, so Hearst folded the division by the end of the year.[135] Publisher's Distributing, another major national player in distribution and publishing, also had little motivation to support comic books.[136] It had been carrying the headline-making and "objectionable" *Crime Does Not Pay* for Lev Gleason Comics. Blamed for starting the crime comic book fad in the first place, Gleason was gone by 1956.[137] Publisher's Distributing did, however, leave Harvey Comics undisturbed; it was the only publisher that survived the crash without strong support from a distributor. Its success was likely due to the company's astute move into licensing kids' comics, which kept it going through the early 1990s.

The smaller independent distributors proved just as likely to cut comic books from their rosters; they could not afford to support a deteriorating medium in which they had no real financial investment. Ace Magazines, which published and distributed just eleven comic books (only five of these were crime or horror), dropped them all in 1956 to focus on its paperbacks; the move helped it hold onto its distribution division into the 1970s when it was bought out by Simon & Schuster.[138] Lastly, there was Kable News Co., which started as a small science fiction distributor,[139] and had more than half its business in comics. When its president George Davis testified to the subcommittee in 1954, he seemed eager to please the senators and more than willing to drop the comic book publishers who had put him in this unwelcome position.

Indeed, four of them were out of business the following year. The only one of Kable's clients that held on was Farrell Comic Group. But according to a lawsuit that publisher brought in 1958—the year it finally folded—Kable had been taking refunds from the publisher on unsold comics since 1955, only to resell those titles on the black market.[140] It appears Farrell had been driven out of business by a distributor that wanted nothing to do with it. For distributors who were not heavily invested in comics, there was little motivation to give the medium the additional support it needed following the Senate hearings. Of the dozen publishers distributed by these companies, only Harvey survived the decade.

The Demise of American News Company

A number of histories have attributed some of the comic book industry's problems to the demise of American News Company, which, depending on the account, folded entirely or just partly after facing a lawsuit from the Department of Justice.[141] The company's exit from the comic book market was actually a little more complicated than that, but it nonetheless had an immense effect on the future of the medium and, for a time, on the entire publishing industry. By 1954, American News Co. distributed, exported, and sold newspapers, magazines, and books, and also operated restaurants, soda fountains, tobacco shops, toy stores, and ice-skating rinks. It was the largest wholesaler of books and the largest retailer of magazines in the world,[142] and it handled about half the comic book industry's volume.[143] Its size and power had helped the comic book industry blossom, but 1955 brought a slew of problems that had nothing to do with the CCA and that went above and beyond the kinds of troubles other distributors had been facing.

The crisis began in June 1955, after a year of quietly declining sales, when American News began losing major publications.[144] Time Inc. left first, bringing *Time, Life, Sports Illustrated,* and *Fortune* to a competitor.[145] Weeks later, the company faced a hostile takeover from a former newsstand dealer named Harry Garfinkle, who immediately began changing company policy.[146] In July, it lost more publications, and in August the company faced a strike that halted deliveries in New York, the epicenter of the publishing business.[147] In September, Garfinkle settled an antitrust suit the Department of Justice had filed back in 1952 that barred its distribution operation from working directly with its retail outlets.[148] American News soon laid off eight thousand employees and sustained losses of $8 million.[149]

Interestingly, the company's prominent role in comic book distribution may have played a role in its troubles with the Department of Justice. American News was the largest distributor of crime and horror comics in the nation but, unlike many of its competitors, chose not to discontinue titles that were considered objectionable. To make matters worse, the distributor had sent its vice-president, William Eichhorn, to testify at the subcommittee hearings, where he was asked to discuss the aggressive sales and distribution tactics that were also at issue in the ongoing antitrust suit. His tone with the senators was dismissive and, much like Bill Gaines, he did not make any political friends that day, despite the fact that his company was sorely in need of allies in Washington.[150] The deal with the Department of Justice closed a year later.

In response to all of this chaos, American News Co. dramatically altered its business strategy. Previously, the company's large and powerful vertically integrated distribution network had allowed minor publications to skate by unnoticed;[151] that was no longer going to be the modus operandi. In the midst of this transition, which happened to coincide with the nadir of the comic book crash in 1955, five comic book publishers distributed by the company folded.[152] Two years later, in May 1957, ANC announced it would close its distribution sector entirely. Of note, the closure probably had little to do with the antitrust settlement, which ANC had been in blatant violation of for some time.[153]

The decision did, however, come just weeks after Dell—the nation's largest and most reputable comic book publisher—announced that it too would be leaving American News. Not only was the distributor about to lose Dell's $30 million newsstand business, but without Dell as a client, it was at risk of losing even more publications whose executives felt nervous about the resulting "diminished newsstand coverage."[154] At this point, it made more sense for the company to sell the real estate of its wholesale branches and refocus its attention on merchandising and restaurants. In the long term, American News Co. emerged "more profitable than ever."[155]

The effect of this decision on the rest of the industry was immense. According to *Business Week,* magazine distribution was "in for a period of disruption" and a "seriously chaotic situation."[156] With the disappearance of American News's wholesale outlets (constituting one-third of the nation's total), other wholesalers had to manage a "deluge of publications" they did not have the capacity to handle.[157] Distributors meanwhile would be unable to ensure any continuity in delivery; their established networks were in total disarray.[158] Publishers, though, would face the greatest challenges of all. The general consensus was that smaller publications with lower circulations, "the poor-quality magazines, the comic books and lurid sensation-ridden periodicals," would suffer the most because they were unimportant to wholesalers. One executive explained that "with all magazines crowded into one house, everyone is going to suffer to a greater or lesser degree. . . . Some fringe publishers will find themselves squeezed out entirely simply because they won't have the strength to command even a minimum distribution effort."[159]

Accordingly, Preferred Comics, Magazine Enterprises, and Standard Comics, whose 88 collective titles had been distributed by American News, all closed their doors within the next two years. Of the twenty comic book publishers that folded between 1953 and 1959, nine had been distributed by American News Company, and among them were some of the largest victims of the crash.[160] These challenges reinforce how important it was for comic books to have strong support from their distributors. Even though the company had acted monopolistically, its size and power had protected publishers from having to face the local monopolies of individual wholesalers.[161] This was exactly why Bill Gaines had been so excited to replace his weaker distributor—he would no longer have to do business with wholesalers.[162]

While Gaines, though, on the heels of American News's closure, was able to take his single remaining publication *Mad Magazine* to Independent News (as did Marvel), National was not opening its doors to any additional comic book publishers. Its top executives had played a major role in the creation of the CCA, which had the specific intention of eliminating such competition. Control over crumbling distribution networks during a moment of transition for the publishing and newsstand industries provided an easy avenue to accomplish this goal. Accordingly, when American News Company—whose monopolistic power had transformed it into a home for independents—left magazine distribution, these publishers, along with any new potential entrants, were left with nowhere else to go. In a span of three years, an industry that initially had no significant barriers to entry had become an exclusive club, impermeable to anyone without prior standing and without one's own preestablished distribution network.

FREE-MARKET CENSORSHIP

Despite the attention given to the Comics Code and the changes it demanded, the ability of publishers to survive this crisis seems to have had very little to do with content. National Comics and other major publishers had power on their side, power that enabled them to frame the debate as it played out on a national stage, and power rooted in their very real ability to put their own comic books on newsstands and prevent certain competitors from doing the same. Their creative capacity in the years that followed—to experiment with content, to respond to readers' interests, to pursue titles that appealed to fans, and eventually to develop their catalogue in creative and innovative ways—all flowed from that initial ability to build infrastructure that supported their own growth and success. This power also depended on their willingness to limit competition by restricting the access of others.

While government censorship is associated with oppressed and closed societies and competitive business practices are associated with free and open ones, there are remarkable similarities between these two frameworks. Both censorship and the deregulation of markets tend to bestow upon a small number of actors immense power to regulate industry and limit its expansion. Free-market economies can see the strength of established networks of circulation grow to the point where they cannot be easily substituted or replaced and, as such, become bottlenecks for products trying to reach consumers. When distributors that control these networks limit access to only favored producers, further consolidation becomes inevitable. When content and conduits are united under one roof (or even just closely linked, as they were in comic books), distributor-producers are even more likely to erect barriers to entry, cutting competing producers off from the broad circulation that sustains their products.

The media business has undergone profound transformations since the 1950s, but these competitive tendencies appear again and again throughout its history. There are other continuities as well; distribution has worked in similar ways over time, from analog to digital, and across various media. There is, for example, the practice of tie-ins. This strategy allowed magazine distributors to withhold their most desirable products in order to force upon retailers their least desirable products. It had as an antecedent the block-booking employed by film distributors in the 1930s. It was also a precursor to today's practice of cable bundling, in which programmers package their less popular channels with more successful ones. In the case of both tie-ins and block-booking, retailers/exhibitors contested this distribution strategy by appealing to the government on moral grounds—claiming that it prevented them from exercising their own discrimination in choosing products of high quality. The Justice Department rejected that argument officially, attacking block-booking on the basis of antitrust legislation instead, and threatening to do the same with tie-ins. Such a threat never materialized in response to cable bundling in today's deregulated media environment.[163]

But morality campaigns have nonetheless repeatedly and successfully served as justification for tighter regulation of industries. This detail was likely not lost on established comic book publishers, who spent fifteen years publicly differentiating themselves from lesser elements within their business. The tendency of the U.S. government to reward such activities was, by that time, relatively well established. Twice during the 1920s, the federal government restricted priority access to the airwaves (which function in radio as channels of distribution) on moral grounds. Reserving the most desirable licenses for wealthier and more reputable commercial broadcasters, federal agencies promised that regulation of distribution would protect Americans from both propaganda and potentially threatening cultural forms like jazz.[164]

In practice, though, this approach to ordering the airwaves had the primary effect of reinforcing already entrenched industry power; it kept network broadcasters "profitable at the expense of the independents."[165] As media scholar Michele Hilmes has noted, federal radio regulation of this kind ultimately led to a "restricted-access, vertically integrated oligopoly, dominated by two large corporations and supported by increasingly blunt and intrusive commercial advertising, [that] exerted what could be a called a stranglehold on radio programming."[166] This situation is remarkably similar to what developed within the comic book industry by the 1970s as just two companies—DC and Marvel—came to dominate the market completely. Both had relied on strong distribution from Independent News to survive the 1954 crash, and DC had acted very strategically in winnowing the market down.

These historical reoccurrences point to a remarkable consistency in the way distribution, as a mechanism of censorship, expands its reach into other areas. As a regulating force, distributors contain not just content, but many other aspects of industry. This was true of radio in the 1920s, when the pursuit of morally acceptable programming blocked outsiders and independents from accessing the medium's best distribution channels. It was also true of film in the 1930s, when the major studios' distribution and exhibition arms enforced the Production Code, not just to placate censors, but to ensure their industry's financial stability into the future. In the 1950s, distribution also became a mechanism of self-censorship within the comic book industry, which, like Hollywood, sought economic and political stability through elimination of, or control over, unpredictable competition. In all of these cases, the greatest threat was not the censorship—which called itself out by name—but the maneuverings these censorship campaigns rendered invisible; away from the public eye, established industry players were reinforcing their advantages and constraining the development of these media for decades to come.

In theory, attention to the media industries through public events like the Senate subcommittee hearings could shine a light on these unsavory and potentially anticompetitive business practices. And a mandate to improve failing industry practices in response to such events could entice new producers to enter the fray and give it a try. In practice, however, public controversies and their resolutions tend to serve a restrictive function and embolden those already in power. The potential for more sweeping or structural change can quickly recede in the face of well-orchestrated public relations campaigns and promises to pursue self-censorship (it should be noted that the "self" part of "self-censorship" generally only applies to the most powerful parties involved, since minor actors are subjected to something closer to "competitor-censorship"). In short, the public cannot trust either the government or industry itself to expose business operations that make companies seem unjustifiably powerful or controlling.

The broader communication networks that characterize today's digital environment may be offering alternative avenues for transparency. In recent years, the tendencies of cable operators and ISPs (contemporary media's most powerful distributors), particularly those that have united with content providers to restrict access and creativity, have been widely recognized by academics and media activists. The ability of those distributors to influence government policy on the issue, and not only avoid or win antitrust suits but shape the law in their favor, has also received interest from the public, particularly in the case of the FCC's dealings regarding net neutrality. As a result, there is more skepticism toward public conversations hijacked by corporate PR departments and more ire toward the vertically integrated companies that back these campaigns. But the dangers posed by consolidated distribution channels linked with oligopolistic content providers continue to pose a threat. Big and growing media companies have, in recent years, realized that distracting the public with controversy (e.g., Donald Trump's war with CNN) can sometimes draw attention away from the real issue at hand (the anti-competitive nature of vertical integration). Visibility thus remains a crucial issue in the fight over media consolidation; it is hard to fix what cannot be seen.

CONCLUSION

Though they are often disregarded, distribution networks play a particularly important role in determining the course of evolution for most media forms—both creatively and industrially. This was certainly the case for comic books; distribution functioned as an organizing force within the business for many decades, profoundly shaping production and consumption in significant and tangible ways.[167] The structural significance of these physical and relational networks was on full display at the Senate subcommittee hearings of 1954, which briefly put the spotlight on a distribution system in disrepair. Contrary to collective memory about these hearings and the anti–comic book crusade that preceded them, these affairs were neither a witch hunt nor a plot to eradicate subversive artistic expression. They were considerably more ordinary and bureaucratic than that. Whatever their personal motivations, the senators involved were trying to find a way to encourage industry to help itself, and in so doing, they supported a very American ideal of commercial self-rule.

The negative public sentiment comic books encountered in that moment was also quite ordinary, and similar to what many new media encounter: broad suspicion accompanied by some amount of fear. How the industry managed it was how many media industries have managed such doubts before and since, which is strategically. What perhaps distinguishes the comic book scare was the fact that the medium was simultaneously facing so many other problems, most of which related to distribution. The implementation of self-censorship, in addition to placating the public, also worked to disentangle the industry from this wider range of issues. So while it may have been prompted by a public relations crisis, regulation worked primarily to reorganize and stabilize the comic book business. This transitional moment allowed industry leaders to rewrite the rules of the business in ways that were better aligned with their needs. They wanted financial security, opportunities for licensing, and less volatility. So moving forward, the comic book industry—disciplined by content codes and constricted distribution networks—became less contentious, more predictable, safer for investors, and less open to independents. It became more corporate.

What remains difficult about reimagining these events is the extent to which the established conception of them has shaped comic book culture. The overstated significance of Wertham, Gaines, and the evils of censorship have long portrayed comic books as a medium besieged by opponents and beleaguered by unfair restrictions. Many continue to view the medium as a cultural form that comes from a fundamental place of political defiance and cultural opposition. It may well be true that as an art form, comic books have always been and continue to be distinct, unruly, even revolutionary.

But as a product, produced, distributed, and sold by a culture industry that has long resembled every other American culture industry, comic books were protected and promoted by the very same and very powerful mass media institutions that popularized radio, film, and television. Hemmed in by the infrastructures that supported their growth and survival, comic books emanated from a place of corporate intention far more than they did a place of subcultural opposition. This need not have remained the case in the decades that followed, as the industry and the form evolved. The next three chapters will assess to what extent it did and did not.

3

Super Origins

Authorship, Creative Labor, and
Copyright in the 1960s–1970s

Two days before Christmas, in 1975, comic book creators Jerry Robinson, Jerry Siegel, and Joe Shuster gathered in front of the CBS Evening News to bask in their recent victory.[1] The final story of the night was about them. Walter Cronkite explained how Siegel and Shuster "dreamed up a super idea and then saw others race away with it faster than a speeding bullet." The duo had created Superman back during the Depression and sold it for a mere $135, "with all rights turned over to the publisher." They looked to the courts for help, "hoping to win royalties and their names back on the comics, but they lost their case and their jobs." Forty years later, the character had made millions in comics, radio, television, and film, but Siegel and Shuster were living in "near poverty," barely able to support themselves. As the nearly blind Joe Shuster explained, "It was our American dream. And our American dream became an American tragedy." And that's when they were rescued. After a nationwide campaign on Siegel and Shuster's behalf, the owners of Superman, Warner Communications, "bowed to public pressure," granting them annual pensions of $20,000 and other benefits, with their byline restored as well.

The reporter concluded that it was "a victory for truth, justice, and the American way." Cronkite echoed the sentiment: "And that's the way it is."[2] It was his standard sign-off, but he spoke for all Americans in commending the story's resolution. Siegel and Shuster's campaign for credit and compensation had been a national story for weeks.[3] Journalists had been visiting the "nearly destitute" creators,[4] trying to bring media attention to their plight. And it worked; the story hit a nerve. The public agreed that the corporate greed Siegel and Shuster were battling was "almost inconceivable" in its unfairness and reflected "quite adversely upon the morality of [the] times."[5] In the face of this growing public outrage, Jay Emmett, an executive vice-president at DC Comics' parent company Warner Communications Inc. (WCI), explained to the press that although they had no legal obligation to the creators, they did have compassion and "a moral obligation" and, as such, had agreed to compensate the duo generously.[6]

The sordid details of this saga were not new to the company. Jay Emmett had actually been personally involved in the drama for more than twenty years. He founded Superman Inc. in the 1950s, and built a career on his successful exploitation of the character; the future executive had been something of a maverick and visionary with respect to marketing and licensing in the early days of character franchising.[7] He had a knack for good PR too. Siegel and Shuster had been fighting for recognition and compensation since 1947, but not until this moment did DC Comics feel obliged to relinquish anything. The law had not required it to, and still did not. But American society had changed. Attitudes toward pop culture were in transition, as new ideas about creativity, mass culture, and corporate media took shape. Conglomerates like WCI understood this and acted accordingly.

Siegel and Shuster's story is known by many as "one of the most shameful and heartbreaking episodes in publishing history."[8] There is, unfortunately, nothing particularly exceptional about what happened to them. Their fate was predictably dictated by an entrenched legal system enforcing centuries-old notions about authors, publishers, and the nature of intellectual property. A common assumption behind the story—that the system failed when it came to giving Siegel and Shuster the protection and profit they had earned from their creative labor—could not be farther from the truth.

This is not to say that Siegel and Shuster did not deserve more compensation, more respect, and better working conditions; they most certainly were due all of these things. Instead, it is to say that commercial media and the legal infrastructure upon which it was founded functioned *exactly* as they were designed to. This was a quintessential example of cultural production in twentieth-century America: a large collective of creative laborers worked to create a text that would primarily benefit a corporation that claimed ownership for itself. Public credit for original authorship with no attendant legal rights, meanwhile, went to just two men, while the many other workers involved remained under-compensated and *also* wholly unacknowledged. This is the logical outcome of our intellectual property regime as it exists today, and in fact as it has always existed.

And yet, in the years leading up to Siegel and Shuster's victory, this legal infrastructure faced very little public scrutiny. It operated effectively and, for the most part, invisibly in facilitating mass media production. Creators in all variety of media adhered to it mechanically, taking for granted its basic principles and assigning to producers ownership of their work as a matter of standard practice. This was just the way things were done. This was always how they had been done, and every facet of the media business—employment, distribution, financing—relied on the regularities and assurances copyright rules provided. It was only after mass media began to benefit from increased cultural legitimacy that such protocols came into question. Emerging rhetoric about the value of creativity in previously lowbrow media like comic books seemed, rather suddenly, at odds with the outcomes that copyright law was producing. It caused a kind of rupture in the system, one that brought unwanted attention to the legal foundation upon which media corporations operated. In response, these companies capitulated to a "moral obligation," as Jay Emmett eloquently phrased it, but declined any "legal obligation" that might demand fundamental changes in the architecture of the U.S. copyright regime; in other words, they worked to shift public attention back to the social dimension.

In the years since, the story of Siegel and Shuster—their downfall and their resurrection—has experienced near-perpetual circulation within comic book culture. It operates as a structuring myth within the community, representing both the instability of work in the creative sector, but also the promise of great windfall and reward. It tends to pit authors against corporations, suggesting that these two sides work in opposition instead of in symbiosis. But it is fundamentally hopeful in reassuring the many writers, artists, and editors who proudly create for an industry that has historically undervalued their efforts that working conditions and opportunities are always improving.

This chapter challenges this narrative by examining the legal infrastructure that has long dictated the terms of the debate, creating an environment in which corporate owners and individual creators rely on each other even when they are ostensibly at odds. At play in this reconsideration is the complex relationship between intellectual property law and public conceptions of authorship. In the case of comic books, the

prevailing cultural narrative about creativity and the seemingly contra-
dictory industrial mobilization of copyright law actually acted as mutu-
ally reinforcing discourses; both tended to serve the needs of corporations over those of actual working writers and artists. As a result, the
comic book industry's major publishers were able to use the growth of
authorship and the expansion of fandom in strategic ways that supported new ventures into licensing and multimedia production. Fans,
authors, and the cultural norms they established were helping expand
the medium, but were also complicit in the corporatization of the industry so many of them tended to critique.

First, though, it is worth considering the intellectual, industrial, and
legal context in which Siegel and Shuster's story began and, with that,
an explanation as to why their experience was so typical and, for most
Americans, so unproblematic.

CREATIVE WORK IN A NEW CULTURE INDUSTRY (1940s)

There is very little romance in the realities of working in a brand-new
culture industry: long hours, low pay, disrespect, and the very real pros-
pect of failure. For every great success story—your Steve Jobs or your
Stan Lee—there are thousands of individuals whose diligence never
pays off and who continue to toil away in obscurity. This is less an acci-
dental by-product of cultural innovation than a fundamental feature, a
precondition for the growth of new media and any novel cultural form.
And yet, those individuals who defy the odds to attain fame and fortune
for their creative work tend to be the most visible of all creative workers. This was certainly true of comic books, where Siegel and Shuster's
success and notoriety proved the exception, not the rule. Their lives and
legacy reveal much about how creators produce cultural meaning and
exactly how this meaning does and does not generate industrial value.

Siegel and Shuster's story begins in 1938, when they sold their rights
to Superman for $130 (in today's dollars, roughly $2,200). The duo had
intended for the character to star in a newspaper strip, but National
Comics' editors wanted Superman for their new magazine *Action Comics* #1. So the young men turned their panels into a thirteen-page story
and mailed it off to New York. Two weeks later, they received their pay,
at a standard rate of ten dollars a page, along with an agreement that
assigned the perpetual rights for the character to National. Siegel and
Shuster signed the contract and returned it to the publisher.[9] They also
cashed the check. A popular narrative assumes this was a tragic decision.

In practice, it was their only choice, and a rather shrewd one at that. The pair had already been trying to sell their Superman character for four years. In the meantime, they had sold a number of other creations, all of which were doing well, and none of which they owned the rights to. That the editor of the brand new *Action Comics* was even interested in their story, and had happened to come across it to begin with, was something of a fluke.[10] So their willingness to accept such a fee was hardly surprising, and really quite natural. An editor at DC Comics noted in the 1970s that it was just "standard practice back then. It still is. Everyone who does art work for us signs a release saying we own the copyright."[11]

In the case of Superman, owning the copyright, however, turned out to be a matter of another magnitude. Once it was clear to editors that the character was popular on newsstands, he became the star of *Action Comics* and was soon featured in a handful of other comics as well— including his own, titled *Superman.* Over the course of the following year, the character got a nationally syndicated newspaper strip (which ran continuously through 1966) and his very own radio show, premiering on February 12, 1940. *The Adventures of Superman* got such high ratings that it was picked up by Mutual Broadcasting, which ran it three times a week to audiences of millions—adults and kids alike. The series ran for eleven years, until the title was picked up for a nationally syndicated television series that ran for an additional six years (1952–1958). In the meantime, Superman also starred in a series of high-profile animated shorts (1941–1942), financed by Paramount and created by Fleischer Studios, as well as a number of very successful matinee film serials produced by Columbia (*Superman,* 1948, and *Atom Man vs. Superman,* 1950).[12]

As a result, in the years that followed, Siegel and Shuster found themselves luckier than almost all of their contemporaries. Their unexpected and extraordinary success with Superman secured them steady jobs with National Comics, which, as one of the more established comic book companies, did not engage the exploitative freelance workshops on which most publishers relied.[13] They negotiated a ten-year contract with the highest page rate in the business, and were able to set up their own shop in their hometown of Cleveland, hiring six full-time artists to help them keep up with the workload.[14]

Even as their only specialty—superheroes—declined dramatically in popularity after World War II, Siegel and Shuster continued to get steady pay, reportedly making $100,000 annually (in today's dollars, more than $1.2 million).[15] The pair lost these working conditions only after they decided to sue their employers in April 1947, the year before their contract was set to expire. They challenged the original release they had signed, asking for $5 million (even in light of Superman's success, this was an extraordinary amount of money) in addition to all the rights for the character. They promptly lost the suit. The contract they had signed, which transferred sole and complete ownership of Superman to the publisher in perpetuity, held up in court for decades.[16]

Other creators in this nascent industry contended with far worse working conditions. And according to some, many of them had far more talent than Siegel and Shuster. Influential fan and critic Ted White referred to their work as "amateurish" and rudimentary, and the famed publisher Bill Gaines said the two were just "a flash in the pan."[17] Other creators, meanwhile, mostly art school graduates with limited job opportunities, were more than willing to work under a less accommodating factory-like system of production. The pay was not particularly good, and the deadlines were too tight to produce high-quality work. But these were not prestigious positions to be proud of in the first place, and most expected to find other lines of work in the future.[18] Even creators who went on to become luminaries in the medium had been skeptical about the job. Acclaimed artist Bernie Krigstein admitted, "I had a prejudice that comic books, as a form of art, were beneath my serious attention. . . . I never signed them; they were hack work of the purest distillation."[19]

In the freelance workshop he ran in the late 1930s, the celebrated creator Will Eisner also used pseudonyms. He had found that anonymity helped him maintain steady and continuous work. Not interested in building any kind of personal reputation, he purposefully used different names and different styles on each of his features. It was "better business," because it kept publishers from thinking that only one man was doing all the work for a particular book.[20] Whether or not they were fooled by these attempts, the publishers benefited from this practice too. They were more than happy to let their freelancers remain anonymous or, at the very least, without distinction. And as with many new industries, there was no regulatory infrastructure to prevent these kinds of practices from taking hold. The laws policing creative labor had long favored employers' interests, providing little protection to workers, and the social norms dictated by public opinion offered little corrective or even criticism.

Cultural discourse of the postwar era actually tended to reinforce this suppression of authorship. Intellectuals brought mostly negative attention to the products of mass culture and the individuals who created them. Critics like Dwight MacDonald and Clement Greenberg expressed a loathing for almost anything popular, criticizing the industrial practices that characterized their production for alienating artists from their art. And yet, the neglect and mistreatment of these creators, in a cultural industry where "writers don't even sign their work," warranted only disparagement, never concern. The low status of comic book artists was not a problem to be rectified but a rationalization of mass media's plainly evident lack of value.[21] Following a circular logic, it provided further justification for the rightfulness of publishers' continued erasure of creative labor.

In short, from the perspective of prominent cultural critics, publishers looking to maximize profit, and even the creators themselves, their labor was undeserving. The absence of proper compensation, decent working conditions, and credit were simply the fundamental nature of lowbrow cultural labor. As for the public, Siegel, Shuster, and other creative workers remained invisible. Neither the material conditions under which they produced culture for the masses nor the legal framework that supported their employment (and exploitation) drew any attention or interest in postwar America. That Siegel and Shuster actually fought for recognition in the 1940s defied the logic of this historical context. Two decades later, as attitudes about the value of popular culture began to change, these creators' desire to receive acknowledgment for work in mass media became far more commonplace and, before long, standard. In this way, Siegel and Shuster's struggle for recognition was ahead of its time, and as such has continued to resonate with later generations of fans and creators.

SUPERMAN AND THE COURTS (1939)

Siegel and Shuster's anachronistic sense of entitlement did not materialize out of nothing. There was one place, even back then, where their creativity did matter: the courtroom. Copyright law, then as always, emphasized "individual authors, individual works, and the notion that creativity is an individual act."[22] Its protections are justified by the need to compensate authors for the intellectual labors they expend in the process of creative work. That the origins of Superman could be traced to two particular men was a fact Superman's publishers sought to emphasize in court even if they downplayed it elsewhere.[23] Because copyright makes little room for collaborative authorship and tends to deny creativity as either a social phenomenon or a derivative and referential process,[24] it was equally important to downplay the contributions of anyone other than Siegel and Shuster, be it hired hands who helped draw the character or sources of inspiration that came before Superman.

And so it was when, in 1939, Detective Comics (soon after, called National Comics) sued Bruns Publications for infringement, claiming that Bruns's book *Wonder Comics* plagiarized its new Superman character in *Action Comics* (see figures 1 and 2 in chapter 1). The case, which Detective Comics won, marked a decisive turning point for Jack Liebowitz and Harry Donenfeld, who ran several other comic book companies (which all came under the name of National in 1946). Their attempt to prevent other superheroes from competing with their own growing portfolio (which would soon include Batman and Wonder Woman) ultimately failed; the character type became too popular too quickly for National to achieve a monopoly. But superheroes did become National's trademark genre, and remained so for decades. Additionally, the legal muscle National flexed during this case established it as a force to be reckoned with,[25] an industry leader with regards to both sales and political and legal clout, which it would exercise repeatedly in the years that followed.[26]

"A poor thing, but mine own"

In order to achieve this very early legal victory, though, Liebowitz and Donenfeld needed a living, breathing author; they needed Jerry Siegel, a man they would have little use for ever again. More specifically, the publisher had to assert its rightful claim to the copyright of Superman, without which it had no legal basis for suing Bruns. This required then, as it does now, that first there be a tangible expression of the character: the thirteen-page comic strip that debuted in *Action Comics* #1. Second, it had to be an original work of authorship, a requirement reflecting copyright law's long and inextricable link with liberal notions of individual and entrepreneurial intellectual labor. Jack Liebowitz took the stand early on in the trial, helping to establish that Superman was indeed a work of individual original authorship. He testified, "One man writes it, and the other man draws. Two men do the work." Siegel himself, just hours later, testified to the contrary, that he and Shuster had already begun outsourcing their work to other artists, exchanging the sketches through the mail.[27]

The presiding judge, however, made quite clear that he was interested in neither their actual working practices nor the process of conception that led to Superman's creation. His priority was instead, in his own words, to "tie up these authors of [Superman] as much as possible with the person who is claiming a copyright to it," the executives at National. This involved an examination of both the contract in which Siegel and Shuster assigned away their rights and the $130 check they received in return. When lawyers began quibbling about whether the pair sold their character as independent contractors (they did) or whether they were in the employ of the publisher and created it as work for hire (they did not), the judge commented that it did not "make the slightest bit of difference. . . . We just don't pay attention to those things."[28] Employer control of the creative work of employees—whether or not they were employees at the moment of creation—was simply assumed, as was the tendency for firms, and not authors, to own copyrights. The issue of work for hire would come up again decades later and be of considerable importance.

That Siegel and Shuster had perhaps been undercompensated or were being exploited by a publisher was also of no interest to the court. When Siegel took the stand to testify to the originality of his authorship, the court repeatedly expressed utter indifference to and impatience with his story.[29] For all involved in the proceedings, Siegel's only purpose was to provide evidence (via the dates of early drawings and letters about the character) that it was not directly modeled on or copied from someone else's work.[30] The appeals court would again treat Siegel with disdain, referring to his work "as foolish rather than comic." And yet, the case ultimately relied heavily on Siegel's presence at the trial. The final decision explained that Siegel had done genuinely creative—if low-quality— work and that the story indeed embodied "an original arrangement of incidents and pictorial and literary form." As author, he deserved to say of it "a poor thing, but mine own." It was an implication that it was *his* property to protect, however shameful. This claim destroyed Bruns's best defense, that Superman was no more than a general archetype. The possibility that National should not own this property, *his* property, was not considered.[31]

Whether Superman was an appropriate subject of copyright came up again, a decade later, when National sued another competitor of Superman, Fawcett's popular superhero Captain Marvel. Again, the court decided in favor of National, relying on the decision in *Detective Comics v. Bruns* to establish Superman's originality via Jerry Siegel.[32] In the aftermath of the decision, Fawcett folded its comic book division, and National actually purchased Fawcett's intellectual properties, adding Captain Marvel to its own back catalog to exploit later as the character

Shazam. It was the first of a number of buyouts National pursued in the 1950s, all of which dramatically strengthened the publisher in the decades that followed, as licensing increasingly drove profits. The creativity of the individual artist had little significance in this strategic shift. So, despite the immense success of the character they helped to create, Siegel and Shuster remained dependent on and virtually defenseless against the corporation responsible for both popularizing and exploiting their intellectual labors.

Meanwhile, the dependence of copyright law on their originality and individuality gave them a sense of proprietorship and ingenuity. In a fascinating display of the power of our legal framework to inscribe itself into culture and even shape individual identity, the role Jerry Siegel had played during the copyright trial began to spill into life outside the courtroom. In the years that followed the 1939 trial, Siegel would time and again represent himself as a creative genius of sorts, an independent author whose originality and intellectual labor entitled him to reap the profits from his literary property. An important part of this self-portrait was Siegel's oft-repeated claim that the character came to him whole on a single sleepless night, in a kind of flash of genius.[33] For a time, this method of conception (instant, as opposed to invention via tinkering) was a literal requirement for patentability. Though it was never required in copyright cases, it certainly helped bolster claims of originality and individual authorship, both of which Siegel was forced to testify to in *Detective Comics v. Bruns.*

Collaborative Creative Work and Superman

Numerous accounts, historical records, and more detailed histories suggest that Superman was not and could not have been conceived on "one sleepless night" and, perhaps more importantly, that the character was neither particularly original nor attributable to the creativity of Siegel alone. It is now widely acknowledged that Siegel and Shuster spent at least three years developing the superhero. They had included a story called "The Reign of Superman" in a 1933 issue of their fanzine, and had made a number of significant changes to the character on the path to publication in 1938, including transforming him from a villain into a hero.[34] Even if Siegel had, contrary to this historical record, dreamt the character up whole, there is also the unavoidable existence of the half-dozen men who were essential to bringing Superman to fruition on the page.

First among them was Joe Shuster, Siegel's constant collaborator from 1931 to 1949.[35] Since comics are as much a visual medium as they are literary, the necessary collaboration of artist and author already serves to distinguish this work from the more highbrow, individually created manuscripts that early copyright law was designed to protect. There was also the significant contribution of Max Gaines, who had found Siegel and Shuster's proposed newspaper strip while working for the McClure Syndicate and thought it might be a good fit for National's new action adventure comic book. He then passed it along to editor Vin Sullivan. Both men then looked over Siegel and Shuster's work and advised the pair on how to edit it by literally cutting and pasting the strip into a thirteen-page story. Ted White has argued that the credit for Superman thus most appropriately belongs to Gaines and also notes the recognizable contributions of the other artists working on the strip.[36]

There is also the question of influence and inspiration. Cultural historian Peter Coogan has executed an exhaustive study on the long derivation of the superhero, an archetypal figure with origins in nineteenth-century fiction that evolved through dime novels, pulp fiction, silent films, and comic strips. By 1933, when Siegel and Shuster wrote their first Superman story, every aspect of the character—the name, the costume, the origin story, the superpowers, and the psychological motivations— had appeared elsewhere in popular culture. Coogan's research shows that the pair was likely familiar with all of these antecedents.[37] This evidence suggests that Superman was original in only the most basic sense required by law. Scarcely more than a general type, the character was at least an original arrangement of incidents and forms, but hardly the result of a flash of genius or the work of a wholly independent author.

Despite these collaborative and derivative origins, Superman was still unquestionably an important innovation. The character's phenomenal success actually helped establish both the medium and the industry that produced it. Nearly as importantly, by opening the door to tremendous licensing opportunities, Superman set the industry on its future course of development. Eighty years later, Superman remains one of the world's most recognizable characters and has taken up a permanent, highly visible, and ubiquitous position within American culture. Certainly, some of this success can be attributed to the work of Siegel and Shuster, who helped generate a character whom the public adored and whom corporations found exceedingly easy to sell. But it is impossible to know how instrumental these two *particular* men were, and whether or not one or two or many dozens of other men would have made possible these same developments had Siegel and Shuster not been there to do it first.

Ultimately, though, their particularness is less important to understand than their averageness. The communal nature of their creative process was typical, and it supported the rather typical circumstances they faced: lack of proper compensation, public indifference to their struggle and even their identity, and unsympathetic treatment by the law. The critique of mass culture that dominated the public sphere did not recognize or value collaborative creative practices, assuming instead that mass media was the result of factory production and had no real authors. Their struggle was invisible and unremarkable. Employers used this fact to their advantage, giving their workers only what they had to. As long as these industrial norms did not violate a social sense of decency or conflict with the basic tenets of American ideology—around entrepreneurship and the value of popular culture—circumstances were not going to change.

In short, Superman's origins typified media practices at the time. Inspired by, if not explicitly based on, cultural texts and objects widely available, the character was brought into being by a team of creative workers. The two officially recognized creators were compensated for their labor in a manner that if anything exceeded the standards of their industry. The publishers, meanwhile, followed the usual protocol in attaining the rights to the character and profiting from it in a manner that foretold later strategies in licensing and franchising. They also defended that copyright in court by invoking a living and breathing author who could testify to its originality, despite its collaborative and derivative nature. That this process resulted in a creative laborer with an exaggerated claim of original authorship for an intellectual property owned by a large and powerful firm is hardly surprising. Siegel and Shuster acted exactly as they were supposed to act, and copyright law did exactly what it was designed to do. If there is any injustice in their story, then, it has little to do with Superman, National Comics, or Siegel and Shuster, and everything to do with the system they inhabited.

A BRIEF HISTORY OF AUTHORS AND PUBLISHERS (1710–1960)

This system, characterized by a symbiotic relationship among copyright law, media corporations, and discourses of authorship is structural to all three entities. Discussing its origins during the Enlightenment, Mark Rose argues that distinguishing between these institutions is nearly impossible, since the legal infrastructure that supports them is so "deeply rooted both in our economic system and in our conception of ourselves."[38] More specifically, as the set of rules that dictate the means and relations of cultural production, copyright law has become, as Jane Gaines has noted, "indistinguishable from the mode of production" itself.[39] As a result, the ways in which our copyright regime has for centuries shaped cultural standards too often remain invisible. Scholarship from Rose, Gaines, and many others has worked to remedy this by tracing the development of these laws within the context of the contemporary discourses and the social and economic institutions that shaped them. In theory, copyright law found its justification in granting authors exclusive control of their intellectual creations in order to encourage dissemination for public benefit. In practice, though, "copyright is about money."[40] And as this scholarship has discovered, more often than not, this money belongs to publishers, sellers, and companies, instead of to the authors and inventors whose names are often used to justify the regulations imposed.

This initial connection between firms and copyright dates back to the very first intellectual property laws in seventeenth-century Britain. Faced with a wave of piracy facilitated by new print technologies, the central bookselling guild lobbied the government for more stringent and expansive restrictions on publishing. They argued that even intangible labor should result in the creation of property from which individuals could reap a benefit. At the core of this argument was an increasingly popular faith in free enterprise; there was also an understanding that individuals would have the right to transfer their newly won intellectual property rights to others, namely the publishers who were lobbying on their behalf.[41] Indeed, booksellers turned out to be responsible for nearly all the copyright cases brought forward in the century after Britain passed the Statute of Anne in 1710.[42] The same was true in America, after Congress passed the Copyright Act of 1790, which the founding fathers had hoped would support individual economic independence. In its first decade, almost half the registrations belonged to someone other than the original author.[43]

Authors stood to benefit too. Before these early laws were passed, authorship was not, in fact, a proper profession at all. Writing did not become an economically feasible occupation until after these new rules helped commodify literature.[44] Unsurprisingly, this did not change the actual everyday creative practices that characterized writing. It was still in most cases a collaborative process that relied as much on the derivation of prior works as on originality, as it had been for centuries before copyright law.[45] Poets, novelists, and essayists of the eighteenth, nineteenth, and eventually twentieth century were thus dependent upon copyright law for their livelihoods—but not because it defined their creative practices or gave them a monopoly on their creative endeavors. Copyright law mattered because it transformed the writer into a valuable commodity for publishers and for the public.

In practice, then, intellectual property was never really the domain of authors; rights tended to belong to publishers who were consequently in a better position to pay creators. The prominence of the author in legal rationalizations was thus primarily that, a means of validating a law that stood to benefit publishing firms already in positions of some power. It was not, notably, an assurance to creators that they would reap the fruits of their labor. And yet the very identity and notion of authorship was rooted in this legal framework, justified on their behalf. The relationship was reciprocal, then, at least to an extent. While authors needed copyright law and the publishers who fought for it in order to maintain cultural capital, publishers needed authors to justify the profits they reaped as owners. If there was a semblance of balance, though, there was also, according to media scholar Thomas Streeter, an inherent "tension between the romantic image of creativity in copyright and the un-romantic results of copyright's application."[46]

This discrepancy between theory and practice, and the resulting complexity of the social and cultural relationships they impacted, intensified as legislators slowly extended the scope of copyright. Among these expansions was the work-for-hire exception, established first by precedent in 1900, and shortly after by legislation. It established that copyrights for work done at the request and expense of an employer automatically belong to the firm and not the individual. It was a reflection of the increasingly common belief that employers were entitled to own all the intellectual creations generated in the workplace, whether the workers actively signed them over or not.[47]

Popular and Romantic conceptions around the artist—themselves rooted in early copyright law[48]—had generated some resistance to the idea that an individual could so easily and, now perhaps unintentionally, assign away ownership of his creation.[49] When it came to purely commercial art and entertainment, however, the public expressed less sympathy for creators and more readily accepted employers' expanding rights. These mass media creations were considered lowbrow, in part a result of the industrial and collective nature of their production. Such origins seemed to justify copyright's expansion and the subordination of creative laborers to employers.[50] And so, without public controversy or attention, the courts were increasingly able to grant the benefits of authorship solely to corporations, often showing no interest in the fact that the creators had no rights at all. This was, of course, consistent with the development of copyright law over the two centuries prior, and characteristic of the court's treatment of Jerry Siegel.[51]

So even though the language of copyright law continued to rhetorically elevate the symbolic status of authors, courtroom decisions were serving to marginalize them, particularly if they created in mass media. Key to this increasing marginalization was the increasing prevalence of collaborative creative labor in the new culture industries. Unlike novels, visual media of the twentieth century (most notably film and television) were a grander affair and relied on the collective work of dozens and sometimes hundreds of creative laborers. Since the rhetoric of copyright law relied so heavily on idealized conceptions of individual creator-geniuses, commercial media's reliance on cooperative work on a massive scale provided further justification to deny its laborers ownership.

Despite its power and rootedness, however, this legal infrastructure still relied on public support and the willing consent of the workers who agreed to its principles and put them into practice. As social norms began to change, then, its straightforward operation grew a little more thorny. By the 1960s, the public had begun to show mass media products the same respect once reserved exclusively for highbrow forms. It was part of a generational shift as baby boomers came of age and rejected many of the values their parents held dear. This elevation in the status of popular culture brought a heightened interest in the formerly anonymous and overlooked creators behind it. And this interest brought visibility. Although it had been operating quite effectively on its own terms and out of sight, the American copyright regime would come under increasing public scrutiny.

THE COMIC BOOK INDUSTRY IN TRANSITION (1956–1981)

This reckoning coincided with an interesting time of transition in the comic book industry. Publicly, DC and Marvel had been cultivating a burgeoning fan community, in part by providing their creators more acknowledgment and deference. Privately, meanwhile, these companies were marginalizing creators as licensing superseded publishing and corporate buyouts fundamentally altered internal priorities and worsened working conditions. The conflict here—about the role creators should play within the industry moving forward—provided a stage for Siegel and Shuster and a path to their redemption. Their fight for fair treatment brought visibility to the inherent injustices in the labor practices and revenue models that underlie cultural production. Unfortunately, this visibility was fleeting, and their victory resulted in very little enduring or systemic change. Instead of fixing the infrastructure itself, media corporations found ways to change the conversation, using the increased legitimacy and affection for creators to their advantage. The discourse of authorship had in fact always, paradoxically, been a part of the copyright regime and was fundamentally consistent with and supportive of a legal investment in corporate ownership. New cultural developments, including the upsurge of respect for popular media, the introduction of theories of commercial authorship, and the growth of fandom, ultimately served to fortify that system.

Fans, Authors, and Superheroes (1956–1966)

In 1960, the editors at DC embarked on an effective audience strategy that did not spread to other media for decades: they began marketing their product to fans. The industry had been exceptionally responsive to and supportive of readers since the late 1930s. However, a recognizable version of comic fandom did not emerge until the early 1950s, in response to and in support of EC Comics. As fan historian Bill Schelly argues, EC publisher Bill Gaines played a big role in mobilizing this community. He helped popularize comic book letter columns and printed the full names and addresses of the writers, connecting these fans to one another through the mail. Before long, he was inviting fans to visit EC headquarters in New York, giving them copyrighted material for their fanzines, and helping publicize these zines in his comics. He also created the official EC Fan-Addict Club, providing members a bulletin, ID cards, and special pins. The fandom remained active for years, even after EC Comics itself disappeared.[52]

Comic book fandom did not extend beyond an EC affiliation until after the 1955 market crash. At that point, the steady deterioration of the audience turned fandom from an industry curiosity into an essential marketing strategy. This new era arguably began in 1956, with the Silver Age revival of the superhero. At first, these characters seemed an odd choice for new content; although popular during World War II, superheroes had practically disappeared by 1952. DC Comics was alone in preserving the genre, presumably for strategic reasons.[53] Having used strong distribution and licensing to turn these characters into household names in the 1940s, it behooved the publisher to keep the titles in front of con-sumers as long as possible, maintaining a strong claim to its copyrights and trademarks, and thereby future licensing potential, even when sales sagged. While the intellectual property rights of most comic book char-acters are easy to protect in court, those of superheroes tend to be even easier. Their vivid costumes (with embedded logos), catchy names, and clearly defined origin stories resulted in the kind of consistency, memo-rableness, concrete visuality, and extractability from the text that met all the legal requirements of copyright and trademark protection.

There were other reasons to bring back superheroes too. The stories were often patriotic and tended to be tame enough to pass the morality requirements publishers had established through the 1954 Comics Code. But even more important, and the factor that compelled the rest of the industry to jump on the superhero bandwagon, was the way in which these characters appealed to fans. In 1960, DC Comics editor Julius Schwartz took a page from Gaines's playbook and invited Jerry Bails into his New York office. An avid reader of superhero comics dur-ing the 1940s, Bails represented a slightly older reading demographic, one with more disposable cash. Galvanized by Schwartz's revival of The Flash in 1956, Bails had started writing to the comics' letter columns. Schwartz, unlike previous editors, many of whom had stumbled upon pulps and then comics by happenstance, had a particular affinity for both media, having once been an avid science fiction fan himself.[54] When Bails arrived at the DC office, Schwartz regaled him with tales of the good old days, hoping to inspire him. He did, and so began a new relationship between the industry and its most loyal readers. Several weeks later, Schwartz began publishing the names and addresses of all the letter column writers, and Bails promptly started contacting them, co-publishing a fanzine within months.[55]

Around the same time, DC also began occasionally publishing credits for writers and artists, who up until that time had remained anonymous. In response, the fans began—within the pages of the newly personalized letter columns—a guessing game over authorship in which they would debate who the writer, penciler, and colorer were in the many issues that still lacked creator credit. Shrewdly, the editors let this game around creator identity continue. Schwartz slowly revealed the names of more and more writers and artists, boosting their reputation among fans along the way. By 1966, everyone was receiving full credit, and the guessing game came to an end, but comic book fandom and authorship had been born.[56] Comic book scholar Will Brooker has noted how the letter columns worked to give voices to readers and creators at the same time. They enabled a "pleasurable to and fro with the editors" that "effectively shaped the concept of the comic book author . . . at the same time they were building their own fan-networks."[57]

The extent to which this promotion of authorship helped intrigue, connect, and eventually motivate a developing community of fans may have been somewhat surprising at the time, but in the years since, this association has become almost routine. As digital technologies have allowed audiences to connect through their mutual admiration for a text and the individual most associated with authoring it, creators have increasingly become the focal point around which many of popular culture's larger and more loyal fandoms rally around. Creators also tend to function as a kind of justification for fan activities. When fans unravel texts, compare them with an author or director's other works, and search for reappearing motifs and themes, media that outsiders may still perceive as lowbrow begin to acquire the marks of high culture.[58]

In the early 1960s, though, when mass media was still breaking free of its low cultural status, there must have been something revelatory in the discovery that creator acknowledgement could actually excite fans *and* elevate perceptions of the medium.[59] And it appears to have been a lesson learned fast and made much use of. Over the next several years, older superhero fans were joined by newer fans in their teens and early twenties, many attracted by the more realistic and morally ambiguous superheroes published by Marvel.

Seeing DC's success, Stan Lee had worked quickly to solidify the growth his rival began, and he too counted on the power of creator acknowledgment, most notably his own. Appealing to Marvel's readers personally and directly, he and artist-writer Jack Kirby cultivated unique personas and worked to address fans as hip, sophisticated, and knowing readers. Asking writers of letter columns to call them "Stan and Jack," they followed DC's lead in expanding creator credits, and then further personalized them through nicknames. Even occasionally appearing in stories with their characters, Lee and Kirby established themselves as auteurs, a role Lee continued to foster and exploit until his death.[60] The success of superheroes at DC and Marvel gradually spread across the industry as Charlton, Archie, and Harvey all experimented with the genre. Even after the Silver Age ended (around 1970), the industry continued to pursue the fans it had won over, gradually reorienting their product to appeal to this significantly narrower but far more loyal audience.

As comics scholar Bart Beaty notes, fan activity continued to center on creators. Fanzines, for instance, showed them a particular reverence; adhering to notions of intentionality, articles and features would seek to cover the "truth behind the work" as determined by the authoritative voices of the medium's most beloved artists and writers.[61] Similarly, early comic book awards organized by the fan community were largely motivated by a desire to single out and distinguish the industry's best creators. There was, for example, Bails's creation of the Alley Awards. In March of 1964, fans assembled at Bails's house to tally votes; it was the medium's first informal convention, a tradition that eventually became an incredibly important staging site for the industry.[62] As for short-term benefits, the Alley Awards at first reserved most of its recognition for the characters that Julius Schwartz helped edit. This development must have been validating for Schwartz, whose efforts to establish a relationship with Bails had paid off quickly. Publicly and visibly acknowledging both the fan community and the creators they loved proved an important strategy for many decades, not just for DC, but for every publisher who remained in the business.

This move constituted a significant shift in a business that had, for decades, worked to conceal the creative process it was now publicizing so proudly. Notably, though, this effort was not actually at odds with the doctrine of copyright, which had always relied on a rhetoric of authorship. In this way, the legal infrastructure that dictated the rights and treatment afforded to creators (which were not particularly good) was not under any threat, at least not yet. As long as new notions of authorship conformed to old ideas about individual creativity without questioning the fundamental rights of employee ownership, they would in fact remain quite consistent with industry needs and values.

Theories of Authorship in the 1960s and 1970s

The way in which discourses of authorship evolved did, ultimately, do just this. With a preference for individual genius over collective creativity and an embrace of titles marked clearly by corporate ownership, theories about authorship in mass media tended to align well with business imperatives. The handful of critics and fans who were writing about comic books at the time—and there were more each year—did not develop a full-fledged theory of auteurism in the same way film critics of the same era did. However, there was a great deal in common between what was happening in comic book culture in the mid-1960s and what was happening in film. It is unlikely that cinematic auteurism directly influenced the letter columns of comic books (or vice versa), but the similarities between the two perspectives are nonetheless illuminating.

In both cinema and in comics, authorship helped to elevate the status of media previously considered too lowbrow for the notice of serious intellectuals. Just as collaborative sweatshop working conditions and a refusal to assign credit to creators had in the 1940s damned comic books as an unworthy cultural form, the introduction of the author in the 1960s helped legitimize both media. This gradual embrace was partially due to the way in which theories of authorship were able to elevate material otherwise perceived as dry or manufactured. Film critics like Andrew Sarris, who popularized auteur theory in the U.S., found purpose in uncovering the connections, internal meanings, and authorial signatures that more casual viewers and readers either missed or dismissed.[63]

Rival critic Pauline Kael disparaged Sarris and his ilk for this very reason. She accused them of making "silly films" and "trash" their chosen province of analysis, and she argued that their auteurist method was all about working "embarrassingly hard trying to give some semblance of intellectual respectability to a preoccupation with mindless, repetitious commercial products."[64] Kael also identified the moral tendencies that characterized this theory as emanating from the business world; its proponents emphasized style over substance and reserved their highest critical praise for company products made by frustrated men working against the many limitations of the material they were given.[65]

Her observation here keenly acknowledges the extent to which auteurism was able to resolve the contradictions that emanated from the vast space between conceptions of art as art and of art as commerce. In identifying artistic value in the recognizable directorial styles that made a film marketable, and in celebrating the tensions generated by corporate practices of cultural production, cinematic auteurism neutralized them and helped transform commercial mass media into art. Comic book auteurism was doing the same; the ability of a writer or artist to use style and ingenuity to transform a company-owned and copyrighted superhero into an artistic masterpiece revolutionized popular conceptions about the value of popular entertainment. These revelations were a boon to a business that no longer had to apologize for mass-producing culture.

Sarris and other auteurists were also very interested in generating fixed evaluative standards to determine quality.[66] He created a pantheon of directors, a list of great men "weighted toward seniority and established reputations."[67] Early comic book fans were engaged in a strikingly similar task in the late 1960s and early 1970s as they focused on creating checklists and catalogues of the medium's greatest hits and the writers and artists responsible for them. In 1973, for example, Jerry Bails began publishing his four-volume *Who's Who in American Comic Books* (a follow-up to his 1964 list *Who's Who in Comic Fandom,* yet another reminder of the strong connection between fandom and auteurism).[68] The publication came just five years after Sarris released his 1968 book *The American Cinema: Directors and Directions.* Both works established a hierarchy that revolved around star talent and that impacted production, marketing, and reception for years to come.

This approach eventually came under fire. As film theorist Peter Wollen noted back in 1969, auteur theory disregarded as "noise" any element of the film that was indecipherable or not pertinent to the director and his vision, considering it all "logically secondary, contingent, to be discarded . . . [as] inaccessible to criticism."[69] Included among these irrelevant aspects of a film were contributions made by all other personnel, like producers, cameramen, and sometimes hundreds of other individuals from set designers to grips. The same was true, although to a lesser extent, within comic books. Fans of the medium were certainly interested in the collaborative nature of comic book publishing. But attention to a handful of select creators, the Jack Kirbys of the medium, tended to marginalize the role of both the publisher and its employees as well as the contributions made to comic book narratives and characters within other media, including radio, television, and even merchandising.

In this way, the theories of authorship that first developed in the 1960s, in both comic book and cinema culture, were often as blind to the practices of collaborative creative labor as were the Romantic notions of authorship that validated copyright law. Both discourses preferred to imagine one individual genius (or two or three) as responsible for a work of art—be it a poem, a novel, or a mass-produced commercial product—rather than recognize the contributions made by dozens or hundreds of creative workers. For this reason and many others, cinematic auteurism faced increasing criticism in the United States and, despite its lasting impact on cinema culture and the movie business, lost favor among many film theorists and scholars. Within comic book culture, the impact of authorship had at least as great an impact. Because the publishing business was barely staying afloat in the late 1960s and 1970s, it was growing more dependent on the loyalty of fans. And fans were increasingly demanding creators with big names and recognizable styles. Appealing to those tastes became a necessary strategy if comic book editors wanted to survive.

But this was only part of the industry's strategy. Publicly, creators were elevated and fans were sought after as both groups moved to the center of comic book culture. Internally, though, creators were experiencing the same mistreatment they always had. The everyday material conditions of their labor remained the same, or got worse, and they continued to follow the same old protocols when it came to signing away rights. Their ability to create new intellectual properties was actually becoming even less significant as publishing relied increasingly on older characters, whose strong copyrights they had long controlled. It was those characters, after all—the superheroes—that had helped cultivate fandom and authorship in the first place, and those same characters were facilitating the industry's pivot toward multimedia production. So while comic book fandom rhetorically emphasized the role of authors, licensing led to a decline in their operational importance. The perceived increase in the status of writers and artists taking place at this time generally remained confined to a symbolic sphere.

Licensing Supplants Publishing (1966–1979)

Despite the growth of an increasingly loyal fan base, the comic book industry was still facing too much competition from television and too much opposition from a changing distribution system to turn things around. Superheroes and fans had merely slowed the medium's steady decline; sales through the 1960s remained basically flat before beginning to fall again in the 1970s.[70] By 1974, only six publishers remained in business: DC, Marvel, Archie, Charlton, Gold Key, and Harvey. Those last two had built their business on popular licensed characters targeted at kids, a strategy that helped them survive into the 1980s before they closed their doors. DC and Marvel had used the reverse approach, licensing their characters out into other media.

In 1979, the *New York Times* reported that licensing revenues in the comic book industry had officially surpassed those generated by publishing.[71] This shift had been aggressively pursued for at least two decades prior, though, and was in fact an ambition since the medium's inception. Superman had begun the trend toward licensing in 1939, with others following suit throughout the 1940s. During the 1950s, when the medium hit tough times, it was rare to find adaptations of comic books in other media, but *The Adventures of Superman* (1952–1958), starring George Reeves, was a noted exception. The program was so popular, it boosted sales of Superman merchandise and comics, prompting National to launch titles built around characters like Superboy and Jimmy Olsen. It also helped forge early ties between the comic book industry and Hollywood.

Most notably, Superman Inc., a company created to effectively exploit the popular character, had morphed into the Licensing Corporation of America (LCA), which soon handled merchandise licensing for more than thirty popular culture properties. In 1966, it became a subsidiary of National Periodical Publications (previously National Comics, later DC Comics), kicking off a new era of licensing.[72] By this time, LCA had become one of the most attractive entertainment companies in the country. Annual profits were estimated at $100 million, but its real value was in the expanding licensing possibilities it offered larger companies interested in pursuing new synergies. While the particular term *synergy* was not yet in wide use, the idea it represented was beginning to impact corporate strategy. Jack Liebowitz believed that National's intellectual properties had the potential to generate revenue in every subsidiary it owned, and that their exploitation across media would only increase their value.[73]

While Liebowitz was way ahead of his time, he was certainly not alone there. Steve Ross, president of Kinney National Services, had similar aspirations and decided to purchase National in 1967. He explained to stockholders that, in acquiring National, they got not only DC Comics, whose characters held "universal" appeal, but also LCA, which held "enormous opportunities." The acquisition gave him a foothold in the entertainment industry, and in 1969 he upped the ante, purchasing Warner Bros. and transforming Kinney into Warner Communications Inc., a major multimedia conglomerate.[74] These purchases, along with the simultaneous buyout of Marvel by Cadence (then called Perfect Film and Chemical), roughly coincided with the return of comic books to mainstream media. Most notable were the live-action ABC series *Batman* (1966–1968) and, later, a stream of comic-book-based cartoons and live-action series on television.

Despite this success in *licensing* though, the health of comic book *publishing* continued to suffer.[75] Shrinking audiences and a still deteriorating distribution system continued to marginalize the thirty-two-page floppy, threatening the very existence of comic books as a physical medium. Against the backdrop of major successes in corporate-backed licensing, the publishing sector's continued failures shone even more brightly, and they ushered in a new operating paradigm that disrupted traditional business practices including, importantly, those related to labor. The interests of the new owners at both DC and Marvel, namely licensing and merchandising, trickled relatively quickly into everyday life within the industry. The emerging ethos within the comic book community that revolved around fans and creators was not, meanwhile, having any great impact on everyday working relations. New ownership and management were instead turning individual creators and workers within the business—artists, editors, and secretaries alike—into cogs serving larger corporate entities.

Corporate Working Conditions (1967–1979)

Jack Liebowitz had, for many years, tried to run DC Comics like a modern corporation; he made acquisitions, used subsidiaries to boost efficiency, and took advantage of an American legal infrastructure that supported established industries. But there remained many aspects of the business that more closely resembled a cottage industry. DC Comics had retained the same key employees for decades and depended upon those individuals heavily.[76] Its catalog of titles was built on individual tastes and personal relationships; most editors were fully entrusted with overseeing content and talent, and many writers and artists had been in the business from its inception. Marvel too was a very personal and close-knit operation, with Stan Lee having worked his way up from an office boy in 1939 to hiring, managing, and collaborating with most of the writers and artists himself.

When vast conglomerates moved in on smaller media companies in the 1960s and 1970s, comic publishers like DC and Marvel—as well as animation studios, book publishers, and record labels—gradually found that to thrive within their new corporate frameworks, these old ways of doing business had to change.[77] More conventional operating practices that relied more heavily on contractual agreements created a need for new middlemen, and agents and managers began doing the work that editors and producers had done before.[78] And whereas lifetime employment had once been typical, even the most experienced employees now found that they were fundamentally replaceable.[79] At comic book companies, senior employees tended to bear the brunt of these changes, but writers and artists also faced upheaval. Driving this transformation was the increasing focus on licensing that began with Kinney's buyout of DC. Because newsstand sales had been on the decline for over a decade, the executives at Kinney (which became Warner Communications Inc. in 1971) believed comic books were only valuable when and if they could generate either licensing fees or content in more profitable media like film and television; they were a loss leader for Warner's other entertainment subsidiaries.[80]

Within a year of its takeover, the corporation's disinterest in the publishing business and frustration with its diminishing value began affecting the staff. Writers at DC responded by forming a union and demanding better pay and a piece of the concepts they created, so they could profit from the licensing that had moved to center stage. In 1968, however, their requests were ill-timed and many lost their jobs.[81] In their place came younger workers, many of whom had their roots in the fan community and were willing to do anything to work in their beloved medium, including, not surprisingly, accepting lower wages than their predecessors had. In fact, any wage was a welcome change to some of these young men, who had for years contributed to fanzines without any pay at all in the hope of breaking into the industry.[82]

Just two years later, workers in comic book publishing again got behind an attempt to boost their side of the business by forming the Academy of Comic Book Arts (ACBA), an organization designed to promote popular appreciation for the form and to address industry working conditions. Promoting comic book authorship was a significant part of this strategy, which included awarding the best creators in the field. Neal Adams, a popular artist with young fans, served as the president, but he owned his own art studio, unlike other creators who felt too vulnerable to make aggressive demands of their employers. Lacking support, ACBA floundered, and it had dissolved by 1975.[83]

Sales had fallen so dramatically by then that most publishers in the business had folded.[84] At Warner Communications, domestic publishing actually began losing money; both *Mad Magazine* and Independent News (the distribution arm) were in the black, indicating that DC and their trade publishing division were performing very poorly.[85] A handful of creators seeking more stability tried to get out of the field entirely.[86] For those who stayed, the situation would get worse before it got better. Executives were considering shutting down the publishing side of the business altogether.[87] Instead, they brought in a new publisher, Jenette Kahn, in 1976, replacing the legendary Carmine Infantino. She was a twenty-eight-year-old children's magazine editor with experience in licensing, who promised to reorganize the company. Just two years later, she did, dramatically cutting the number of titles and overhauling distribution. The move became known as the DC Implosion.[88] Marvel followed suit, axing many of its titles and also bringing in a new editor-in-chief, Jim Shooter, also twenty-eight years old.

According to Marvel historians Jordan Raphael and Tom Spurgeon, early in his decade-long tenure, Shooter "established a streamlined, top-down structure that gave him greater influence over the editorial and production flow . . . [and] the company completed its transformation from a family-run hack shop to a corporate publishing house." Shepherding in an era at Marvel known for "blatant profit-seeking" and "lifeless retreads" of older works, he quickly became known as a "tyrant" and "the most reviled figure in comics."[89] In 1979, just one year after he started, the *New York Times* quoted staffers at Marvel as saying, "the dissatisfaction is so thick, you can touch it." They blamed "power-thirsty" editors for creating a "callous and inhuman" atmosphere that was driving many workers to threaten quitting. The reporter noted that this kind of warring was usually seen only in corporate environments and attributed it to an increasing emphasis on licensing that saw Stan Lee spending "most of his time on the West Coast, striking deals with Hollywood" and staff members being reassigned to "working with licensed products exclusively."[90]

This treatment was not consistent with the values of fans. Creators had been paraded out for their pleasure by Stan Lee and Julius Schwartz, and as news leaked out that such public posturing did not reflect actual office dynamics, bad publicity became a problem. If for no other reason, it was undesirable to have the fans poking about in everyday business; no company wants its internal systems revealed and dissected by an interested public. And the continued loyalty of these dedicated consumers still mattered—their commitment to the medium had a material impact—but that dedication was coming under threat. The priorities of the two sides then, the fans and creators on the one hand and the executives on the other, were misaligned. Unfortunately for the former, the executives were the ones with the infrastructural power—it was their prerogative to change (or not change) whichever internal systems they determined needed changing. So if the promotion of the new culture of comics (which was focused on creativity and loyalty) was going to survive, it would have to do so within the boundaries of this emerging corporate culture.

Creator Rights (1974–1981)

It was in this context that Siegel and Shuster reemerged into comic book culture. Despite their legal dispute in the 1940s, Siegel had managed to find employment at DC Comics again in the early 1960s. But again, he and Shuster filed a lawsuit against the publisher, trying again to challenge DC's ownership of Superman as established in the 1938 contract. Again, Siegel lost his job, and after eight years of legal battles, they lost their suit (again) in 1974. The court held that Siegel and Shuster had transferred *all* rights to DC in their 1938 agreement, and had then reaffirmed that transfer in a 1938 employment contract as well as in their 1948 settlement.[91] At this point, DC's repeated legal victories had made its contractual advantage seem ironclad; it could continue exploiting the character in other media without further legal trouble. The following summer, two French producers, Alexander and Ilya Salkind, announced that they had purchased the movie rights to Superman for $3 million. They told the press they had lots of ideas about how to adapt the character, whom they perceived as "unrealistic."[92]

Jerry Siegel was irate about this news. In his frustration, he wrote an angry letter and sent out a thousand copies, hitting every major media outlet in the country.[93] A month later, an alternative arts paper in Southern California finally picked up the story, inciting an outpouring of sympathy, including from artist Neal Adams. With ACBA having collapsed, he was gearing up for his next fight for creator unionization, and Siegel and Shuster's story had the kind of mythic possibility he needed to make his case. Their campaign soon reached far beyond the comic book community; it drew in literary luminaries like Kurt Vonnegut and Norman Mailer, all of whom were invested in a discourse of authorship that extolled the virtues of original and individual contributions to art and literature.[94] Times had changed, and so had public opinion regarding the artistic value of mass media. No longer would consumers accept the disparagement and mistreatment of creative workers, even in a once-reviled industry like comic books. Accordingly, WCI had to be more concerned with appearances.

The annual pensions and benefits it offered Siegel and Shuster were a reasonable cost to end the bad press. The bigger sticking point had reportedly been credit, but WCI ultimately gave in and agreed to return Siegel and Shuster's byline to all future Superman products. In exchange for the voluntary payment and restored byline, however, Siegel and Shuster had to reaffirm the publisher's ownership of all rights to Superman, a legal

FIGURE 10. Jerry Siegel (left) and Joe Shuster (right) pose for a photo at the New York Press Club in early December 1975. Behind them is a drawing, by supporter Neal Adams, of Superman rescuing his two downtrodden creators. Photo by Robert Walker. Redux Pictures / New York Times.

settlement they were well aware would jeopardize any future efforts to reclaim rights or more money. On several occasions, agreements like this—which came out of settlements and reaffirmed older contracts—were later used against the duo to shore up DC's overriding claim of ownership.[95] Unfortunately, then, their winning public credit had very little to do with their financial security. In their sixties by this time, the pair had little hope of using the publicity to find future work; Shuster had been partially blind for decades and could not hope to draw, and Siegel had given up writing. Still, the creators wanted to be known as authors, whether or not they could profit from it (see figure 10).

Siegel and Shuster were hardly the first creative laborers in history willing to exchange the promise of compensation for credit, and they would not be the last.[96] This interest in credit certainly drove Neal Adams, who was also celebrating at the signing of that 1975 contract, along with Jerry Robinson.[97] The story continued generating press for several years, as Adams campaigned for moral rights, in the United States and then in Britain, boasting to reporters how he had appealed to the publisher's morality and most importantly had gotten Siegel and Shuster's "names [back] on the comics; there for all to see."[98] When Warner Bros. released

Superman in 1978, an opening credit proudly declared that the character was "created by Jerry Siegel and Joe Shuster," and the comic book community again happily rejoiced in the victory.

But the fight for creators was only just beginning. That the importance and profiles of writers and artists had risen within the fan community precisely when their relevance to corporate publishers had virtually disappeared temporarily exacerbated conflict within the industry. When creators again tried to unionize under the Comics Creators Guild in 1978, infighting doomed their effort. The new generation of creators that had been brought in cheaply to replace the old guard in the late 1960s had been emboldened by the rise of auteurism and ultimately felt even more entitled to recognition and benefits than their predecessors. More established writers worried that their younger colleagues' demands were too unrealistic to be effective; publishers, meanwhile, found the whole concept of creators' rights unnatural and unreasonable.[99] Even Stan Lee, who had helped invent comic book auteurism, felt by this point that writers and artists had become so self-indulgent, writing only what pleased themselves, that they were destroying the business.[100] For those at the top, comics were useful primarily in their ability to generate licensed products and possible franchises; anything outside that was a distraction, including the perception that these successes had been built on the backs of uniquely talented writers and artists.

There was, nonetheless, a way for publishers to respond to creator complaints (and those of the fans that supported them) without giving up the copyright ownership that was driving profits. Using the financial buffer created by additional licensing revenues while simultaneously placating the fan community, freelance creators, and staff, Jenette Kahn helped reposition DC Comics as a "creative rights company." In 1981, she instituted a royalty policy that awarded creators 5 percent of revenue after the first hundred thousand sales of each comic book they produced.[101] Marvel followed DC's lead later that year, creating the "Marvel Incentive Plan," which like Kahn's strategy promised increased benefits to creators on issues that sold more than a hundred thousand copies.[102] With the average comic selling around one hundred fifty thousand issues, creators stood to make as much as a few thousand dollars extra each year—not an insignificant amount for an artist.[103]

At the same time, these fees did not threaten the companies' bottom lines, a fact DC's executives had to prove to their parent company before the changes could go through.[104] In 1981, the publishing division brought in profits of $14.8 million; the figure was up nearly 40 percent from the year prior, the result of royalty income from the distribution of *Superman II* (Warner Bros., 1980).[105] By this time, licensing was in fact accounting for two-thirds of revenue. As long as Shooter and Kahn were able to maximize profits in that space, they had a lot more leeway to pay creators. There was far less flexibility, however, when it came to control of copyright. So Kahn's other creative rights policy, an agreement to give creators 20 percent of licensing fees, was perhaps less meaningful. The plan only applied to characters created since 1976, and so had little impact on most licensing deals, which focused almost entirely on well-established characters (like Superman) created decades earlier.[106] Similarly, Shooter's incentive plan gave a nod to original creators by promising them a 1 percent bonus for high sales, but even that small royalty applied only to characters created after 1982.[107]

While these measures did not make any changes to the legal framework through which revenues and wage structures were formed, they promised some financial benefit and were greeted warmly by the creative community. As Paul Levitz, a top DC executive at the time, has noted, nobody was making good money anyway, so the mere hope of higher profits made a discernible difference.[108] Creative workers were also shifting their agenda away from working conditions and ownership, and towards the issue of moral rights championed by Neal Adams. This was the "view that an author's rights should include not only transferable economic rights to exploit a work commercially, but also rights personal to the author to safeguard the artistic integrity of his or her work."[109]

The concept of moral rights had developed gradually in Europe, and put authors at the center of the culture of copyright there. It did not, however, cross the Atlantic, as the American legal framework continued to rely on a utilitarian approach that largely ignored any potential artistic rights.[110] As comic book scholar Ian Gordon has noted, for members of the comic book community, in which the intellectual properties already belonged to the publishers, "the ability to assert a moral right is an ability to claim a form of ownership beyond the economic" and thus proved quite meaningful to many within comic book culture.[111]

With the artistic community pursuing moral rights—which were legally unenforceable and successfully separated attribution from economic reward—comic book publishers found themselves in a strong position. They could maintain ownership of their most licensable properties, those whose copyrights and trademarks were strong after decades of protection, and simultaneously negotiate contracts that promoted artistic integrity. In the process, they gave creators increased incentive to do good work while facing only minimal financial loss. The cultural shifts that had occurred over the 1960s and 1970s had at first appeared to be at odds with the imperatives of the legal infrastructure and the labor practices it helped establish. Workers' struggles—Siegel and Shuster's more visibly than any others—threatened to shine light on this tension. But the comic book industry figured out how to use these changes to its advantage. The deep and historical entanglement, and symbiosis, between theories of authorship, copyright law, and the interests of publishers ultimately helped defuse the conflict.

INDUSTRIAL CREATIVE LABOR AND THE COURTS (1976–PRESENT)

In the forty years between the first publication of Superman in *Action Comics* #1 and the release of the 1978 film, thousands of people had contributed to the character in a variety of media. Each had a hand in shaping the vision that began with Siegel and Shuster, but none were credited alongside them on screen. The writers of the radio program, for example, were responsible for Superman's famous tagline, "faster than a speeding bullet," as well as the character's ability to fly and a number of the hallmark characters in his mythology, including Perry White and Jimmy Olsen. Through the 1940s and 1950s, radio voice Bud Collyer, cartoon animator Max Fleischer, and TV producer Robert Maxwell each gave Superman new dimensions as they introduced the character to wider audiences and new generations of fans. Even with this expansion across media, Superman might have faded away as "just a fad" had it not been for a creative renaissance in the comic books beginning around 1958, the result of work from longtime artist Wayne Boring, writer Otto Binder, editor Mort Weisinger, and dozens of other DC employees.[112]

The inability of either the discourse of copyright or the discourse of authorship that grew out of it to account for these collaborations ultimately hindered a wider embrace of the actual working practices shaping popular culture. The fate of Jerry Siegel and Joe Shuster was deeply intertwined in this complicated web of legal justification and cultural value. An early-twentieth-century legal regime that favored publishers over authors dictated the basis of their early employment, while changing conceptions about mass media authorship restored their cultural legacy. But the limitations imposed by the logic of both copyright and authorship continued to prevent a more expansive understanding of the everyday creative labor that brought Superman into being.

In this way, the lionization of Siegel and Shuster served to disavow the very collaborative working practices that generated and sustained Superman, and indeed constitute all mass media production. It remains unclear to what extent glorifying these "original" authors at the expense of more rank-and-file creative workers helped either current or future generations of laborers. Public acknowledgment of their contribution to popular culture could have provided an opportunity for systemic change. But the nature of their victory—which emphasized credit over stable employment and which exalted initial invention over development and collaborative creativity—set a poor precedent for future talent. The industry was still in a state of turmoil, with conditions at Marvel worse than ever and the Comics Creators Guild floundering. And Siegel and Shuster were simply not representative of what the industry had become in the years since Superman first appeared. The medium was becoming even more derivative than it was at the start, meaning their supposed victory would have little applicability or impact moving forward.

More specifically, most of the popular books coming out of the 1970s featured superheroes, and most of those superheroes had been created either back in the 1940s or in the early 1960s. So creators were not just borrowing different elements of established archetypes as had Siegel and Shuster, but taking wholesale the work of others and updating it. And this would remain true well into the 1980s as the medium's most renowned emerging auteurs made their name on old-time superheroes and relaunches of previously well-known and heavily protected characters (e.g., Frank Miller with *Dark Knight Returns* in 1986, Alan Moore with *Killing Joke* in 1988, and Neil Gaiman with *Sandman* from 1989 to 1996). Accordingly, most creators had little hope of owning copyrights to either the books that made them famous or, as was more important financially, those that might generate big media adaptations.

So while it seemed to hold out some kind of intangible promise, DC's decision to restore the duo's byline was no more than a minor concession—the company's willingness to prioritize good public relations over an old feud with employees who refused to drop a lawsuit they had no hope of winning. And the move did ultimately help the company's public image, with both a general mass audience (that included Walter Cronkite, no less) and its increasingly narrow target reading demographic. Notably though, in establishing more forcefully the role of individual writers and artists in their books, publishers were not only pleasing readers, but *also* establishing more forcefully their rightful claim to protect those books under copyright law, both legally and in the court of public opinion. The visible presence of living, breathing authors was still useful, just as it had been in the legal sphere thirty years earlier in *Detective Comics v. Bruns*.

In the cultural sphere, holding up individual authors in front of the public could help justify the ever-increasing legal protections to which they and other corporate copyright holders were laying claim. For centuries, intellectual property holders in a wide swath of media had looked to authors whenever they sought to expand their rights and strengthen their cultural monopolies. As labor law historian Catherine Fisk notes, looking for "creative ways to shore up the legitimacy of their legal rights and to quell resistance," industries' appeal to authors who could put a human face on the benefits of broad protection is a "strategy as old as copyright."[113] Corporations were at this game again in the late 1970s, lobbying for yet another expansion of copyright's reach.

Termination Rights for Siegel and Shuster

The primacy of the corporate copyright holder became even clearer with the passing of the Copyright Act of 1976. Critics argue that it "looked like a gift" to the major media corporations who had spent a decade lobbying for it.[114] But in order to expand the scope of copyrightable work and extend terms of protection, the Act also had to pledge some gains to individual authors, in whose names these rule changes were publicly justified. Most important here was the addition of termination rights, which allow creators to terminate contracts in which they awarded perpetual rights to another party. This opened the door for authors to unwind old deals and renegotiate terms, a particularly useful opportunity if a property became more valuable after an original transfer of rights.

Fortunately for the media industries, works made for hire—which constitute the vast majority of their creative production—have been excluded from this provision; because authors of these works never owned the copyright to begin with, there is no agreement to terminate.[115] Siegel and Shuster again proved to be an exception here. Although the judge in 1939 cared little about whether they were employees creating works for hire or independent contractors, this distinction in employment status suddenly gained monumental importance in their struggle. And so the surviving heirs of Siegel and Shuster, who passed in 1996 and 1992, respectively, reinitiated their fight against DC Comics. Since the 1975 deal, the families had maintained good relations with the publisher, which had increased their stipends, awarded them additional bonuses, and extended additional benefits to family members.[116]

The Copyright Act of 1976, however, changed the rules of the game. Siegel had been reluctant to go back to court in his old age, so his wife waited until 1997, the year after his death, to take action, terminating the original 1938 contract. Paul Levitz, who succeeded Kahn as DC publisher, and had started his career as a fan and then writer, bore no ill will toward this renewed legal action and believed it was in DC's best interest to honor the now legendary struggle of Siegel and Shuster. He promised to continue paying Siegel's widow the voluntary stipend as long as they worked together on negotiations, which held up until 2002.[117]

After that, the two sides, which later included Shuster's heirs as well, fought out the intricacies of the case in court, to great interest from Hollywood and less and less concern from the public. This reaction was reasonable, considering the course the legal battle took. The flurry of suits, counter suits, and appeals took up as their primary focus mundane legal minutiae; a cultural narrative about creator exploitation and artistic integrity was replaced by close analysis of antiquated rules and the relationships they dictate.

For example, there were continuing disputes over accounting—as the heirs tried to attain their precise portion of profits—which made for less compelling drama than a mythic tale of corporate greed. DC also took Siegel's heirs' lawyer Marc Toberoff to court, accusing him of conning his clients into awarding him half of any rights recovered.[118] This claim might have elicited public sympathy for the families had they not received over $4 million since the 1975 deal, not including benefits, bonuses, and possible future profits, which may be considerable.[119] Whether or not old contracts hold up in court under new laws was also a repeated concern in these cases. But for most of the public, contract law lacks the sexiness of origin stories.

Diminishing interest among comic book fans and creators in the affairs of Siegel and Shuster's heirs may also have had something to do with the possible consequences of their legal actions, which became clear with one decision handed down in March 2008. In it, the judge proudly asserted that "Jerome Siegel's heirs regain what he granted so long ago—the copyright in the Superman material that was published in *Action Comics*, Vol. 1." This temporary victory was less complete than it sounds. The material contained in that single issue (and a small number of other works whose copyrights were also granted to Siegel) constituted only a few of the characteristics that make Superman Superman, for instance, his super strength, his blue and red costume, and his alter ego Clark Kent. Meanwhile, many other elements of the Superman mythology—such as Kryptonite, his ability to fly, and characters like Lex Luthor—which were created either by Siegel and Shuster after they became employees or by other individuals entirely, remained the property of DC Comics.[120]

This split in the copyright would have made future exploitations of the character a significant challenge, since all three parties would have to enter into an agreement with each licensee, a daunting task. Fortunately for fans and industry alike, that decision was overturned, so this scenario did not come to pass. For now, the legal battle seems to have come to an end, with DC maintaining full rights to the character, and franchise production humming along into the foreseeable future.[121] But Siegel and Shuster's disputed status as independent contractors and their temporary ability to terminate their contract revealed a kind of rupture in the careful balance that the copyright regime maintains. During the two decades (from 1975 to 1997) in which the duo retained public credit for Superman but were barred from asserting attendant legal rights, that balance held up. In that moment, the discourses of auteurism and copyright, both of which rely on a rhetoric of individual authorship, were in perfect accordance.

With termination rights, however, the purely rhetorical glorification of creators without copyright ownership obtained some legal muscle. So the fiction of solitary authorship came into contact with the reality of working practices based on collaboration. Siegel and Shuster could represent creative laborers on the level of cultural discourse, but their families' claim to the financial and legal rights that accompany that claim to authorship exposed the incompleteness of their creation. Hundreds of people helped make Superman who he was; awarding Siegel and Shuster ownership of their contribution meant severing the character in two. Authors in transmedia are only ever partial authors.

It is for precisely this reason that almost all creative labor in the media industries is executed as work for hire, protecting corporate copyright holders from complications like termination rights. Were Superman a less lucrative intellectual property, Hollywood might already have given up on him. Ongoing legal disputes have been known to hold up the development of films and television programs based on preexisting characters.[122] No producer wants to find himself embroiled in the kind of costly lawsuits that result from copyright disputes, or risk the possibility he will have to offer profits to a previously unknown rights holder.

Work for Hire for Jack Kirby

This is exactly the scenario Disney faced after its 2009 purchase of Marvel, when the heirs of Jack Kirby launched a legal battle that very much resembled Siegel and Shuster's. One of the most beloved artists in the history of comic books, Jack Kirby helped to create properties like the Avengers, the X-Men, and the Fantastic Four. Rising to prominence in the 1960s, he was at the center of comic book culture's new elevation of writers and artists. But there were considerable discrepancies between the industry's promotion of his authorship and the reality of the creative collaboration on the ground.

Publicly, Stan Lee boasted about Marvel's new editorial structure, bringing visibility to previously obscured creators and their working practices. There was the Marvel Bullpen Bulletin (which provided readers with staff photos and other personal details) and also promotion of the new "Marvel Method." According to this method, Lee would personally talk through a story with an artist, who would subsequently create the issue based on that outline. Later, Lee would add dialogue for a letterer to finish. While it nodded, quite impressively, to the power of collaboration in pop culture, the Marvel Method emphasized the significance of Lee, and sometimes Kirby, above anyone else, giving Lee a reputation as a "gloryhound."[123] Meanwhile, Kirby maintained throughout the 1970s and 1980s (against the claims of the Marvel Method) that he had actually worked quite independently in creating many of Marvel's marquee characters.[124]

The conflicting assertions of creative genius here are hardly surprising, since such statements are essential for whoever hopes to meet the requirements of copyright law and claim ownership. The result is an exceedingly murky picture of the actual working practices at Marvel. What is clear is that Kirby felt entitled to a stake in the ownership of the characters he created (or helped create). If Jerry Siegel was emboldened by the discourse of copyright he encountered in the courtroom, Kirby found his audacity in the new cultural environment that had spun up around him. Suddenly, publishers valued fans and fans valued authors, and since licensing had become so important, everyone assumed authors would see rewards related to copyright ownership. Despite this new visibility, however, such an outcome was not mandated by law, nor did it align with corporate financial imperatives. And unfortunately for Kirby, termination rights could not come to his rescue. Siegel and Shuster had created Superman before they were hired by DC; Kirby was already employed at Marvel when he brought his characters to life. Accordingly, there was no contract to terminate or negate in court, only the question of whether Kirby's creative labor really was executed as work for hire. If it was, he had no viable claim.

Marvel and parent company Disney have prevailed here, with courts supporting their ownership and determining that Kirby was indeed a contracted employee, his intellectual labors belonging to his employer.[125] Intriguingly, though, the mundane details of this case, which include whether or not Kirby purchased his own pencils or worked from home, have received less press than the issue of credit. When *The Avengers* (Walt Disney Studios) came to theaters in the summer of 2012, a number of comic book critics encouraged a boycott of the film based on Marvel's treatment of Kirby, and a controversy arose around whether or not Kirby would receive a screen credit.[126] As it happens, like Siegel and Shuster, he did receive such a credit, allaying the concerns of many fans, even though this recognition would have no bearing on his legal rights or financial compensation. Regardless, Kirby's heirs decided to cease their appeals process, having "amicably resolved" their dispute with Disney.[127] It seems, then, that credit continues to be a sticking point within comic book culture, as the narrative around authorship continues to conceal a legal infrastructure that fully supports corporations' ability to maintain full control of their most valuable properties.

Of course, were all creators, writers, artists, directors, and actors able to retain the rights to the creative contributions they made to every intellectual property, mass media production as we know it would cease to exist. As Ellen and Bill Seiter note in their book on creative rights, anyone interested in further exploiting a title—in sequels, merchandising, spinoffs, or even distribution in other windows—would have to hand-stitch a "motley quilt of copyright assignments obtained one by one from [their] motley crew." Work-for-hire agreements are ultimately what make large-scale multimedia production possible.[128] And the protocols and directives of copyright form a legal infrastructure on top of which everything else in the entertainment industry is built.

Noncollaborative, nonderivative authorship has become increasingly rare with the rise of mass media and the dominance of the franchise, so the work-for-hire exception that consolidates copyright ownership into the hands of a single corporate owner has remained an essential legal mechanism. Notably, the discourse of individual and original authorship has proved just as essential. It carries out the erasure of collaborative labor within the cultural sphere in the same way the language of copyright does in the political and economic sphere.

AUTHORS AND PUBLISHERS TODAY

There is a considerable dependency between authors and industry, and between ideologies of auteurism and those of capitalism. In spite of, or maybe because of, this fundamental connection, a kind of animosity developed within comic book culture, in the years after Siegel and Shuster won their 1975 campaign, between the industry's major publishers and its major creative voices. On numerous occasions, artists and writers have declared that these companies do not understand the medium, that they depend on factory production, that they cower in the face of censorship, and that they fear any amount of change.[129] These accusations may be true, but their vitriol tends to belie the underlying symbiosis between them; the continued production of comic books relies on a system that inextricably intertwines the needs and motivations of both sides. The established industry architecture—for better or worse—always has and always will play a fundamental role in shaping mass media. For decades, comic book publishing and all those who worked within it remained totally dependent on the corporate backing that kept distribution systems intact despite perpetually declining sales and sometimes nonexistent profits.

Creator-Centered Publishers

As time wore on, comic book writers and artists were finding that they could finally venture out on their own to create work and sell it to readers. So independent publishers rose up in this murky space between authors and industry, offering an antidote to building tensions in the industry. Their success was uneven, though, and their independence only partial. Taking advantage of the increased visibility of creator rights struggles in the late 1970s and early 1980s, the first wave of independents offered disgruntled writers and artists like Jack Kirby full ownership of the titles they created. Since some of these firms already had a foot in distribution (like Eclipse and Capital City), revenue from licensing was less important.[130] But when distribution problems mounted, as they often do (difficulty with retailers, competition for publications, etc.), or sales had an off year (like a minor market crash in

1987),[131] there was nothing to fall back on. In 1984, for example, when rumors of financial difficulty at Pacific Comics spread, creators who owned their own titles simply defected, taking their comics with them and hastening the publisher's demise.[132]

Amidst many closures and an exceedingly unsteady existence for those who have survived,[133] there has been one notable star in the independent sector: Image Comics. The six prominent creators who founded Image in 1992 after very publicly defecting from DC and Marvel vowed never to own or interfere with any of the creative work of their writers and artists. Their titles quickly defied expectation and rose to the top of sales charts. The comic book community celebrated their success as proof that fans were more loyal to the creators than to either DC or Marvel or the superhero franchises they published.[134] That Image persisted through the mid-1990s, even after creator-owned imprints at DC, Marvel, and Dark Horse all shuttered, further showed that if publishers were serious about supporting their artists' work, it could in fact be done.[135]

But Image nonetheless faced operational challenges, created distribution problems for mom-and-pop retailers, and possibly even contributed to the 1993 market crash.[136] The company also suffered from infighting and experienced a partial breakup; one founder, Jim Lee, sold his division to DC, expressing a desire to get back to the creative work he loved most (as of 2018, he is the co-publisher of DC as well as the chief creative officer at DC Entertainment, overseeing the company's biggest media adaptations). As critic Ray Mescallado notes, it was soon clear that creator-owned imprints would not revolutionize or save comic book publishing and that neither Image nor any other publisher could eliminate the practice or need for work-for-hire arrangements. In fact, by the late nineties, the independents were acting more and more like the majors, adopting a "corporate mentality" and perhaps even learning "the benefits and necessities of toiling as a cog," particularly in an industry in a "downward spiral."[137]

In this way, and many others, the independents have long been rather dependent on the IP-based success of DC and Marvel and the licensing-rich environment those corporate-financed publishers first created in the late 1960s and 1970s. While the comic book industry can now support both creator ownership and independent publishing, market volatility and distribution challenges make it hard for almost anyone to succeed in this space without pursuing media adaptations.[138] This has clearly been true for publishing's other major players, Dark Horse (founded in 1986) and IDW (founded in 1999), both of which have relied on successful licensing deals (adapting comic books in other media, and other media as comic books) to prosper. Notably, the majority of film and television deals, and certainly the most lucrative ones, are still negotiated for company-owned titles, not the original auteurist work that has often excited the fan community.

There remain creative dependencies too, as many writers and artists find themselves alternating between work they own and work for hire. This back-and-forth still proves the best way to establish artistic credentials, allowing creators to grow a loyal fandom through marquee franchises from big publishers. As comic book scholar Matthew McAllister argues, even Image creators continued to rely on the "mainstreamed, superhero version of content" invented and sustained for decades by DC and Marvel, where they all "cut their creative teeth." And according to Mescallado, some of the best comic books still come out of work-for-hire relationships—when recognized auteurs take on the iconic characters or "toys" of the major publishers.[139]

Transmedia Auteurs

Auteurist claims have more recently been moving into even less likely contexts. Just as lofty notions of the individual creator-genius traveled from highbrow forms like poetry into more collaborative and previously lowbrow media like cinema and comic books, these theories continue to follow that trajectory, increasingly informing the most collectively produced mass media texts. Throughout popular culture, then, audiences are more frequently identifying singular personalities as guiding, sometimes divinely inspired, forces behind productions that are in actuality generated by armies of creative workers. This has been true of television series, websites, film franchises, and even vast transmedia narratives. Many fans regard Kevin Feige, for example, as the architect of Marvel's expanding universe, while they credit the success of the *Avengers* film franchise to Joss Whedon (see figure 11). The cultural products these auteurs create, of course, not only depend on vast and talented workforces, but also stand on the shoulders of decades' worth of creative labor, labor that invented, honed, and ingrained characters into the fabric of American culture.

As media scholar Henry Jenkins has pointed out, quite often these individual authors, imagined as "The Guiding Spirit" of the texts they care for, are positioned in opposition to "The Powers That Be," the networks and corporations charged with making practical production

FIGURE 11. Joss Whedon signs autographs for excited fans at an *Avengers: Age of Ultron* red-carpet event in 2015. Whedon's popularity with fans and his reputation for guiding successful transmedia projects helped him get this high-profile directing job. Photo by Mark Schiefelbein. AP Images.

decisions based on economic calculations. Accordingly, even as most fans are more than willing to disagree with the auteurs they adore, they still put faith in this antagonism between creator and corporation. Such trust can help manage frustrations around the text and reconcile the sometimes visible conflict between art and commerce.[140] In this way and many others, then, auteurism continues to be a useful model for consumers thinking through conceptions of creative production and its many pitfalls. As media industry scholar John Caldwell has noted, even while negotiated and collective authorship have long represented the dominant paradigm in Hollywood, "the auteur myth still very much lives on" in discourses that maintain the illusion of personal creativity.[141]

Although he wrote decades before this development, Michel Foucault's description of authorship offers perhaps the best explanation as to why it has become so useful and therefore so prevalent. Acknowledging how intellectual property rights helped establish the conception of the author in the first place, he argues that authors remain, first and foremost, "a function of discourse." Constructed as unifying, rational entities with transcendent powers of creativity and profundity, they become capable of resolving unevenness and neutralizing any incompatibilities and general contradictions within the text.[142]

In this respect, contemporary transmedia—which often expands in unruly ways—can actually benefit even more from "the author function," as Foucault called it, than traditional titles have. It is the very multitude of creative hands and the disarray that can characterize their production practices that demand the organizing and prioritizing force an identifiable author can provide, if only discursively. In addition, more than ever before, audiences need help classifying the worth of texts and distinguishing between content they care about and content they would prefer to discount, a process that can be simplified through the use of author "brands."[143]

The author has thus become an essential mechanism for media producers—both independent and corporate backed—who seek to embrace grassroots, user-driven circulation systems. Accordingly, media scholar Jonathan Gray explains, the entertainment industry has been working hard to "actively create artistic aura" in the texts it distributes, creating author figures behind their origins and insisting on the uniqueness and authenticity of what are otherwise standardized industrial products, thereby rendering them works of art.[144] In this way, digital culture has supported a version of authorship that continues to bolster the interests of corporate producers who have little in common with the individual artists on whose aura they so heavily depend. This discourse has become a structural and seemingly permanent feature of contemporary multimedia production, which relies more than ever on a copyright regime founded on such notions.

Creative Work in a New Culture Industry (Present)

Unfortunately, the ever-increasing levels of respect for creativity in pop culture have generally failed to make significant strides in improving working conditions for laborers. And systemic change in the legal framework that supports media production and determines those working conditions remains well out of reach. Most mass culture is still produced in the way it always has been—indeed, the way most highbrow culture has been as well—collectively. This tendency toward collaboration and derivative products has only intensified amidst the rise in franchised properties. The result is a public culture that idealizes and romanticizes original authors and an industry that rarely creates the kind of media that could give such authors an opportunity to thrive. In film, for example, as industry scholar Eric Hoyt notes, "the market for original screenplays has eroded dramatically as risk-averse studios gravitate toward pre-branded material" so that a "new generation of original screenwriters finds it harder to sell scripts, see them made, and earn a produced screenwriting credit—a prerequisite to getting steady studio employment."[145]

The failure of auteurism to effect broader change is at least in part due to its fundamental connection with copyright law. As long as intellectual property remains fundamental to the functioning of the culture industries, corporations will continue to fight for protections to expand into every crack and crevice of digital culture. Along the way, each of these spaces will necessarily be reimagined in ways that suppress any complicating details, particularly those that point to the collaborative, derivative, and messy nature of almost all creative work.[146]

The myth of Superman's real-life origin, in the way it glorifies original solitary authors, unfortunately contributes to this artifice around creative labor and, in so doing, reinforces a proprietary logic with regards to artistic and financial credit. The emphasis the comic book community places on moral rights and proper attribution in particular threatens to justify an approach to production that replaces good compensation and employee stability with the promise of recognition. The importance of receiving credit for creative labor, be it internal or public, functions as an important industry narrative that degrades working conditions, but it is hardly the only one.

The culture industries' continued suppression of details around labor has recently been accompanied by narratives about the joys of creativity in the digital age and the flexibility of freelance employment. Marxist scholar Jyotsna Kapur has pointed out that many have hoped that "meaningful and creative work" would rescue everyday workers from the fragmented labor that used to characterize the culture industries. Some have even described it as "an expression of creativity" not unrelated to more Romantic conceptions of authorship. Meanwhile, a higher and higher volume of cultural work is outsourced internationally each year, often to what Kapur calls "soul-destroying sweatshops," while most creative workers face worse conditions than ever.[147]

Catherine Fisk has also documented degraded working conditions for creative laborers. Freelancers are increasingly exchanging job security for greater flexibility and the promise of "greater human capital development opportunities" and increased mobility, although not typically ownership of their intellectual properties.[148] When these workers agree to become independent contractors, employers can avoid federal and state labor protections including the Fair Labor Standards Act, the National Labor Relations Act, and the Civil Rights Act.[149] In trying to understand how corporate media producers have been able to shore up power in this way and maintain a constantly "churning workforce," John Caldwell has also pointed to industry narratives. Trade stories told between workers create an "ethos of the survival of the fittest," which heightens job insecurities and personal anxieties as an increasing amount of labor is offloaded onto "underpaid/overworked aspirants."[150]

Because nearly all employment contracts in contemporary culture industries define all work as work for hire, most creators will never have the opportunity to claim their own copyrights. Despite the fundamental and original purpose behind copyright law, the only legal and financial benefits most authors reap from their own intellectual labors are those explicitly delineated in their contracts. The occasional willingness of workers to exchange tangible benefits (like better compensation or increased job security) for the intangible promise of moral rights, a byline, or internal recognition from colleagues thus serves to prop up corporate interests in ways that do not collectively serve employees. The same can be said for any industry myth that gives rank-and-file creative workers the notion that properly attributed credit—could such a thing even exist in most multimedia production—will one day help them strike it rich.

CONCLUSION

While the battle for ownership of Superman involves a number of exceptions, it nonetheless typifies the ways in which legal frameworks serve as a structural foundation for both cultural production and reception. The infrastructure of copyright helped determine Siegel and Shuster's worth as creators to themselves as individuals, to the industry, and to the public. After 1975, DC Comics proved willing to recognize the men as creators, rhetorically elevating their status, but denying them legal and economic rights. This was fundamentally consistent with the company's strategy all along and indeed with the intentions and legacy of copyright law more broadly. And it was also quite consistent with theories of authorship. These theories tend to glorify individual artistic ambitions in ways that celebrate and help legitimize mass media texts. In the process, these cultural and legal discourses also helped justify and obscure the baser tendencies of commercial cultural production, including, in this case, poor labor practices and overreaching intellectual property claims.

The debate over moral rights, the rise of auteurism, and the glorification of individual creator contributions have oftentimes seemed to offer a corrective to bad working conditions and other problems within the creative industries. By extension, the prominence of these discourses within comic book culture, particularly as they emerge in the mythological telling of Siegel and Shuster's long struggle, has occasionally framed the entire medium as a kind of antidote to these problems throughout media. Understood by many to be a quintessentially auteurist art form, shaped by noble battles over creative control and creative rights, comic book publishing seems at times like a fringe medium, with the potential to change the way other media industries approach their workers, their fans, and even their content.

But within the industry, the rise of fandom, auteurism, and creative rights—all of which were shaped by an exceedingly powerful legal discourse—was a boon to business that almost always aligned with commercial imperatives. And that success was, in turn, always consistent with conglomerate power; the way in which auteurism rose up alongside the growth of large multimedia corporations suggests that the two trends are neither oppositional nor disconnected. Indeed, the strength of the corporate author was built on the strength of the romanticized creator-geniuses who made the gradual justification of mass media more palatable, culturally and legally. The story of Siegel and Shuster without the sheen of rebellion, victory, and glory suggests that comic books are auteurist only inasmuch as that auteurism promises to support the collaborative corporate authorship to which it is supposedly set in opposition.

4

Tales of the Comic Book Cult

Quality Demographics and Insider
Fans in the 1970s–1980s

In 1994, insiders working on *Tales from the Crypt,* a horror anthology
series on HBO, were ramping up production on every front they could
imagine. The show was a huge hit, and this was going to be the "Year of
the Crypt Keeper." The name belonged to the series' narrator, a wise-
cracking ghoul who was on the verge of becoming his own "billion-dollar
industry."[1] Debuting in 1989, *Tales from the Crypt* cost $1 million per
episode, quickly gaining the distinction of being the "most expensive half
hour in TV."[2] The producers had financed the show on deficit, without the
possibility of earning ad dollars on HBO. So they hoped to make their
money back in syndication, foreign broadcast rights, and a robust ancillary afterlife.[3] Their gamble paid off. The show was HBO's first real hit
and quickly became a phenomenon. The producers sold it into syndication
on Fox, which broadcast it to high ratings during prime time. It was then
adapted as a Saturday morning cartoon on ABC (*Tales from the Cryptkeeper,* 1993–1999). Next came two feature films in wide release (*Demon
Knight,* 1995, and *Bordello of Blood,* 1996, both released by Universal)
and even a children's game show (*Secrets of the Cryptkeeper's Haunted
House,* CBS, 1996–1997). All of these venues made possible various lines
of merchandise, for both kids and collectors, or as licensors described
them, "the cultist who's been following the Crypt Keeper for years."[4]

Originally based on horror stories published by EC Comics in the early
1950s, this series reappropriated a brand that was specifically identified
as the essence of bad taste. The publishing company had been the subject

of nationwide condemnation when its grisly comics become the subject of televised Senate hearings in 1954 on the threat comic books posed to America's youth. HBO had revived the title just as it was trying to rebrand itself as a home for good taste, or as its tagline promised, "simply the best." At the time, "quality cable television" still seemed to many to be a kind of oxymoron, but with a new slate of original programming, public perception of the medium was about to change. *Tales from the Crypt* helped HBO establish a valuable network of talent and a foundation of legitimacy on which the company subsequently built a stronghold of quality television. By the end of the decade, HBO had incited a creative renewal for the medium, and by some estimates, initiated a second "Golden Age" in television. In elevating EC Comics from the nadir of quality to its peak, HBO also helped satisfy the longtime expectations of a community of dedicated EC fans who believed these were "some of the best comic books ever published."[5] For decades, this loyal fandom had generated a continuous stream of criticism, giving the brand a subcultural visibility and unique cultural cache. They hoped that EC's titles would be spared from being among comics' many "forgotten titles."[6]

They were spared, and indeed, the brand's transformation on HBO marked a milestone for the comic book industry, which had been unable to generate a higher quality track record of adaptations in other media. Licensing had long been a core aspect of the comic book business; there were toys, bedspreads and t-shirts, kids' cartoons, campy live-action television series, and B-movies. But quality media had remained disappointingly out of reach until 1989. In July of that year, Warner Bros. released the first major *Batman* film to strong reviews and huge box office numbers. While the premiere of *Tales from the Crypt* on HBO a month earlier made fewer headlines, the inroads the series made for comic books were perhaps more significant and longer lasting.

In very little time, the public saw other high-quality adaptations— media made for adults with serious tastes. There were *Lois & Clark* (ABC, 1993–1997), *The Crow* (Miramax, 1994), *Spawn* (HBO, 1997–1999), and *Blade* (New Line Cinema, 1998), among others (see Appendix A for a complete list of adaptations). These were not generally the superhero tentpole franchises that began dominating the box office in the 2000s. But they constituted a crucial step toward achieving that future. *Tales from the Crypt* and the high-quality adaptations that came in its wake brought cultural legitimacy to comic book media. In redefining what comic books were capable of, these adaptations sparked industry interest and allowed comic book fans in the business to make a case for a bigger investment in the medium moving forward. (Chapter 5 picks up this story in the 1990s to explain what else had to happen *after* quality media to help comic books transform into a cinematic juggernaut.)

The comic book industry's approach to demographics was the cornerstone of this reassessment. Since the late 1950s, comic book publishers had been cultivating a narrow but highly engaged consumer base of privileged adult males. In the 1990s, shrinking audiences began to plague other sectors of media. Simultaneously, consolidation was altering the underlying architecture of the entertainment industry and heightening the need for audiences that would loyally consume titles across platforms, following properties for long ancillary lives. In this environment, *who* was watching was almost always as important as *what* they were watching. More often than not, this meant that viewers of a higher socioeconomic status—typically educated, wealthy, urban, white, and male—were more valuable to advertisers. The human networks comic book fans had formed through zines, conventions, and specialty shops were thus appealing to producers, who looked to build new audience strategies on the foundation that fan communities had built. So while comic book readership had narrowed intensely, its distinctiveness caught the interest of film and television executives who were increasingly seeking out a high-quality demographic.

The Crypt Keeper never did take over Hollywood as some had hoped. But the success of *Tales from the Crypt* on HBO was a testament to the value comic books offered multimedia production in the niche environment that was beginning to characterize this era of convergence. Demographic boundaries had taken on new significance after deregulation had altered the structural organization of the film and television industries. New economic imperatives in cable in particular had created an opening for a new kind of media product, and comic books—shepherded by a network of fans within the industry and outside of it—came to occupy that space. Within this quickly evolving landscape, the comic book industry, small in comparison to other media businesses, could have faded from view. But its demographic strategy raised its profile and potential.

SOLVING DISTRIBUTION (1956–1993)

The winnowing of the comic book audience was a gradual process that began in the 1950s. At that time, competition from television, problems in distribution, market saturation due to overproduction, public apprehension, and the threat of government oversight all worked together to cause a dramatic decline in sales. Of this wide-ranging set of difficulties, issues related to distribution were closest at hand, so the industry's strategies for survival typically revolved around this sector. Unfortunately, decade after decade, distribution never seemed to be a problem that could, once and for all, be solved. So major industry players did whatever they could to stay afloat.

This meant pursuing solutions that were available and intelligible, and rarely employing unproven tactics. Over time, publishers replaced old networks of relationships with new ones, changed the way they financed operations, and shifted away from outdated editorial practices. These adjustments to the industry's infrastructure allowed for a transformation of the medium: by changing the way they did everyday business, comic book companies were able to form a new kind of relationship with their audience, which paved the way for a revolution in content, in turn, stimulating additional changes in infrastructure. This interplay between operational improvements, evolving social relations, and creative developments is worth examining in some detail here. The material details of this history help to explain exactly how and why comic book culture changed in the way that it did.

Notably, there is no simple reason or singular explanation as to why this process resulted in a gradual niche-ing. But in general, the fringes of comic book culture tended to manifest a dramatic influence upon the mainstream. Supported by an increasingly robust network of independent publishers, distributors, and retailers, and aligned with practices of artistic modernism, these forces from the periphery pushed against the medium's mainstream. Accordingly, both structural and creative innovations often moved from the margins to the center in ways that transformed comics from something that seemed fundamentally mass into a subculture that was anything but. A fringe or outsider sensibility began to pervade the comic books themselves and the industrial and consuming community around them. This aura of cult, along with a large number of educated and loyal adult male readers, would eventually make comic books a highly valuable commodity in the multimedia landscape.

This fate, however, could not have been known by the handful of publishers who found themselves in control of the industry in the late 1950s. Their first move after the market crash in 1955 was a return to the superhero genre. Successful back in the early 1940s, superheroes proved to be strong intellectual properties and tended to travel well across media, succeed in licensing, and attract corporate financing. They

FIGURE 12. In the late 1940s, Nadine French King, pictured here, worked for Archer St. John, a publisher known for romance and western comics. Originally a letterer, King took on secretarial tasks and did editing work under Marion McDermott, another female employee. St. John left the comic book business in 1958, shortly after his distributor, American News Co., closed shop. Photo courtesy of Fantagraphics Books (www.fantagraphics.com).

also appealed to an emerging fan community that represented a more loyal demographic of young adult men, many of whom had been comic book fans as kids. Female readers, meanwhile, began to fall by the wayside. Although female creators had been working in genres like teen and romance throughout the 1940s, most of them were gone by the late 1950s (see figure 12). They left behind older men to edit, write, and draw for an audience they did not understand.[7] When DC and Marvel discovered a male college-age audience for their new superhero stories in the 1960s, the publishers' inattention to more feminine preferences only intensified.[8] The pursuit of fans was also leading DC and Marvel away from younger audiences, a demographic that was increasingly left in the hands of Archie, Harvey, Dell, and Gold Key.[9]

While Silver Age (1956–1970) superheroes helped stabilize the industry and temporarily forestall declining sales, the gains faded away in the 1970s.[10] Problems in distribution dating back to the mid-1950s were still visibly damaging the comic book business. There was the continuing decline of mom-and-pop newsstands during this era, caused by suburbanization, and the rise of chain stores that were less interested in carrying comics, which had low profit margins.[11] There was also a flourishing black market, an outgrowth of second-hand circulation.[12]

Publishers in search of cost-cutting measures had stopped demanding that wholesalers asking for refunds return the covers of unsold books, replacing that proof of destruction with an honor system based on affidavits. Wholesalers and distributors would collect money from publishers on reportedly "unsold" comics only to turn around and sell those same comics to a growing number of specialized sellers. Farrell Comic Group had accused its distributor Kable News of this practice back in 1958, but few paid attention.[13] By the 1970s, the problem had become rampant and was dramatically impacting revenue industry-wide.[14] Defects in the distribution chain were becoming intractable obstacles to growth.

Underground Comix (1968–1973)

It took the major publishers another decade to figure out how to restructure the system. The impetus ultimately did not come from within these companies. By their own doing, they had been protected, and perhaps sheltered, creatively and structurally. So the first sign of innovation arose out of the medium's most oppositional faction, Underground Comix. The movement had roots in the early 1960s, when artists—some of whom were inspired by EC Comics and *Mad Magazine,* began creating edgy, antiauthoritarian, and sometimes obscene comic strips in college newspapers and humor magazines.[15] With the rise of the free press, their work moved into underground publications by mid-decade. Gradually, these creators, together with independent publishers and distributors, formed a creative and entrepreneurial community based out of San Francisco, where they kicked off what became a highly influential artistic movement. The release of Robert Crumb's *Zap* in 1968 marked its official start, and this alternative art form became known as Comix, quickly attracting a national readership and supporting a small but thriving industry (see figure 13).[16]

These works looked like mainstream comic books in terms of format, but they were ironic, funny, political, hip, sometimes deeply personal, and also at times extremely sexual and violent.[17] As comic book scholar Charles Hatfield has noted, they embraced a "new formalism" within the medium, narratively and aesthetically, and opened the door to "the idea of comics as an acutely personal means of artistic exploration."[18] The movement also attempted to break taboos, satirizing authority figures and mocking established institutions. Included among these was the comic book industry, which Comix creators perceived as sanitized, unsophisticated, and overly commercial.[19] In their work,

FIGURE 13. Co-founder Dave Moriaty at Rip-Off Press, one of the original and seminal publishers of Underground Comix. On the press is Richard Corben's *Grim Wit* #1. San Francisco, November 28, 1972. Photo courtesy of The Estate of Clay Geerdes.

Crumb and his cohort "took back the comic book and redefined what it could do," rescuing a medium "hitherto associated with anonymous, industrialized entertainment, and transformed it into a vehicle for self-expression in a highly romanticized and radical way."[20]

In this respect, Underground Comix had much in common with contemporaneous avant-garde movements in other media. Across the country in New York, for example, Jonas Mekas and other experimental filmmakers of the New American Cinema had spent the 1960s developing intensely first-person, diaristic styles that worked to refocus the form on their own generational concerns and liberate it "from the bonds of Hollywood" and its "overprofessionalization and overtechnicality."[21] The creators behind Underground Comix tended toward a similar self-reflexivity and irony that, once turned inward, grew increasingly preoccupied with the medium itself and their rejection of it.[22] This was becoming a familiar artistic move, one that both deeply engages with and in some ways admires the established medium, but also seeks to denigrate its formulaic and fundamentally mass nature. In its desire to distance itself from commercial culture, then, Underground Comix had, perhaps unknowingly, aligned with postwar modernism and higher institutions of art and culture; it was rejecting one kind of "establishment" (commercial comic book publishing) in favor of another, actually more respected one.

In moving in this direction, Underground Comix was also exacerbating (or improving, depending on the perspective) something of an audience problem. Like other forms of modernist art, the Underground's critique of popular comic books was largely aesthetic and narrative; its participants had relatively little interest in the social problems that plagued mainstream publishing. So while Comix was inspired by genuinely radical political motives, its pioneers did little to push against the medium's rather traditional social hierarchy, specifically, its ever-increasing bias toward male, college-age readers, a demographic it shared with other countercultural and avant-garde movements. Creator Trina Robbins, who experienced the movement first hand, has pointed out that the Underground was just reproducing an "alternative version of the old boys' club" that had long existed at the major publishers. In 1972, she and others formed the Wimmen's Comix Collective to counteract this bent, along with Comix's tendency to depict women and blacks in violent and sometimes demeaning ways.[23] But the group arrived at the tail end of the Underground movement, and its push for better representation made little impression on mainstream comic book publishing.

What did leave an impact was the Underground's irreverent attitude, its auteurist tendencies, and, most importantly (although most frequently overlooked), its infrastructural innovations. Due to the obscene nature of its work, the Comix community could rely even less on traditional newsstands than could mainstream comic books. Accordingly, publishers and dealers had to generate an alternative distribution network that consisted primarily of mail-order catalogs, head shops, and counterculture record stores. For a time, these retail sites were tremendously successful at getting Comix to their desired target audience (college-age men) without interference from more traditional market actors. But a Supreme Court ruling on the definition of obscenity in 1973, along with new anti–drug paraphernalia laws, left head shops vulnerable. Many either closed their doors or refused to continue carrying Comix, which now carried the threat of government interference.[24]

As a result, the Underground quickly faded. The movement lasted just five years, but in that time had intensified the medium's appeal to an audience of educated young men. And in its auteurist nature, Comix moved it spiritually, if not tangibly yet, in the direction of respectable culture. This creep is ironic, given the obscene and in some cases illegal nature of the content. Official culture's initial rejection of the Underground was ultimately blunted by the rising status of its practitioners—white college-educated men who would eventually be embraced by more traditional art and literary circles. The Underground also demonstrated a new kind of distribution system that did not have to rely on the declining newsstands, reluctant chain retailers, and dishonest national distributors who had been driving mainstream comic books to ruin. Another possibility for the medium had finally emerged.

Phil Seuling and the Rise of the Direct Market (1973–1993)

Between the success of the Underground, the growth of collector-fans, and the rise of fanzines, there was increasingly enough specialty interest in the medium to support small-scale dealers and shops. There had long been stores that carried ephemera like pulps and movie press kits, and also devoted space to used comics. But shops that carried only comics, and brand-new comics, suddenly started popping up in the early 1970s. They arrived first in cities like Berkeley, where Comix had thrived, but gradually opened nationwide (see figure 14).[25] Responding to their growing demand, Phil Seuling, an active fan who organized some of the first comic book conventions, set up Seagate Distribution in 1973. Offering an alternative to the independent national distributors, Seagate bypassed traditional wholesalers entirely. Seuling got a 60 percent discount from publishers by promising to keep all unsold issues and then passed a 40 percent discount on to his retailers. He provided for them a far superior mix and quantity of comics that catered to the fan audience both he and they knew so well, a familiarity that minimized the usefulness of an increasingly costly return system. With this innovation, known as the direct market, publishers could avoid the many problems associated with traditional distribution. Seuling also promised new specialty retailers more reliable schedules for new comics, allowing fans to expect greater consistency in access to the titles they desired.[26]

For most of the decade, used and independent comics dominated these specialty stores. Independent publishing began with the newly emerging category of fan-oriented "groundlevel comics," which applied a reflexive, Undergroundesque, and more personal sensibility to familiar genres like sci-fi and fantasy. The space they occupied, somewhere between the mainstream and the margins, borrowing characteristics of both, was gradually becoming a kind of sweet spot for the medium as a whole. These early successes in the direct market paved the way for new independent publish-

FIGURE 14. Gary Arlington at the Cosmic Comic Company, the shop he founded in San Francisco's Mission District. At the time of this photo, in 1972, the store was a hub for Underground creators. But Arlington continued to run the shop for decades after Comix's brief heyday, selling all variety of comics to the city's comic enthusiasts. Photo by Patrick Rosenkranz.

ers who began issuing inexpensive, often black-and-white comics, through these same distribution and retail channels.[27] Their sales tended to be very small, but the direct market could sustain them nonetheless.

This meant that after twenty years of inaccessibility, the barriers to entry in the comic book business were, once again, exceedingly low, although this time the business model was structured to promote, not broadly popular genre fads (as was the case in the late 1940s), but increasingly subcultural tastes. The comic book publishing industry had shifted away from mainstream interests and broad audiences to a niche appeal and a very narrow readership. Notably, a significant percentage of the readers who remained were active in fan communities and engaged in formal criticism (through fanzines and letter columns) and organizing (through conventions and other trade and collecting networks).

In other words, they were in a position to continue building out informal infrastructures that supported the medium as it increasingly catered to their particular tastes. In addition, these fans tended to be well educated and well read in a wide variety of media. This background gave them cultural capital that allowed an embrace of the core of comic book culture as well as disruptions of and challenges to that core. Their privilege supported a complicated and nuanced relationship with the medium not available to all fans of mass media. As might be expected, this had an enormous and long-lasting impact on comic book production and culture.

Stifled by a dying distribution system, meanwhile, the larger publishers faced declining sales for most of the 1970s.[28] Finally, in 1982, Marvel and DC decided to fully embrace not only this new distribution system, but its creative mode, and began issuing fan-oriented direct market exclusives, titles like Marvel's *Dazzler* and DC's *Camelot 3000*. The industry's other major publishers, namely Gold Key, Harvey, and Charlton, which had largely targeted children, were all forced to close their doors by the early 1980s (although Harvey would briefly resurface on the strength of good licensing).[29] Archie Comics alone managed to sustain itself on a small number of newsstand sales to kids, leaving mainstream comic book publishing to just two companies, DC and Marvel.[30]

Although comic book sales continued to decline through 1983, this nadir was followed by an industry-wide boom.[31] The two big publishers and a growing number of independents continued to feed the direct market, which soon accounted for up to 75 percent of comic book sales; by the end of the 1980s, it also spawned as many as six thousand specialty shops.[32] Historians estimate the number of publishers in this market at well over one hundred by 1993, although most were so small they issued titles with print runs of fewer than twenty thousand copies.[33] Unfortunately, with this growth, and the loosening chokehold of the major publishers, came a certain amount of volatility. The boom that began in 1983 led to such a rapid expansion of the market that it crashed in 1987, putting a number of independent publishers and retailers out of business. This was followed by yet another, larger crash in 1993.[34]

Still, the direct market had helped bring the comic book industry economic growth and creative innovation in the mid-1980s. It was a brief glimmer of success that came on the heels of nearly three decades of decline.[35] Phil Seuling, the emerging specialty shops, and the fans who supported them had solved the problem of distribution. Their success meant that comics would never again be sold in the way they once had. But they were not quite the same product they had been, either; as Paul Levitz at DC Comics noted, "Everything changed around it."[36] Comic books now reflected the interests and preferences not of a broad audience the industry hoped to reach, but of an exceedingly narrow readership of loyal fans (mostly educated young-adult men interested in art or literature) to which they had already established a connection.

CARVING OUT A NICHE (1973–1993)

There were a variety of reasons that comics no longer appealed to the masses, including competition from other media and the form's reputation as children's entertainment. Unfortunately, the growth of specialty shops only exacerbated the matter. As media industry researcher Patrick Parsons has noted, even though the direct market saved "the industry from collapse," it also reinforced "existing demographic trends." With the popular market now withered away, "a smaller, more specialized audience gathered at and was limited to the specialty store."[37] For fans, this proved a great beacon; shops provided comic book culture with a physical space in which they could "consolidate their identity" as fans.[38]

But any time a community affirms its identity, it also tends to affirm the borders of that identity, ascertaining what is inside by distinguishing what is outside. Within fan communities, that outside tends to be defined as the ordinary viewer/reader of popular culture. Media theorist Mark Jancovich has suggested that, "rather than simply accepting the fans' construction of the authentic subcultural self and the inauthentic mass cultural other" as an accurate dichotomy, it is important to challenge their homogenization of more conventional audiences and examine the complexity of relationships within these communities.[39] Of particular interest in comic book culture was the way in which this ordinary "other" audience tended to be conflated with "woman," and the extent to which these potential readers were excluded from fandom. This exclusion was not just a theorization of identity, a vague sense of us versus them. It was a marginalization imposed through the community's deepening network of relationships, enforced within retail spaces, and reiterated by the practices that characterized publishing.

In appealing to a particular demographic that increasingly coalesced around a relatively coherent identity, the comic book industry and the culture it cultivated was increasingly alienating any real or perceived outsiders. Alongside this marginalization came a doubling down on the medium's prevailing center—educated adult men who had come to occupy space throughout comic book culture. These were the individuals who started comic book companies, worked at them, and made hiring and editorial decisions; they also wrote about comics, established networks of fans, organized conventions, and built out new systems of exchange and circulation. As changing infrastructures created the space for a different kind of comic book culture to emerge, these were the people in closest proximity, and they unsurprisingly made comic books a deeper reflection of their own identities and interests.

Freezing Out Female Fans: Part 1

Specialty shops became the epicenter of this inscription and exclusion. They lacked visibility in that consumers who were not specifically seeking comic books, and thereby willing to enter a specialty shop, no longer had the opportunity to peruse comic books or even see them on the shelves at general chain stores. To the limited extent that comic books could still have appealed to a broad, if diminished, audience, the medium's repositioning out of traditional retail outlets eliminated that possibility and worked to further marginalize the medium. The creation of a niche audience in this instance, as well as the extent of cultural visibility, were both functions of distribution. Changes to wholesale and retail networks have a huge impact not only on *how* a medium is accessed, but also on *who* can and will access it; even those means of distribution that seem accessible to all in theory, in practice may only welcome a small portion of the potential audience.

For most everyone else—women, kids, and really anyone who was not already a fan—comic shops tended to be alienating. More than anyone else, women felt very out of place within their space, and were often deterred from reading. Trina Robbins has offered this description: "If you're of the female persuasion, odds are you take one look at the scene before you shrug, and decide you'd really rather read a novel."[40] It is highly likely that the exceedingly masculine nature of the comic shop grew at least in part out of the exceedingly masculine nature of the comic book industry it mirrored. Populated almost entirely by men throughout the 1960s and 1970s, the publishing business remained rather unapologetic about its very obvious male bias.[41]

Well after the rise of second-wave feminism, the industry's most visible personalities remained unapologetically unwelcoming to women. In 1975, for example, DC editor Julius Schwartz said, about the character Lois Lane, that she might be "some sort of women's libber . . . [but] I don't know in my heart if she is or not. Like any woman, she's not very consistent."[42] Marvel's Stan Lee meanwhile, in 1978, vehemently denied the existence of "women's liberation" in the company's comics, noting that "in thinking about female characters . . . we usually don't think of them as women. It's usually a case of trying to get a good character."[43]

These kinds of comments were unfortunately only the beginning. It was an "open secret" among the few women who did work in comics that Julius Schwartz was rather "handsy." After his passing in 2004, several female creators went on record to accuse him of harassment, and in at least one case, assault. Despite these rumors, DC had kept the editor around as an official goodwill ambassador through his death, suggesting that such behavior had long been normalized, or at the very least, deemed tolerable. This attitude seems to have been widespread, given the sexual harassment complaints filed formally or aired publicly in recent years and the near total absence of a response from any of the top publishers (all of whom have been implicated by such claims).[44]

By 1979, Lee was beginning to acknowledge that he wanted more women working for him and that his male staff was becoming "more conscious of women's lib." However, considering how difficult this environment remains for women today, attracting and retaining female creators back then must have been nearly impossible.[45] By the 1970s, then, just before the direct market boom, the industry seems already to have acknowledged its failure in attracting both female workers and readers. Unfortunately, the growth of specialty shops in the years that followed seems to have repelled them even further. The assumption of a male audience thus became self-fulfilling, in that it inhibited greater effort on the part of publishers and distributors from reaching out to women or building a distribution infrastructure that could more effectively bring them into the fold. In so doing, male publishers institutionalized what may have been merely an inclination; the tendency to exclude or dismiss women became part of the new architecture of the industry.

There were also broader social trends that may have contributed. Cultural theorists Angela McRobbie and Jenny Garber have suggested that the social mores and female consumption patterns that characterize girls' lives historically limited their access to trends that centered outside of the home and the bedroom.[46] These boundaries likely played a role in keeping women out of the nascent comic book community of the 1960s and 1970s that rose up around collector bins, head shops, and early specialty stores. Scholars like Dick Hebdige have described fandoms of this type, which emerge out of mainstream culture but restyle it in a more oppositional nature, as subcultural communities.[47] The efforts of these cult communities to define themselves against a commercial mass often mean defining themselves against a certain kind of femininity. More specifically, as feminist media scholar Joanne Hollows has noted, "The characteristics associated with subcultures are those commonly associated with masculinity and the characteristics derided in portraits of the mainstream are those associated with femininity."[48]

For this reason, feminists have long been critical of the ways in which subcultures "hinge on a collective disregard for women."[49] McRobbie and Garber note that the "very term subculture has acquired such strong masculine overtones" that it has long threatened to make invisible both female participants and possible female counterparts.[50] Comic book fan and scholar Suzanne Scott has echoed these sentiments with regards to comic book fandom, noting that "female fans of comic books have long felt 'fridged,' an audience segment kept on ice and out of view."[51] This conversation has begun to shift in recent years, as the popular and academic presses increasingly claim for female fans and female characters a greater stake in both the past and present of comic book culture.[52]

Current data on the gender divide remains inconclusive, though, if not especially promising.[53] Regardless, even a modern-day uptick in female interest unfortunately cannot eliminate a long history in which women were kept away, sometimes aggressively, from the center of the medium. The exclusion was not only narrative (marked by the dearth of female characters) and social (marked by majority male fan communities), but industrial (marked by mostly male staffs, mostly male creators, a work environment that was hostile to women, and a distribution system that did not reach out to female consumers).

This does not mean that there were not female comic book fans. Women have always read comic books, and many more might have read them had the industry sought them out. It is important to emphasize, then, that the exclusion of women from comic books' ever-narrowing target demographic was neither total nor necessary, but a consequence of the structural and creative decisions the industry made between the late 1950s and the 1980s. Comic books had become a masculine medium, created for men, by men, and about men. In this environment, individuals of any minority status—women in particular—fell out of visibility within the industry and the community around it.

While this invisibility and the exclusionary tendency behind it has recently created a host of public relations problems for comic books,[54] there was a long period of time during which it created ease. The upper-class masculinity that became associated with the medium was a boon for business for many decades before it became a liability, not least because it reflected the identity of those who produced most mass media products, thereby opening some important doors.

Continuity and the New Comic Book Audience

As far as Marvel and DC were concerned, then, by the late 1980s, their audience was quite distinct, and it did not include women. Marketing surveys at the time tended to confirm this hypothesis, defining the average comic book reader as a very literate male in his mid-twenties who spent up to twenty dollars a month on the product.[55] With new easy access to this demographic through the direct market, mainstream and independent publishers alike were able to model their product with this audience in mind and, for better or worse, had made a practice of "consciously aiming their efforts directly at the fan market as their chief area of growth."[56]

This fan strategy had a number of implications in terms of both creative content and everyday business practices. In the 1940s and 1950s, publishers had assumed that comic books were essentially ephemeral products and that readers—inconsistent in their purchase patterns—would not follow ongoing stories. Irregular distribution patterns only reinforced this assumption, which led publishers to eschew serialized narratives. This began to change in the early 1960s, when the Silver Age attracted more college-aged readers in addition to more "literal-minded youngsters." These audiences began to demand stories that better adhered to their own narrative logic. According to a Superman editor in 1962, "Kids today are much more sophisticated. . . . There are a lot of things they just won't accept nowadays."[57] Audiences of the sixties had evolved past the narrative and aesthetic techniques of comic books' origins, and the comic book publishers followed them forward.

By the 1980s, specialty shops could guarantee the regular return of established fans, who would shop weekly or monthly to purchase their favorite series. These readers, already more sophisticated in their preferences, could also now access back issues more easily—through their local shop and also through the growing network of collectors and sellers connected through these stores, collector-oriented publications like *The Overstreet Price Guide,* and comic book conventions.[58] Out of this fan network came a greater push for continuity, a textual logic that brought together separate comic book stories into unified and essentially rational narrative universes. As a result, stories could become more connected to each other with continuity growing more and more complex.[59] It was a narrative shift that grew directly out of the operational changes brought by direct market distribution.[60]

These evolving reading practices were also notable for the role they played in conferring on comic books a higher cultural status. Nuanced and often self-reflective, appreciative of narrative complexity and visual originality, the fans' approach to the text had a great deal in common with the way established intellectuals handled great literature and fine art. This parallel can be interpreted as an endorsement of the medium's intrinsic value, but it probably says more about the similarity of the readers in question than it does about the similarity of the texts. As the social theorist Pierre Bourdieu has argued, the ways in which people relate to culture are very closely linked to their education and bound up with their social position and lifestyle. Even years after schooling is over, "the manner in which culture has been acquired lives on in the manner of using it," meaning that connoisseurs continue applying the skills of discernment they have acquired wherever they go, no matter what the text or context. Bourdieu explains that "taste classifies, and it classifies the classifier," which is to say that taste does *not* classify, nearly as effectively, the objects it intends to.[61]

Applied here, this theory suggests that readers' demand for continuity and their collective delight when publishers gave it to them was all about the readers themselves and the backgrounds they hailed from; they were asking from comic books what they knew to ask from any text they encountered. The comic book itself, a thirty-two-page floppy filled with pictures and words, could have been a vehicle for any kind of story or style or purpose. That it evolved as it did—into a profoundly intertextual, multilayered, genre-twisting, auteurist vehicle often featuring superheroes—is a reflection of the tastes, reading practices, and interests of the individuals who shaped it. The workers who produced comic books and the fans who read them were imprinting their tastes onto the medium and, along with their tastes, their social and cultural status. Their ability to do this stemmed directly from their close proximity to the physical, financial, and social infrastructures that were supporting the medium throughout this era of change.

Continuity and the New Television Audience

What comic books were experiencing in this moment resonates considerably with what television is experiencing today. In the twenty-first century, television has grown increasingly complex, layered, experimental, serialized, and auteurist. The shift is at least in part a result of a parallel shift in reception. Television scholar Jason Mittell has argued that the internet gave rise to television websites that (much as comic specialty shops did in the 1970s and 1980s) helped to "facilitate collective discussions" among viewers and spread decoding practices within communities of viewers. There has been a general willingness (among television executives and critics alike) to assume that their preferences are "indicative of broader tendencies" in the overall population, thereby "making such fans an important and influential minority viewership."[62]

Television producers' willingness to cater to these preferences, embracing continuity and complexity, is interesting in light of the way in which this same approach in the comic book industry ultimately alienated some readers and foreclosed the potential of an expanding fan base. But in both cases, the opportunity to secure loyal fans (whose backgrounds generally resembled that of the producers) amidst an overall decline in audiences was worth the risk. Notably, the strategy was only possible due to the introduction of new distribution mechanisms that could reach narrower but more engaged consumers through narrower but more reliable and predictive pipelines. The result in both media was a very particular kind of narrative and stylistic innovation, less reliant on the technology itself than on the access to fans that technology offered. And despite its drawbacks, this creative strategy—built on the strength of structural innovation—was ultimately able to bring some stability to both industries at times of crisis.

In the case of comic books, the audience had gotten much smaller, much narrower, and indeed more critical, but it had also gotten qualitatively better. By the 1980s, amidst the emerging multimedia landscape, there were benefits to maintaining an extremely loyal audience with a cult sensibility and a complicated mode of engagement, composed of privileged, eighteen- to thirty-four-year-old men. This demographic was, by this time, the most coveted for advertisers, and thus highly desired by producers, programmers, and distributors too.[63] The industry's ability to leverage this highly prized readership into licensing and merchandising opportunities would become an incredibly profitable asset to a business that continued to face volatility. The attractiveness of this demographic also helped to bring about a convergence between comic books, which had been facing shrinking audiences for decades, and television, which in the late eighties was only just beginning to encounter this problem.

LEGITIMATING COMIC BOOKS

Still, the comic book audience could not simply be sold to the highest bidder (it was not an intellectual property to be licensed off or assigned away). The value it promised was indirect and came largely through the increased legitimacy it brought to the medium and the way that legitimacy could translate to the other cultural products comic books touched. More specifically, its determination of value brought improved prospects for multimedia licensing. These kinds of opportunities are increasingly important for all variety of media production, but for at least four decades, they were a prerequisite for financial stability in comic book publishing. So the medium's struggle for legitimacy was of great consequence.

In the mid-1950s, public controversy and widespread animosity toward comic books led to a nearly decade-long hiatus in cross-media licensing that publishers worked aggressively to reverse. And when comic-book-based products returned to popular culture in the late 1960s and 1970s, the kind of media produced (animated children's series, live-action television camp, low-budget features) reflected current tepid but improving attitudes toward the medium. So when creators of the Underground and their successors in the direct market began moving toward a more serious and sophisticated mode of address, they opened the door for future adaptations that could also be more serious and sophisticated. It was not simply that there was new and better source material (although that certainly helped), but that the material had been publicly recast. As the status of the medium within the mass culture hierarchy shifted, its increased cultural value translated very effectively into increased economic value through lucrative licensing opportunities.

Marvel and Mainstream Legitimacy (1970s)

A shift in perception toward comics began in the 1960s; it emerged from within the burgeoning fan community and gradually spread outward. By the early 1970s, the popular press started taking notice of the medium, touting its sophistication. This coverage was initially rooted in a fascination with fandom itself. Mainstream publications like the *Washington Post* were noting the increasing number of comic book conventions, expressing awe at their high attendance.[64] The collectors' market proved even more captivating. Journalists would describe the intricacies of valuations—early superhero comics, for example, "must be in excellent, or mint, condition"[65]—and then list the increasingly high costs of a growing number of comics.[66] To be sure, some articles were dismissive of the form as well as of the fans, whom they characterized as overgrown boys who still live with their parents.[67]

But a different angle began to surface. A number of journalists took special note of some fans' very impressive resumes; there were Harvard graduates, professors with PhDs, and "doctors, lawyers and successful businessmen." There were even bold declarations, like an observation from the *Los Angeles Times* in 1974 stating, "Suddenly comic books are respectable, hurtled into museums and classrooms by the rush of legitimacy that followed their blindingly successful incursion into the college market. . . . If comics get any more respectable, they'll have to be sold with two pairs of trousers."[68] It was common for publications to attribute all of this to Marvel's Silver Age superheroes, who were more realistic than those launched in the early 1940s. They gave the credit specifically to Stan Lee, who "literally created the college market all by himself."[69] While Marvel and DC had indeed attempted in the early 1970s to bring greater sophistication and realism to their stories, though, their efforts were primarily a public relations strategy that played to reporters but lacked genuine radicalism.[70]

Maus *and Legitimacy of the Form (1986)*

Scholars, meanwhile, have tended to attach this shift in perception to a handful of notable comic books that helped change the public discourse around the medium. As Bart Beaty points out, these works surpassed "the threshold for aesthetic greatness established by the fields of literature, visual arts, and academic criticism."[71] Art Spiegelman's *Maus,* in particular, received such immense support from fans, and eventually from art and literature critics, that it actually helped lift the whole form to a new level of respect. It changed "the cultural perception of what a comic book can be," making it okay for educated people "to have an opinion about cartoons."[72] Charles Hatfield agrees that the crossover success of *Maus* "served to ratify comic art as a literary form" and "suddenly made serious comics culturally legible, recognizable, in a way they had not been before."

Not surprisingly, given its overall importance and incredible influence on the mainstream, *Maus* represents yet another comic book milestone with roots in the Underground. Initially appearing in 1980 as a serialized story in the alternative comic *Raw,* Spiegelman's work came out of the auteurist, highly personal, and self-reflexive fringe of comic book culture to which Comix had first given life.[73] Like other alternative comics, it had relied on the new independent network of publishers, distributors, and retailers that had been reorganizing the industry. And as a breakthrough work that was ultimately too big for the industry's existing infrastructure, it additionally helped forge yet another innovation in distribution: comic books' move into bookstores. The growth in popularity of the graphic novel category made this opportunity possible. Graphic novels, book-length comics that have never been published in classic comic book form (the standard thirty-two-page floppy), were another of the creative innovations that independent and alternative publishers initiated, and which DC and Marvel soon took up. The trade paperback, a bound collection of previously published issues, usually united by a single story-arc, was also gaining in popularity.[74]

Maus's popularity as a bound book, the great respect it was afforded as a work of literature, and the attention it brought to the graphic novel as a form helped generate a level of broad consumer interest in comic books that had long since disappeared. And starting in 1986, the year *Maus* was first available in book format, the big comic book publishers began winning shelf space in national book chains like Waldenbooks, Barnes & Noble, and Dalton.[75] This move meant gradually regaining access to a broad public that had been neglected by the growing direct market. So while the Underground and its successors worked to disparage mainstream comics, in offering an alternative, these movements ultimately helped elevate the medium as a whole. The contributions of these oppositional traditions have since become constitutive of the comic book tradition writ large. Their innovations and successes—creative and economic—helped shape a comic book future into something more respectable than it might otherwise have been, in part by supporting a wider and stronger system of distribution and retail.

EC Comics and the Legitimacy of the Audience (1955–1989)

Even with this structural growth, however, the accomplishments of *Maus* and other similarly brilliant works were not enough, at least on their own, to change cultural perceptions of the medium. Artistic norms and the standards of good taste were in constant flux throughout the second half of the twentieth century. What was once disparaged might later be praised, often by the same institution that did the initial disparaging. What tended to shift less often was *who* was capable of bestowing the praise and prestige that changed cultural hierarchies and that translated into profitability. Whereas women and less educated and wealthy individuals—whose tastes were consistently associated with the lowbrow—were often shut out of this process, educated white men, particularly those with control over cultural production, often found their tastes reaffirmed.

Through their social, cultural, and economic status, this demographic, which constituted the core of comic book fandom, helped the medium move toward respectability. The importance of social identity in processes of legitimation, especially with regards to the elevation of comic books, is particularly clear in the metamorphosis of EC Comics. The case study that follows demonstrates that comic books' new legitimacy ultimately had less to do with the nature of particular books than with the audience these books addressed. Transformed from a symbol of vulgarity into one of quality in less than a generation, this publisher rose to respectability on the backs of a subset of very powerful fans. The ability of these individuals to influence and guide the cultural mainstream explains much not only about this particular brand, but about comics' surge in respectability more generally and their closely correlated convergence with television.

In 1950, EC Comics editors Bill Gaines and Al Feldstein introduced the Crypt Keeper, the freakish, sardonic narrator of *Tales from the Crypt,* to set up and explain their new horror stories. He had a hallmark sarcasm that attracted bright and engaged comic book readers—both young and old, but primarily male—to the EC brand. Gaines actively reached out to his emerging fan community years before such tactics were typically employed in any medium, comic books included. Regularly publishing eloquently written fan letters within the comics, Gaines also established the EC Fan-Addict Club, offering members secret pins and a regular *Fan-Addict Club Bulletin* that advertised EC-dedicated fanzines.[76] Despite his success with loyal readers, Gaines faced aggressive competition from other publishers and lost his distributor; by 1956, he had no choice but to cancel every title save *Mad Magazine,* which became his sole focus.

In the years that followed, a number of EC fans went on to draw or write comics for the Underground; to publish fanzines, comic criticism, and comic history; and to collect and sell comics in the emerging specialty market.[77] Their work was important; their ideas helped the growing fan community articulate why comics mattered, and the networks they established helped the medium evolve in new ways. Art Spiegelman himself was an avid fan of the publisher as a kid, and was deeply informed by its catalog.[78] There had been fewer than eighteen thousand members of the original fan club, and just a small percentage of them went on to participate in fan activity later on.[79] But this small community's affection for comic books generally and EC in particular, and its members' prominence within their cultural communities, clearly

FIGURE 15. Creators Sergio Aragonés (left, seated) and Harvey Kurtzman (right, seated), famous among fans for their work on EC Comics' *Mad,* sign copies of the magazine for eager, primarily adult male, attendees of the Portland Comic Convention in 1977. Photo by Patrick Rosenkranz.

outweighed their small number (see figure 15). It was an early example of how an audience that was undersized could still prove highly visible and valuable through intense engagement and social capital. They constituted what Bart Beaty has called an "elite fan base, self-conceptualized as connoisseurs."

Indeed, prominent creators in a variety of media looked back fondly on EC's comics, with many citing the publisher as a source of inspiration in their work. In the 1980s, this list of fans included a number of Hollywood's best and brightest, including Steven Spielberg, George Lucas, John Carpenter, and Stephen King.[80] At this point in time, these former EC fans, mostly baby boomers, were entering their thirties and forties, and rising in wealth, fame, and influence. As they did, instead of championing the same high art traditions that previous generations of social elites had, this new elite—informed by the countercultural revolution of the sixties and all it implied—began to shepherd new traditions. More specifically, they shunned official high culture and instead resurrected their most beloved childhood texts and popular forms, among them the comic book. Not coincidentally, then, the horror genre more generally and EC in particular re-entered the cultural zeitgeist.

That EC in particular held a special fascination with creators of the 1980s is not especially surprising. The publisher's roots were in the mainstream of the early 1950s, but the brand developed a deep association with experimental and alternative comics of the 1960s and 1970s. This timing was perfect for reaching baby boomers, and positioned EC Comics squarely between the mass and fringe impulses of the medium. Despite its small circulation, it had the possibility, albeit small, of reaching a slightly older subset of fans who read them as boys as they were published. But more significantly, after the 1954 Senate hearings on juvenile delinquency, in which they played a prominent role, they began to reach a new group of fans. These readers were slightly younger and often discovered EC as contraband during the sixties, in collector bins at emerging specialty shops alongside the Comix targeted at male college-aged audiences. Eventually, they would be circulated within the hallways of film schools too.

One of these younger fans, Hollywood power producer Joel Silver, described how he used to see old EC Comics at friends' houses, noting that "if you found one you'd pull it out and say, I gotta read this, they were like some kind of forbidden fruit. Everyone knew they weren't ordinary comic books."[81] Practically speaking, they were very much ordinary comic books—cheaply produced and cheaply bought right alongside the five hundred other titles hitting newsstands in the early 1950s. But they retained a subcultural and oppositional aura. This was, of course, the result of the company's very public shaming; the very fact that the government used the publisher as an example of bad taste quickly began to generate positive interest in the brand. EC held a similar appeal to director Robert Zemeckis, who remembered the comics as a beloved "guilty pleasure."[82]

Tales from the Crypt *and the Legitimacy of Cult Media (1989)*

The 1970s had seen two film adaptations of EC comics, *Tales from the Crypt* (1972) and *The Vault of Horror* (1973). Both came from Amicus Productions, a British exploitation film company that ran on efficiency, low budgets, and favorable deals with distributors. While the movies were neither prestigious nor huge earners, EC's titles fit a financial model that was working well at a time when Hollywood was in transition. The same was true in the late 1980s, when Zemeckis and Silver, along with three other highly regarded Hollywood producers, transformed the long-defunct *Tales from the Crypt* into a hot property. A reflection of most workers in their industry, all five producers were white, educated men, and—like many other men in their forties interested in the arts and popular culture—they were all longtime comic book fans.[83] When they decided to pitch the project to HBO, they got an immediate green light. It was exactly the kind of series the pay-cable network had been looking for.[84] The producers and executives who got behind this title were passionate about it and hoped to expose it to others who would also be passionate about it. The impulse to do this is, of course, quite natural and long-standing among producers and connoisseurs of culture. Admirers of high art worked tirelessly throughout the nineteenth and twentieth centuries not only to fund painting, literature, and opera, but to do outreach and teach the general public to appreciate these works just as they did.[85] Those who have social and economic power often use that power to spread the culture they love.

Operagoers and literature professors may not have recognized it, but this was what was happening in 1980s popular culture. Films, advertisers, and television networks were refocusing their attention on young male audiences, a group whose tastes and identity closely reflected those of many American producers and creators. In the mid-1990s, producer Barbara Maltby explained the phenomenon this way: "Hollywood has traditionally been run by men—now mostly young men. The reason for this is simple: action-adventure movies that aspire to be blockbusters must appeal to the young men who will see the movie four or five times; so who better to understand the viewers' taste than other young men?"[86] Perhaps, though, it was not the product that demanded a particular workforce, but a particular workforce that had demanded this product. Men, and young men in particular, had *always* run Hollywood.[87]

What had changed was the media landscape, as shifts in the basic organization of the media industries had made the aggressive pursuit of young men more viable. HBO's interest in *Tales* was very much a response to the changing economics of television. Ad sales, and therefore high ratings, may have driven television profits in the past, but television of the deregulated future would succeed through ancillary growth.[88] As media conglomerates gobbled up cable networks and cable operators, television and film studios, benefits would come not from big business in any one channel, but from the ability of a title to move across all of them, generating interest through each and every distribution outlet and subsidiary. In this environment, which spurned uninterested mass audiences in favor of loyal niche ones (who would presumably follow titles over multiple iterations), producers had the ability to pursue different kinds of cultural products. Not surprisingly, they tended to support those they personally loved. For HBO, the answer to the political and economic circumstances of this transitional moment was the kind of quality original programming embodied by *Tales*, a forbidden text with a notorious fan following, and great affection among many industry insiders. A fundamental shift—in demographics and infrastructure—had opened the door to media texts like *Tales from the Crypt*.

The debut of *Tales from the Crypt* was at least as momentous as the medium's move into bookstores. Among several contemporaneous projects that reintroduced the medium into mainstream American consciousness, *Tales* was one of comic books' first entries into *quality* mass media. And in that space, comic books held a lot of promise. They represented a form of cult media, and as television scholars Michael Newman and Elana Levine have pointed out, cult status promises not just cultural legitimacy, but consuming power, "in the form of DVDs, episode guides, action figures, comic books, and other ancillary paraphernalia that avid fans covet."[89] Once the viability of comics was established there, they were poised for an expansion into mass media and, in particular, the blockbuster film. This leap from niche to mass may seem uncorrelated, or even paradoxical. But the accrual of legitimacy in the right sphere, however narrow, can be a bridge to a wider cultural embrace. As Newman and Levine note, "When the textual traits and reception practices associated with cult forms gain use in more 'mainstream' contexts, the cultural distinction claimed by the marginality of cult also translates. Legitimation allows a particular text to be both 'cult' and 'blockbuster' at the same time, the idea being that the text is of such exceptional quality that a larger audience than the fringe cult must necessarily appreciate it."[90]

Comic books eventually made the leap to blockbuster status. But proving their cult worth in quality media like *Tales from the Crypt* was a necessary first step. That television became the medium in which this reassessment took place would have come as a surprise at the time; television had long been associated with all the trappings of mass and none of the benefits of fringe. But the 1980s brought tremendous changes for television—in the way it was regulated, what laws it followed, how it was organized, how it made money, and how it selected content. By the decade's end, these structural shifts had opened up new creative possibilities for the medium, and it gradually became a home for cult media that once would have been deemed antithetical to the form.

HBO and the Legitimacy of Television (1970s–1990s)

The well-worn critique of television as a vast wasteland has always retained a clear demographic dimension. Ratings data tended to under-count racial minorities, children, and the elderly, emphasizing instead white, middle-class, adult, female viewers.[91] In this way, the television business was following in a long cultural tradition of conflating mass with feminine, washing out difference in a genuinely diverse audience to collapse and reimagine unruly masses into an idealized female consumer. For decades, then, television had a reputation amongst executives, critics, intellectuals, and audiences as a feminine medium.[92] And it faced scorn for this fundamental association with the wrong kind of viewer.

Not surprisingly, executives were perpetually trying to reach younger, better-educated, and higher-income families who would have evaded this derision and more closely reflected their own upper-middle-class homes and social circles.[93] Over time, this approach gained ground. A gradual wane in the advertising of small-ticket consumer goods targeted at housewives saw sponsors slowly lose interest in overall household ratings and the housewife demographic they were imagined to represent.[94] In their place, networks were doing more business on their ability to attract more discrete demographics.[95] *Variety* noted in 1987 that "virtually no national advertiser anymore, even package goods manufacturers, wants boxcar, household numbers," with almost all ad buys guaranteed on the basis of some particular demographic.[96]

In this context, young men, aged eighteen to thirty-four, preferably urban and educated, gradually came to replace middle-class women as the medium's most desirable demographic. The industry offered a number of reasons why this group was so valuable. There was a broad perception that their disposable income was for the taking, and that this money would be going disproportionately to technology, blockbuster movies, and beer, categories that were constituting a larger and larger portion of the products marketed on television and elsewhere.[97] According-ing to industry trades, meanwhile, there was an even simpler explana-tion. This was the most difficult audience to reach, and therefore the most desirable, with scarcity driving value.[98] Of course, over the four decades prior, the opposite was true; housewives were desirable because they drove big ratings, their appeal proportionate to their numbers. In this demographic shift, then, came the reversal of the medium's long-established goal of reaching the many over the few. The television industry's most fundamental operating logic had undergone a tremendous change; but then, so had its organizational infrastructure.

Nowhere were these changes more visible than in cable, and nowhere in cable were they more extreme than at HBO, a company so successful it gradually reshaped the center of television and popular culture both economically and culturally. The extent of the network's influence was partly the result of shrewd decision-making from forward-thinking executives. But to an almost surprising degree, as industry scholar Jennifer Holt has argued, HBO's rise was the product of explicit government favor and "impeccable" timing or, in other words, the luck of asking for the right accommodations at the right time.[99]

For decades, the FCC had worked to prevent horizontal and vertical integration, keeping various media industries structurally disconnected and holding back the development of cable.[100] The tide began to turn in the late 1970s as a new chaotic and uneven deregulatory regime began to alter the entertainment landscape.[101] In the 1977 HBO Decision, the U.S. Circuit Court of Appeals of the District of Columbia struck down some of the FCC's most restrictive rules, giving pay cable much greater First Amendment protection. It was a huge win for the company, which began to build its brand around its freedom from government censorship.[102] Before long, HBO established a virtual monopoly in pay cable, and surprisingly, the Department of Justice actually worked to preserve it, suing film and television studios that tried to compete with it.[103] Later, the government decided to selectively squash a number of mergers in Hollywood, but let HBO grow through numerous acquisitions. As a result, the network was able to transform from being merely a distribution platform into a major film producer. Financing films by preselling the TV rights to itself, the network filled its programming pipeline and increased profit participation in what it was airing.[104]

By 1987, HBO was the biggest financier of motion pictures in the world, and Time Inc.'s biggest cash cow. Both studios and broadcasters were incensed by the way the network used its clout in its dealings, acting as a great—and dangerous—"unregulated monopoly."[105] This power within the industry, however, made the subsidiary the unsung star of the 1989 merger between Time. Inc and Warner Communications; though the press was largely focused on the deal's impact on the film business, cable accounted for more than a third of the new conglomerate's profits, exceeding those from publishing, music, and film/television production.[106]

HBO also promised to strengthen and support the company's large and always expanding cable service operators, open up international distribution markets by appealing to a global middle-class audience, and satisfy—through the film and television content it financed, produced, and distributed itself—the conglomerate's multiplying programming needs across platforms.[107] Most elusively, though, the HBO brand promised to bring with it a new kind of highly valuable consumer. As CEO Michael Fuchs explained to the press, the intention was never massive ratings.[108] Instead, the network wanted to seek out an engaged niche audience to help enhance its reputation as a quality network.[109] The hope was that these highly loyal fans would be willing to follow content through multiple iterations across the conglomerate.

HBO thus found itself in a unique position. Liberated from the perceived encumbrance of pursuing mass (female) audiences, the network could envision a new style of television, more exclusive in appeal and masculine in nature. To accomplish this, executives built a roster that made up for, in either shock value or critical interest, what it lacked in broad appeal. These series included *Dream On* (1990–1996), a relatively standard sitcom but for an abundance of sex and nudity; *The Larry Sanders Show* (1992–1998), a highly reflexive comedic critical darling; and *Tales from the Crypt* (1989–1996), with a brash display of violence, gore, sex, and nudity.

This first successful wave of programming ended in 1996, as new leadership came on to transform HBO from an occasional-use luxury brand into a regular-use network more integral to viewers' daily lives and social identity.[110] The strategy was a success. By the end of the decade, business was booming and critics were crediting HBO's inspired executives and creative talent with revolutionizing television.[111] Notably, though, the network could not have pursued a new creative strategy had the regulatory regime not been in its favor early on, and had deregulation not subsequently changed the entire industry. The company's creative potential flowed directly from the position of economic and political power it occupied. According to Fuchs himself, had it not been for HBO's savvy business strategy, which took a diversified approach to the entertainment landscape, the company would not have even survived through to the 1990s, much less been able to launch a major creative revolution.[112]

Most critical and scholarly attention has been on the network's second and more acclaimed post-1996 wave of original programming, which included *Sex and the City* (1998–2004) and *The Sopranos* (1999–2007). But the focus here, on *Tales from the Crypt*, is on foundations—how this series helped lay the groundwork for economic and creative success, and how it helped reconceptualize the quality TV genre by realigning it on HBO. The company's decision to forge an association with good taste via a title that represented bad taste may seem paradoxical. However, it says a lot about the potential of comic books and the value of comic book fans in the emerging media landscape.

Steve Ross—the visionary CEO of Warner Communications—had made his initial move into the entertainment industry by purchasing National Periodicals, a leader in comic book publishing, magazine distribution, and media licensing. His eye had been primarily on the latter, and already, comic books had proved their worth in the growth of branding and cross-media adaptations. Now that Time Inc. (with its subsidiary HBO) was joining Ross's empire, comic books would again lead the way—although this time, it was the comic book audience and the cachet they brought that stood out as valuable.

RESURRECTING *TALES FROM THE CRYPT* (1989–1996)

> *Tales from the Crypt* should not be confused with serious,
> adult fare . . . yet it is not pretentious. You'll never get highbrow
> points for watching. Call it a guilty pleasure, like comic books.
> And television.[113]
>
> —Scott Williams, *Washington Post*, 1991

While *Tales from the Crypt* has largely been forgotten in critical circles, it played a major role in forming HBO's early nineties programming and branding strategy. Producers thought the material was too racy for broadcast and too risky for film, so they needed a sweet spot between the major studios and the major networks, a place where they could make "the sort of film [they] couldn't do otherwise." HBO became that place for them, and would soon be the same for scores of other producers with similar needs. Boasting a perfectly cult sensibility, innately controversial and obscene subject matter, a recognizable brand, and a built-in audience that perfectly matched HBO's desired core demographic, *Tales from the Crypt* was an ideal match.

Since it shared these characteristics with dozens of other comic book properties, it also helped prove the viability of the medium as a source for high-quality niche adaptations. The title's success on pay cable was not yet proof that comic books would appeal to mass audiences, but it was an important step in the right direction. As for HBO, *Tales* was able to generate buzz that spoke directly to the heavyweight creative talent with whom the network was eager to be in business; it was a group with a perhaps disproportionate number of EC fans.[114] Bringing in this particular talent pool became an essential tool as HBO expanded its roster of original programming.

FIGURE 16. Final panel from ". . . And All Through the House . . ." by Johnny Craig in EC Comics' *Vault of Horror* #35 (March 1954). Illustration copyright © Johnny Craig. Courtesy of Fantagraphics Books (www.fantagraphics.com).

The anthology series itself was built around twenty-five-minute episodes, each based on an original EC Comics horror story written in the 1950s, meaning that no stories or characters—save the Crypt Keeper as narrator—reappeared or continued. Staying true to their source material, the plots featured twist-endings with sardonically delivered morality lessons. The show's anthology structure allowed for a rotating talent pool; each installment brought in a new director and a new set of actors, many of whom were well known from impressive careers in film.

One fairly typical episode, titled "And All Through the House" (based on a 1954 Johnny Craig story), features a woman who murders her husband on Christmas Eve while her daughter sleeps upstairs. She is subsequently visited by a homicidal mental patient dressed as Santa Claus. After a gory chase, her little girl innocently invites the blood-soaked Santa into the house (see figures 16 and 17). As the newly widowed woman screams her brains out, deranged Santa asks forebodingly, "naughty or nice?" The episode ends with a commentary from the Crypt Keeper. He assures viewers the little daughter will be fine: "This particular Santa preferred older women . . . in pieces, that is! Well, it just goes to show, be very careful what you *axe* for on Christmas, you might just *get it!*"

Not surprisingly, many critics were sure to note that *Tales* was decidedly *not* highbrow.[115] Pointing out the "bad taste" level that characterized the series, the press, at least at first, harshly criticized its predictability, lack of subtlety, formulaic quality, and excessive use of violence, sex, and gore.[116] Repeatedly, the critics blamed these flaws on *Tales'*

FIGURE 17. Publicity still from Season 1 of the HBO anthology *Tales from the Crypt*, 1989. The series borrowed heavily from the vibrant imagery of the original comic book source material. Photo from the Cinefantastique Magazine Records of the Margaret Herrick Library, Academy of Motion Picture Arts and Sciences.

comic book source material, which suffered from "built-in limitations" and trite twist-endings.[117] It was the very elements the critics rejected, however, that connected so effectively with media-savvy HBO audiences and the new generation of Hollywood power players who were rallying behind it. Indeed, executives reported that viewers were watching it "with more loyalty than anything the cable channel has offered."[118]

The critics' inability to perceive in these aspects of the show something that was irreverent and playful was part of what made the series appeal to its most hardcore fans. These viewers warmly embraced the show, not because it had realism and narrative complexity, but because it actively rejected those features, and nonetheless maintained its cultural capital. It was a sophisticated approach to pop culture that at least some of the series' fans had honed over a lifetime of reading comic books and consuming other cult media.

Notably, the ability to eschew the markers of high culture while maintaining cultural legitimacy would have been considerably less likely had the genre in question been feminine, and the audience female. Because mass culture is so frequently gendered as feminine, the visible aura of masculinity around EC Comics in and of itself helped distance the property—particularly when it migrated to the small screen—from the mass femininity with which television was so often associated.[119] In walking this fine line, the connection the television series retained with the original comic book source material proved to be invaluable. By associating itself with this once-disparaged print medium, and with the most disparaged brand within that medium, HBO could take up a position adversarial to highbrow art. It stood in marked contrast to the culture of an older generation of gatekeepers, and instead aligned itself with the countercultural taste politics that were coming to define New Hollywood.

Persuading the Hollywood Elites

Over the course of the 1970s and 1980s, a subset of television series had begun to win for the medium an increased level of respect. High-quality series like *Hill Street Blues* (1981–1987, NBC) and *St. Elsewhere* (1982–1988, NBC) were marked by high production values, esteemed actors, visual stylization, a cinematic feel, and a complex structure that encouraged more active viewing.[120] *Tales from the Crypt* was obviously not one of these programs. It eschewed their typical cinematic seriousness and deep literary symbolism, instead opting for the irreverent tone of comic books. With single-installment episodes, it also lacked the complex and interweaving narrative structure that has defined so much quality TV, from the seventies through today.

Nonetheless, costing $1 million per episode, it had one of the biggest budgets in television at the time, making for visibly high production values that created an "eye-catching package" and "an unmistakable cinematic look."[121] The series also prioritized an innovative, often auteurist, visual style closely associated with its use of respected creative talent, both behind the camera and in front of it. According to the series' promotional machine, in directing the first three episodes, the producers worked to establish a "sensationalist and totally nonconformist" feel. They used direct address, extreme wide-angle lenses, and an overall visual "funhouse mirror unorthodoxy." The producers subsequently pushed each episode's new set of creative talent to "do everything they were trained *not* to do" and "go all out and have fun." As a result, each installment had "an individual look" associated with its distinctive creative team.[122] Enamored by these possibilities, or at least the promise of them, Hollywood elites flocked to the show. The strategy here was not unlike the current approach Disney takes to the Marvel Cinematic Universe. While the franchise's entries are united in tone and theme, the studio invites individual auteurs to spearhead each film, attaching to it his own (and it has invariably always been a *he*) distinctive personal vision.

Some twenty years before Marvel conceived of this formula, *Tales from the Crypt* perfected it and built up a "cachet in the industry that few other television opportunities could match." Before long, "stars and directors were calling [the producers] asking for a chance to do a segment. . . . It became a mark of prestige."[123] According to Zemeckis, it gave directors a chance to return to the kind of short films they did in school, in a form that wasn't "completely ham-strung and censor-ridden, the way broadcast television is. You don't have to worry about commercial breaks or censorship of any kind. You just have to do it with complete abandon and go for it."[124] Producers paid even the biggest names low or scale wages. But because production was typically only a week long—with no added expectation of handling distribution or marketing—high-profile directors and actors were willing to fit the show into their busy schedules.[125] HBO's innovative operations were helping create an unconventional path toward respectability.

Still, the production culture of the show initially failed to impress reviewers. They complained of the first season that, despite "big-name directors" and cinematic production values, the episodes simply were not special or scary or dazzling enough.[126] But gradually, the social capital *Tales* built up within the industry spilled over into critical discourse. Although members of the press found the product to be more "noticeably uneven" in later seasons, they warmed up to the style considerably. Reviews began making more note of its great casting, "stylistic fun," redeeming "wit, malice, and humor," and overall superior execution: "nowhere in television is formula, 30-minute drama done better."[127] This shift in attitudes, of course, did not happen all by itself. It was HBO's job not only to convince industry insiders of the network's rising value, but to convince journalists and critics on the fringe of the industry as well, so that they, in turn, could convince the public.

Howard Rosenberg, television critic at the *Los Angeles Times* throughout the 1980s and 1990s, remembers HBO's publicity team as functioning in a far more engaged way than he had previously experienced. Before HBO, television seemed a landscape littered with more misses than hits.[128] The medium lacked the kind of established institutions and critical networks that could match the magnitude of the task of improving the form's reputation.[129] Into this vacuum stepped HBO's public relations arm. The network's representatives made an effort to understand critics' individual tastes, connecting with them on a personal level, and treating both HBO's product and the critic's profession with more intensity and seriousness than was common at the time.[130] Before long, the popular press, which benefited from the way in which HBO was elevating the status of television criticism, started taking greater notice of the cable network.[131] Writers increasingly described HBO as a brand worthy of attention, with the potential of raising the bar for the whole medium.[132]

Part of the pitch, intriguingly, was the air of exclusivity that HBO was cultivating. In one *Los Angeles Times* piece, a major film producer admiringly referred to the network as "elitist," reassuringly noting that HBO offers "totally satisfying work. It's not déclassé in any respect."[133] The downside of this exclusivity, namely the fact that the actual HBO audience had remained small and that *Tales from the Crypt* (or any other of its series for that matter) and the cultural references it conjured were too obscure, seems not to have been a problem. As media scholar Christopher Anderson has noted, the network's publicity machine was able to defy limitations and function as a kind of "echo chamber of cultural production." It effectively created the widespread impression that HBO's programming was playing "a disproportionately major role in American culture," even as it continued to define its audience exceedingly narrowly.[134] The network had this in common with comic books.

Freezing out Female Fans: Part 2

If exclusivity was not a problem, neither was the series' or the network's decidedly male bent. Years before *The Sopranos* made the Bada Bing! strip club a regular set piece and *Game of Thrones* (2011–2019) made "sexplication" a buzzword, the *Los Angeles Times* blithely pointed out *Tales'* "penchant for setting scenes in topless-dancer bars."[135] Reviewers also noticed the frequency with which the show's graphic sex and murder scenes hinged on either the "brutal and bloody murder of a young woman" or a symbolic punishment for her vices.[136] *Variety* once described an episode in which the "viciousness" of one "nasty" woman was curbed by a potion that turned her into a nymphomaniac,[137] and the *Washington Post* even included quotes from the series:

> Sample dialogue: "Women: you can't live with 'em, you can't cut them up in little pieces and tell the neighbors they're in Palm Springs."
> Euw, gross! . . .
> Sample dialogue: "Women: you can't live with 'em, you can't fit more than one in the trunk."
> Euw, gross!

The critic's explanation for the pattern—cheeky, but telling nonetheless—was that "UCLA film school graduates tend to think alike."[138] Ultimately, industry insiders, HBO audiences, and the critics agreed that even the most exploitative scenes were "very well executed"; it was all "class trash."[139] The series was, after all, a "sexually and viscerally explicit horror-comic anthology where most femmes are fatales," and the rule seemed to be, "the more tasteless, the more delicious."[140]

Already, then, HBO had begun to craft a new approach to lewdness. At first, critics had seen it as a cheap ploy—nudity and violence to attract boys or men flipping fecklessly through channels.[141] But it is clear from critics' evolving and amused reactions to the series' excessive gore and sexuality that the network was in the process of redefining cable's relationship to obscenity. Because of the 1977 HBO decision, which gave it greater speech protections, the network was in a unique position to build indecency into its brand, not as titillation but as a creative tool to achieve either realism or camp.

Because of its fabled past, the EC Comics brand was able to help frame this obscenity as an ironic or subversive rather than commercial impulse. With content like this, as well as a superb public relations department, HBO was able to make controversial content that could have been a marker of bad taste (which is what violence and sex often represent in less rarefied contexts) instead serve as a marker of quality. Notably, this claim to artistic legitimacy depended on the assumption that HBO's elite audience could respond to controversial content in an appropriate and respectable way.[142]

In this respect, *Tales'* cult status and its simultaneous rejection of both mainstream cultural norms and more highbrow approaches to visual media may have given it a kind of cover. The series seemed justified in its refusal to conform to notions of appropriateness with regards to representations of women. And to a certain extent, the series' treatment of women and its sometimes visceral tastelessness may have itself been responsible for its cult status. Subcultural communities, comic books included, have a history of exhibiting indifference and, at times, disrespect for women.[143]

As that culture migrated to a new medium, it seemed to bring that disregard along with it. This replication was by no means inevitable, though; the violence and gore on which *Tales from the Crypt* hinged did not have to be a violence disproportionately meted out against women. But the series' misogynistic edge and male address is part of what distinguished it from programming on network television, which was still, in the late 1980s, interested in targeting women. Some women enjoyed comic books in general and EC Comics in particular, but the fact that most people (within the television industry and outside of it) imagined comic book fans to be men was helpful in generating the sense that HBO viewers were not typical. The network had reimagined the television audience as male, and its programming was projecting this reimagining to the public and to those within the industry.

The string of series that came after largely followed the same approach. Almost all of the network's offerings during the 1990s featured white, affluent male baby boomers as protagonists, telegraphing the target audience.[144] It is unlikely that producers and executives at HBO intentionally sought to alienate female viewers, just as it is unlikely that comic book publishers and retailers had sought to alienate female readers. But in both cases, the exclusion of women from the target demographic seems to have been an acceptable and untroubling byproduct of appealing effectively to a core fan base of privileged men with cult sensibilities.

Leaving a Legacy (kind of)

Perhaps due to its masculine aura, and certainly because of its hospitability toward auteurism, *Tales from the Crypt* helped attract a Hollywood elite to HBO. In the years that followed, HBO became a "haven" for the industry's best and brightest, widely known for offering creative talent freedom from focus groups, censors, and network executives.[145] And on that reputation and the network of relationships it supported, HBO built a slate of programs that raised the aesthetic and narrative standards in the medium. Again, the appeal of the EC brand and of comic book material in general helped facilitate this development. The allure of *Tales from the Crypt,* a beloved and subversive pop culture artifact from the 1950s and 1960s, was essential in attracting creative baby-boomer luminaries from Hollywood. The film industry had transitioned into the era of the blockbuster, and, increasingly, the town's most respected artists (many of whom got their start making B movies) were individuals who embraced aspects of lowbrow culture and treasured cult media like *Tales.*

Critics never celebrated *Tales from the Crypt* in the way they did other quality television, like *Hill Street Blues* before it or *The Sopranos* after it. But they did support it—even at its most violent, sexual, and misogynistic turns. It was a significant departure from the critical reception the same stories had met thirty-five years prior in comic book form. Social mores had changed, but the title's tremendous transformation in cultural worth had involved a far more complicated set of value conversions. The *Tales from the Crypt* series had earned itself a unique and venerable position with an increasingly convoluted artistic hierarchy. More akin to cinema than television in terms of budget, big-name talent, and aesthetics, it used the credibility of the series' respected auteurs and the affluence of its audience to justify its ostensible "tastelessness."

After six seasons, by which time it had cemented HBO's status as a refuge for Hollywood's creative geniuses, the series was canceled. As an anthology show, it had more limited appeal in this new era, which favored intensely serialized narratives. But the series had nonetheless made enormous strides in the way it was able to highlight the more cinematic and masculine side of HBO as a brand, and of television overall. The support of comic book fans—both behind the scenes and in affluent living rooms—helped make that reconceptualization possible.

THE POWER OF CULT AUDIENCES

In every aspect of the network's move toward legitimacy was the specter of audience composition. While economic shifts in broadcast television brought a gradual shift in address from masses to elites, structural imperatives at HBO demanding an affluent male audience (smaller in size, but higher in value) were more exaggerated. Without the need to attract women and the high ratings they were associated with, HBO could pursue a version of the quality genre that was more visibly exclusive and masculine. It was a world populated by gangsters, prisoners, and athletes that looked more like cinema, experimental video, and comic books than anything on the broadcast networks. And it appealed immensely to the critics and industry insiders who celebrated its high quality.

The cultural legitimacy achieved here was both elitist and gendered in nature. Designations of quality in American media often are. Media historian Mark Alvey has pointed out that, dating back to the 1970s, television producers interested in legitimacy have often had to actively disavow programming that appealed to elderly, rural, uneducated, and black audiences; the gradual embrace of the medium ever since has thus relied on classist and racist assumptions that he argues represent a fundamental "betrayal of the medium's democratic promise."[146]

The same patterns emerge in the legitimation of other subcultural forms, which tend to rely on gendered norms and the elitism of established cultural hierarchies. While cult communities often present themselves as oppositional, as Mark Jancovich and Nathan Hunt argue, "Their specific reading strategies not only are the product of a situation of relative privilege and authority within the cultural field, but also frequently reproduce relations of power and authority within it."[147] Joanne Hollows offers a similar thought, pointing specifically to the compounding of "cultural distinctions and cultural hierarchies along the lines of gender" and the "processes of othering" on which they rely.[148]

In the case of comic books, there has been a long, deliberate, and impactful campaign for increased respectability, one stewarded by creators, fans, critics, and scholars, many of whom have argued for the medium's rightful place alongside other high art forms.[149] Increasingly, this position is gaining ground, but proponents of comics have long felt they were facing an uphill battle. As comic scholar Jeffrey Brown lamented in the late 1990s, fans and critics have been "disempowered" because their aesthetic preferences threaten "dominant cultural hierarchies" and "challenge what the bourgeois have institutionalized as natural and universal standards of 'good taste.'"[150] This has resulted in a widespread perception of fans' marginalization.[151] The distance that remains between them and producers has relegated many in the comic book community into becoming what both Bart Beaty and media scholar John Tulloch refer to as a "powerless elite."[152]

Absent from these observations, unfortunately, is a recognition of the social context by which such reorganizations—of the boundaries between good taste and bad, high culture and low—were occurring. While individuals who were part of comic book fandom may have felt shut out of the "official" culture Brown references, many if not most of them belonged to a higher social class that has historically benefited from the power to determine the standards by which that culture is defined. Indeed, the most prominent and unwavering characteristic of high culture, since there has existed such a thing, has been not any single or fixed artistic standard, but the fact that it has been enjoyed by an elite class.

Marx and Engels theorized in *The German Ideology* that the class that controls the material forces of society necessarily also controls mental and intellectual production. But this necessary link between social and cultural power has hardly been confined to leftist theory. Critics like Matthew Arnold, F.R. Leavis, and Dwight MacDonald have at least partly understood culture to be whatever things elites believe they must, out of political and social responsibility, bestow or even force upon the masses. As MacDonald noted in 1957, that "all the great cultures of the past were elite cultures" was not a coincidence as much as it was their constituting characteristic.[153]

Mass culture, in turn, has long been defined in direct opposition to elite, high culture. Whatever forms of entertainment were enjoyed by those peoples who were not educated and powerful, and thereby white and male, were necessarily denigrated as culturally inferior. As Clement Greenberg wrote in 1939, there was "on one side the minority of the powerful—and therefore the cultivated—and on the other the great mass of the exploited and poor—and therefore the ignorant. Formal culture has always belonged to the first."[154] He accordingly criticized comic books, a cheap and mass form still, at the time he wrote, in its infancy, as being restricted by an unworthy audience composed of the "contemporary American literate middle classes."[155] A half century later, as academics and fans were forcefully making the case for the medium's cultural worthiness, this was no longer the case. Having long since abandoned a mass audience, the medium was the domain of eighteen- to forty-nine-year-old males with higher levels of education. Historically, this demographic made up society's elite class; more than any other social group, men of this age and position held the power to dictate, or at least shape, cultural standards.

As the twenty-first century approached, however, everything *seemed* to be changing. The advance of postmodernism was breaking down traditional barriers between high and low culture, and as Fredric Jameson observed, mass culture increasingly existed in a "field of stylistic and discursive heterogeneity without a norm." In this context, television, comic books, and other cult media could be reimagined as sources of genuine art and authentically high-quality media. But a correlated notion advanced by Jameson, that elite classes were no longer dictating the dominant or hegemonic cultural ideology, had not come to pass.[156] Social status still impacted the arts since it continued to determine which individuals were best positioned—by way of education, community ties, and cultural capital—to access the means of cultural production and criticism.

The ability to influence the course of development of almost any art form still tended to reside with the very same group it always had: educated, white, adult men. Cultural politics and the postmodern aesthetic may have been complicated, but they were not random. As media scholar Lynn Spigel has noted, there were "social agents and material processes through which the mergers between high and low took place."[157] Comic books, a formerly lowbrow cultural form that was increasingly incorporated into higher-quality media, were thoroughly implicated within these material processes. The means by which comic books found increased respectability in the late twentieth century was neither predetermined nor certain, nor was it unrelated to the inherent merits of the form. But the gradual cultural ascendance of the medium was never an unlikely or unnatural occurrence.

Comic books benefited from supporters who were relatively privileged. Fans not only brought to the medium a sophisticated approach to reading, but more importantly, they brought the power of their social networks and a closer proximity to the gears of change within the media industries. By no means did all comic book fans—or even a large percentage of them—become media producers. But a disproportionate number of media producers since the 1990s have tended to be fans, and have been able to push comic books, television, and film in directions that reflected personal and community tastes. In addition, many fans, whether they boasted ties to the media industries or not, typically enjoyed preferential treatment as a coveted demographic. As the growth of the internet in the mid-1990s facilitated a more fluid interaction between producers and early adopters, this community's technological and cultural savvy (also a result of social status and educational background) only intensified its status as a favored demographic with a disproportionate influence on popular culture.[158] In this respect, the legitimation of both comic books and comic-book-based media reveals itself as being far less radical than it first appears.

Over the last three decades, *Tales from the Crypt* and *Maus* have both reached genuinely mass audiences, whether in their original form or via adaptations in other media. But these creative milestones were products of a distinctly privileged subculture. At their height in the 1950s, EC's titles never reached an audience larger than three hundred thousand, and the population of enduring fans was probably less than 1 percent of that. The independent publishing scene that supported Spiegelman survived on issuing titles that typically reached fewer than twenty thousand readers, sold exclusively to the collectors' market through specialty shops famous for their alienating atmospheres.[159] Even DC and Marvel were "mainstream" in only a very generous sense; well-performing titles of the 1980s were selling around two hundred thousand copies an issue, but many comics struggled to break even the hundred-thousand-copy mark, with half of these sales in the direct market.[160]

While this narrowing perpetually threatened the vitality of comic book publishing, it allowed the form to cultivate an elite legitimacy that made its incorporation into other media more viable and valuable. Similarly, throughout HBO's cultural revolution of the 1990s, the network's overall market penetration remained basically fixed, capturing only a quarter of American homes.[161] And only a small percentage of those homes were tuning in to "hit" shows like *The Sopranos*. Of course, as cultural scholar Lawrence Levine has noted, "exoteric or popular art is transformed into esoteric or high art at precisely that time when it in fact *becomes* esoteric, that is, when it becomes or is rendered inaccessible to the types of people who appreciated it earlier."[162] In the very act of rejecting television's mass base and the female viewers who composed it, HBO made genuine strides toward a greater level of respectability. And comic books, merely in pursuing artistic developments that excluded the broad audience that once defined it as popular, were coming a great deal closer to achieving the elevated cultural status that so many fans and academics long believed the medium deserved.

CONCLUSION

The changing demographic boundaries of both television and comic books could theoretically have remained neutral, and never prompted a reassessment of artistic worth. But the composition of the audience of both comic books and television did help legitimize both media. And that cultural worth brought with it distinct economic benefits, particularly as intellectual properties began supporting longer lives across an ever-expanding matrix of different media outlets and distribution channels. At the heart of this process of (re)valuation was the rising importance the entertainment industry attributed to media subcultures and their supporters.

Over the last twenty years, producers across Hollywood have tried to replicate the success of Marvel, DC, and HBO, using powerful audiences to build powerful branded content. But producers only rarely succeed in these efforts, which often require preestablished relationships with demographics the producers and advertisers deem valuable. The comic book industry spent nearly four decades cultivating its readership of educated, media-literate, mostly adult male fans. Over the last twenty-five years, HBO has done the same, although far more deliberately, and with only some reliance on preexisting properties from comic books, video games, and toys.

But for most other producers, comic books and their built-in audiences continue to bring tremendous value to the creation of a wide array of media products. Not only do the medium's strong intellectual properties serve as solid foundations for budding franchises, but its fans promise a built-in audience as well as a subcultural cachet that carries value both within the entertainment industry and outside it. Ironically, then, in actively narrowing their target audience and limiting their product's appeal, comic book publishers ultimately helped to expand their reach. The cultural strides that HBO's *Tales from the Crypt* made helped justify other niche comic book adaptations over the course of the 1990s.

New Line Cinema bet on a minor comic book in *The Mask* (1994) and had a smash hit. Miramax Films found success with *The Crow* (1994), United Artists attempted it with *Tank Girl* (1996), and HBO followed up *Tales* with another comic book cult hit in Todd McFarlane's *Spawn* (1997–1999). Some of these products were financially successful; some were not. But none were mocked or denigrated for putting real Hollywood talent and muscle into adaptations of independently created comic books that targeted miniscule populations of cult fans. Comic books had achieved cultural legitimacy and had been embraced by the entertainment industry as acceptable source material for a wide range of media products. It was a crucial step along the path to the full exploitation of comic books as franchise fodder, a status the medium would not reach until the early 2000s.

Reaching that next milestone was another matter entirely. There were a number of hurdles to overcome before the film industry was ready to embrace comic books as a reliable source for big-budget, mass-market action movies. Among these were questions about whether or not the blockbuster itself, as a mode of production, had a permanent role to play in the entertainment landscape. As a result, it took more than a decade from the debut of *Tales from the Crypt* before comic book movies hit their stride. Chapter 5 explores this long journey to blockbuster status in more detail, paying particular attention to the evolution in film financing during this time. Notably, though, it proceeds forward based on the conclusion reached here, that in order to gain access to a mass audience, comic books had to prove their appeal to an elite one first.

As comic books made the final leg of the journey to mainstream mass media via the tentpole franchise film, the movie industry's transformation followed the same pattern covered here. It began with changes in infrastructure, shifts in distribution and retail systems, community networks, financial incentives, regulatory frameworks, and internal organization, which began to open up new possibilities for new kinds of media products. The individuals in closest proximity to these changes found themselves in a position to bend this new cultural production in ways that better reflected their own identities and tastes. While media producers remain financially and creatively constrained by often restrictive industrial frameworks, to the extent that these individuals have a choice, they typically choose themselves, their art, their culture.

Fortunately for comic books, the 1990s was only the beginning of an influx of industry elites who loved comic books.[163] Power players like Nicholas Cage, Sam Raimi, Tim Burton, James Cameron, Lana and Lilly Wachowski, Darren Aronofsky, and Kevin Smith all considered themselves fans.[164] It was generally the comic book as artistically stylized, narratively complex, and deeply intertextual that they identified with; for this rising group of media producers, comic books were fully and unquestionably part of legitimate culture—there was no more justification required. And there was no sign of abatement in the ranks of fans streaming in to fill industry positions. In 2001, Avi Arad, the head of Marvel Studios, boasted that when hot new filmmakers graduate from USC, the first thing they do is call him, asking to make comic book movies.[165] By this point, it was beginning to seem as though the fans had triumphed, or as one creator commented, "comic books won the battle."[166] Looking back nearly twenty years later, there can be no denying this truth.

5

Mutant Risk

Speculation and Comic Book Films
in the 1990s–2000s

As a result of a boom in the direct market, the 1980s saw a steady
increase in comic book sales. In April 1993, numbers reached an all-time
high and annual revenue was on its way to $850 million.[1] But then, once
again, the market crashed; sales were down by half the following April.
Retail shops were hit hardest, with thousands closing their doors. "It's
just been brutal," reported one owner, we "have been getting creamed."[2]
The crisis was widely blamed on speculation, which, in its various forms,
would cause a lot of problems for the comic book industry in the 1990s.
In this instance, collectors seemed to be at fault; after years of news stories about the high value of back-issue comics, people started buying
them up in droves, hoping they could make a profit down the line. The
extra business, in addition to easy terms offered up by distributors,
spurred growth in retail. Hundreds of new shops opened up, and quite a
few new independent publishers as well, leading to an oversupply of
titles and a surplus of orders. The industry had been here before, back in
the early 1950s, and the fallout was just as bad this time around. When
collectors realized their investments were worthless and dropped out of
the market, everything came tumbling down. It was a "bloodbath," said
one industry analyst.[3]

Each of the previous chapters in this book began with a big news story
from the comic book world. Despite its severity, this crash was not one of
those big stories. The national press was not especially interested in the
ups and downs of comic book publishing, and there had been lots of ups

and downs (another crash just six years earlier, for example). But unless you owned a comic book shop, the impact of these booms and busts was not especially noticeable. Even the comic book companies themselves, the large ones in particular, were only marginally impacted.[4] Huge conglomerates had bought up the major publishers back in the 1960s, securing their finances and detaching them from the repercussions of the publishing cycle. Then, in the 1970s, as comic book cartoons and TV series began to flourish, licensing supplanted publishing as the industry's major source of revenue. Trends in publishing were nonetheless still impacting the industry's trajectory forward. The rise of fandom and authorship in the 1960s, the narrowing of demographics in the 1970s and 1980s, the increasing sophistication of the medium in the 1980s, and the rise of independent publishing in the late 1980s and early 1990s all had a discernible impact on how comic books were perceived and on what kinds of cultural products comics would generate in other media.

But by the mid-1990s, even the marginal influence of publishing was waning. To be a comic book company in this era meant, by and large, to be an entertainment company. The fate of DC and Marvel in particular—which together boasted an 80 percent market share at the start of the decade—no longer rested on publishing. Paul Levitz, publisher of DC, had come to understand that his company was to serve as no more than a self-financing R&D operation for Warner Bros.' bigger projects.[5] Meanwhile, Marvel's owner at the time, Ron Perelman, barely even noticed the 1993 dip in sales wreaking havoc for retailers. He too was a speculator, but he ultimately caused a lot more harm than the collectors. His story, in contrast to theirs, saw quite a lot of press. With no background in publishing and no particular interest in comic books, Perelman seemingly bought Marvel on a whim; he had a sense the company was worth something, or that it would be in the future.

This was a sea change in the industry. The business had at one time revolved around a physical product, and distribution (the physical transfer of these physical products) had been a major driver of change for decades. Although the industry's fate had long hinged on the strength of its intellectual properties, it now seemed that those properties need not even be exploited, on film or television or in merchandise, to generate revenue. To make money, all a financier needed were the property rights—the mere option to exploit. The immaterial possession of intangible characters and stories had become the business's most valuable currency, and this made the comic book industry subject to intense speculation.

This chapter thus pivots away from publishing to focus on the speculative dealings that drove this industry in the 1990s and early 2000s, particularly as it relates to the comic book film. Though comic book adaptations had been very popular on television, and merchandising was an industry mainstay, theatrical films based on comics had been few and far between. As the new millennium approached, comic book companies still believed that major motion pictures could bolster the entire business, but this holy grail of licensing remained largely out of reach.

The problem was, again, speculative in nature. On the one hand was narrative speculation; a kind of lore developed in Hollywood about the viability of these films. Brand awareness was high and there was an influential built-in audience, but these projects required big budgets. Without evidence to predict their likelihood of success, most industry insiders determined the genre could not guarantee a return on investment, and as a result, they wavered on potential projects. Based largely on conjecture and apprehension, this narrative about comic book films as inherently risky was itself uncertain, and as such, subject to change.

The driver of this change, unfortunately, was also quite speculative: financing. While shifting social norms, artistic and cultural developments, and advancements in technology all effect change in the media industries, economics underlie most decision-making as well as most myth-making. Movies are big business, and the industry does not move in any direction unless that move guarantees bigger profits (if not for all, then at least for the biggest players). What distinguishes the 1990s is that once-straightforward economic decisions were growing more complex and less visible, heightening uncertainty. Financial innovations were introducing new ways to fund filmmaking, and these strategies were slowly reshaping the industry's economic infrastructure, changing the business relationships and networks built on top of it. In the case of comic books, investors began valuing comic book properties according to their potential sale price as opposed to their actual existing market value (i.e., the revenue they produced as source material for comic books, films, toys, etc.). The increasing intensity of this speculative strategy had a major impact on the fate of the comic book film, and on perceptions about its inherent level of risk.

With attention to the dynamic relationship between narrative and financial speculation, this chapter examines how changing economic circumstances were articulated through ideas about the viability of comic book films. While the industry's corporate infrastructure (production capacity, distribution outlets, ancillary networks) could support the scale of major comic book movies by the early 1990s, widespread feelings about their riskiness kept the genre at bay until the early 2000s, when it suddenly exploded. The intricacies of film financing and nuances of industry accounting practices become essential to understanding the decision-making that slowed, and then fast-tracked, this trend.

Yet, despite its central role, the financial infrastructure of Hollywood often remains invisible, with most creative (and creative-adjacent) workers preferring to focus on plot points over stock prices. Despite this neglect, however (or perhaps because of it), these details impact not just what gets made, but the narrative that develops around that decision-making process. The industry's understanding of itself is deeply, often imperceptibly, shaped by the financial fine print on deals most producers and executives would rather leave to the lawyers. This was particularly true at the intersection of the film and comic book industries, where budgets were high and speculation higher.

THE EXPLOSION OF COMIC BOOK FILMS (2001)

The first feature film based on a comic book premiered in 1941, and was quickly followed by a string of very popular film serials. Despite this auspicious start, comic-book-based films were quite rare in the years that followed. From 1950 to 1990, only twenty appeared in theaters. And by and large, these were not particularly successful, interesting, or high-quality films (see Appendix A for a complete list of adaptations). There were a number of exceptions. Warner Bros. launched Superman and Batman franchises in 1978 and 1989, respectively, on the conviction that these two very iconic superheroes had enough brand awareness to transcend the medium. Then, over the course of the 1990s, a number of interesting and successful comic book adaptations hit theaters, including *Teenage Mutant Ninja Turtles* (1990, New Line) and *The Mask* (1994, New Line) (see Appendix B for a complete list of films and box office grosses).

But comic book movies were by no means a trend. And while there were often high hopes among comic book fans, they certainly had no expectation that their favorite books would soon be inspiring their favorite movies. This was because Hollywood insiders had no particular interest in the medium. Comic books were a potential site of source material—as were cartoons, old television series, and even folk tales. But there was nothing special about the medium, no reason to mine its characters or to prioritize comic book titles over any other kind of intellectual property.

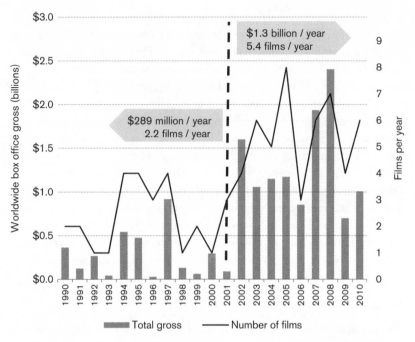

FIGURE 18. Comic book film grosses, 1990–2010. Average box office performance of comic films gradually increased throughout this period. But in 2001, production noticeably surged. Together, these two factors led to a dramatic increase in box office take. Grosses for each film from *Box Office Mojo* (www.boxofficemojo.com).

This attitude changed emphatically in 2001 (see figure 18). The summer before, *X-Men* (20th Century Fox) had blown industry expectations out of the water when it made nearly $300 million at the box office. The first modern superhero film, *X-Men* did not shy away from its comic book roots and took its source material seriously. Just two years later, *Spider-Man* (Sony) exploded into theaters and made so much money, according to one analyst, it created a "new paradigm in terms of what a movie can do."[6] Reactions to these back-to-back successes within the industry were swift. Comic book creator (and soon-to-be film director) Frank Miller noted that "it was a real turning point. . . . Unless I'm completely misreading the Hollywood people I've talked to, there's a sense now that we've got something."[7]

Comic book films were moving into production at studios all over town, and as *Variety* noted, "Hollywood is scouring comic publishers' vaults for more movie-worthy characters."[8] For years, most film executives had shown little faith in the genre, only believing in adaptations that starred iconic characters. But suddenly, the whole comic book universe was fair game. No character was too strange (e.g., *Hellboy* in 2004), no premise too ridiculous (e.g., *League of Extraordinary Gentleman* in 2003), no story too obscure (e.g., *30 Days of Night* in 2007) to warrant a full studio effort, including shocking budgets, massive marketing campaigns, and staggeringly wide releases.

And from there, the excitement only intensified. After Marvel Studios launched the Marvel Cinematic Universe with *Iron Man* in 2008, comic book film mania reached a fever pitch that, at the time of publication, has yet to diminish. Over the next decade, thirty-three films adapted from Marvel comic books hit theaters, bringing in over $20 billion at the box office. And Marvel was not alone. There have been twenty-three DC Comics movies since 2005, making $8 billion in theaters, and ten Dark Horse films since 2004.[9] By 2020, major comic book adaptations will be rolling into theaters at the rate of about ten per year, not including lower-budget films or adaptations of independent comics.[10] The medium has achieved a privileged place in the American film landscape. Comic book fans have come to expect adaptations of popular and obscure characters alike, and industry insiders perceive comic books as a separate and favored category of source material.

Why Comic Book Movies and Why Now?

Considering the magnitude of this trend and the way it has conquered the box office, there has been no shortage of ideas offered about its underlying cause. Explanations from fan websites, industry trades, and scholars tend to fall into a few major categories: 1) the influence of prominent industry insiders who happen to be comic book fans, 2) an intensification of interest in presold films, 3) the rise of CGI technology, 4) the increasing importance of international markets, and 5) a social-cultural psychic need. None of these causes, notably, account particularly well for timing; they generally point to trends that originated in the 1970s or 1980s and gradually intensified—but did not suddenly explode in quite the way the comic book film did. These explanations do, nonetheless, explain a great deal about how comic book films responded to broad trends in the industry at the dawn of the twenty-first century, and how the genre became so significant.

In his book on the comic book film, media scholar Liam Burke describes several of these causes, but emphasizes the first. He points out how "comics are increasingly positioned as pitch-ready material by a generation of filmmakers more enthusiastic about comics than any before."[11] Although this inclination seemed more apparent in the 2010s, this "changing of the guard" dates back to at least 1989. That was when power players Joel Silver and Robert Zemeckis sold the horror-comic anthology series *Tales from the Crypt* to enthusiastic executives at HBO. This first generation of fanboy-filmmakers came of age in the 1960s and 1970s, when comic book publishers first began to aggressively target well-educated and culturally literate young men. They rose through the ranks of Hollywood in the late 1980s, and as chapter 4 explains, they took advantage of changes in the media landscape to begin bringing their beloved pastime to a broader audience. As a result, media companies slowly embraced comic books, particularly those from independent publishers, as viable source material for high-quality niche media. In the years after Zemeckis and Silver first became fans, the national comic book audience actually shrank, so that fewer people were reading comics during the 1990s than ever before. But notably, it was not until that smaller generation of readers matured and secured credits and executive titles in Hollywood, during the early 2000s, that comic book movies really exploded.

The increasing value of branded entertainment is a second factor often cited for the comic book movie boom. Although film franchises stretch back to the late 1970s, the 1990s saw an intensification of the trend as media conglomerates began to rely heavily on titles that could pull built-in audiences across multiple distribution channels and subsidiaries for long ancillary lives. Comic book fans proved loyal and willing participants in these transmedia exploitations. Additionally, because comic book properties generally benefit from strong copyright protections, they were particularly appealing source material as studios began digging into their vaults to mine old characters for new adaptations. By 2002, it was clear to industry observers that comic books were "a marketing executive's wet dream: their logos and tag lines are already invented, widely recognized and just waiting to be writ large across the screen."[12]

Industry trades at the time, as well as creators and critics, were also drawn to a third explanation, one that focused on the development of digital special effects. Producers told journalists that computer-generated imagery (CGI) had finally caught up with filmmakers' imaginations. Stories that had been impossible decades earlier, because they would have looked "hokey," were now a "perfect vehicle to take advantage of the revolution in computer animation."[13] But again, better special effects technology was a gradual development, not an explosion that could explain the studios' sudden interest in comic books after 2001.

The same was true of a much older development in Hollywood, globalization, a fourth cause explaining comic book films' soaring popularity. Extending their reach into previously untapped international markets, studios set out to conquer Europe in the 1980s and East Asia after that.[14] As they shifted away from domestic profits, executives maintained that only a particular kind of film worked for foreign audiences. It could not contain too much social or emotional nuance or be too driven by dialogue (so as to avoid both language barriers and specific cultural contexts). So special effects–driven action films were favored over both comedies and dramas.[15] Because these films required ever-increasing budgets, their prominence intensified according to a circular logic: their huge costs entailed risks that made international success more important over time, thereby fueling a need for ever more global blockbusters with ever-growing budgets, further emphasizing the need for more international success. Comic book movies were good contenders to support this rising trend; way back in 1978, the original *Superman* (Warner Bros.) had brought in more dollars through foreign theaters than domestic.

With these explanations generally focusing on trends that evolved over ten, twenty, or thirty years, some have explained the particular timing of the comic book movie trend with a final cause, a cultural narrative. Reflecting on audience surveys, marketing materials, and the musings of filmmakers like Sam Raimi (director of *Spider-Man*, 2001) and Jon Favreau (director of *Iron Man*, 2008), Liam Burke argues that the events of September 11, 2001, played a central role in the popularity of the genre. Featuring New York City prominently, offering ritual functions (like nostalgia, escapism, and wish fulfillment), and displaying a "sociopolitical inflection," these films struck a chord with audiences overcoming the trauma of that moment.[16] Others agree with this assessment, noting that as post-9/11 politics grew increasingly polarizing and complicated, comic books offered a much-desired "moral clarity" whose ethical dilemmas spoke to the moment.[17] But the films that triggered the comic book boom were in production well before 2001. After the smash debut of *X-Men* in 2000, Fox was already very committed to the 2003 *X2*. And the marketing campaign for Raimi's mostly completed 2002 *Spider-Man* had already begun.[18] While some films, like *V for Vendetta* (2005), were clearly a response to a post-9/11 political climate, the center of the comic book boom—the superhero genre—

did not significantly expand again until 2008. At that point, the United States had arguably entered a new socio-cultural era.

Stuck in the Nineties

In the ten years leading up to comic books' takeover of Hollywood, CGI technology improved, the international box office grew, the desire for prebranded franchises intensified, and more comic book fans seem to have become movie producers and studio executives. But by 1990, each of these developments was well understood and established enough to support the production and release of major comic book films. In fact, the success of *Batman* in 1989 served as proof that such films were not only viable, but an excellent means of capitalizing on emerging structures in the film industry. Since the release of *Jaws* in 1975, Hollywood had transformed itself to better accommodate a certain kind of film: one with a big budget, big effects, and big cross-promotional opportunities, for big audiences. Films based on comic books were good at delivering this oversized set of goods, and they held personal and nostalgic appeal for many producers and executives in positions of power.[19] And yet, the 1990s saw few comic book adaptations make it to theaters. And those that did tended to have relatively humble aspirations, and almost always adapted comic books from independent publishers.

As a result, many of these films were not recognizable as comic book adaptations at all. The medium was providing source material, but projects were not presold as comics; very few moviegoers had heard of comic books like *Tank Girl* (1995, United Artists) or *Judge Dredd* (1995, Hollywood Pictures) before their adaptations' release. Although a couple of these films broke out to become hits, they mostly hoped to bring in modest returns from smaller audiences. The big comic book films, meanwhile, were languishing in development; they were getting stuck somewhere along the way to production. Producers, directors, and actors had wanted to make them, studios had heard their pitches and signed deals, and screenwriters had written scripts. But then everything stopped. Considering the factors listed above, why exactly did these movies not got made? If industry machinery was ready for the comic book film back in 1989, why did it not catch fire until 2001? There was one facet of industry infrastructure that still lagged behind: studio financing had not yet evolved to support the level of risk these films entailed, or at least the level of risk that most decision-makers *believed* they entailed.

BRUCE WAYNE, DICK TRACY, AND JEFFREY
KATZENBERG (1989–1991)

As Hollywood entered the 1990s, film budgets were steadily increasing, but the industry was still not wedded to the blockbuster. Between successive waves of media mergers, Hollywood was in transition and experiencing growing pains. It seemed as though the large conglomerates taking over entertainment could support bigger films, and perhaps capitalize on the scale and synergy they promised, but nobody was yet sold on this new paradigm or ready to adopt a new approach to picking projects. There were, in fact, signs of resistance and resentment about the changes underway. The uncertainty of the moment, about how a shifting infrastructure might rewrite the everyday rules of doing business, intensified existing anxieties about the inherent riskiness of the movie business. Despite having many fans in Hollywood, comic book films, and fears about the extent of their appeal, were deeply entangled with these concerns. Unfortunately, once established, perceived common wisdom about genres can be very difficult to reverse.

And the 1980s had proved devastating for conventional wisdom about comic books on the big screen. *Conan the Barbarian* (1982, Universal) and its sequel *Conan the Destroyer* (Universal) performed well enough, but these films seemed unrepresentative, since sword and sorcery was not widely perceived as a comic book genre at all. Meanwhile, female-centered films like *Supergirl* (1984, Tri-Star) were critically panned and failed to recoup their modest budgets. The 1978 release of *Superman* (Warner Bros.) had proved a massive hit, but was also considered an outlier; Superman was already so famous, his appeal did not seem reproducible. Furthermore, 1980s installments of the franchise ran into serious trouble, with each subsequent entry dipping dramatically in box office take. In 1987, *Superman IV* (Warner Bros.) made only $15 million at the box office, less than its $17 million budget.

But that failure was minor in comparison to that of *Howard the Duck* (Universal). The biggest flop of 1986, this adaptation of a niche Marvel comic cost $34 million but made less than $10 million in U.S. theaters. Despite the "abundant amount of special effects," *Variety* wrote, the "film just about dies in the first 15 minutes."[20] Within a few months, critics were categorizing it alongside *Heaven's Gate* (1980) as the very worst of Hollywood's offerings—expensive, meaningless, and a danger to the industry (see figure 19).[21] Big-budget films like these "took a beat-

FIGURE 19. *Howard the Duck.* Film Critic Gene Siskel noted tersely, "the story has no center; the duck is not likable." Photo from the Core Collection Production Photographs of the Margaret Herrick Library, Academy of Motion Picture Arts and Sciences, 1986.

ing" from 1985 to 1987, and their failure made many doubt the viability of the blockbuster film, still a relatively new studio innovation.[22]

When it came to comic book movies, *Howard the Duck* cast an even darker shadow. These adaptations were too expensive to make, and their box office appeal too uncertain. Even merchandisers were hesitant. They worried that comic book characters were too faddish—that once they appeared on film, they were prone to the kind of oversaturation that brought doom to established brands.[23] Stan Lee, a master of self-promotion, had become known for his inability to close deals, and began giving away film rights on the cheap.[24] DC was also guilty of this crime. The company sold the rights for *Batman* to a team of producers led by Michael Uslan, "a kid in his twenties" whose chief accomplishment was having taught the country's first college course on comic books.[25] In the 1980s, comic books had taken great strides toward achieving cultural legitimacy and had become a staple for cartoons. But when it came to film, as one fan later wrote, they were delivering nothing but "heartbreak and a lump of box office kryptonite."[26]

The Power of Industry Lore

Once this narrative of risk and failure was established, it became hard to disprove. There needed to be not just one success, but a string of them, to demonstrate the reliability of the genre. And to the extent that these successes appeared to be outliers, they would still fail to alter established skepticism. Of course, making a comic book film that did *not* look like an outlier became tremendously difficult, since studios believed these films were unsafe investments. Another bit of circular logic, this thinking was characteristic of Hollywood's famously risk-averse behavior, a response to the uncertainty of audience preferences.[27] It also represented the power of what media scholars have referred to as industry lore.

Decades ago, media sociologist Todd Gitlin found that executives in Hollywood tended to rely on a seemingly arbitrary set of rules about what does and does not appeal to audiences. These axioms, about sure-fire genres or doomed formats, were no more scientific or trustworthy than gut instinct (on which many executives also depended). But the rules provided them a useful discourse for explaining their decision-making to anyone who questioned their thinking. As such, they were used often in everyday situations, and gained the force of habit; they persisted, in short, "by being applied." Lore about what kinds of movies would work and what movies were risky, however "flimsy, flexible, ad hoc," thus became quite powerful: they dictated what pitches executives agreed to hear and what projects studio bosses would green-light.[28] Notably though, because these narratives were so flexible, new ones could emerge as old ones changed. Industry scholar Timothy Havens provides a useful framework for understanding this process of change, which tends to occur in "moments of significant political, economic, and regulatory change in the world's media systems." During these transitions, particularly those that alter the financial or organizational infrastructure of the business, uncertainty tends to reach new levels. As a result, executives are forced to seek out new kinds of cultural products and new ways of imagining how and why those products will connect with new kinds of audiences.[29] This anxiety-induced process of reinvention, as John Caldwell has noted, results in new "trade stories," or new narratives that industry personnel at all levels tell themselves about the work they do.[30] As different workers pursue different needs, Havens notes, they compete to shape these narratives in ways that will benefit their interests and those of the organizations that employ them.[31]

Along the way, the nuanced economic demands of the business get coded into industry culture and eventually into concrete representational practices via the media it produces. This process of formation means that industry lore is less rooted in "the collective imagination" of executives than it is in "the material conditions within which they work and the historical processes that influence their perspectives." In making the chaos of the media industries seem more manageable, predictable, and human, industry lore becomes "part and parcel" of the process of material change it represents.[32] Comic books, a form deeply and historically incorporated into the emerging practices of conglomerate-owned, corporately produced multimedia, had a perhaps heightened symbolic value in the formation of this industry lore. That legacy and the string of failures attached to the medium in the 1980s were more than enough to create a negative narrative about the inherent riskiness of comic book films, despite the medium's growing number of high-powered fans in Hollywood. Correcting it would require a change in the material processes at the core of industry lore—new financial conditions and changes in corporate organization big enough to alter everyday protocols of decision-making; a new narrative would require a perceptible shift in industry infrastructure.

Batman (1989)

A watershed year in the structural convergence of the media industries, 1989 presented a window of opportunity for just this kind of transition. Hollywood was moving toward a paradigm shift, and comic books held a lot of potential in this moment. A number of major acquisitions, spurred by the deregulatory activity of the eighties, saw six mega studios take over Hollywood, marking the beginning of an era of conglomerate filmmaking.[33] This organizational shift, as well as the flurry of changes it brought to everyday business practices from development to exhibition, created room for innovation. In television, executives at HBO turned to *Tales from the Crypt,* a niche title with appeal to a quality demographic of adult males. In film, Warner Bros.—which was on the verge of a merger with Time Inc.—released *Batman,* an extremely expensive and surprisingly dark superhero film. Most industry insiders had dismissed the character as worthless back in 1968, after ABC cancelled its campy television series. Warner Bros.' film thus seemed extremely risky, both creatively and financially. Its production moved forward "shrouded in secrecy, ballyhooed in superlatives and plagued by controversy." Not only was it considered "the summer's biggest gamble," but "if it does poorly," worried many in the comic book industry, "it will kill a lot of other properties."[34]

Fortunately, *Batman* did not do poorly. It grossed more than $400 million at the box office, with another $400 million in home video.[35]

This success served as proof of concept for the vertical reintegration of Hollywood that was underway. As Jennifer Holt notes, the film was "a shining example of how to combine your corporate media holdings into wildly popular, synergistic entertainment." It "provided the vision for a developing conglomerate aesthetic, one in which a film's narrative would be designed to capitalize on all potential revenue streams and corporate holdings."[36] For a time, the excitement seemed to generate an industry-wide afterglow as creators and executives all over town reportedly began "dipping into the inkwell of comics" for inspiration on their next projects.[37] Well over a dozen superhero films were reportedly in active development,[38] and it seemed to industry observers as if the "comic-book sensibility" had "never been more widespread."[39]

And yet *Batman*'s immense success was not enough to erase the memories of *Howard the Duck*. It was far from clear that comic books provided any kind of answer to the industrial challenges of that moment. It was, at this point, not even clear that big-budget films were the right response to the emerging paradigm. Generating the kind of content that could satisfy the proliferating subsidiaries of media conglomerates was important. But nobody was certain this was the best way to take advantage of the growth of the home video market or to serve changing audiences. So most producers were left wondering what the future would hold; 1990 turned out to be a year of soul-searching, as Hollywood went about the work of "rethinking its summer menu."[40] Amidst the uncertainty, all the studios hoped they would find another runaway hit like *Batman,* if not a caped crusader, then "maybe a crime-stopper in a yellow trench coat."[41]

Dick Tracy *(1990)*

Not surprisingly then, wrote one reporter, "the biggest question mark of the season hangs over Warren Beatty's *Dick Tracy*"(see figure 20).[42] Although the film was adapted from a comic strip rather than a comic book, this distinction was lost on most; to the uninitiated, Dick Tracy was a crime-fighting superhero, just like Batman. Batman, however, was a global icon, and had been a presold property for decades, while Tracy was relatively unfamiliar, especially to younger viewers. So on top of a $40 million production budget, Disney dedicated another $55 million to marketing and distributing the film.[43] Although *Dick Tracy* ended up performing well at the box office, crossing the $100 million mark, it did not meet the studio's heightened expectations and left Disney executives deeply unsatisfied.

In fact, the film has perhaps the most famous postmortem in Hollywood history. In January of 1991, Disney Studios chairman Jeffrey Katzenberg wrote a twenty-eight-page memo or "manifesto," as it became known, and sent it home with executives for their weekend read. It was intended for internal use only, but the document was faxed all over town within days, and reprinted in its entirety in *Variety* a few weeks later. Attention gravitated, at least at first, to Katzenberg's "scathing assessment of *Dick Tracy*."[44] Sure, the film was a critical success, and it made its money back; but along the way, he opined, it "made demands on our time, talent and treasury that, upon reflection, may not have been worth it." Katzenberg had to lavish too many company resources and too much personal attention, only to have it "savagely disparaged" for failing "to achieve *Batman*-like success." He warned that such expectations, and the "blockbuster mentality" behind them, were leading Hollywood to ruin.[45]

Many dismissed Katzenberg's memo as an apologia, "self-serving palaver" designed to shield himself from criticism.[46] He was trying to account for a disappointing year and protect against another on the way.[47] But there was clearly more to this memo than a justification of prior actions. Katzenberg observed that a looming recession and aggressive corporate takeovers had catapulted the industry into a "period of great danger and even greater uncertainty." An "atmosphere of near hysteria" had ensued. Like any ambitious leader, he wanted to diagnose the problem and recommend a remedy—in this case, a new formula for better decision-making.

So, he determined, the time had come to cut back, to stop pursuing the next *Batman,* to stop giving celebrities gargantuan salaries, to stop targeting ancillary markets, and instead, to get "back to basics." By focusing on "authentic, great Ideas," and executing them well, Katzenberg insisted, they could recreate the "magic" and win back audiences.[48] It was this incredibly hopeful and heartfelt message that was immortalized a few years later in the opening scenes of *Jerry Maguire*, which fictionalized the memo's creation and distribution.[49]

But in terms of its prescription, Katzenberg's ideas were somewhat reactionary and perhaps even naïve. His call for great stories was nothing new, a well-established rallying cry in Hollywood. It was where he located those stories—in modest, original, adult-targeted films—that was a throwback. He wanted Disney to build a wide slate of films produced on mostly mid-range budgets in the hope of a few breakout hits. This was a rejection of an emerging paradigm that favored big films with big built-in expectations and big opportunities across a whole conglomerate. It makes sense, then, that the distress Katzenberg expressed was meted out disproportionately on *Dick Tracy*, and articulated pointedly through a deep annoyance with *Batman*. He was not alone in either his anxiety about or his aversion to this new direction—or, unfortunately, in his disdain for comic book films, which symbolized the transition he was resisting.

Industry trades observed that the memo quickly became a "source of anger, resentment, debate and jokes within Hollywood," not for its defensiveness, or hyperbole, but because it struck a chord, or, as some even claimed, "stated the obvious." All across town, people were agreeing that Katzenberg was right, and that "things had to change."[50] And they did, or so Hollywood claimed. Budgets quickly became "an anxious topic" as talk of "enormous belt-tightening" promised to bring an end to the town's long "history of free spending." Within just a few months, the narrative went, "recession mentality has replaced blockbuster mentality."[51] In response to a complicated moment, the industry had produced a logical and principled collective narrative about its direction forward. Movies like *Dick Tracy* and *Batman* had been too expensive, and consequently too risky.

The appeal of this narrative was undeniable, and it doomed comic book movies. In the year that followed Katzenberg's memo, nobody in Hollywood wanted to be perceived as pursuing the next *Batman*. Even though both that film and *Dick Tracy* had succeeded at the box office, the logic behind their production and execution had come under direct fire. Just as quickly as *Batman* had lit a flame for all things comic books, *Dick Tracy* and its infamous postmortem extinguished it. Producers and executives who had been pushing big comic book films moved on to other projects. *Batman* had become an undeniable success, and Warner Bros. would continue to pump out sequels at declining levels of quality and popularity. But comic book movies otherwise were relegated to mid-range status. When they were made at all, they were made on the cheap, and their comic-book-ness was largely denied.

OTHER PEOPLE'S MONEY (1989–1997)

It was one thing for comic book films to be marked as risky by industry lore. But this negative narrative was supported by material conditions, at least during the early to mid-1990s. Comic book films were not actually doing poorly at the box office; there were not enough of them in theaters to know how they would perform. The problem was that comic book properties, from Marvel in particular, had become an object of financial speculation. As a result, they had gotten caught up in some highly visible and highly risky endeavors that did not help the medium's already blemished reputation. These ventures, which relied on financial engineering more than actual cultural production, worked to create more reliable profit streams from film, a business that tended toward unpredictability. In time, Hollywood would tweak these financial schemes until they could do just that. But in the late eighties and early nineties, these strategies remained tentative and thrived on the periphery of the business and in its margins. This was of course where comic book films lived. As a result, the comic book industry found itself on the front lines of new, rather risky, and often questionable, approaches to financing.

To the extent that these new funding tactics shared a common goal or theme, it was quite simple: reduce studio exposure to vast uncertainty by investing other people's money. Successfully demonstrating this objective in 1992, producer-director James Cameron set up twelve films in a highly enviable arrangement with Fox. Unlike the studio's other deals, this was a "partnership," one that allowed Cameron's production company Lightstorm to retain a portion of the rights and evolve into a self-contained global distribution firm. The key to the deal was that Cameron was bringing financing with him; an undisclosed portion of the funding came from equity sources, in this case, Japanese investors who were especially excited about his upcoming *Spider-Man* film.[52]

Cameron's unnamed foreign partners were hardly the only investors looking to get into entertainment in the 1990s. As media economist Harold Vogel explains, large-scale financing began materializing in "unexpected places," including private sources in Japan, German public equity, Middle Eastern sovereign wealth, and a number of foreign banks. Driven in large part by a desire to participate in the movie business, they were often willing to accept relatively low returns on their capital.[53] In response, studios began pushing hard for films that could attract funding from external sources.[54] One producer summarized the new approach to deal-making this way: "The idea to get the big money for these slates was to find someone who was willing to take on the risk. . . . They were never great deals for the people who took it on. But there were always people out there willing, and the studios took advantage of that to some degree."[55]

The Independents (Late 1980s)

In the few years before these external investors started proliferating, studios had come upon an even simpler strategy to reduce financial exposure. They got into the distribution business with independent producers. They could take a distribution fee of 18 percent on an investment of just 8 percent, leaving themselves with a significant profit, completely risk-free.[56] Meanwhile, the independents behind these deals, which included Cannon, De Laurentiis Entertainment Group, New World, and New Line, were writing the book on how to exploit capital from external investors. These firms rose up amidst the high-yield or "junk" bond market of the late 1980s and early 1990s, largely on the strength of dubious approaches to accounting.

Their bread and butter was lower-budget action movies, which they financed by preselling distribution rights (in international theatrical, home video, or television); they then rolled ancillary revenue from successful films directly back into new projects.[57] When they needed to bridge gaps in funding, they took on heavy debt, often from foreign banks like Credit Lyonnais. Investor confidence in this approach to financing, supported by faith in the growing home video market, floated these companies throughout the boom years of the 1980s.[58] But debt spiraled out of control as these firms expanded their interests and tackled bigger and bigger films (pushing them from low-budget to mid-range projects). After the stock market crash in October of 1987 and a decline in theater attendance in 1988, these companies began to suffer huge, and very visible, losses.[59]

The comic book business, unfortunately, became entangled in the fallout. The still somewhat marginal status of comic books in the 1980s had made the medium ideal source material for the B-movies these companies were pushing.[60] This was not good for comic book films' future potential. As one critic noted, "what killed many of these film superheroes was not their archenemies but their low budget made-for-TV formats."[61] As long as these companies were trying to produce comic book films on budgets of $20 million, studios were unlikely to invest blockbuster dollars on the same material. More importantly, though, as the 1990s approached, these independents' financial precariousness and the exclusive options they maintained on many comic book rights held back these titles' potential development elsewhere.

For example, Cannon, a significant player in comic book optioning, had a particularly egregious financial record. Having long used highly questionable accounting practices, the company faced an SEC investigation in 1986, and emerged from it nearly a billion dollars in debt.[62] Despite this abysmal record, Cannon's woes at the time were attributed to the poor box office performance of *Superman IV* in 1987;[63] it was terrible publicity for the franchise and for comic book movies in general. The French firm Pathé ultimately stepped in to save Cannon, but only after borrowing another $250 million on the company's back, and hurling its pending production of *Spider-Man* into a decade of litigation.[64]

Captain America also got caught up in Cannon's mess. The company had bought the character rights in the early 1980s, but never moved forward on it. When company head Menahem Golan parted ways with Pathé in 1989, he took the option with him, forging ahead on production immediately.[65] The result "wasn't merely a bad film, but a creatively desperate one" that ended with a direct-to-video release.[66] *Fantastic Four* met a similar fate. It was acquired for a small fee by a German production company, Constantin Film, which was becoming another independent player in Hollywood. But because, according to the company's head, "Marvel superheroes were still an untested property," he could not get interest from any major studio. Wanting to hold on to his option until the property was more valuable, he decided to make the project with B-film legend Roger Corman. Together they produced an unreleasable film in 1994.[67]

Corman, incidentally, was also the founder of New World Pictures, another significant player in this independent space. In 1983, Corman sold the company to two entertainment lawyers, Larry Kupin and Harry Sloan, who wanted to transform New World into a media empire. One of their biggest acquisitions was Marvel Entertainment, in 1986, for just over $40 million. Their interest in the comic book company was almost entirely about licensing potential, or as Sloan put it, the "steady stream of ideas and characters for animation, theatrical features, live-action television production and made-for videos."[68] Of less interest was the comic book publishing business they also haphazardly acquired, which Kupin and Sloan reportedly "know nothing about."[69] By 1988, New World also began facing serious financial trouble. It tried to offset its $262 million of debt through junk bonds, but the company's aggressive expansion into television and rumors they were playing the stock market with borrowed money scared away investors.[70]

In November, Kupin and Sloan decided to sell Marvel to Andrews Group, a holding company controlled by Ronald Perelman, the chairman of Revlon, for $82.5 million.[71] In just two years, the former attorneys had doubled their money. The only movie they had made was *The Punisher* (Live Ent., 1989) yet another unreleasable film. But while Marvel had not given them any tangible successes, *as an asset*—with potential but unrealized worth—the company had generated tremendous value. This fact would dramatically shape Marvel's future, as well as the future of comic book films, which did not actually need to get made in order to create profits; the promise of these films, at this particular moment, was seemingly more valuable than their concrete existence.[72] It was still not enough to keep New World afloat though, so in April of 1989, Kupin and Sloan sold the rest of their media empire to Perelman for another $145 million.[73]

The only one of these independent studios to thrive beyond the late 1980s was New Line Cinema.[74] The company stuck to its roots, producing low-budget niche films while simultaneously maintaining a strong distribution business.[75] In 1990, New Line picked up *Teenage Mutant Ninja Turtles* from a Hong Kong–based firm, Golden Harvest. An animated television series and merchandise had made the title characters hugely popular with kids, and the film only cost $12 million, making it an exceedingly safe bet.[76] It went on to make more than $200 million at the box office and become the highest-grossing independent film at that time.[77] The major studios had missed a major opportunity. One of the film's producers explained that executives "were so turned off by the silly title and concept that they failed to do their homework" and realize that "this wasn't *Howard the Duck*."[78]

More surprising, though, was the studios' failure to learn from this mistake. Despite the phenomenal success of *Teenage Mutant Ninja Turtles,* and for that matter *Batman* and *Dick Tracy,* studios largely chose to continue avoiding comic book movies. With an industry narrative about cost-consciousness still in play, mega superhero flicks were decidedly unfashionable. The role of debt-ridden independents in the genre and their track record of inaction (most notably on *Spider-Man*) and failure (in *The Punisher, Fantastic Four,* and *Captain America*) further poisoned the well. Unfortunately, things would get worse before they got better.

Ron Perelman's Shell Game (1989–1997)

Like Kupin and Sloan before him, Ron Perelman knew very little about comic books, and ultimately had very little interest in learning about the business he bought or the people who worked for it. It was Marvel's licensing potential, as opposed to the publishing operation, that had attracted the tycoon, just as it had every buyer since the 1960s.[79] So it made sense when, shortly after Perelman's takeover, Stan Lee and other Marvel executives began hyping the company's "increasingly proactive stance in Hollywood" as they set out about town to make film and television deals. The brand had a disappointing record; *Howard the Duck* was the company's most notable film adaptation. Nonetheless, for a brief moment in the early 1990s (before the Katzenberg memo, in particular), comic books seemed to be everywhere, and Marvel's more sophisticated titles held out promise for an audience of young adults.[80]

Potential profits from merchandising only sweetened these prospects. Warner Bros.' release of *Batman* had increased merchandise sales for the company fourfold, and Marvel hoped to replicate this success.[81] Notably, this down-market ancillary revenue stream was actually preferable for Perelman. As *Variety* explained, "the carrot for Marvel is the fat margins from merchandise" which ran as high as 80 percent, "rather than royalties from the programs and films themselves" at rates of just 10 percent.[82] Unfortunately, this was the strategy of a business man, not a publisher or a producer. In addition to almost completely ignoring the comic book business, this approach to growth also inadvertently dismissed Hollywood.[83]

Perelman was approaching deal-making in film the same way he approached everything else, with a total reliance on other people's

FIGURE 21. Ron Perelman (right) celebrates Revlon's 1996 IPO with company spokesmodel Cindy Crawford (middle) and NYSE chairman Richard Grasson (left). The Revlon stock offering injected $150 million into the company, but it did little to reduce the $2 billion debt that Perelman had amassed in his 1985 junk-bond-funded buyout, which continued to beleaguer the cosmetics giant well into the 2000s. Photo by Richard Drew. AP Images.

money (see figure 21). Though he refused to put up any of the production or marketing costs for films based on Marvel's characters, he insisted on retaining option and consulting fees, royalties, and, most importantly, merchandising rights, which the studios were determined to retain for themselves."[84] At another moment in time, this strategy might have worked. But just like Perelman, Hollywood executives were increasingly determined both to find external sources of financing and to avoid collaborators who demanded too large a share of the profits. Marvel's approach may have made sense financially, but as one executive commented, it was "too good, too airtight"—it provided no incentive to studio heads looking for safe investments and well-behaved partners.[85]

With the licensing business at a standstill, Perelman began pursuing other means of boosting merchandise, or at least of boosting his own

bottom line. In July 1992, he used Marvel's assets as collateral to purchase a trading card company, Fleer Corporation for $286 million.
Then came Panini, an Italian sticker maker (for $158 million), Skybox,
another trading card company (for $150 million), two independent
comic book publishers, Malibu Comics and Welsh Publishing, and
finally Heroes World, a regional comic book distributor. These purchases saddled Marvel with a mountain of debt, more than $580 mil-
lion by the end of 1995. Along the way, Perelman made one acquisition
at no upfront cost: Marvel took on minority ownership (46 percent) in
a small toy manufacturer called ToyBiz in exchange for a perpetual, *no-
fee* license to produce Marvel toys.[86] The deal ate into an important
source of value and growth for Marvel, but it put Perelman on the
board of yet another company, and brought short-term cash flow to his
swiftly expanding empire.[87]

Throughout this buying spree, Perelman seemed unfazed by signs of
trouble, even as comic book publishing (and card-trading and sticker
manufacturing) faced serious problems after 1993. In fact, he personally
dealt an additional blow to the publishing sector in 1995, when he shifted
all of Marvel's business (more than 30 percent of the market) to its newly
acquired distributor, Heroes World. The move pushed the industry's
other publishers (DC, Image, and Dark Horse) to also pursue exclusive
distribution deals (they all signed with Diamond Comic Distributors).
This realignment forced retailers, who often relied on a single distributor,
to open new accounts with multiple firms, changing the way they ran
their stores. Meanwhile, Heroes World lacked the infrastructure to handle all the new volume. It folded after just two years, but not before also
handing its business over to Diamond, the only distributor left standing,
and, to this day, the only major comic book distributor in operation.[88]

These upsets had significant costs for the many individuals who
worked in the comic book industry. There were the many shop owners
who went out of business, as well as Marvel employees who faced lay-
offs in 1994 and again in 1996.[89] Their fate was of little interest to Perelman, however, as long as the banks continued to back his expanding
interests in the company—which they did, for a surprisingly long time.
Good buzz early on had made investor support easy to come by. After
an initial public offering in 1991, amidst talk of a wave of comic book
film and television adaptations, Marvel's stock prices had soared 400
percent.[90] Perelman's personal stake at that point was more than $2.5
billion. His financial outlook remained bright even after the shares took
a dive in 1994, as he borrowed an additional $300 million to acquire

more shares, now available at a considerable discount; in the game Perelman was playing, bad performance still had its upsides. Throughout this time, and well after the *Wall Street Journal* dubbed the stock "dead money," Marvel continued to expand—at Perelman's behest—largely by directing whatever revenue it generated to pay down the additional debt he was incurring on the company's behalf.[91]

By 1996, it was finally clear that this expansion into merchandising would not work as long as Marvel's dry spell in film and television persisted. Perelman made one final deal, selling shares in ToyBiz he had never actually bought to fund a new $100 million venture, Marvel Studios.[92] The company's announcement, which once again promised a wave of Marvel adaptations on the near horizon, finally failed to convince investors. When the company's stock was officially downgraded, Perelman—unashamedly and unironically—stepped forward to help.[93] He offered to "save the company" he had nearly destroyed, claiming a desire to protect its "many constituents, including its employees." His initial proposal was to personally purchase 400 million new shares of the company, now at an even steeper discount. When bondholders, led by activist investor and millionaire Carl Icahn, balked at his audacity and stock prices plunged, Perelman had to file for Chapter 11. Icahn and his lawyers were able to push Perelman out by the spring of 1997.[94]

Intellectual Property Speculation

Perelman had made an initial personal investment of $10.5 million in Marvel—he had borrowed the remainder of the $82.5 million purchase price.[95] By the time he was finished with the company, he had taken out at least $200 million more than he had put into it, far more by some accounts. Although he had failed dramatically in achieving his supposed goal of building an entertainment empire, or really anything of value at all, he walked away from the ordeal a much wealthier man.[96] In all these respects, his strategy bears a strong resemblance to that of the private equity funds that began investing in the media industries in the early 2000s.[97]

As media industry scholar Andrew deWaard has noted, these firms tend to follow a predictable formula: they raise enormous levels of debt to acquire a company at a high cost, saddle the company with the debt resulting from its purchase, restructure operations, lay off employees, and within a few years, "exit the investment with a profit achieved through financial engineering."[98] Although Perelman may have intended to grow

Marvel and stay with the company longer, the end result—a swift and profitable departure that left destruction in its wake—was the same.

Reeling from the trauma, and briefly operating under the control of Carl Icahn, Marvel waited. The company hoped for a buyout offer from a major studio. Disney and Time Warner were both rumored to be considering a bid, along with Fox, Universal, and Sony.[99] But nothing materialized. An executive at DreamWorks explained the lack of interest, noting, "it's hard to imagine the rights to these characters are worth hundreds of millions of dollars."[100] In hindsight, this mistaken prediction appears imprudent—how could the studios have overlooked Marvel's potential to generate not just hundreds of millions, but *tens of billions* of dollars? At the time, though, the company's value was anything but clear, and executives wholeheartedly believed that comic-book-based films were not worth the risk their budgets entailed.

Industry lore was partly to blame. But Marvel's low value was also a product of its temporary existence as the personal financial instrument of a tycoon. Marvel had failed to produce a single film adaptation throughout Perelman's tenure. This failure was hardly an accident. With no examples to point to, neither Hollywood executives nor Wall Street investors could presume much of anything about the brand's licensing potential. This void invited wild speculation about the company. Some believed its characters were "priceless," while others thought the hype was not just exaggerated, but "insane." As the company sat in limbo, its value remained "murky," somewhere in a range of $150 million to $400 million.[101]

This uncertainty likely worked to Perelman's advantage, as he used fluctuations in value to shift debt and reorganize his interest in the company through periodic stock purchases. Comic book films were more valuable to him as theoretical projects than they were as real ones; he traded in hype and bluster, not product. This strategy may have worked for Perelman in the short term, but in failing to create long-term value, it put Marvel in a very precarious position. By late 1997, once it was clear no studio bid would materialize, ToyBiz head Ike Perlmutter put forward his own reorganization plan that both the banks and courts approved. He took over the company in 1998, selling off the trading card and sticker subsidiaries, and forming a new corporation, Marvel Enterprises (parent of ToyBiz, Marvel Studios, and the publishing division). Perlmutter promised to pay back investors with additional shares and yet another assurance that a wave of Marvel adaptations in film and television was on its way.[102]

DEVELOPMENT HELL (1992–1997)

Throughout the Perelman era, comic book films had been stuck in limbo. This was a predictable outcome, given Perelman's financialization of the company's assets, a strategy he also applied to Marvel's intellectual properties; bought and sold to generate cash flow and stock fluctuations instead of actual movies, the rights were destined to sit idle. It is very common for films to get waylaid in preproduction—it just became particularly common during this time for comic book films. Notably, though, this was true whether or not they came from Marvel. Even titles that did not carry piles of debt were associated with risk. In short, for a comic book film to get made during these years, it had to practically sneak into production.

At first, Marvel had claimed it was pursuing a more aggressive approach to film production. But in optioning both marquee and minor characters to producers and executives all over town, the company pursued deals that were ultimately less proactive than they were haphazard. For example, the company repeatedly promised the same characters to different entities (for example, Captain America would be licensed to one producer, and the entire Avengers team to another).[103] Whether this was a result of duplicity or negligence is not entirely clear.[104] *X-Men* producer Bill Todman, Jr. was able to snag an option on Wolverine, Ghost Rider, and Dr. Strange on a cocktail napkin after a single meeting with Stan Lee.[105] The initial deal was only for 90 days, and it cost Todman nothing, but longer options for bigger characters could be quite costly.

By 1992, Marvel had collected $3.5 million in nonrefundable fees for a *Spider-Man* option that soon got tied up in litigation, with multiple parties claiming the rights.[106] By 1997, the company was stockpiling sums on more than a dozen other options too, with an executive commenting that "it was like being a landlord collecting the rent."[107] Many of these deals were front-loaded, providing quick cash flow for Perelman's many ventures, with lesser benefits coming to the company later on.[108] But that hardly mattered, since the terms gave studios little incentive to move into production anyway. Furthermore, the company's instability, financial volatility, and unreliability (e.g., double-licensing) meant that a studio might end up in court or renegotiations to hold on to whatever rights they managed to successfully exploit.

Overall, it seemed a losing proposition. And yet, producers continued to pay for options, and most of the major studios put at least one Marvel film into preproduction. But these were largely defensive moves.

Studio heads were too scared to bet $100 million on a film franchise for any superhero not named Batman or Superman, but they were more than happy to spend $100 thousand to make sure *someone else* would not do it either.[109] This seemingly childish strategy has long been a common move in Hollywood, where risk-averse behavior takes on sometimes strange dimensions. The result of such maneuvering has, for decades, been a heavy backlog of projects perpetually stuck in preproduction, known by many as development hell.

Why Films Languish

Throughout the nineties, the Hollywood trades regularly reported on at least twenty different comic-book-based films set up with major producers (some reports suggested the number was as high as forty or fifty).[110] These accounts made it seem like, as one executive claimed, "everybody who does movies wants to do comics."[111] But at any given time, the studios had as many as twenty-five hundred movies in active development, with only a small handful ever making it to actual production; like many other projects, comic book films were getting stuck along the way. The path to development hell was familiar to most: after optioning a property (reserving the exclusive right to develop it for a designated period of time) or buying the rights, and often commissioning a script, studio executives stepped on the brakes. They decided the story needed to go in a different direction, that a different writer could do a better job, that the project needed more actors attached before proceeding, or simply that other projects were more deserving of their time and energy.[112] Even if a film was championed by an enthusiastic producer, most projects needed to pass through multiple layers of a studio hierarchy, each with the power to say no, and only one with the capacity to green-light, or approve, the movie for production.[113]

Marvel's head of film development, Avi Arad, remembers that "it was literally a daily fight . . . trying to open people's eyes to what was right in front of them."[114] Bill Todman, Jr. also recalls a lack of interest and unawareness. Despite all the buzz in the trades, "nobody really had their eye on the comic book world." Marvel characters, in particular, being full of teenage angst, "were not well understood."[115] Unfortunately, Marvel's own management generally did little to improve this unawareness, since they were some of the worst offenders. At one point in the early 1990s, Perelman's team approached Warner Bros., which had successfully exploited several DC characters, with a request. They wanted to know which Marvel titles would make good movies, presumably because they had little personal knowledge of their own catalogue and little faith in their own editorial team to fill them in.[116]

With too much money at stake, and neither enthusiasm from the parties involved nor an industry fad to propel them forward (as there might have been after *Batman*), Marvel's projects were easy to neglect. Even if a producer had personal enthusiasm for a comic book project or one had earned the support of a studio, there were additional obstacles. Development hell tends to become a good deal more hellish when corporate buyouts or reorganizations enter the picture, intensifying the usual progression of disruptions.[117] Marvel's financial woes therefore created a serious additional impediment on the path to production.

Spider-Man Entangled

No film better epitomized this tendency than *Spider-Man*. Production on the film was first announced in 1990.[118] When it finally hit theaters more than a decade later, it became such a massive box office success, it changed the future of comic book films and of blockbusters more generally. This had in fact been the expectation, or at least the hope, all along. Unlike other comic book films, people had been desperate to make *Spider-Man* throughout the 1990s. Those vying for the opportunity believed the character was just like Batman and Superman—an iconic superhero with exceptional brand awareness that made his exploitation on screen worth the investment, no matter how large. The title became Hollywood's very own "hope diamond."[119] This was in fact part of the problem; the character was *too* sought after.

Things had not started out this way. When the Superman franchise began to wane in the early 1980s, everyone assumed superheroes were done for. So Menahem Golan, head of junk bond–funded Cannon Films, purchased a five-year option on the character for $225,000. Golan commissioned scripts and budgeted the film at $15 million, a price tag Cannon could not afford, so the film went nowhere. After Pathé, which later merged with MGM, bought out Cannon, Golan renegotiated the rights with Marvel, taking *Spider-Man* with him to his new debt-financed company, 21st Century. Capitalizing on the short-lived excitement around superhero films in 1990, he sold off distribution rights to Viacom and Columbia and made a production deal with independent production company Carolco and big-name director James Cameron.[120]

Then things started to get complicated. James Cameron, for whatever reason, refused to give Golan a producing credit. And then it turned out that the lawyers drafting the deals had made mistakes (and promises they could not keep).[121] Multiple parties were convinced they had the same exclusive rights. Raising the stakes (and stirring the pot), Wall Street investors made clear they thought the movie would be a hit—meaning that winning control of the rights could boost a company's stock price.[122] So everyone went to court. By 1994, there were at least five lawsuits involving at least seven companies and eighteen different contracts. Cameron claimed the movie was moving forward, but to make a blockbuster like this, he needed bank financing and insurance, and those institutions were not about to ensnare themselves in this legal mess.[123]

To make matters worse, the companies involved began facing serious financial trouble. Both of Golan's brainchildren, Cannon and 21st Century, went bankrupt, followed not long after by Carolco. MGM bought all three firms, conceivably guaranteeing its claim on the rights. The only problem was that MGM was itself struggling (also a result of debt and foreign takeovers) and lacked the financial muscle to actually produce the film (or bring an end to litigation with Viacom and Columbia). Meanwhile, Marvel also declared bankruptcy and Cameron eventually gave up and moved on to other projects.

With all of these competing claims, shifting assets, and corporate dramas, the contractual rights of the creative laborers involved in the film were neglected completely. So just as it looked like *Spider-Man* might disentangle itself from this legal web, the film became the center of a new dispute for writing credit; various screenwriters who had worked on the film over the course of seventeen years of development began fighting over whose version would finally make it to the screen.[124] Ironically, the heated battle over *Spider-Man* seemed to have the effect of making the character more valuable, instead of less. Everyone's desperation to get the rights had shown that people believed in this film; that blind faith had the effect of increasing its worth. Whether or not it was ever actually going to get made was almost beside the point.

DC, Dark Horse, and the Independents

As *Spider-Man*, Marvel's best-positioned property, demonstrates, the company's woes during the 1990s were considerable. But notably, other comic book publishers fared only slightly better, with DC Comics also falling behind in production.[125] As a subsidiary of Warner Bros., the publisher faced none of Marvel's existential challenges; its ownership and financial backing were sound, and fellow subsidiary Warner Bros. Pictures had no need to worry about losing rights to a competitor or missing out on the benefits of merchandising.

But according to publisher Paul Levitz, these were still "fairly crummy years." DC never gave up working on a new Superman film, as well as projects for Wonder Woman, Sgt. Rock, and several other key properties; stacks of scripts commissioned for these projects accumulated, but they never seemed to go anywhere. Just like Marvel, DC was up against a lack of excitement and faced fears around a high-risk genre that everyone believed was unproven. That Warner Bros. did not have to worry about losing rights to a competitor actually worked to intensify the studio's inhibitions. The lack of competition pulled the heat off of any project that might otherwise have been enticing.[126] The big two publishers thus faced a Goldilocks scenario, with Marvel's properties too encumbered, and DC's properties too accessible.

Somewhere in the middle were the smaller publishers. They ultimately had the most luck, in large part because they were able to pursue long-term value through deals not hampered by short-term corporate imperatives. They also were not selling iconic superheroes, and as such, did not have to emphasize their stories' comic-book-ness. At the time, Dark Horse and Image billed themselves as "much more than just a comic-book publisher." These companies were simply just a good source of ideas and stories. Not only did their titles have the benefit of R&D (having already been tested with the comic book audience) but they also provided a kind of visual blueprint. One producer explained, "All you have to do is walk in with a comic book and show it to a studio executive. . . . The person doesn't have to use much imagination to know what he's going to get."[127] Approaching content in this way, independent publishers were often able to evade the negative industry lore about comic book films' excessive risk and unproven content. Economic anxieties were not attached to these projects in the same way they latched onto big superhero movies.

Over the course of the nineties, studios pushed a handful of niche projects into production, often at lower budgets (generally less than $20 million). There was *Tales from the Crypt* for horror lovers, *Tank Girl* for the indie crowd, and *The Crow* (1994, Miramax) for action and exploitation fans. With modest box office aspirations, studios could use the titles' comic book origins to market the films to the distinct demographics to whom such an association was legible and valuable. For slightly bigger comic book adaptations with increasingly hard-to-come-by mid-range budgets, the origin of the source material was often less visible.

Dark Horse in particular had always thrived in the lucrative space between publishing and licensing, finding early success adapting movies (like *Aliens* and *Star Wars*) into comics, and soon after, adapting comics into movies. After doing *The Rocketeer* (1991, Buena Vista) with Disney, the company signed a deal with prominent action-film producer Larry Gordon at Twentieth Century Fox,[128] and eventually got *The Mask*, *Timecop* (1994, Universal), and *Barb Wire* (1996, Gramercy) to theaters. None were sold as comic book films. Unfortunately, the results were still very mixed, with only *The Mask* proving a breakout hit, largely due to star Jim Carrey and producer/distributor New Line, whose track record with low-budget comic book and action films had become very strong.

The only film that did actively promote its origin as a comic book ended up being the biggest failure of them all, further cursing the genre. Based on a popular British comic book, and starring Sylvester Stallone, *Judge Dredd* cost nearly $100 million to make; it was a huge sum for Disney's Buena Vista Pictures, particularly after the studio was burned on *Dick Tracy* and *The Rocketeer*.[129] Expectations were very high, with a sequel "at the starting gate" and one hundred thousand avid fans praying for its success.[130] Ultimately panned by critics as one of the worst films of the year, it made only $35 million at the U.S. box office (although twice that in international theaters). The movie had failed to set the right tone (was it a dark political allegory or a comedic action flick?), and it seemed other comic book films would be doomed to repeat its mistake. Critics and filmmakers started writing about these movies as "treading a thin line" between seriousness and camp, and with increasingly silly Batman sequels hitting theaters, these adaptations seemed exceedingly "tricky" to make.[131]

As Marvel emerged from bankruptcy, this narrative was as strong as ever.[132] So when Sony released *Men in Black*, a Will Smith action comedy about intergalactic secret agents, the studio downplayed its comic book origins.[133] Also on the near horizon was *Blade*, which went into production in early 1997 with a mid-range budget.[134] The film had been in development for more than five years, initially with LL Cool J, and eventually with Wesley Snipes, who had been busy in active development on a Black Panther film.[135] Once again proving its comic book acumen, New Line gave *Blade* a strong release in the summer of 1998. But the studio again deemphasized the movie's source material. Avi Arad would later note that *Blade* was "barely a comic book" at all.[136] Both *Men in Black* and *Blade* turned out to be huge hits, exceeding box office expectations and winning over audiences. Though these movies were not initially sold or perceived as comic book films, they immediately spawned sequels that would be. Released in 2002, both *Men in Black II* and *Blade II* became part of the impending explosion of the genre.

RISK AND REASSESSMENT (1998–2002)

When Hollywood turned to embrace comic books at the turn of the millennium, it was not the result of a reassessment of the quality of their stories. The industry's homegrown fanboys had been quietly promoting the medium, but a dominant industry narrative about overhyped and cartoonish blockbusters persisted through at least 1998, as critics widely prognosticated the death of the blockbuster, yet again.[137] What changed were the economic realities on the ground. While many remained resistant to the changes wrought by corporate reorganizations in the late eighties and nineties, their impact was getting hard to ignore. Executives may have been lukewarm on comic book films, but they had never stopped making movies with big effects, big budgets, and big opening weekends—despite industry narratives that warned against them. Media conglomerates had built machinery for big movies, not modest ones. And evolving financial strategies, moving from the margins of the industry to the center, were pushing in the same direction. Comic book films could deliver these goods. Industry rhetoric of the 1990s may have pushed comic books out of the limelight and into development hell, but the economics of the next decade were about to fast-track them for production. The genre was fully supported by a new financial model now firmly in place and thriving. It would not take long for a new narrative to develop to justify its embrace.

The Middle Drops Out (1996–2001)

In 1996, just five years after Katzenberg's memo condemned Hollywood's "blockbuster mentality," it was already clear to most how wrong he had been. As *Variety* columnist Peter Bart put it, the memo had "set forth all the right information, [but] advanced the wrong prognosis." Katzenberg had thought blockbusters were the problem, but "event pictures [had] proven to be the salvation of Hollywood. Megapics yield megabucks."[138] Far from diminishing the power of blockbusters, all the talk of risk had made executives even more likely to bet on established talent and big special effects, just not when those effects were in comic book films.

By the mid-nineties, studios were devoting so many resources and so much energy to blockbusters that their profitability became a kind of self-fulfilling prophesy.[139] The studios were coming to believe that risk actually *diminished* as they spent *more* money; one producer called this counterintuitive logic "a crazy making aspect of the industry."[140] Crazy or not, the appealing and moralistic narrative about saying no to films that were too expensive and too big was giving way to a renewed and increasingly energetic pursuit of these exact films. When studios wanted to save money, they were not turning to cheaper movies. They just looked for smarter ways to make money from the "event" films they had come to rely on.[141]

Blockbusters had, of course, always been billed as special occasions, but the exhibition practices that supported these weekend-long events reached a new height around 2001. A theater-building binge in the late nineties created a glut of multiplexes, facilitating wider releases, and putting more pressure on huge opening weekends.[142] This practice of front-loading benefited studios in a number of ways. As distributors, they would typically collect 80 to 90 percent of the box office take during the first week, leaving theater owners only a 10 percent cut (plus basic costs for running the theater). Each week or two the film was out, theater owners would get an additional 10 percent in the split. The arrangement worked for everyone when films were in theaters for weeks. But short theatrical runs with big openings and sharp declines were tough on exhibitors, who became increasingly angered by a trend that was deliberately limiting their share of the profits. Ultimately though, the studios had the upper hand. They were in charge of green-lighting films, and they were eager to push through the expensive films that benefited their interests, not the theater owners'.[143]

Blockbuster films that did well on opening weekends also tended to do well internationally—often better than local productions, even—further heightening their appeal.[144] In addition, many in the industry had come to believe that frontloading films made them critic-proof. Instead of relying on a film's positive buzz with audiences, studios were becoming ever more dependent on "blitzkrieg" marketing strategies. They were pouring tens of millions of dollars into multimedia campaigns that reached an overwhelming crescendo in the few weeks leading up to a global release. If the marketing worked, and viewers flocked to see the movie on opening weekend, it ultimately would not matter if critics hated it, or if word of mouth was poor. A huge fall-off in the second weekend—usually a sign of unhappy audiences—was still not a particularly desirable outcome. But the idea that it ultimately did not matter, that you could make enough money (or close to it) without having to worry about negative reactions from fickle audiences, was extremely appealing to risk-averse executives (and still is).[145]

This new emphasis on event films did not mean the end of either "good stories, well-executed" or the industry lore that championed them. This opposing impulse and the low-budget films (which cost less than $20 million) it generated had come to constitute an "independent" market, where movies could recoup costs through a small theatrical release to a discrete and discerning audience.[146] What really suffered, then, were the mid-range films. Executives were increasingly declining to make romantic comedies, period pieces, dramas, or any other film costing between $20 and $60 million. Movies of this size failed at the box office more consistently than any other, and after a while, they became toxic to studio heads. By the end of the decade, the middle ground was effectively dead.[147]

This trend put comic book films in an interesting circumstance. Because superheroes were perceived as too risky to command big budgets, they had been consigned to mid-range status. In the late eighties, debt-ridden low-budget action producers like Cannon had scooped up titles. And when those firms disappeared, smaller comic books from the smaller publishers became fodder for niche projects and other modest films. But this middle ground had gotten squeezed in the late nineties and was about to disappear entirely. If comic book movies were going to survive at all, they would have to make the jump to blockbuster status. Fortunately, the growth of big-budget films was reaching a new level of intensity. With new approaches to exhibition, and new funding strategies, the financial infrastructure of the business was undergoing another shift, and it created lots of room at the top of the budget spectrum.

The Risk-Free Film

The problem was never that comic books lacked popular appeal; the fear was that they lacked *enough* appeal to justify the financial risk they entailed. That was about to change. For years, industry insiders had hypothesized a revenue floor on big-budget films, a kind of no-risk bottom. Well-marketed, high-profile movies could attract built-in audiences for big opening weekends, thereby guaranteeing robust ancillary afterlives in international theaters, on home video, and eventually on cable television. In other words, they were foolproof. Katzenberg, among others, had insisted that this idea was a fallacy and that "any film can fail at the box office."[148] But as the decade wore on, the blockbuster naysayers were proven wrong. Increasingly, it seemed like even blockbusters that appeared to be flops were still finding ways to make back their investment.

There was, for instance, *Godzilla*. The most anticipated (and expensive) film of 1998, Sony's monster remake quickly gained distinction as the "the summer's biggest disappointment."[149] But this was more rhetoric than reality. Taking advantage (and possibly proving the existence) of critic-proof opening weekends, *Godzilla* had actually seen the biggest debut of the year. Bad word of mouth had incited a sharp fall-off in the second week, but a big take in international theaters more than made up for it.[150] Sony quietly noted at the time that the film would earn a profit, and it eventually did. Over the next few years, other poorly received films were replicating this backhanded success. As film industry scholar Thomas Schatz notes, the global movie marketplace was getting "so lucrative that it was difficult for Hollywood-produced blockbusters *not* to make money."[151]

Publicly, this was not a message most studios were eager to broadcast. They benefited from the fact that most people believed their industry was ruled by volatility and uncertainty, and that only a small fraction of films (allegedly one out of five) was making any profit at all. According to media economist Sergio Sparviero, this persistent bit of lore around risk not only allowed conglomerates to justify their existence to policy makers but also helped studios negotiate favorable terms with potential partners.[152] Meanwhile, according to investigative reporter Edward Epstein, studio executives were more and more frequently finding ways to "reduce the risk [of a film] to practically zero."[153] It was a goal reached through the combination and culmination of strategies developed over the decade prior. Initial funding (and therefore actual risk) was no longer coming from the studio, but from other people—private partners, foreign investors, and banks.

Then, to ensure it was the studio, not the investor, who benefited from the "shared risk" in the end, Hollywood looked to "creative accounting." Harold Vogel has written that "some of the most creative work in the entire movie industry is reflected not on the screen but in the financial offering prospectuses."[154] Indeed, Hollywood had come a long way from relying on simple formulas to determine profitability. Comparing the domestic box office to the production budget (or perhaps multiplying that budget by two to find a break-even point) had become exercises in futility.[155] The cost of a film was far too dispersed, its sources of revenue too scattered, and the stakes of various parties involved too complex. This was of course by design, since the studios themselves maintained the books and decided when, and if, they could pay profits out to investors.

In this way, media conglomerates had transformed into a sort of "clearinghouse," a term Epstein uses to describe the industry's financial infrastructure at the time. Money came into the "clearinghouse" through external investment capital and also through revenue: box office receipts from domestic and international theaters, nontheatrical releases, home video sales, and cable and television licensing. The film division's cut in each of these slices of the pie varied. For example, studios usually took 50 percent of domestic theatrical revenue from exhibitors, although more if the film opened big (see above). For home video, however, which was usually handled by a sister subsidiary, the studio would typically receive just 20 percent of sales, leaving the lion's share of profits (hundreds of millions of dollars for popular blockbusters) to the home video division.[156]

Meanwhile, as Sparviero notes, distribution subsidiaries (domestic theatrical, international theatrical, domestic cable, etc.) would also take a significant cut, collecting 35 percent of each revenue stream they handled, although the actual costs of distribution were far below this.[157] And then there were administrative and marketing overhead fees, as well as interest, at 15 percent. By the time the conglomerate allocated the money for all these "costs," there was typically very little "profit" left remaining for the film studio itself. This meant very little left to pay back investors, as well as an established but dubious record of unprofitability.[158] Through this creative accounting, even if the books showed a film to be officially in deficit, it had usually still made tens of millions for the conglomerate enterprise as a whole; the film division might have officially taken a loss, but distribution and home video subsidiaries had likely come out on top.

That studios were risking less and less of their own money to begin with made the advantages for major media companies even starker. A considerable additional benefit for big conglomerates was merchandising. An event film could often generate massive amounts of money in product licensing and cross-promotions, but these categories were almost never credited to the film or divvied up among partners as part of profit.[159] This was why studios had been loath to give this revenue up in deal-making with Marvel during Perelman's reign. But the landscape was changing. As the era of the risk-free blockbuster approached, comic books were starting to look like much safer bets. And just as this new logic was emerging across Hollywood, Marvel was emerging from bankruptcy, with a new outlook on film development. In short, the financial stars were aligning in comic books' favor.

Marvel's Path to Solvency (1998-2002)

When Ike Perlmutter took over Marvel at the start of 1998, he owed the banks $200 million. With a reputation as a cheapskate, he did what he could to cut costs, rolling back titles, cutting executive pay, and laying off what employees he could.[160] But in order to climb out of the debt, the company needed to find new sources of revenue; this meant developing properties for film and television. ToyBiz executive Avi Arad, who got his start as a toy designer and had been representing Marvel in Hollywood since the early 1990s, quickly pushed a few films out of development and into production.[161]

The news that Marvel had finally emerged from bankruptcy proceedings certainly aided his efforts. But Arad's newfound success, after nearly a decade of disappointment, had a lot to do with changing economics internally and externally. Under Perlmutter, the company was far more serious about making deals and was willing to change its terms, often taking a hit, in order to close. Most notably, Marvel was now willing to split merchandising revenue with partners. The company would still control the rights, so it could manufacture everything through its ToyBiz subsidiary, but profits were subject to negotiation.[162]

In a reflection of Perlmutter's tight-fistedness, however, Marvel still refused to put up financing for films based on its characters. As a result, the revenue the publisher collected on the back end had to be quite low; studios were not interested in collaborators who wanted a big (or any) share of the profits, particularly when they were not willing to share in the risk. This meant that for all the films that moved forward in the aftermath of ToyBiz's takeover, Marvel's take was small. In the much-hyped and litigated Spider-Man deal, Marvel took a $10 million licensing fee and a small percentage of gross revenue; from two films with a combined box office gross of $1.6 billion, Marvel ultimately received just $62 million.[163] And, this was the high-water mark, since the company was usually unable to negotiate any profit share at all.

For three *X-Men* films (a combined box office total of $1.2 billion), Marvel's take was just $26 million. And on *Blade* ($131 million at the box office), their fee was just $25,000.[164] When it came to the enormous ancillary revenue these movies generated for the studios in DVDs and cable licensing, Marvel was excluded completely. Arad later commented that these deals "were kind of ridiculous. . . . We got very little out of it."[165]

Notably, though, the true dollar value of these titles remained incredibly murky. Arad himself admits, "we didn't know our own worth," and nobody else did either.[166] So Marvel had to stick with established standards, making deals that looked like those of any other licensor for every other piece of source material; there was no sense—or at least no reflection of one in the numbers—that these were unique properties, the kinds of stories that could generate not just sequels but whole universes.[167]There was, unfortunately, no real evidence to prove that potential. On the upside, films were moving into production, and their successes gave Marvel leverage to move more into production.[168] In just a few years, these efforts turned around the company's finances. Although the films brought in few licensing dollars, they did generate tremendous toy sales (even if Marvel had to share in these profits), just as Arad and Perlmutter—and Perelman before them—had suspected they would.[169]

X-Men *(2000)*

Avi Arad first made a deal for X-Men in 1992. In the years since, it had gone from Columbia to Fox and survived several sets of writers, directors, and producers—and several years of neglect.[170] Driven by a "pack mentality," as *Variety* called it, the industry had been hesitant to pursue the title.[171] But by the late 1990s, big-budget event films were not as risky as they had been before, and Marvel's terms had gotten much better. Twentieth Century Fox boss Tom Rothman still equivocated when it came to the film's comic book roots, noting in interviews that "the issue is not is it a comic or not a comic."[172] But he also insisted that he believed in the project, and by all accounts, this was true; the studio enthusiastically pushed the movie into production.[173]

That *X-Men* ended up being the first of this new batch of comic book films for a new era of Hollywood filmmaking was no accident. Though it lacked the iconicness of Batman, Superman, and Spider-Man, X-Men had been the industry's best-selling comic books throughout the 1990s. With the rise of *Ain't It Cool News* and other online gossip sites, the preferences of these fans had become more important to the studios.[174] They also complemented the interests of a cadre of fanboys inside

Hollywood's ranks, who remained eager to promote a medium they viewed as completely legitimate source material. The title's animated cartoon, a hit with kids throughout the nineties, also promised a sizable youth audience.[175]

Furthermore, the studio had found a way to make the film on the cheap—relatively speaking. Originally budgeted at $150 million, Fox brought the number down to just $78 million. They went with cheaper shooting locations (Canada), opted for smaller stars with smaller salaries (Hugh Jackman was basically unknown), and kept everything as "lean" as possible.[176] In short, the film ended up being a relatively safe bet. It was a comic book film—and a rather serious one at that—but Fox had put strong pedigree behind the camera (Richard Donner was a producer and Bryan Singer had come on as director), the budget was not jaw-dropping, and the licensing deal came without profit participation. Furthermore, as Rothman noted, it had "nearly universal awareness and a lot of positive interest. . . . It gives you a tiny bit of security."[177] Still, none of this eased anxieties about the film's release. Even if *X-Men* was likely to turn a profit, it was not clear it would be a big enough hit to support the sequels Fox was planning or to satisfy the "legions of comic book fans" praying for its success.[178] The industry had determined that this was "a test case" for "superhero spectaculars." Marvel had everything riding on it as Stan Lee, only half-joking, commented that it was "of paramount importance for *X-Men* to do well—we've got to prove ourselves after *Howard the Duck*."[179]

The anticipation closely paralleled what had preceded the release of *Batman*. And like that film, *X-Men* turned out to be a massive hit, beating out predictions to save the summer and break box office records.[180] But the film industry had changed significantly over the decade prior, and this time, there would be no memo beeping through fax machines to condemn the movie's opening weekend aspirations and cartoonish source material. The economic infrastructure of the business now fully supported, and in fact desperately needed, movies of just this nature, and that need had opened the door to a new conversation about what kinds of movies Hollywood should make. The exact product the industry needed in this particular moment, *X-Men* "opened the floodgates" for major comic book adaptations, even for characters unknown to the general public.[181] Fanboy critics and producers all over town were coming out of the woodwork to praise the film's pitch-perfect adaptation and their hopes for more just like it.[182]

Before long, Marvel was "back in a big way," and Arad was closing deals all over town—although now, they were actually rolling swiftly out of development and into production.[183] Time Warner was also now taking its own properties, via its subsidiary DC Comics, more seriously, mandating that its vault of characters be exploited.[184] Exemplifying the industry's change of attitude regarding comics was an explosion of interest in San Diego's Comic-Con. In years prior, the studios had given away buttons and posters, but after *X-Men* staged a more serious promotion in 2000, the stakes were raised. In 2001, the event drew seventy thousand people, including a growing number of producers and executives down from Los Angeles, who were beginning to consider it a hot ticket. The press proclaimed Comic-Con a "mecca for pop culture" and it became a "one-stop marketing venue" for the event films and budding franchises on which the studios were now pinning their hopes and finances.[185] The comic book movie was quickly on its way to becoming a Hollywood staple.

Spider-Man *(2002)*

Fortunately for Marvel, the publisher's marquee title *Spider-Man* was already well underway when the tide began to shift. The film had ended up in the hands of Sony, which after years of losses was looking for a big film with big potential. When MGM suffered a few major setbacks in litigation, Sony stepped in with cash, helping Marvel make a settlement with the struggling studio (a few years later, Sony would step in again, this time to buy MGM outright—with the help of external investors, of course). Sony forged ahead on the film quickly; this speed was one of Marvel's stipulations. Without a big licensing fee or significant profit participation, the publisher needed the film *in theaters,* to spur merchandise sales and other adaptations; the mere promise of films was no longer enough to pay down the company's debt.[186] The $140 million movie made back $115 million at the U.S. box office in just three days. And fans loved it.[187]

Spider-Man's success was bigger than the comic book community, though. As one marketing executive noted, it changed "the whole idea of how big a movie can open. The side effect will be increasing pressure on all of us who do these jobs to get those big weekends."[188] Whatever shred of hesitation remained in Hollywood regarding comic book movies, or franchise event films, was now certainly gone. There would be no more prognostications of the death of the blockbuster. Demonstrating the shift in thinking, Fox fast-tracked another Marvel adaptation, *Daredevil* (2003). In response to the success of *X-Men* and *Spider-Man*'s positive buzz, the studio transformed what had begun as a modest mid-budget action film, about a character with very little awareness outside fandom, into a big-budget ($80 million) event film with a big star (Ben Affleck).[189] The film ultimately disappointed audiences, but that hardly seemed to matter. It made lots of money anyway, and Fox immediately moved forward on a female-starring spin-off (*Elektra*, 2005, with Jennifer Garner). The economics of superhero films had clearly changed. A product that had once seemed like Hollywood's biggest gamble was starting to look like its safest bet.

THE MARVELOUS MR. MAISEL (2003–2005)

In the early 2000s, comic book adaptations rolled out all over town, basking in the afterglow of *X-Men* and then *Spider-Man*, and trying to replicate their phenomenal success. The trend may have persisted like this for years, with various studios launching franchises around various characters, with varying levels of success (although, in the end, almost always profitably). But there was another economic shift on the horizon; the entry of private equity into Hollywood was about to alter the business's financial infrastructure yet again. Private equity and hedge funds pool capital from wealthy individuals and institutional investors, including pension plans, insurance companies, and endowments. Providing large amounts of money (several hundred million dollars), these funds began financing films for major studios around 2004.[190] Amidst this transition, the reversal of risk on comic book films became even more unambiguous. These massive projects became incredibly reliable, in large part, because they could now capitalize on the same speculation that had almost driven them to ruin a few years earlier. They were ideal investments for the financiers who were rewriting the economic rules of the industry.

At least at first, financialization represented an intensification of earlier business practices, as opposed to a total break with the past. Studios treated these funds as merely the latest in a long line of external sources of investment eager to get into moviemaking; as one executive explained, "when one door closes another one will open."[191] Just as they had before, studios managed to maintain a superior position in these deals. Through fees and creative accounting, they could get their investment back first and keep a larger share of total earnings in the end.[192] Given this inherent asymmetry, private equity investors had only one truly important means of reducing their risk: they diversified their investment by backing an entire slate, a carefully calibrated set of films planned by the studio to achieve balance and profitability.[193]

These slates were increasingly relying on one or several "tentpole" films, event movies so large they could support the studio's other smaller projects and any possible flops. These were not just big-budget movies. They were bigger—projects the studios made numerous exceptions for in the belief they would deliver certain economic returns, drive future film production, and offer other intangible benefits.[194] Because of their built-in audiences, their iconic nature, and their penchant for big effects and universe-building, comic books were great candidates for these tentpoles. Tentpoles' increasing strategic importance meant that what could have merely been a comic book movie fad came to permanently dominate the cinematic landscape.

Legendary and Merrill Lynch

From the very start, comic book films played a key role in this emerging financial trend; they were at the center of the industry's first major private equity deals. In 2005, two investments—one in Marvel films and one in DC films—injected huge amounts of cash into comic book blockbusters at a very low risk to studios. Ultimately proving quite successful, these deals heightened investor interest in Hollywood and helped boost the already rising profile of superhero movies.

In June, Legendary Pictures, a production company backed by a consortium of Wall Street investors, agreed to put up $500 million to finance twenty-five films at Warner Bros. The deal reportedly had a standard structure in which the equity fund would finance half the budget and share in half the profits, but only after the studio recouped its standard fees and paid money out to other participants.[195] Legendary opted for a huge slate to reduce its risk, and the strategy worked, largely because its investment in the relaunched Batman and Superman franchises proved very profitable.

Other investors at the time were not as lucky. As Andrew deWaard notes, many of the initial private equity deals in Hollywood ultimately went sour. Not only did financiers encounter creative accounting practices that denied them profits, but many soon realized they had been shut out from the studios' most reliable projects, having unknowingly funded incomplete slates filled with riskier films.[196] Warner Bros., in contrast, had included its superhero juggernauts in Legendary's slate.[197]

Despite recent excitement over comic book movies, Warner Bros. likely remained doubtful about the genre's financial prospects and was willing to offload the films' inherent risk, even if that meant sharing the profits. Batman and Superman were simultaneously the properties that had likely attracted Legendary to begin with. These were the kind of iconic event projects that private equity investors, who were not as influenced by Hollywood lore, were eager to back. The deal was win-win. It transformed Legendary into a permanent player in Hollywood and helped Warner Bros. relaunch both iconic superheroes, previously stuck in development.

Just two months earlier, Marvel made an even more impressive deal, involving a bit more complexity. For starters, Marvel Studios was not an actual studio. The film business that Avi Arad had been running since the early 1990s (Perelman had officially christened it in 1996) was actually a licensing operation; it did not make films, it really only sold rights—for rather low fees—in the hope of generating revenue in merchandising.[198] This approach had restored Marvel to good health, but it was not a strategy for long-term growth. So Marvel began pursuing the same thing everyone else in Hollywood was after: other people's money. First came a modest financing and distribution deal with Artisan Entertainment, later merged with Lionsgate, that served as proof of concept for Marvel's new financial whiz, David Maisel.[199]

Though he had limited knowledge of the characters themselves, David Maisel understood financing (see figure 22). In April 2005, he made a deal with Merrill Lynch that one executive called "the most impressive piece of pure intellectual structuring I'd ever seen."[200] Marvel would get a seven-year revolving credit line of $525 million to finance any film costing less than $180 million. Paramount happily agreed to distribute the films for its regular fee (but put up no investment capital), with Marvel to receive a producing fee in addition to, impressively, all of the films' profits, including revenue from all ancillary markets.[201] For collateral, Marvel put the rights to ten of its own characters on the line, including the Avengers; in this, the theoretical value of the company's unexploited intellectual properties was still the key to its future. Unlike Perelman, though, David Maisel was leveraging their worth for long-term stability instead of short-term cash flow.

If the movies bombed, the insurance company Ambac would get the rights moving forward, but Marvel would still be able to earn revenue on

FIGURE 22. David Maisel poses for the press in 2007. Despite the impressive financing deal Maisel had recently orchestrated, many industry observers continued to believe that Marvel's upcoming films *Iron Man* and *Incredible Hulk* were excessively risky. Photo by Stephanie Diani. Redux Pictures / The New York Times.

merchandising. This meant that in the worst-case scenario, the company would be in basically the same position it was in without the deal (since it had not earned much on licensing anyway).[202] In short, as the *Hollywood Reporter* noted, "Marvel would put up no cash and assume no risk." Maisel described his own deal as "too good to be true" and pointed out how "novel" it was that a studio could "get the financial upside from its films without having to take any material financial risks."[203]

Whether the deal was as unique as he claimed is unclear, but he certainly was not the first or the last financier to attempt such a feat. The first film that came out of the Merrill Lynch deal was *Iron Man* in 2008. In addition to making $585 million at the box office, the film launched the Marvel Cinematic Universe and solidified the dominance of the comic book film in Hollywood. Its success also caught the eye of Disney. Maisel arranged a meeting between Ike Perlmutter and Disney boss Bob Iger in early 2009. By August, Iger had announced that Disney would buy the comic book company for $4 billion, citing the strategic value of Marvel's "treasure trove" of characters as motivation.[204]

"The Story Is Still the Thing"

Disney's valuation of Marvel had many skeptics, but the comic book company's swift rise from a failing publishing and licensing operation to the most valuable film studio in Hollywood was not unfathomable. The causes offered at this chapter's start—a rising need for presold films with international potential and big CGI effects—provided some explanation. For those more intimately involved or interested, though, there arose an even simpler rationalization: it was all about the story.[205] In 2002, explaining the recent success of *Spider-Man* and Hollywood's sudden interest in comic books, Marvel front man Stan Lee offered up a familiar perspective: "You still need a compelling story with elements of surprise and characters who must be believable and empathetic. . . . The story is still the thing."[206]

This was, of course, the standard party line of the film industry. It has always been all about the story, since long before Stan Lee, or even Jeffrey Katzenberg. When Katzenberg preached this message back in the early nineties, he was talking about the awfulness of big comic book films and the greatness of *other* kinds of "good stories," namely those in original mid-budget films. They were his best guess in that particular moment; he was trying to chart a successful path forward in a time of great uncertainty and profound change. He misread the situation and turned out to be wrong; the blockbuster was not the industry's downfall, but its savior.[207] Over the course of the nineties, big-budget films became the cornerstone of the studios' programming strategy. These tentpoles shored up the industry's entire production model, and comic book films happened to make great tentpoles.

They were a product uniquely attuned to Hollywood's wide list of strategic and economic needs. And when private equity entered the equation, these films very effectively met a new set of financial demands, largely through their ability to fill out a slate in a way that satisfied Wall Street. Investors, especially those who had no experience in entertainment, could comprehend the theoretical value of an iconic comic book character and its ability to launch a franchise. The movies need not actually exist in order to generate material worth through that investment. For a time, this special superpower had put comic book films, and perhaps the comic book itself, in mortal danger. Financiers like Ron

Perelman treated Marvel's intellectual properties like personal playthings. But in the 2000s, with some strategic planning and innovative financial engineering, comic book stories began fulfilling their economic destiny as virtually risk-free tentpole franchise films.

Along the way, the narrative about what kinds of movies Hollywood should make changed. It shifted to better reflect the economic realities on the ground. Industry lore about how to pick winning projects has always been, first and foremost, about risk—which movies are worth it and which are not. A "good story, well-executed" always mattered—the idea remained king. But what kinds of stories could be considered great, and what it meant for a movie to be well-executed, seemed to hinge on what was economically viable and best utilized existing studio infrastructure.

But if you only listened to the way executives talked about comic book films, money and strategic thinking had nothing to do with it. Tom Rothman explained at the time that Fox made *Daredevil* solely "because it's a great story. This guy is deeply interesting. He's a hero who is human. He is morally complex, he bleeds, he hurts, and he is a flawed person."[208] This reflection was obviously part of a marketing effort around that film, but these sentiments were remarkably widespread.

As this new wave of comic book films rolled into theaters, Hollywood was humming with discussions of authenticity, character complexity, strong backstories, and respect for the original material.[209] Critics and producers were spreading a well-polished industry narrative about how decision-making happens, and that narrative revolved completely around the dimensions of story. The effect, intentionally or not, was to obscure the importance of financial considerations, which were, at that time, remaking Hollywood from the inside out. The studio boss behind *Spider-Man* explained, "One would like to say it's a rational business, but the fact of the matter is, it's all gut." His top executive agreed: "I just want to make good movies."[210] This was, of course, not even half the story behind *Spider-Man*'s long journey to the big screen.

Avi Arad and David Maisel

Nowhere is the "great story well told" narrative more vivid, and its economic counterpart more absent, than in accounts of great movie men, the individuals responsible for cinematic innovations. Since Disney's buyout of Marvel in 2009, a narrative of this type has centered squarely on Marvel Studios president Kevin Feige. His feel for the characters, respect for the universe, and dynamic control over creative development (not too much, not too little) have earned him credit for the company's many creative and box office successes.[211] But before Feige took on this particular role, it belonged to Avi Arad, who spearheaded Marvel's film development from 1992 to 2006 and played the part of company hero in the trade press.

Smart and entrepreneurial, Arad was known for his business savvy and knack for brand-building.[212] But it was his love of comic books that stood out most. Enthralled by the medium his whole life, Arad took it seriously. He treated comic books as literature and saw in each character an underlying metaphor for life. And because he knew them backward and forward, he knew exactly how to sell them, to anyone and everyone who would hear him out. Famous for being good in the room—supposedly nobody could pitch these characters the way he could—Arad energized investors, inspired collaborators, and when the time called for it, exerted the creative control the projects required. He was ebullient, just like "a kid in a comic book store."[213] His counterpart in charge of financing, David Maisel, meanwhile, displayed "none of the playfulness you'd expect from someone whose job is to make movies about guys in tights. Instead he talks endlessly about Marvel's business plans."[214]

They may not have been quite as exciting as speeches about mythic superheroes, but those business plans mattered quite a lot to those heroes' future. When David Maisel came to Marvel in 2003, the company had been aggressively making a case for itself in Hollywood for three decades. Stan Lee had been doing the rounds since the 1970s.[215] Year after year, he tried to sell the same old comics, pushing the same old story about relatable and compelling superheroes; "The characters must be believable," he was preaching back in 1988, "that's the key."[216] Taking over for Lee in the early 1990s, Arad began selling his version of this same narrative. At first, he seemed to be getting more traction, and was praised for closing deals on *X-Men, Black Panther,* and *Doctor Strange.*[217] But those movies sat in development hell—no amount of salesmanship could make them seem less risky.

So starting in 1996, with the help of Perelman and then Perlmutter, Arad began selling the dream of Marvel Studios. If the company could just exert more control over preproduction, he believed, it could get the movies out of development; he knew what titles were key and in what order they should come. He could find the scripts, assemble the creative team, and coordinate the timing of releases.[218] Marvel Studios became a real entity, and movies began to roll into production, but Arad never got the control he was after or achieved the vision he laid out for the company—not until he brought on David Maisel to get the money, seven years into the venture.

Over the course of a whole decade, Marvel's creative strategy had remained exactly the same. The pitch skills of Avi Arad, however impressive, were not enough to make things happen. What finally moved the needle was the financing: internally, first through better terms offered under Perlmutter and subsequently by Merrill Lynch's capital investment, and externally, as studios moved toward increasingly creative funding structures. Studio bosses did not suddenly begin believing in the power of superheroes or in the need for Marvel's cinematic independence. Comic book films moved into production as soon as those productions no longer entailed the financial risk that was holding them back.

Writing about Marvel's success during these years, media industry scholar Derek Johnson has argued that the company's move into independent production "constituted a significant reorganization of Hollywood modes of production." Recognizing the importance of industry lore, Johnson reads Marvel's plan for creative control and its wide appeal to self-destiny as an attempt to culturally negotiate and legitimate its new role.[219] But the revelation remaking Hollywood in these years was not Marvel's rhetorical declaration of independence, it was the slate financing that enabled it. And executives were not fighting its takeover (as some had in the early 1990s); they were all just trying to figure out how to reap its potential windfalls.

It was that new economic reality that changed the narrative around comic books. Marvel's unchanging pitch about the importance of story, character, believability, and its own unique ability to ensure its stories' integrity was immaterial by comparison. Furthermore, this narrative was already written; Hollywood believes in good stories and always has. Fortunately, those good stories can come from anywhere as long as the economics are behind it. Financing tends to choose the winners and then wait for industry narratives to catch up and call those winners great storytellers.

CONCLUSION

Although the relationship between economics and narrative may seem incidental (does it matter if the tail wags the dog?), it remains an important distinction to make, particularly as financialization is transforming

American filmmaking. As Andrew deWaard has pointed out, the new financial structures that undergird the entertainment business are increasing consolidation, heightening inequality, and weakening media diversity. Financialization remains a "little-understood, yet profoundly transformative—and often destructive—force within the cultural industries."[220] As long as there are cultural narratives that conceal its power and obscure its methods, this financial transformation will continue to quietly wreak havoc. Overall invisibility is part of the problem, since equity deals often move forward without much interest from the press, from industry workers, or from media scholars. But specificity also plays a role, since it is often the obfuscating details of these financial deals that effectively conceal their influence.

So while many attribute new cultural trends to the industry's broad strategic needs, less attention has been given to the nuances of funding structures, or the role of speculation or external capital investment. And it is the combination of these forces, evolving corporate imperatives *together with* emergent financing strategies, that have reshaped Hollywood in recent decades. The appearance of new types of investors and innovative funding opportunities has been an increasingly significant factor in determining exactly which projects reach the public. Our ability to continue reading media effectively, to accurately understand what it says (or does not say) about culture and society, hinges on our willingness to understand these particulars of decision-making in the culture industries. And financing is an incredibly important part of that process.

In the case of the comic book film, shifts in Hollywood's financial infrastructure around the new millennium enabled a reassessment of the genre's level of risk. Studio machinery—its accounting practices, exhibition strategies, marketing techniques, and internal organization—had evolved to better accommodate films of this nature. And as importantly, the financial speculation that had plagued comic book films for more than a decade began to work in their favor. When the first equity investors in Hollywood targeted comic book films, they were following in a well-established tradition of speculators—the junk-bond independent producers who bought up comic book options in the 1980s, the collectors who flocked to comic book shops in the early 1990s, and the financier who used Marvel as the command center of a debt-financed empire in the mid-1990s. These strategies had begun on the dubious outskirts of the industry, where comic books thrived. When this evolving approach to financing moved to the fully sanctioned center, it brought comic book movies with it.

Something about the comic book industry seems to have made it appealing to such speculation. Perhaps it was the business's intense volatility over the years or its resilience in enduring one ordeal after another (morality crusades, market crashes, disappearing audiences, to name a few). Or perhaps it was simply the iconic power and longevity of its characters, which seemed as good a bet as any in an unpredictable cultural environment. Regardless, at the end of this brief and intense clash with speculation—both narrative and financial—the comic book industry turned a corner. The speculative appeal of the medium helped secure its future as it entered the 2010s. A business that had evolved through periods of intense crisis and transformation, and which had faced many different kinds of risk along the way, had secured a vaunted and well-protected position at the center of contemporary entertainment. It remains there, unscathed, today.

Epilogue

A Powerful Medium

With great power there must also come—great responsibility.

—*Amazing Fantasy #15* (1962)

This very quotable line of dialogue, from Spider-Man's origin story, is probably the most hackneyed phrase in comic book culture. I think its enduring fascination within that culture has to do with the community's deep-seated interest in the nature of power. Power is of course at the heart of much of the medium's mythology, since so many of its iconic characters have had such complicated relationships with strength, ability, authority, and legitimacy. Notably, Bruce Wayne, Tony Stark, and even Bruce Banner, Peter Parker, and Clark Kent are (and always have been) people of privilege. Superheroes in general have tended to be college-educated white males, with respectable day jobs in business, science, journalism, or education. These were never individuals without power. And though they had marked weaknesses—physical, social, or emotional—they of course also benefited from underlying, usually superhuman strengths. The core of their narratives has often been about figuring out how to grow into all of this power, how to master it, and perhaps most importantly, how to use it for good. Usually, in their long and winding journeys, these heroes prevail. But understanding when and how to use their power effectively and responsibly never stopped being difficult.

As I close this book, this ongoing struggle seems as good a metaphor as any for the challenges the comic book industry faces today. For many decades, comic books and comic book audiences seemed to occupy a subcultural space relegated to the margins of modern entertainment.

Audiences were always declining, sales were volatile, and media adaptations were underwhelming. In addition to that were storied clashes with censors, the rebellion of the Underground, heated auteurist battles, and renowned cult fandoms. This cultural history provided an aura of valiant resistance to a medium that seemed assailed, undervalued, and misunderstood.

Although some onlookers may still see comic books in this light, as a kind of cultural underdog, this representation was always something of a red herring. Today, the medium's role as a powerful commercial force is practically irrefutable. Comic books have never actually generated a particularly resistant or outsider culture. A favored form of contemporary society's elites, the medium sits atop the cultural hierarchy that organizes art and media in the digital age. A variety of factors—artistic, aesthetic, narrative, and technological—have contributed both to comic books' legitimation within more refined taste communities and their simultaneous rise in mainstream popularity. But the medium's underlying strength springs from a much deeper and older place than these factors, or the standard cultural narratives that promulgate them, reveal.

Socially and structurally, comic book culture is hegemonic. This is clear in the context of the medium's history, particularly that of its industrial and infrastructural features, which show that the form's incorporation into contemporary conglomerate multimedia is neither new nor coincidental. The medium and the industry that has supported its survival have long been deeply intertwined with entrenched media systems, and have benefited immensely from significant state and corporate support. The industry was bolstered by government intervention and internal regulation, shored up by a legal system intent on protecting its properties into the distant future, sustained by corporate networks that facilitated its transition into the modern era, and underwritten by a financial system that circulated its stories across every platform and product category in every corner of the globe.

The medium's ability to survive and eventually thrive hinged on these secret abilities, rooted in infrastructures which often remained invisible to outsiders and fans alike. Comic books were never without power; the culture around them emanated from a place of economic, political, and social strength. There was, perhaps, a legitimacy or popularity problem of sorts for a time, as the medium temporarily faded from prominence. But this is no longer the case. Comic books—as a cultural form if not as a material product—are quite popular today; they reach a genuinely mass audience of billions of people worldwide. In short, if the medium's image used to take after Peter Parker, it now tilts decidedly toward Spider-Man.

Comic books have great power, and with that must also come great responsibility. Unfortunately, doing good is not a simple matter of desire or will. Understanding how to exercise power effectively and responsibly is difficult, because power is complicated and often works in mysterious ways. It is the role of scholars and the goal of this book to make those ways less mysterious.

. . .

The 2010s saw a lot of criticism directed at the comic book industry over its failures, most notably its lack of diversity on the page and screen as well as behind the scenes.[1] The public wants mainstream culture to better reflect more lives as they are actually lived, to provide children and adolescents with something they can learn and grow from, and to offer society something more valuable and productive. For a long time, the comic book industry (and Hollywood more generally) responded poorly to these critiques, or not at all. As this book goes to press in the summer of 2018, it feels as if the tide may be turning. There are promising signs that the comic book industry—which is now a complicated mix of publishing house, licensing operation, film business, and multimedia clearinghouse—has begun to take the responsibility of its cultural power more seriously. Specifically, after a decade of tentpole franchises featuring white male superheroes, DC debuted *Wonder Woman* (2017, Warner Bros.) and Marvel introduced *Black Panther* (2018, Walt Disney Studios). Both films were wildly successfully with critics and fans, as well as at the global box office.

Notably, these films came out of formidable film studios at the top of their game. Disney in particular has been at the apex of the entertainment industry for some time and enjoys almost limitless power (economic, political, social) to create whatever kind of content it pleases.[2] Often, as this book has shown, producers use opportunities like these to advance their own cultural interests. When opportunities for new kinds of media products arise, those products usually end up reflecting the identity and tastes of those in closest proximity to the gears of change. Recently, though, these companies have decided to broaden their appeal and their message. They have boosted diversity on screen and are reportedly making better efforts to do the same off screen.[3] They are also engaging in more responsible storytelling and beginning to practice more informed cultural politics. They are using their power for good, and they are doing so respectfully and appropriately.[4] I hope these ink-lings of change become widespread and permanent.

Of course, in keeping with this book's broader argument and its fundamental premise, it is important to acknowledge that these steps forward did not occur in a vacuum. *Black Panther* was not green-lighted because a kind executive with a good idea wanted to do something nice. That is not how decisions get made at multinational media conglomerates navigating highly complex entertainment environments. Culture is built on top of and through infrastructure. Its production and circulation rely on vast distribution networks both physical and intangible, legal frameworks and organizational structures that establish labor standards and protocols of exchange, and financial practices that keep operations moving. When these systems do not support change or cannot facilitate it, change does not happen. In all likelihood, then, the progress the comic book industry has made has been progress that was legible within and already supported by established infrastructure. That both *Wonder Woman* and *Black Panther* were so phenomenally successful financially and culturally suggests that the industry machinery supporting and facilitating the headway they represent was already in place. This is a good start.

But for a better cultural future to fully materialize, neither this nor collective goodwill will be enough, even when the right individuals desire change, and even if powerful players agree to act responsibly. The right distribution networks and the right laws need to be in place. Corporate structures need to be accommodating and pliable. And financial backing must be available and accessible. This is particularly important to remember in the current moment, when it seems as if the media and communication industries are amidst another significant period of structural transition. More specifically, the courts have recently given a flashing green light to vertical integration, and a wave of mergers is underway. This year will see AT&T take over Time Warner, Disney purchase 21st Century Fox, and a likely reunification of CBS and Viacom, alongside many smaller acquisitions.[5]

In the near future, we can expect more consolidated distribution channels to team up with more oligopolistic content providers. This merging of content with conduits is hardly new. But it will continue to intensify both with new mergers and with new developments in tech, as media producers like Disney more aggressively pursue streaming, and platforms like Amazon and Netflix (not to mention hardware companies like Apple) move more aggressively into media production. DC

Comics and Marvel are of course deeply entangled in these developments. The comic book industry has always sat close to the heart of media conglomeration, at the intersection of various platforms, and on the front lines of the industry's structural evolution. It is unfortunately too early to know if the right systems will be in place to support responsible actions from these comic book companies or their parent corporations. But this uncertainty—not knowing exactly where the future will lead—also represents flexibility and possibility; moments of change can be moments of visibility, understanding, and most importantly, intervention.

Accordingly, it is important that media and communication scholars continue to bring these changing infrastructures out of the shadows and to assess the extent to which they can and cannot facilitate the kind of progress we collectively desire. Amidst this structural reorganization, I have seen some very familiar industry narratives (re)emerge: tech firms rationalizing astonishing payouts to attract auteurist talent, media moguls justifying unregulated growth by claiming unprofitability, content providers promising advertisers ever-increasing audience segmentation and selectiveness, and investors speculating on everlasting risk-free growth.[6] These narratives, which are the closest thing we have to a public discourse about media infrastructure, deserve far more scrutiny than they currently get.

More research needs to pursue these goals by pointing to specific elements of infrastructure and revealing details about the everyday inner workings of embedded systems. These particulars have material consequences; the exact contours of media infrastructure shape cultural production in nuanced ways that have profound impacts. It matters how a system is built (with intention, usually by powerful players), how a moment of transition allows infrastructure to shift, and how an altered architecture is likely to suit some needs but not others. Only through a deeper understanding of all of these processes can we work to fight for positive cultural changes that may be actually feasible and genuinely long-lasting.

Comic Book Adaptations for Film and Television

Following is as comprehensive a list as possible of American comic book adaptations in U.S. film and television productions. Several characteristics (in addition to year and title) are included: (1) the type of adaptation (live-action or animated, TV or film) with nontheatrical (unreleased, direct-to-video, or made-for-television) film releases noted as such; (2) the publisher of the comic book on which the adaptation was based; (3) the primary or most relevant producer, a sometimes subjective selection given the multitude of producers attached to many projects; and (4) the initial (domestic) theatrical distributor in the case of films, and the initial airing network (as well as, in some instances, the distribution company) in the case of television. The entries are broken up into three distinct eras, marked by dark dividing lines, and explained in more depth in chapter 1: the Establishing Era of Licensing (1933–1955); the Era of Lowbrow Adaptations (1956–1988); and the Era of Quality Transmedia (1989–2010).

Year	Title	Type	Publisher	Producer	Distributor or Network
1940–1951	Adventures of Superman	Radio Series	DC Comics	Mutual Broadcasting	ABC
1941–1943	Superman	Animated Shorts	DC Comics	Fleischer Studios	Paramount
1941	Adventures of Captain Marvel	Live-Action Film Serial	Fawcett	Republic Pictures	Republic Pictures
1942–1948	Hop Harrigan	Radio Series	DC Comics	Mutual Broadcasting	ABC
1942	Spy Smasher	Live-Action Film Serial	Fawcett	Republic Pictures	Republic Pictures
1943	Batman	Live-Action Film Serial	DC Comics	Columbia Pictures	Columbia Pictures
1944	Captain America	Live-Action Film Serial	Timely (Marvel)	Republic Pictures	Republic Pictures
1946	Hop Harrigan	Live-Action Film Serial	DC Comics	Columbia Pictures	Columbia Pictures
1947	The Vigilante	Live-Action Film Serial	DC Comics	Columbia Pictures	Columbia Pictures
1948	Congo Bill	Live-Action Film Serial	DC Comics	Columbia Pictures	Columbia Pictures
1948	Superman	Live-Action Film Serial	DC Comics	Columbia Pictures	Columbia Pictures
1949	Batman and Robin	Live-Action Film Serial	DC Comics	Columbia Pictures	Columbia Pictures
1950	Atom Man vs. Superman	Live-Action Film Serial	DC Comics	Columbia Pictures	Columbia Pictures
1952–1958	Adventures of Superman	Live-Action TV	DC Comics	Superman Inc.	WBTV
1952	Blackhawk	Live-Action Film Serial	Quality (DC Comics)	Columbia Pictures	Columbia Pictures
1955–1956	Sheena	Live-Action TV	Fiction House	Nassour Studios	ABC Films Syndication
1966–1968	Batman	Live-Action TV	DC Comics	Greenaway Productions	ABC
1966–1969	Adventures of Superboy	Animated TV	DC Comics	Filmation / WBTV	CBS
1966–1970	New Adventures of Superman	Animated TV	DC Comics	Filmation / WBTV	CBS
1967–1970	Aquaman	Animated TV	DC Comics	Filmation	CBS
1967–1970	Fantastic Four	Animated TV	Marvel	Hanna-Barbera	ABC
1967–1970	Spider-Man	Animated TV	Marvel	Grantray-Lawrence	ABC
1968–1969	Batman/Superman Hour	Animated TV	DC Comics	Filmation	CBS
1968–1976	Archie Show	Animated TV	Archie	Filmation	CBS
1970–1972	Josie and the Pussycats	Animated TV	Archie	Hanna-Barbera	CBS

Year	Title		Type	Production Company	Distributor/Network
1972	*Fritz the Cat*	Help! / Cavalier	Animated Film	Steve Krantz Productions	Cinemation
1972	*Tales from the Crypt*	EC Comics	Live-Action Film	Amicus / Metromedia	20th Century Fox
1973–1986	*Super Friends (and other variations)*	DC Comics	Animated TV	Hanna-Barbera	ABC
1973	*Vault of Horror*	EC Comics	Live-Action Film	Amicus / Metromedia	20th Century Fox
1974	*Nine Lives of Fritz the Cat*	Help! / Cavalier	Animated Film	Steve Krantz Productions	AIP
1975–1979	*Wonder Woman*	DC Comics	Live-Action TV	WBTV	ABC / CBS
1977–1979	*Amazing Spider-Man*	Marvel	Live-Action TV	Charles Fries Productions	CBS
1977–1982	*The Incredible Hulk*	Marvel	Live-Action TV	Universal Television	CBS
1978	*Dr. Strange*	Marvel	Live-Action TV Film	Universal Television	CBS
1978	*Superman*	DC Comics	Live-Action Film	Alexander & Ilya Salkind	Warner Bros.
1979	*Captain America*	Marvel	Live-Action Direct-to-Video	Universal	CBS
1981–1983	*Spider-Man & His Amazing Friends*	Marvel	Animated TV	Marvel Productions	NBC
1981	*Superman II*	DC Comics	Live-Action Film	Alexander & Ilya Salkind	Warner Bros.
1982–1983	*Incredible Hulk*	Marvel	Animated TV	Marvel Productions	NBC
1982	*Conan the Barbarian*	Marvel	Live-Action Film	Dino de Laurentiis Corp.	Universal Pictures
1982	*Swamp Thing*	DC Comics	Live-Action Film	Swampfilms	Embassy Pictures
1983	*Superman III*	DC Comics	Live-Action Film	Alexander & Ilya Salkind	Warner Bros.
1984	*Conan the Destroyer*	Marvel	Live-Action Film	Dino de Laurentiis Corp.	Universal Pictures
1984	*Sheena*	Fiction House	Live-Action Film	Columbia Pictures	Columbia Pictures
1984	*Supergirl*	DC Comics	Live-Action Film	Alexander & Ilya Salkind	Tri-Star Pictures
1985	*Red Sonja*	Marvel	Live-Action Film	Dino de Laurentiis Corp.	MGM/UA
1985	*Weird Science*	EC Comics	Live-Action Film	Silver Pictures	Universal Pictures
1986	*Howard the Duck*	Marvel	Live-Action Film	Lucasfilm Ltd.	Universal Pictures
1987–1990	*Ducktales*	Dell / Gold Key	Animated TV	Walt Disney TV Animation	Buena Vista Television
1987–1996	*Teenage Mutant Ninja Turtles*	Mirage Studios	Animated TV	Murakami-Wolf-Swenson	CBS
1987	*Superman IV*	DC Comics	Live-Action Film	Cannon Films	Warner Bros.
1988–1992	*Superboy*	DC Comics	Live-Action TV	Cantharus Productions	WBTV
1988	*Incredible Hulk Returns*	Marvel	Live-Action TV Film	New World	Lakeshore

Year	Title	Type	Publisher	Producer	Distributor or Network
1989–1996	Tales from the Crypt	Live-Action TV	EC Comics	HBO	HBO
1989	Batman	Live-Action Film	DC Comics	Warner Bros. Pictures	Warner Bros.
1989	Punisher	Live-Action Direct-to-Video	Marvel	New World	Live Entertainment
1989	Return of the Swamp Thing	Live-Action Film	DC Comics	Lightyear	Millimeter Films
1990	The Flash	Live-Action TV Film	DC Comics	WBTV	CBS
1990–1993	Swamp Thing	Live-Action TV	DC Comics	MCA Television	WBTV / USA Network
1990	Dick Tracy	Live-Action Film	Comic Strip	Walt Disney Pictures	Buena Vista Pictures
1990	Teenage Mutant Ninja Turtles	Live-Action Film	Mirage	Golden Harvest	New Line Cinema
1991	Teenage Mutant Ninja Turtles II	Live-Action Film	Mirage	Golden Harvest	New Line Cinema
1991	The Rocketeer	Live-Action Film	Dark Horse	Walt Disney Pictures	Buena Vista Pictures
1992–1995	Batman: The Animated Series	Animated TV	DC Comics	Warner Bros. Animation	Fox Kids
1992–1997	X-Men	Animated TV	Marvel	Saban Entertainment	Fox Kids
1992	Batman Returns	Live-Action Film	DC Comics	Warner Bros. Pictures	Warner Bros.
1992	Captain America	Live-Action Direct-to-Video	Marvel	21st Century Film	Columbia Tri-Star
1992	Human Target	Live-Action TV	DC Comics	WBTV	ABC
1993–1997	Lois & Clark	Live-Action TV	DC Comics	WBTV	ABC
1993	Batman: Mask of the Phantasm	Animated Direct-to-Video	DC Comics	Warner Bros. Animation	Warner Bros.
1993	Teenage Mutant Ninja Turtles III	Live-Action Film	Mirage	Golden Harvest	New Line Cinema
1994–1996	Fantastic Four	Animated TV	Marvel	New World	Genesis Entertainment
1994–1996	Iron Man	Animated TV	Marvel	New World	Genesis Entertainment
1994–1997	Duckman	Animated TV	Dark Horse	Paramount Television	USA Network
1994–1998	Spider-Man	Animated TV	Marvel	Marvel Films Animation	Fox Kids
1994–1998	Weird Science	Live-Action TV	EC Comics	Universal Television	USA Network
1994	Fantastic Four	Live-Action Film (unreleased)	Marvel	Constantin Films	—
1994	Richie Rich	Live-Action Film	Harvey	Silver Pictures	Warner Bros.
1994	The Crow	Live-Action Film	Caliber	Dimension Films	Miramax

Year	Title	Medium	Publisher	Production	Distributor/Network
1994	*The Mask*	Live-Action Film	Dark Horse	Dark Horse Ent. / New Line	New Line Cinema
1994	*Timecop*	Live-Action Film	Dark Horse	Dark Horse Ent. / Largo	Universal Pictures
1994	*WildCats*	Animated TV	Wildstorm	Nelvana	CBS
1995	*Batman Forever*	Live-Action Film	DC Comics	Warner Bros. Pictures	Warner Bros.
1995	*Judge Dredd*	Live-Action Film	2000 AD	Hollywood Pictures	Buena Vista Pictures
1995	*Tales from the Crypt: Demon Knight*	Live-Action Film	EC Comics	Universal Pictures	Universal Pictures
1995	*Tank Girl*	Live-Action Film	Independent	Trilogy Ent.	United Artists
1996–2003	*Sabrina the Teenage Witch*	Live-Action TV	Archie	Paramount Television	ABC
1996	*Barb Wire*	Live-Action Film	Dark Horse	PolyGram	Gramercy Pictures
1996	*Bordello of Blood*	Live-Action Film	EC Comics	Universal City Studios	Universal Pictures
1996	*The Crow: City of Angels*	Live-Action Film	Caliber	Dimension Films	Miramax
1997–1998	*Ninja Turtles: The Next Mutation*	Live-Action TV	Mirage	Saban Entertainment	Fox Kids
1997–1999	*Night Man*	Live-Action TV	Marvel	Glen Larson	Tribune Broadcasting
1997–1999	*Todd McFarlane's Spawn*	Animated TV	Image	HBO Animation	HBO
1997	*Batman & Robin*	Live-Action Film	DC Comics	Warner Bros. Pictures	Warner Bros.
1997	*Men in Black*	Live-Action Film	Malibu (Marvel)	Amblin Ent.	Columbia Pictures
1997	*Perversions of Science*	Live-Action TV	EC Comics	HBO	HBO
1997	*Spawn*	Live-Action Film	Image	Todd McFarlane	New Line Cinema
1997	*Steel*	Live-Action Film	DC Comics	Warner Bros. Pictures	Warner Bros.
1998	*Blade*	Live-Action Film	Marvel	Marvel Ent. / New Line	New Line Cinema
1999	*Mystery Men*	Live-Action Film	Dark Horse	Dark Horse Ent.	Universal Pictures
1999	*Virus*	Live-Action Film	Dark Horse	Dark Horse Ent. / Valhalla	Universal Pictures
2000–2002	*Sheena*	Live-Action TV	Fiction House	Columbia TriStar Television	Sony Pictures Television
2000	*X-Men*	Live-Action Film	Marvel	Marvel Ent. / 20th Century Fox	20th Century Fox
2001–2002	*Witchblade*	Live-Action TV	Image	WBTV	TNT
2001–2004	*Mutant X*	Live-Action TV	Marvel	Fireworks / Marvel Studios	Tribune Entertainment
2001–2011	*Smallville*	Live-Action TV	DC Comics	WBTV	The WB / The CW
2001	*From Hell*	Live-Action Film	Top Shelf	Underworld Pictures	20th Century Fox
2001	*Ghost World*	Live-Action Film	Fantagraphics	Granada Film	United Artists

Year	Title	Type	Publisher	Producer	Distributor or Network
2001	Monkeybone	Live-Action Film	Mad Monkey	20th Century Fox / 1492	20th Century Fox
2001	The Tick	Live-Action TV	New England	Columbia TriStar Television	Fox
2002–2003	Birds of Prey	Live-Action TV	DC Comics	WBTV	The WB
2002	Blade II	Live-Action Film	Marvel	Marvel Ent. / New Line	New Line Cinema
2002	Men in Black II	Live-Action Film	Malibu (Marvel)	Amblin Ent.	Columbia Pictures
2002	Road to Perdition	Live-Action Film	DC Comics	Zanuck Company	DreamWorks
2002	Spider-Man	Live-Action Film	Marvel	Marvel Ent. / Columbia	Sony Pictures
2003–2009	Teenage Mutant Ninja Turtles	Animated TV	Mirage Studios	Mirage Studios	Fox / The CW
2003	American Splendor	Live-Action Film	Dark Horse	Good Machine	HBO / Fine Line
2003	Bulletproof Monk	Live-Action Film	Image	Lakeshore	MGM
2003	Daredevil	Live-Action Film	Marvel	Marvel Ent. / 20th Century Fox	20th Century Fox
2003	Hulk	Live-Action Film	Marvel	Marvel Ent. / Universal Pictures	Universal Pictures
2003	League of Extraordinary Gentlemen	Live-Action Film	DC Comics	20th Century Fox	20th Century Fox
2003	X2	Live-Action Film	Marvel	Marvel Ent. / 20th Century Fox	20th Century Fox
2004	Blade: Trinity	Live-Action Film	Marvel	Marvel Ent. / New Line	New Line Cinema
2004	Catwoman	Live-Action Film	DC Comics	Village Roadshow	Warner Bros.
2004	Hellboy	Live-Action Film	Dark Horse	Revolution Studios	Sony Pictures
2004	Punisher	Live-Action Film	Marvel	Marvel Ent. / Lionsgate	Artisan
2004	Spider-Man 2	Live-Action Film	Marvel	Marvel Ent. / Columbia	Sony Pictures
2005	A History of Violence	Live-Action Film	DC Comics	BenderSpink	New Line Cinema
2005	Batman Begins	Live-Action Film	DC Comics	Legendary	Warner Bros.
2005	Elektra	Live-Action Film	Marvel	Marvel Ent. / New Regency	20th Century Fox
2005	Fantastic Four	Live-Action Film	Marvel	Marvel Ent. / Constantin	20th Century Fox
2005	Man-Thing	Live-Action Film	Marvel	Marvel Ent. / Lionsgate	Artisan
2005	Sin City	Live-Action Film	Dark Horse	Dimension Films	Miramax
2005	Son of the Mask	Live-Action Film	Dark Horse	Dark Horse Ent.	New Line Cinema

2005	*V for Vendetta*	Live-Action Film	DC Comics	Silver Pictures	Warner Bros.
2006	*Art School Confidential*	Live-Action Film	DC Comics	United Artists	Sony Pictures Classics
2006	*Blade: The Series*	Live-Action TV	Marvel	Marvel Ent. / New Line	WBTV / Spike TV
2006	*Superman Returns*	Live-Action Film	DC Comics	Legendary	Warner Bros.
2006	*Ultimate Avengers II*	Animated Direct-to-Video	Marvel	Marvel Animated / Lionsgate	Lionsgate
2006	*Ultimate Avengers: The Movie*	Animated Direct-to-Video	Marvel	Marvel Animated / Lionsgate	Lionsgate
2006	*X-Men: The Last Stand*	Live-Action Film	Marvel	Marvel Ent. / 20th Century Fox	20th Century Fox
2007	*300*	Live-Action Film	Dark Horse	Legendary	Warner Bros.
2007	*30 Days of Night*	Live-Action Film	IDW Publishing	Dark Horse Ent. / Ghost House	Sony Pictures
2007	*Doctor Strange: The Sorcerer Supreme*	Animated Direct-to-Video	Marvel	Marvel Animated / Lionsgate	Lionsgate
2007	*Fantastic Four: Rise of the Silver Surfer*	Live-Action Film	Marvel	Marvel Ent. / Constantin	20th Century Fox
2007	*Ghost Rider*	Live-Action Film	Marvel	Marvel Ent. / Columbia	Sony Pictures
2007	*Painkiller Jane*	Live-Action TV	Event Comics	IDT Entertainment	Sci Fi Channel
2007	*Spider-Man 3*	Live-Action Film	Marvel	Marvel Ent. / Columbia	Sony Pictures
2007	*Superman: Doomsday*	Animated Direct-to-Video	Marvel	Warner Bros. Animation	Warner Home Video
2007	*The Invincible Iron Man*	Animated Direct-to-Video	Marvel	Marvel Animated / Lionsgate	Lionsgate
2007	*TMNT*	Animated Film	Mirage	Imagi Animation	Warner Bros.
2008	*Batman: Gotham Knight*	Animated Shorts	DC Comics	Warner Bros. Animation	Warner Home Video
2008	*Dark Knight*	Live-Action Film	DC Comics	Legendary	Warner Bros.
2008	*Hellboy II*	Live-Action Film	Dark Horse	Relativity Media	Universal Pictures
2008	*Iron Man*	Live-Action Film	Marvel	Marvel Studios	Paramount Pictures
2008	*Justice League: The New Frontier*	Animated Direct-to-Video	DC Comics	Warner Bros. Animation	Warner Home Video
2008	*Next Avengers: Heroes of Tomorrow*	Animated Direct-to-Video	Marvel	Marvel Animated / Lionsgate	Lionsgate
2008	*Punisher: War Zone*	Live-Action Film	Marvel	Marvel Ent. / Lionsgate	Lionsgate
2008	*Incredible Hulk*	Live-Action Film	Marvel	Marvel Studios	Universal Pictures
2008	*Middleman*	Live-Action TV	Viper	ABC Family	ABC Family
2008	*The Spirit*	Live-Action Film	DC Comics	Dark Lot Ent.	Lionsgate
2008	*Wanted*	Live-Action Film	Image	Spyglass / Relativity Media	Universal Pictures

Year	Title	Type	Publisher	Producer	Distributor or Network
2009	*Green Lantern: First Flight*	Animated Direct-to-Video	DC Comics	Warner Bros. Animation	Warner Home Video
2009	*Hulk Vs.*	Animated Direct-to-Video	Marvel	Marvel Animated / Lionsgate	Lionsgate
2009	*Superman/Batman: Public Enemies*	Animated Direct-to-Video	DC Comics	Warner Bros. Animation	Warner Home Video
2009	*Surrogates*	Live-Action Film	Top Shelf	Touchstone Pictures	Walt Disney Studios
2009	*Haunted World of El Superbeasto*	Animated Direct-to-Video	Image	Film Roman	Anchor Bay Films
2009	*Watchmen*	Live-Action Film	DC Comics	Legendary	Warner Bros.
2009	*Whiteout*	Live-Action Film	Oni Press	Silver Pictures	Warner Bros.
2009	*Wonder Woman*	Animated Direct-to-Video	DC Comics	Warner Bros. Animation	Warner Home Video
2009	*X-Men Origins: Wolverine*	Live-Action Film	Marvel	Marvel Ent. / 20th Century Fox	20th Century Fox
2010–2011	*Human Target*	Live Action TV	DC Comics	WBTV	Fox
2010–now	*Walking Dead*	Live Action TV	Image	AMC Studios / Valhalla	AMC
2010	*Batman: Under the Red Hood*	Animated Direct-to-Video	DC Comics	Warner Bros. Animation	Warner Home Video
2010	*Iron Man 2*	Live-Action Film	Marvel	Marvel Studios	Paramount Pictures
2010	*Jonah Hex*	Live-Action Film	DC Comics	Legendary	Warner Bros.
2010	*Justice League: Crisis on Two Earths*	Animated Direct-to-Video	DC Comics	Warner Bros. Animation	Warner Home Video
2010	*Kick-Ass*	Live-Action Film	Icon	Plan B	Lionsgate
2010	*Planet Hulk*	Animated Direct-to-Video	Marvel	Marvel Animated / Lionsgate	Lionsgate
2010	*RED*	Live-Action Film	DC Comics	DC Ent.	Summit Ent.
2010	*Scott Pilgrim vs. the World*	Live-Action Film	Oni Press	Big Talk Films	Universal Pictures
2010	*The Losers*	Live-Action Film	DC Comics	Silver Pictures	Warner Bros.

Comic Book Film Adaptations, 1956–2010

The following chart catalogues the total box office receipts—domestic, foreign, and total—of all American comic-book-based films released between 1956 and 2010. Transitional years (1989, 1991, 1998, and 2003) are marked by dark dividing lines and are explained in more depth in chapter 5. Films that did not receive a theatrical release are not included. Publisher, producer, and distributor information can also be found in Appendix A.

Year	Title	Publisher	Producer	Distributor	Domestic Gross (millions)	Foreign Gross (millions)	Global Gross (millions)
1972	*Fritz the Cat*	Help! / Cavalier	Steve Krantz Productions	Cinemation	$25.0	$65.0	$90.0
1972	*Tales from the Crypt*	EC Comics	Amicus / Metromedia	20th Century Fox	$2.0	—	$2.0
1973	*Vault of Horror*	EC Comics	Amicus / Metromedia	20th Century Fox	$0.6	—	$0.6
1974	*Nine Lives of Fritz the Cat*	Help! / Cavalier	Steve Krantz Productions	AIP	$1.2	—	$1.2
1978	*Superman*	DC Comics	Alexander & Ilya Salkind	Warner Bros.	$108.2	—	$108.2
1981	*Superman II*	DC Comics	Alexander & Ilya Salkind	Warner Bros.	$134.2	$166.0	$300.2
1982	*Conan the Barbarian*	Marvel	Dino de Laurentiis Corporation	Universal Pictures	$39.6	$29.3	$68.9
1983	*Superman III*	DC Comics	Alexander & Ilya Salkind	Warner Bros.	$60.0	—	$60.0
1984	*Conan the Destroyer*	Marvel	Dino de Laurentiis Corporation	Universal Pictures	$31.0	—	$31.0
1984	*Sheena*	Fiction House	Columbia Pictures	Columbia Pictures	$5.8	—	$5.8
1984	*Supergirl*	DC Comics	Alexander & Ilya Salkind	Tri-Star Pictures	$14.3	—	$14.3
1985	*Red Sonja*	Marvel	Dino de Laurentiis Corporation	MGM/UA	$6.9	—	$6.9
1985	*Weird Science*	EC Comics	Silver Pictures	Universal Pictures	$23.8	$15.1	$38.9
1986	*Howard the Duck*	Marvel	Lucasfilm Ltd.	Universal Pictures	$16.3	$21.7	$38.0
1987	*Superman IV*	DC Comics	Cannon Films	Warner Bros.	$15.7	—	$15.7
1989	*Batman*	DC Comics	Warner Bros. Pictures	Warner Bros.	$251.2	$160.2	$411.3
1989	*Return of the Swamp Thing*	DC Comics	Lightyear	Millimeter Films	$0.2	—	$0.2
1990	*Dick Tracy*	Comic Strip	Walt Disney Pictures	Buena Vista Pictures	$103.7	$59.0	$162.7
1990	*Teenage Mutant Ninja Turtles*	Mirage	Golden Harvest	New Line Cinema	$135.3	$66.7	$202.0
1991	*Teenage Mutant Ninja Turtles II*	Mirage	Golden Harvest	New Line Cinema	$78.7	—	$78.7
1991	*The Rocketeer*	Dark Horse	Walt Disney Pictures	Buena Vista Pictures	$46.7	—	$46.7
1992	*Batman Returns*	DC Comics	Warner Bros. Pictures	Warner Bros.	$162.8	$104.0	$266.8
1993	*Teenage Mutant Ninja Turtles III*	Mirage	Golden Harvest	New Line Cinema	$42.3	—	$42.3
1994	*Richie Rich*	Harvey	Silver Pictures	Warner Bros.	$38.1	—	$38.1
1994	*The Crow*	Caliber	Dimension Films	Miramax	$50.7	—	$50.7

Year	Title	Publisher	Production	Distributor			
1994	*The Mask*	Dark Horse	Dark Horse Ent. / New Line	New Line Cinema	$119.9	$231.6	$351.6
1994	*Timecop*	Dark Horse	Dark Horse Ent. / Largo	Universal Pictures	$44.9	$56.8	$101.6
1995	*Batman Forever*	DC Comics	Warner Bros. Pictures	Warner Bros.	$184.0	$152.5	$336.5
1995	*Judge Dredd*	2000 AD	Hollywood Pictures	Buena Vista Pictures	$34.7	$78.8	$113.5
1995	*Tales from the Crypt: Demon Knight*	EC Comics	Universal Pictures	Universal Pictures	$21.1	—	$21.1
1995	*Tank Girl*	Independent	Trilogy Ent.	United Artists	$4.1	—	$4.1
1996	*Barb Wire*	Dark Horse	PolyGram	Gramercy Pictures	$3.8	—	$3.8
1996	*Bordello of Blood*	EC Comics	Universal City Studios	Universal Pictures	$5.8	—	$5.8
1996	*The Crow: City of Angels*	Caliber	Dimension Films	Miramax	$17.9	—	$17.9
1997	*Batman & Robin*	DC Comics	Warner Bros. Pictures	Warner Bros.	$107.3	$130.9	$238.2
1997	*Men in Black*	Malibu (Marvel)	Amblin Ent.	Columbia Pictures	$250.7	$338.7	$589.4
1997	*Spawn*	Image	Todd McFarlane	New Line Cinema	$54.9	$33.0	$87.8
1997	*Steel*	DC Comics	Warner Bros. Pictures	Warner Bros.	$1.7	—	$1.7
1998	*Blade*	Marvel	Marvel Ent. / New Line	New Line Cinema	$70.1	$61.1	$131.2
1999	*Mystery Men*	Dark Horse	Dark Horse Ent.	Universal Pictures	$29.8	$3.7	$33.5
1999	*Virus*	Dark Horse	Dark Horse Ent. / Valhalla	Universal Pictures	$14.0	$16.6	$30.7
2000	*X-Men*	Marvel	Marvel Ent. / 20th Century Fox	20th Century Fox	$157.3	$139.0	$296.3
2001	*From Hell*	Top Shelf	Underworld Pictures	20th Century Fox	$31.6	$43.0	$74.6
2001	*Ghost World*	Fantagraphics	Granada Film	United Artists	$6.2	$2.5	$8.8
2001	*Monkeybone*	Mad Monkey	20th Century Fox / 1492	20th Century Fox	$5.4	$2.2	$7.6
2002	*Blade II*	Marvel	Marvel Ent. / New Line	New Line Cinema	$82.3	$72.7	$155.0
2002	*Men in Black II*	Malibu / Marvel	Amblin Ent.	Columbia Pictures	$190.4	$251.4	$441.8
2002	*Road to Perdition*	DC Comics	Zanuck Company	DreamWorks	$104.5	$76.5	$181.0
2002	*Spider-Man*	Marvel	Marvel Ent. / Columbia	Sony Pictures	$403.7	$418.0	$821.7
2003	*American Splendor*	Dark Horse	Good Machine	HBO / Fine Line	$6.0	$2.0	$8.0
2003	*Bulletproof Monk*	Image	Lakeshore	MGM	$23.4	$14.4	$37.7
2003	*Daredevil*	Marvel	Marvel Ent. / 20th Century Fox	20th Century Fox	$102.5	$76.6	$179.2
2003	*Hulk*	Marvel	Marvel Ent. / Universal Pictures	Universal Pictures	$132.2	$113.2	$245.4

Year	Title	Publisher	Producer	Distributor	Domestic Gross (millions)	Foreign Gross (millions)	Global Gross (millions)
2003	*League of Extraordinary Gentlemen*	DC Comics	20th Century Fox	20th Century Fox	$66.5	$112.8	$179.3
2003	*X2*	Marvel	Marvel Ent. / 20th Century Fox	20th Century Fox	$214.9	$192.8	$407.7
2004	*Blade: Trinity*	Marvel	Marvel Ent. / New Line	New Line Cinema	$52.4	$76.5	$128.9
2004	*Catwoman*	DC Comics	Village Roadshow	Warner Bros.	$40.2	$41.9	$82.1
2004	*Hellboy*	Dark Horse	Revolution Studios	Sony Pictures	$59.6	$39.7	$99.3
2004	*Punisher*	Marvel	Marvel Ent. / Lionsgate	Artisan	$33.8	$20.9	$54.7
2004	*Spider-Man 2*	Marvel	Marvel Ent. / Columbia	Sony Pictures	$373.6	$410.2	$783.8
2005	*A History of Violence*	DC Comics	BenderSpink	New Line Cinema	$31.5	$29.2	$60.7
2005	*Batman Begins*	DC Comics	Legendary	Warner Bros. Pictures	$206.9	$167.4	$374.2
2005	*Elektra*	Marvel	Marvel Ent. / 20th Century Fox	20th Century Fox	$24.4	$32.3	$56.7
2005	*Fantastic Four*	Marvel	Marvel Ent. / Constantin	20th Century Fox	$154.7	$175.9	$330.6
2005	*Man-Thing*	Marvel	Marvel Ent. / Lionsgate	Artisan	n/a	$1.1	$1.1
2005	*Sin City*	Dark Horse	Dimension Films	Miramax	$74.1	$84.7	$158.8
2005	*Son of the Mask*	Dark Horse	Dark Horse Ent.	New Line Cinema	$17.0	$40.5	$57.6
2005	*V for Vendetta*	DC Comics	Silver Pictures	Warner Bros.	$70.5	$62.0	$132.5
2006	*Art School Confidential*	DC Comics	United Artists	Sony Pictures Classics	$3.3	$0.0	$3.3
2006	*Superman Returns*	DC Comics	Legendary	Warner Bros. Pictures	$200.1	$191.0	$391.1
2006	*X-Men: The Last Stand*	Marvel	Marvel Ent. / 20th Century Fox	20th Century Fox	$234.4	$225.0	$459.4
2007	*300*	Dark Horse	Legendary	Warner Bros.	$210.6	$245.5	$456.1
2007	*30 Days of Night*	IDW Publishing	Dark Horse Ent. / Ghost House	Sony Pictures	$39.6	$35.9	$75.5
2007	*Fantastic Four: Rise of the Silver Surfer*	Marvel	Marvel Ent. / Constantin	20th Century Fox	$131.9	$157.1	$289.0
2007	*Ghost Rider*	Marvel	Marvel Ent. / Columbia	Sony Pictures	$115.8	$12.9	$128.7
2007	*Spider-Man 3*	Marvel	Marvel Ent. / Columbia	Sony Pictures	$336.5	$554.3	$890.9
2007	*TMNT*	Mirage	Imagi Animation	Warner Bros.	$54.1	$41.5	$95.6
2008	*Dark Knight*	DC Comics	Legendary	Warner Bros.	$534.9	$469.7	$1,004.6

Year	Title					
2008	Hellboy II	Dark Horse	Relativity Media	Universal Pictures	$76.0	$84.4	$160.4
2008	Iron Man	Marvel	Marvel Studios	Paramount Pictures	$318.4	$266.8	$585.2
2008	Punisher: War Zone	Marvel	Marvel Ent. / Lionsgate	Lionsgate	$8.1	$2.0	$10.1
2008	Incredible Hulk	Marvel	Marvel Studios	Universal Pictures	$134.8	$128.6	$263.4
2008	The Spirit	DC Comics	Dark Lot Ent.	Lionsgate	$19.8	$19.2	$39.0
2008	Wanted	Image	Spyglass / Relativity Media	Universal Pictures	$134.5	$206.9	$341.4
2009	Surrogates	Top Shelf	Touchstone Pictures	Walt Disney Studios	$38.6	$83.9	$122.4
2009	Watchmen	DC Comics	Legendary	Warner Bros.	$107.5	$77.7	$185.3
2009	Whiteout	Oni Press	Silver Pictures	Warner Bros.	$10.3	$7.6	$17.8
2009	X-Men Origins: Wolverine	Marvel	Marvel Ent. / 20th Century Fox	20th Century Fox	$179.9	$193.2	$373.1
2010	Iron Man 2	Marvel	Marvel Studios	Paramount Pictures	$312.4	$311.5	$623.9
2010	Jonah Hex	DC Comics	Legendary	Warner Bros.	$10.5	$0.4	$10.9
2010	Kick-Ass	Icon	Plan B	Lionsgate	$48.1	$48.1	$96.2
2010	RED	DC Comics	DC Ent.	Summit Ent.	$90.4	$108.6	$199.0
2010	Scott Pilgrim vs. the World	Oni Press	Big Talk Films	Universal Pictures	$31.5	$16.1	$47.7
2010	The Losers	DC Comics	Silver Pictures	Warner Bros.	$23.6	$5.8	$29.4

Notes

1. Peter C. Du Bois, "Superman, Batman and Ivanhoe: Comic Books Have Become Both Profitable and Respectable," *Barron's National Business and Financial Weekly*, September 18, 1961.

2. These surveys were conducted in 1947 and 1948, well before sales peaked in 1954. During this time, comic book content became more mature in nature, so in all likelihood the adult audience only grew larger. Surveys quoted by Norbert Muhlen, "Comic Books and Other Horrors," *Commentary* 8 (January 1, 1949): 81–82.

3. Bradford W. Wright, *Comic Book Nation: The Transformation of Youth Culture in America* (Baltimore: Johns Hopkins University Press, 2003), 57.

4. Peter Bart, "Some Comic Book Men Pine for Sin, Sex as Their Sales Skid," *Wall Street Journal*, February 25, 1959.

5. John Jackson Miller, "Monthly Sales," *Comichron: The Comics Chronicles*, accessed August 11, 2018, www.comichron.com/monthlycomicssales.html.

6. Chapter 4 covers demographic patterns in depth. While there have always been fans who did not fit the long-established reader profile reported by publishers and retailers—educated men in their 30s and 40s—more diverse readers have been far less visible and numerous. Reports since 2014 suggest that this may finally (and hopefully, permanently) be changing, but it is still too soon to tell. Glen Weldon, "Beyond The Pale (Male): Marvel, Diversity and a Changing Comics Readership," *Weekend Edition Saturday*, NPR, April 8, 2017, www .npr.org/2017/04/08/523044892/beyond-the-pale-male-marvel-diversity-and-a-changing-comics-readership; Vaneta Rogers, "Is the Average Age of Comic Book Readers Increasing?," *Newsarama*, February 2, 2017, www.newsarama .com/33006-is-the-average-age-of-comic-book-readers-increasing-retailers-talk-state-of-the-business-2017.html; "ICv2 White Paper: Rise of the New

Comics Customers," *CBR.com,* October 10, 2014, www.cbr.com/icv2-white-paper-rise-of-the-new-comics-customers/.

7. DC Comics co-publisher Dan DiDio expressed his deep concern about the health of the publishing business in a presentation about "The New 52" he gave to students of Transmedia Entertainment at the University of Southern California, September 27, 2011. His actual estimate of the reading public was only 1 million, but others have suggested the number may be somewhat higher. See Heidi MacDonald, "Rough Calculations Suggests 2% of Millennials Read Comics," *The Beat,* December 29, 2014, www.comicsbeat.com/rough-calculations-suggests-2-of-millennials-read-comics/.

8. "Movie Franchises and Brands Index," *Box Office Mojo,* accessed January 13, 2018, www.boxofficemojo.com/franchises/.

9. Chris Arrant, "The Full Comic Book Television Release Schedule," *Newsarama,* October 31, 2017, www.newsarama.com/30432-the-full-comic-book-television-release-schedule.html.

10. Henry Jenkins, "Comics and Convergence Part One," *Confessions of an Aca-Fan* (blog), August 18, 2008, http://henryjenkins.org/2006/08/comics_and_convergence.html.

11. Jenkins, "Comics and Convergence Part One."

12. For examples of the former, see Ian Gordon and Matthew P. McAllister, eds., *Film and Comic Books* (Jackson: University Press of Mississippi, 2007); Matthew P. McAllister and Ian Gordon, eds., *Comics and Ideology* (New York: Peter Lang, 2001); Wendy Haslem, Angela Ndalianis, and Chris Mackie, eds., *Super/Heroes: From Hercules to Superman* (Washington, DC: New Academia Publishing, 2007). For a good example of the latter, see the comments of Scott Bukatman and Greg Smith in a 2011 roundtable discussion: Greg Smith, "Surveying the World of Contemporary Comics Scholarship: A Conversation," *Cinema Journal* 50, no. 3 (Spring 2011): 106–47.

13. Graham Murdock and Peter Golding, "Capitalism, Communication, and Class Relations," in *Mass Communication and Society,* ed. James Curran, Michael Gurevitch, and Janet Woollacott (London: Sage, 1979), 25.

14. Jennifer Holt, *Empires of Entertainment: Media Industries and the Politics of Deregulation, 1980–1996* (New Brunswick, NJ: Rutgers University Press, 2011), 7. See also Herbert I. Schiller, *Culture Inc.: The Corporate Takeover of Public Expression* (New York: Oxford University Press, 1989); Michele Hilmes, *Hollywood and Broadcasting: From Radio to Cable* (Urbana: University of Illinois Press, 1990); William Kunz, *Culture Conglomerates: Consolidation in the Motion Picture and Television Industries* (Lanham, MD: Rowman and Littlefield, 2007).

15. Consider this: overall domestic sales of comic books in 2016, a banner year, totaled just over $1 billion. The domestic theatrical release of *Star Wars* at the end of 2015 earned nearly that amount, by itself, without accounting for home video or television sales. Furthermore, a major film production like *Star Wars* would typically employ more individuals than all the comic book publishers in aggregate. See "Yearly Box Office," *Box Office Mojo,* accessed November 30, 2017, www.boxofficemojo.com/yearly/?view2 = ytdcompare; John Jackson Miller, "Comics and Graphic Novel Sales Up 5% in 2016," *Com-*

ichron, accessed November 30, 2017, www.comichron.com/yearlycomicssales /industrywide/2016-industrywide.html.

16. Walt Hickey provides a nice summary of the former perspective, with statistics to back it up, while Jeffrey Brown defends the latter claim arguing for a "re-found freedom of expression" within the medium. Walt Hickey, "Comic Books Are Still Made by Men, for Men and about Men," *FiveThirtyEight,* October 13, 2014, https://fivethirtyeight.com/features/women-in-comic-books/; Jeffrey A. Brown, "Comic Book Fandom and Cultural Capital," *Journal of Popular Culture* 30, no. 4 (1997): 13–31.

17. *New York Times* comic book critic Douglas Wolk even takes both positions simultaneously, arguing that many independent creators are true auteurs while the major publishers rely on what is essentially assembly-line production. Douglas Wolk, *Reading Comics: How Graphic Novels Work and What They Mean* (New York: Da Capo Press, 2008), 19–35.

18. Brian Larkin, "The Politics and Poetics of Infrastructure," *Annual Review of Anthropology* 42 (2013): 328.

19. Lisa Parks and Nicole Starosielski, "Introduction," in *Signal Traffic: Critical Studies of Media Infrastructures,* ed. Lisa Parks and Nicole Starosielski (Urbana: University of Illinois Press, 2015), 1, 5, 9.

20. Susan Leigh Star and Karen Ruhleder, "Steps Toward an Ecology of Infrastructure: Design and Access for Large Information Spaces," *Information Systems Research* 7, no. 1 (March 1996): 113.

21. Star and Ruhleder, 113. The authors, here and elsewhere, outline eight common dimensions of infrastructures, all of which apply to the industrial infrastructures at the core of this analysis: (1) they are *embedded* or sunk into other structures, (2) they are *transparent* and invisibly support various tasks, (3) they *reach* beyond a single site or event, (4) they are *learned* as part of membership in a community of practice, (5) they are shaped by the *conventions* of that community, (6) they become *standardized,* (7) they are built on top of an *existing base,* and (8) they become *visible upon breakdown.*

22. Geoffrey C. Bowker and Susan Leigh Star, *Sorting Things Out: Classification and Its Consequences* (Cambridge, MA: MIT Press, 1999), 323.

23. Susan Leigh Star, "The Ethnography of Infrastructure," *American Behavioral Scientist* 43, no. 3 (December 1999): 380.

24. Lisa Gitelman, *Always Already New: Media, History, and the Data of Culture* (Cambridge, MA: MIT Press, 2008), 6–7.

25. Star, "Ethnography of Infrastructure," 380.

26. Dade Hayes, "CBS on Carriage Dispute with Dish," *Deadline Hollywood,* November 22, 2017, http://deadline.com/2017/11/cbs-dish-carriage-dispute-remain-far-apart-on-terms-1202213799/.

27. Christian Sandvig, "The Internet as Anti-Television: Distribution Infrastructure as Culture and Power," in *Signal Traffic: Critical Studies of Media Infrastructures,* ed. Lisa Parks and Nicole Starosielski (Urbana: University of Illinois Press, 2015), 236–37, 226.

28. Raymond Williams, "Base and Superstructure in Marxist Cultural Theory," *New Left Review* 82 (1973): 7.

29. Raymond Williams, *Television: Technology and Cultural Form* (London: Routledge, 1974), 133.

1. INCORPORATING COMICS

1. Jackson Ayres, "When Were Superheroes Grim and Gritty?," *Los Angeles Review of Books,* February 20, 2016, https://lareviewofbooks.org/article/when-were-superheroes-grim-and-gritty/; Greg Burgas, "What Should We Call This Age of Comics?," *CBR.com,* May 5, 2012, www.cbr.com/what-should-we-call-this-age-of-comics/.

2. Paul Lopes, *Demanding Respect: The Evolution of the American Comic Book* (Philadelphia: Temple University Press, 2009); Randy Duncan and Matthew J. Smith, *The Power of Comics: History, Form and Culture* (New York: Continuum, 2009); Bradford W. Wright, *Comic Book Nation: The Transformation of Youth Culture in America* (Baltimore: Johns Hopkins University Press, 2003).

3. For further reading on aesthetics, see Scott McCloud, *Understanding Comics: The Invisible Art* (New York: William Morrow, 1994); Will Eisner, *Comics and Sequential Art: Principles and Practices from the Legendary Cartoonist* (New York: W. W. Norton, 2008). On narrative and cultural criticism, see Martin Barker, *Comics: Ideology, Power and the Critics* (Manchester, UK: Manchester University Press, 1989); Duncan and Smith, *Power of Comics;* Paul Gravett, *Graphic Novels: Everything You Need to Know* (New York: Collins Design, 2005). On fandom and comics criticism, see Bill Schelly, *Founders of Comic Fandom* (Jefferson, NC: McFarland, 2010); Dick Lupoff and Don Thompson, *All in Color for a Dime* (New York: Ace Books, 1970); Matthew J. Pustz, *Comic Book Culture: Fanboys and True Believers* (Jackson: University Press of Mississippi, 2000).

4. Henry Jenkins, *Convergence Culture: Where Old and New Media Collide* (New York: NYU Press, 2008), 97.

5. See Bart Beaty's discussion of various attempts to define the medium. Bart Beaty, *Comics versus Art* (Toronto: University of Toronto Press, 2012), chap. 2. Also, Simone Murray's discussion of adaptation studies and historical efforts to denigrate cross-media adaptations as offending artistic and literary standards. Simone Murray, *The Adaptation Industry* (New York: Routledge, 2012).

6. Jared Gardner, *Projections: Comics and the History of Twenty-First-Century Storytelling* (Stanford, CA: Stanford University Press, 2012), chap. 6.

7. For example, Cogan and Massey point to continuity and world-building to explain comic books' success on the big screen. Reynolds and Sommers suggest that the mythological nature of the comics accounts for their success. Brian Cogan and Jeff Massey, "Myth-Taken Identity in the Marvel Cinematic Universe," in *Marvel Comics into Film: Essays on Adaptations Since the 1940s,* ed. Matthew J. McEniry, Robert Moses Peaslee, and Robert G. Weiner (Jefferson, NC: McFarland, 2016), 9–12; Richard Reynolds, *Super Heroes: A Modern Mythology* (Jackson: University Press of Mississippi, 1992); Joseph Sommers, "On the American Comic Book," in *The American Comic Book,* ed. Joseph Sommers (Ipswich, MA: Salem Press, 2014), xxi–xxiii.

8. Leslie A. Kurtz, "The Independent Legal Lives of Fictional Characters," *Wisconsin Law Review* (1986): 439–49.

9. The 1955 Sam Spade case was a landmark in this regard. See Kurtz, "Independent Legal Lives," 450–64.

10. Umberto Eco, "The Myth of Superman" (1962 essay), in *Arguing Comics: Literary Masters on a Popular Medium,* ed. Jeet Heer and Kent Worcester (Jackson: University Press of Mississippi, 2004), 151. *New York Times* comic book critic Douglas Wolk echoes this sentiment in *Reading Comics: How Graphic Novels Work and What They Mean* (New York: Da Capo Press, 2008), 102.

11. Jane Gaines, *Contested Culture: The Image, the Voice, and the Law* (Chapel Hill: University of North Carolina Press, 1991), 210–25.

12. "Action Comics Chief Liebowitz Spawned Superman in 1937," *Variety,* July 8, 1987; Gerard Jones, *Men of Tomorrow: Geeks, Gangsters, and the Birth of the Comic Book* (New York: Basic Books, 2005), 141.

13. Mike Benton, *The Comic Book in America: An Illustrated History* (Dallas: Taylor, 1993).

14. Sixty-one patriotic superheroes debuted between 1940 and 1944, forty-seven before Pearl Harbor. Duncan and Smith, *Power of Comics,* 250.

15. Jean-Paul Gabilliet, *Of Comics and Men: A Cultural History of American Comic Books,* trans. Bart Beaty and Nick Nguyen (Jackson: University Press of Mississippi, 2009), 34.

16. Gabilliet, 31.

17. In 1949, romances replaced westerns and soon became the fastest-growing genre yet, accounting for more than 25% of all titles on the market. See Trina Robbins, *From Girls to Grrrlz: A History of Female Comics From Teens to Zines* (San Francisco: Chronicle Books, 1999), 54. After Gaines introduced EC's New Trend line in 1950, the horror comic took off and, like earlier trends, soon accounted for one quarter of all the titles sold. See Jim Trombetta, *The Horror! The Horror!: Comic Books the Government Didn't Want You to Read!* (New York: Abrams ComicArts, 2010), 31. With the onset of the Korean War, sales of war comics also spiked around 1952, as did science fiction comics. See Benton, *Comic Book in America,* 49–51.

18. Rob Edelman, "Vintage 40s & 50s Film Serials Were Smashes Before TV Did 'Em In," *Variety,* July 8, 1987.

19. Avi Santo, "Batman versus the Green Hornet: The Merchandisable TV Text and the Paradox of Licensing in the Classical Network Era," *Cinema Journal* 49, no. 2 (2010): 60.

20. Les Daniels, *Superman: The Complete History* (San Francisco: Chronicle Books, 2004), 47–54, 92–97.

21. Detective Comics v. Bruns Publications et al., 111 F.2d 432 (2nd Cir. 1940).

22. Benton, *Comic Book in America,* 108.

23. Stanley Kligfeld, "Comic Magazines: Crime, Superman, Love Help Them Set Records for Sales," *Wall Street Journal,* January 12, 1953.

24. Gabilliet, *Of Comics and Men,* 40.

25. Bill Gaines, interview by Rich Hauser, *Spa Fon #5* (fanzine), 1969, reprinted in Fred von Bernewitz and Grant Geissman, *Tales of Terror! The EC Companion* (Seattle: Fantagraphics Books, 2000), 182.

26. Subcommittee to Investigate Juvenile Delinquency, Interim Report of the Committee on the Judiciary: Comic Books and Juvenile Delinquency, 88th Congress, Senate Report 62 (1955), section titled "An Overview of the Organization of the Comic-Book Industry"; Interborough News Company v. The Curtis Publishing Company, 127 F. Supp. 286 (US Southern District of New York 1954).

27. Timothy Havens and Amanda Lotz, *Understanding Media Industries* (New York: Oxford University Press, 2012), 147, 155.

28. J. Howard Rutledge and Peter Bart, "Comic Books: Slight Sales Recovery Leaves Volume below Pre-Clean-Up Days," *Wall Street Journal,* October 5, 1955.

29. After Dell lost its exclusive licenses to competitor Gold Key, its fortunes quickly declined, leading to closure in 1973. Theodore Peterson, *Magazines in the Twentieth Century,* 2nd ed. (Urbana: University of Illinois Press, 1964); "Sidelights: S.E.C. Is Fighting Cuts in Staff," *New York Times,* August 8, 1959; Benton, *Comic Book in America,* 110.

30. Benton, 127.

31. As an assistant and creative executive at DC Comics between 2004 and 2006, I recall going through literal binders full of properties, characters either developed at DC (or one of its imprints) or purchased by the company at some point over the four decades prior.

32. The roots of comic book fandom, of course, precede this moment by several decades, most notably with sci-fi and comic book fanzines of the 1940s and the EC Fan Addicts of the early 1950s. However, 1960 remains a useful starting date, based on Jerry Bails's initial interactions with Julius Schwartz at DC and on Dick and Pat Lupoff's first pieces about comic books. Schelly, *Founders of Comic Fandom;* Duncan and Smith, *Power of Comics,* 177.

33. Daniels, *Superman,* 47.

34. Jones, *Men of Tomorrow,* 291.

35. Liebowitz quoted in Santo, "Batman vs. Green Hornet," 69–70.

36. Henry Jenkins and Lynn Spigel, "Mass Culture and Popular Memory," in *The Many Lives of the Batman: Critical Approaches to a Superhero and His Media,* ed. William Uricchio and Roberta Pearson (New York: Routledge, 1991), 123; Les Daniels, *Batman: The Complete History* (San Francisco: Chronicle Books, 1999), 102–3.

37. Santo, "Batman vs. Green Hornet," 69, 72.

38. Santo, 69–70.

39. "Superman Leaps to the Big Board," *New York Times,* May 27, 1965.

40. Kinney National Service, Inc., *Annual Report,* 1967–1971.

41. They included *The New Adventures of Superman* (1966–1970, WBTV, CBS) and *Spider Man* (1967–1970, Disney, ABC).

42. See, for example, Vincent Canby, "Fighting, Fantasy in 'Conan the Barbarian,'" *New York Times,* May 15, 1982; Richard Schickel, "Cinema: Over-

kill," *Time,* May 24, 1982; Dave Kehr, "Unlovable Duck Makes 'Howard' an Unlovable Film," *Chicago Tribune,* August 1, 1986, sec. N; "'Howard the Duck': Reviewers Still Quacking," *Chicago Tribune,* August 10, 1986, sec. 13.

43. N.R. Kleinfield, "Superheroes' Creators Wrangle," *New York Times,* October 13, 1979; Phillip Gutis, "Turning Superheroes into Super Sales," *New York Times,* January 6, 1985.

44. Patrick Parsons, "Batman and His Audience: The Dialectic of Culture," in *The Many Lives of the Batman: Critical Approaches to a Superhero and His Media,* ed. Roberta Pearson and William Uricchio (New York: Routledge, 1991), 77.

45. Jennifer Holt, *Empires of Entertainment: Media Industries and the Politics of Deregulation, 1980–1996* (New Brunswick, NJ: Rutgers University Press, 2011), 18.

46. Jenkins, *Convergence Culture,* 10–11, 254.

47. Derek Johnson, *Media Franchising: Creative License and Collaboration in the Culture Industries* (New York: NYU Press, 2013), Introduction.

48. Chuck Rozanski, "The Vicious Downward Spiral of the 1990's," Tales from the Database (blog), *Mile High Comics,* 2002, www.milehighcomics.com /tales/cbg36.html.

49. Andrew Ross Sorkin, "Remembering Two Titans' Marvel Duel," *New York Times: Dealbook* (blog), August 31, 2009, http://dealbook.nytimes .com/2009/08/31/remembering-two-titans-marvel-duel/?_r = 0.

50. Gabilliet, *Of Comics and Men,* 101.

51. Lopes, *Demanding Respect,* 155.

52. Lopes, 165.

53. Brigid Alverson, "Manga 2013: A Smaller, More Sustainable Market," *Publishers Weekly,* April 5, 2013, www.publishersweekly.com/pw/by-topic /industry-news/comics/article/56693-manga-2013-a-smaller-more-sustainable-market.html; Laura Hudson, "ICv2 Projects Graphic Novel Sales Down 20%, Digital Comics Up Over 1000% in 2010," *Comics Alliance,* October 7, 2010, http://comicsalliance.com/digital-comics-sales/.

54. For more on shifts in Hollywood's financial system, see chapter 5.

55. Claudia Eller and Ben Fritz, "Warner Shakes Up DC Comics to Compete with Marvel," *Los Angeles Times,* Company Town, September 10, 2009, http:// articles.latimes.com/2009/sep/10/business/fi-ct-warner10.

56. Jenkins, *Convergence Culture,* 2, 254.

57. For more about the development of comic books' core demographic as well as Hollywood's embrace of this audience, see chapter 4.

2. COMIC BOOK CRISIS

1. *Juvenile Delinquency (Comic Books): Hearings before the Subcommittee to Investigate Juvenile Delinquency of the Committee on the Judiciary, United States Senate* (1954), testimony of Bill Gaines (April 21, 1954), 103.

2. Peter Kihss, "No Harm in Horror, Comics Issuer Says: Comics Publisher Sees No Harm in Horror, Discounts 'Good Taste,'" *New York Times,* April 22,

1954; Irving Kravsow, "Senate Comic Book Probers Learn Publisher Attempt at Cleanup Failed," *Hartford Courant,* April 22, 1954; "Comic Book Publisher Boasts of Horror for Child Reading," *Baltimore Sun,* April 22, 1954.

3. Jeffrey A. Brown, "Comic Book Fandom and Cultural Capital," *Journal of Popular Culture* 30, no. 4 (1997): 18. For similar accusations, see "Comic Books Profit by Rush to Legitimacy," *Los Angeles Times,* November 28, 1974; Mark Gauvreau Judge, "Holy Censorship, Batman! Guess Who's Banning Comic Books," *Washington Post,* June 9, 1996; Max Alexander, "Seriously, It's Comics: From Superman to Today," *New York Times,* June 11, 1989, Arts & Leisure; John F. Brodsen, "Tempo: It's Alive! Comic Terror Is Back from the Crypt," *Chicago Tribune,* February 15, 1984, sec. 5; Jim Trombetta, *The Horror! The Horror!: Comic Books the Government Didn't Want You to Read!* (New York: Abrams ComicArts, 2010), 79; Paul Lopes, *Demanding Respect: The Evolution of the American Comic Book* (Philadelphia: Temple University Press, 2009), 51–52; Shirrel Rhoades, *A Complete History of American Comic Books* (New York: Peter Lang, 2008), 58.

4. Digby Diehl, *Tales from the Crypt: The Official Archives* (New York: St. Martin's Press, 1996), 91; Bill Schelly, *Founders of Comic Fandom* (Jefferson, NC: McFarland, 2010), 198.

5. Grant Geissmann, *Foul Play! The Art and Artists of the 1950s EC Comics* (New York: Harper Design International, 2005), 16–17; Howard Rodman, "They Shoot Comic Books, Don't They?," *American Film* 14, no. 7 (May 1989): 34–39; Brian Siano, "The Skeptical Eye: Tales from the Crypt," *The Humanist,* March 1994; Franklin Harris, "The Long, Gory Life of EC Comics," *Reason* 37, no. 2 (June 2005): 64–65; Barbara Carlson, "To Him, the Comics Aren't Mickeymouse," *Hartford Courant,* February 17, 1973; Chris Kaltenbach, "A Comic Book Kingdom: 'Up, Up and AWAYYYY,'" *Baltimore Sun,* December 4, 1983.

6. This was clear as early as the late fifties, when EC fans Fred von Bernewitz and Grant Geissman, frustrated by public criticism, helped establish comic book culture's first and longest-lasting fandom. Similarly, Dick Lupoff and Don Thompson's *All in Color for a Dime* (1970), the very first published volume dedicated to comic book criticism, introduces its purpose with several defenses against Fredric Wertham. Bhob Stewart and Larry Stark's fanzines also sprang to life based on similar defenses. Dick Lupoff and Don Thompson, *All in Color for a Dime* (New York: Ace Books, 1970), 9–11; Fred von Bernewitz and Grant Geissman, *Tales of Terror! The EC Companion* (Seattle: Fantagraphics Books, 2000), 18; Schelly, *Founders of Comic Fandom,* 86, 126. This story continued to impact fandom and criticism well into the 1990s. For examples, see M. Thomas Inge, *Comics as Culture* (Jackson: University Press of Mississippi, 1990), 128; Matthew J. Pustz, *Comic Book Culture: Fanboys and True Believers* (Jackson: University Press of Mississippi, 2000), 42; Brown, "Comic Book Fandom and Cultural Capital," 22.

7. Lopes, *Demanding Respect,* 30, 58–59; Trombetta, *The Horror! The Horror!,* 23, 31.

8. David Hadju, *The Ten-Cent Plague: The Great Comic-Book Scare and How It Changed America* (New York: Farrar, Straus and Giroux, 2008), 6–7.

9. James Burkhart Gilbert, *A Cycle of Outrage: America's Reaction to the Juvenile Delinquent in the 1950s* (New York: Oxford University Press, 1986), 7.

10. Hadju, *Ten-Cent Plague*, 41–44; Lopes, *Demanding Respect*, 32; Gerard Jones, *Men of Tomorrow: Geeks, Gangsters, and the Birth of the Comic Book* (New York: Basic Books, 2005), 168–69.

11. For a variety of these perspectives, see Catherine Mackenzie, "Movies—and Superman," *New York Times,* October 12, 1941, Parent and Child; Bart Beaty, *Fredric Wertham and the Critique of Mass Culture* (Jackson: University Press of Mississippi, 2005), 107; Amy Kiste Nyberg, *Seal of Approval: The History of the Comics Code* (Jackson: University Press of Mississippi, 1998), 114.

12. These publishers also included Lev Gleason and Magazine Management (later Marvel). Nyberg, *Seal of Approval,* 107.

13. Patrick Parsons, "Batman and His Audience: The Dialectic of Culture," in *The Many Lives of the Batman: Critical Approaches to a Superhero and His Media,* ed. Roberta Pearson and William Uricchio (New York: Routledge, 1991), 69.

14. There was, for example, the publication of the December 1944 issue of the *Journal of Educational Sociology,* consisting of seven articles that discussed comics in a positive light (with titles like "Comics as a Social Force"), six of which were authored by academics associated with the industry. Harvey Sorbaugh and Sidonie Gruenberg worked with Fawcett while Josette Frank, Lauretta Bender, and W. W. D. Sones worked with National. Paul Witty has no known associations with the industry. See Harvey Zorbaugh, ed., "The Comics as an Educational Medium," *Journal of Educational Sociology* 18, no. 4 (December 1944): 193–256; Nyberg, *Seal of Approval,* 15.

15. Gilbert, *Cycle of Outrage,* 14.

16. Jean-Paul Gabilliet, *Of Comics and Men: A Cultural History of American Comic Books,* trans. Bart Beaty and Nick Nguyen (Jackson: University Press of Mississippi, 2009), 216.

17. Jones, *Men of Tomorrow,* 239.

18. This last development, a handful of bonfires sponsored largely by religious organizations, notably occurred only in 1948, and thus—contrary to claims in the media—could not have been caused by either the Senate hearings or the publication of Wertham's book, both of which occurred in 1954.

19. Beaty, *Fredric Wertham,* 116–17, 121; Gabilliet, *Of Comics and Men,* 218–19; Gilbert, *Cycle of Outrage,* 101; Nyberg, *Seal of Approval,* 30–34.

20. Jones, *Men of Tomorrow,* 266; Diehl, *Tales from the Crypt,* 89.

21. Jones, *Men of Tomorrow,* 266; Trombetta, *The Horror! The Horror!,* 79; Al Feldstein, interview by Grant Geissman, April 1996, in von Bernewitz and Geissman, *Tales of Terror!,* 87–88.

22. Gabilliet, *Of Comics and Men,* 219; Shawn Selby, "Congress, Culture and Capitalism: Congressional Hearings into Cultural Regulation, 1953–1967" (PhD diss., Ohio University, 2008), 51.

23. Les Daniels, *DC Comics: Sixty Years of the World's Favorite Comic Book Heroes* (Boston: Little, Brown, 1995), 92.

24. Gabilliet, *Of Comics and Men,* 218; Beaty, *Fredric Wertham,* 119.

25. The most notable example is the December 1949 issue of the *Journal of Educational Sociology*. Contributors included Henry Schultz, head of the brand new ACMP, and Frederic Thrasher, whose piece in that publication would serve, five years later, as the Senate subcommittee's primary rebuttal to Wertham's inflammatory theories. Harvey Zorbaugh, ed., *Journal of Educational Sociology* 23, no. 4 (December 1949): 193–247; Subcommittee to Investigate Juvenile Delinquency, Interim Report of the Committee on the Judiciary: Comic Books and Juvenile Delinquency, 88th Congress, Senate Report 62 (1955), section titled "Crime and Horror Comics and the Well-Adjusted and Normal Law Abiding Child."

26. *Juvenile Delinquency (Comic Books)* hearings, testimony of Gunnar Dybwad (April 22, 1954), 119–45; Subcom. to Investigate Juvenile Delinquency, Interim Report, "Crime and Horror Comics."

27. Jones, *Men of Tomorrow*, 241; Gabilliet, *Of Comics and Men*, 218; Diehl, *Tales from the Crypt*, 83; Selby, "Congress, Culture and Capitalism," 50–60.

28. For more on the early years of the Production Code, see Leonard J. Leff and Jerold Simmons, *The Dame in the Kimono: Hollywood, Censorship, and the Production Code*, revised ed. (Lexington: University Press of Kentucky, 2001), 17–36.

29. Mike Benton, *The Comic Book in America: An Illustrated History* (Dallas: Taylor, 1993), 43–44.

30. Max C. Gaines was responsible for three innovations that basically created the comic book industry: he produced the very first comic book, *Funnies on Parade;* he was the first to sell comic books on newsstands; and he discovered Siegel and Shuster's character Superman, which kick-started the whole industry.

31. Frank Jacobs, *The Mad World of William M. Gaines* (Secaucus, NJ: Lyle Stuart, 1972), 63–75; Hadju, *Ten-Cent Plague*, 89–90; Diehl, *Tales from the Crypt*, 18.

32. Geissmann, *Foul Play!*, 10–13; Diehl, *Tales from the Crypt*, 18–26.

33. Diehl, 76.

34. Peter C. Du Bois, "Superman, Batman and Ivanhoe: Comic Books Have Become Both Profitable and Respectable," *Barron's National Business and Financial Weekly*, September 18, 1961.

35. "It Works!," *Christian Science Monitor*, September 16, 1954, Editorials/Features.

36. Gabilliet, *Of Comics and Men*, 40.

37. Kaltenbach, "A Comic Book Kingdom"; Carlson, "To Him, the Comics Aren't Mickeymouse"; Judge, "Holy Censorship, Batman!"

38. Bill Gaines, interview by Rich Hauser, *Spa Fon #5* (fanzine), 1969, reprinted in von Bernewitz and Geissman, *Tales of Terror!*, 180.

39. Diehl, *Tales from the Crypt*, 87.

40. The decision was Robert Hendrickson's, chair of the subcommittee and recipient of the angry letters. Beaty, *Fredric Wertham*, 124–31, 155; Gabilliet, *Of Comics and Men*, 220.

41. Shearon Lowery and Melvin L. De Fleur, *Milestones in Mass Communication Research: Media Effects* (New York: Longman, 1983), 234; Parsons, "Batman and His Audience," 71; Beaty, *Fredric Wertham*, 3–4, 207.

42. Robert Warshow, "Paul, the Horror, and Dr. Wertham," *Commentary* 17 (1954): 596–604, reprinted in *Mass Culture: The Popular Arts in America,* ed. Bernard Rosenberg and David Manning White (Glencoe, IL: Free Press, 1957), 200–02.

43. Frances Ilg and Louise Ames, "Wertham View on Comics Is Questioned by Warshow," *Daily Boston Globe,* November 8, 1954.

44. Norbert Muhlen, "Comic Books and Other Horrors," *Commentary* 8 (January 1, 1949); Munro Leaf, "Lollipops or Dynamite? Millions of Comic Books Devoured with Gusto by Children. With What Effect?," *Christian Science Monitor,* November 13, 1948, Weekly Magazine.

45. Theodore Peterson, *Magazines in the Twentieth Century,* 2nd ed. (Urbana: University of Illinois Press, 1964), 358.

46. Kingsley Amis, "A Threat to Our Culture," *Spectator,* December 30, 1955.

47. Selby, "Congress, Culture and Capitalism," 66.

48. Selby, 56, 67, 74.

49. Amy Kiste Nyberg, "William Gaines and the Battle over EC Comics," *Inks: Cartoon and Comic Art Studies* 3, no. 1 (February 1996): 6–8.

50. Staff director of the subcommittee Richard Clendenen explained how he came to receive Gaines's "Red Dupe" ad during his testimony, which opened the hearings. *Juvenile Delinquency (Comic Books)* hearings, testimony of Richard Clendenen (April 21, 1954), 59.

51. Feldstein interview, in von Bernewitz and Geissman, *Tales of Terror!,* 87–88.

52. Trombetta, *The Horror! The Horror!,* 79.

53. Diehl, *Tales from the Crypt,* 31, 92.

54. See for example, Bill Schelly, *Founders of Comic Fandom* (Jefferson, NC: McFarland, 2010), 198.

55. Wertham's testimony came just two days after the release of *Seduction of the Innocent.* So while Kefauver had already read it (or at least claimed to), the viewing public likely had not. What ultimately matters most in Wertham's legacy, then, was what he actually said that day to Congress, in the moment his ideas had the most potential to influence policy, industry, and broad public opinion.

56. This point is frequently lost in more cursory descriptions of Wertham's research, but he was unequivocal throughout his testimony that comic books could in no way cause juvenile delinquency all on their own and that there "are many, many other factors." See *Juvenile Delinquency (Comic Books)* hearings, testimony of Fredric Wertham (April 21, 1954), 79–96.

57. Subcom. to Investigate Juvenile Delinquency, Interim Report, "Crime and Horror Comics."

58. The close analysis of Wertham's research has been a topic of scholarly interest at least since Shearon Lowery and Melvin de Fleur published *Milestones in Mass Communications Research* in 1983. The authors dedicated a whole chapter to Wertham's version of media effects, dissecting *Seduction of the Innocent* by itemizing its various arguments and pointing out its methodological flaws. More recently, Carol Tilley combed through the doctor's old papers,

seeking out discrete examples of his poor research—instances when he left extenuating circumstances out of his final publication or surreptitiously combined case studies to make his case seem stronger. Tilley's resulting publication was covered widely by the national press, both print and online, suggesting that there is still considerable interest in Wertham's work more than sixty years later. There are dozens if not hundreds of other examples of similar efforts around Wertham's work. Lowery and De Fleur, *Milestones in Mass Communication Research;* Dave Itzkoff, "Flaws Found in Fredric Wertham's Comic-Book Studies," *New York Times,* February 19, 2013; John Farrier, "The Research That Led to the Comics Code Authority Was Faked," *Neatorama,* February 5, 2013, www.neatorama.com/2013/02/15/The-Research-That-Led-to-the-Comics-Code-Authority-Was-Faked/.

59. There are entire websites dedicated to Wertham's follies, countless articles that falsely recount his story, and blogs, Tumblr pages, and Twitter accounts created in his name, designed to further discredit him. Specifically, Wertham has been accused of trading in "hucksterism and salesmanship" and commanding a "monocausal, obsessive, and populist" crusade. One critic longingly imagines him suffering in an "infernal chain gang . . . using his bare hands to lay down hot asphalt along the Good Intentions Expressway." Online, he is referred to, among many other things, as a "quack," a "douchebag," and a "cultural elitist and furious ideologist." Gabilliet, *Of Comics and Men,* 216; Harry Mendryk, "Fredric Wertham's 'Seduction of the Innocent,'" *Simon and Kirby* (blog), August 1, 2008, http://kirbymuseum.org/blogs/simonandkirby/archives/1428; Adrian Wymann, "He Was a Psychiatrist, So People Listened," *Panelology: Where Comic Books Make Sense,* February 2, 2013, www.wymann.info /comics/025-Wertham1940s.html. For an example of a blog, see *Dr. Fredric Wertham, M.D.,* accessed September 14, 2018, www.ep.tc/wertham/soti/blog/. Twitter handles include DrFredWertham. Tumblr accounts include Seduction of the Innocent.

60. More specifically, Wertham hypothesized four "avenues" along which comic books might lead to delinquency. Two spoke to the harmful effects of the products advertised within the books, specifically about how the stories and ads worked together to degrade children's ethics. The subcommittee did reach conclusions in its final report about false claims in ads and the sale of unsafe and illegal goods to minors through the mail, but the senators seemed to disregard completely Wertham's specific thoughts. Another ignored avenue considered proper reading instruction, and the fourth is that which is detailed in the text.

61. A clarification of terminology is necessary here. Wertham wrote and spoke primarily of "crime" comic books. The crime genre, as understood by nearly everyone except Wertham, had peaked in 1948 and 1949 and had declined significantly in popularity by 1954. Wertham, however, was not actually referring to this genre when he said the word "crime." Rather, he meant any book in which any crime or violence was depicted. This category thus included nearly all the popular comic book genres: superheroes, westerns, sci-fi, war, crime, horror, and even love confessionals. See *Juvenile Delinquency (Comic Books)* hearings, testimony of Fredric Wertham, April 21, 1954, 79–96; Fredric Wertham, *Seduction of the Innocent* (New York: Rinehart, 1954).

62. Subcom. to Investigate Juvenile Delinquency, Interim Report, "Specific Examples of Material Dealt with at New York Hearing."

63. Beaty, *Fredric Wertham*, 160–65; Gilbert, *Cycle of Outrage*, 148; Gabilliet, *Of Comics and Men*, 237.

64. Following is the full list of speakers at the Senate subcommittee hearings in 1954. April 21: Dr. Harris Peck (director, Bureau of Mental Health Services, Children's Court, New York), Henry Edward Schultz (general counsel, ACMP), Dr. Fredric Wertham (author, *Seduction of the Innocent*), William Gaines (publisher, EC Comics), Walt Kelly (National Cartoonist Society), Milton Caniff (National Cartoonist Society), Joseph Musial (National Cartoonist Society). April 22: Gunnar Dybwad (executive director, CSAA), William Friedman (publisher, Master Comics and Story Comics), Dr. Laura Bender (director, Children's Ward in the Psychiatric Division at Bellevue Hospital, New York, NY), Monroe Froehlich Jr. (business manager, Magazine Management Co.), William Richter (News Dealers Association of Greater New York), Alex Segal (president, Stravon Publications), Samuel Roth (publisher of pornography), Helen Meyer and Matthew Murphy (vice-president and editor, Dell Publications). June 4: James Fitzpatrick (chairman, New York State Joint Legislative Committee to Study the Publication of Comics), Benjamin Freedman (chairman, Newsdealers Association of Greater New York and America), Harold Chamberlain (circulation director, Independent News Co.), Charles Appel (owner, Angus Drug Store), George Davis (president, Kable News Co.), E. D. Fulton (member, House of Commons in Canada), Samuel Black (vice-president, Atlantic Coast Independent Distributors Association), William Eichhorn (vice-president, American News Co.), Jerome Kaplon (chairman, Juvenile Delinquency Committee, Union County Bar Association).

65. Trombetta, *The Horror! The Horror!*, 79.

66. *Juvenile Delinquency (Comic Books)* hearings, testimonies of Monroe Froehlich, Jr. (April 22, 1954), 167–83; Helen Meyer (April 22, 1954), 196–200; and Harold Chamberlain (June 4, 1954), 222–33.

67. Subcom. to Investigate Juvenile Delinquency, Interim Report, "Current Efforts at Self-Regulation."

68. Subcom. to Investigate Juvenile Delinquency, Interim Report.

69. Parsons, "Batman and His Audience," 71–72; Lopes, *Demanding Respect*, 44–45.

70. Don Smith Somerville, "A Study of Local Regulations and Group Actions on the Circulation of Newsstand Publications" (PhD diss., University of Illinois at Urbana-Champaign, 1956), 18–21.

71. "Comic Book Curb Grows," *New York Times*, July 11, 1955; "Legislatures of 12 States Enact Comic Book Curbs," *Hartford Courant*, July 11, 1955.

72. Peterson, *Magazines in the Twentieth Century*, 359.

73. The Code and Charles Murphy's appointment as new "czar" (head of the CCA) were both announced on September 16, 1954.

74. He had even selected two Harvard researchers to write a new study on the spuriousness of the link between juvenile delinquency and comic books. Nyberg, *Seal of Approval*, 108.

75. Nyberg, 110.

76. Feldstein interview in von Bernewitz and Geissman, *Tales of Terror!*, 86–93.

77. CMAA, "Code of the Comics Magazine Association of America, Inc.," October 26, 1954, *CBLDF*, http://cbldf.org/the-comics-code-of-1954/.

78. See, for example, Jared Gardner, *Projections: Comics and the History of Twenty-First-Century Storytelling* (Stanford, CA: Stanford University Press), 103–104; Hadju, *Ten-Cent Plague,* 321–323.

79. Feldstein interview, in von Bernewitz and Geissman, *Tales of Terror!*, 87–88.

80. Alisa Perren, "Rethinking Distribution for the Future of Media Industry Studies," *Cinema Journal* 52, no. 3 (Spring 2013): 166. Within film studies, distribution has traditionally been defined as separate from exhibition, which refers primarily to theaters. In the context of comic books, however, exhibition is more akin to retail, which might refer to newsstands and other venues of consumption that were often integrated with wholesale and distribution businesses.

81. Lee Grieveson, *Policing Cinema: Movies and Censorship in Early-Twentieth-Century America* (Berkeley: University of California Press, 2004), 131–35.

82. Ruth A. Inglis, "Self-Regulation in Operation," in *The American Film Industry,* ed. Tino Balio (Madison: University of Wisconsin Press, 1985), 384–86.

83. Nyberg, *Seal of Approval,* 156–57; Gabilliet, *Of Comics and Men,* 44–49. Randy Duncan and Matthew Smith similarly attribute the crisis's disproportionate consequences to the industry's "natural boom-and-bust cycle," explaining that only the more established publishers, by relying on proven characters and innovative genres, could weather the downturn of the fifties. Randy Duncan and Matthew J. Smith, *The Power of Comics: History, Form and Culture* (New York: Continuum, 2009), 40–48. Bradford Wright makes a similar argument, showing how four of the larger publishers were able to successfully adapt their titles to respond to a changing market after the crash. He explains how DC Comics and Dell used high-profile characters, supported by licensing in other media, to maintain affluent and wholesome public images that sustained sales. Marvel and Charlton, meanwhile, took a different approach, finding niches in stories about relevant superheroes and the Vietnam War, respectively, that kept them alive into the following decades. Bradford W. Wright, *Comic Book Nation: The Transformation of Youth Culture in America* (Baltimore: Johns Hopkins University Press, 2003), 182–212.

84. J. Howard Rutledge and Peter Bart, "Comic Books: Slight Sales Recovery Leaves Volume below Pre-Clean-Up Days," *Wall Street Journal,* October 5, 1955.

85. Peterson, *Magazines in the Twentieth Century,* 91.

86. These publishers took advantage of a network of independent newspaper wholesalers who agreed to sell their magazines and used the opportunity to create independent national distribution companies. Finally, publishers had an alternative to American News. By the late 1940s, there were thirteen of these distributors in operation, and they worked with around 800 independent wholesalers.

87. "Newsstand Giant Shrinks Away," *Business Week,* May 25, 1957, 70; Peterson, *Magazines in the Twentieth Century,* 91–94; Interborough News

Company v. The Curtis Publishing Company, 127 F. Supp. 286 (US Southern District of New York 1954).

88. *Juvenile Delinquency (Comic Books)* hearings, testimony of William Eichhorn (June 4, 1954), 274–78.

89. Michael Ashley, *Transformations: The Story of the Science-Fiction Magazines from 1950 to 1970* (Liverpool, UK: Liverpool University Press, 2005).

90. Subcom. to Investigate Juvenile Delinquency, Interim Report, "Organization of the Comic Book Industry in the United States according to Distributor, Comic Group, and Publisher, in the Spring of 1954."

91. For example, Toby and Standard—both distributed by ANC—had a handful of big successes like the western *John Wayne Comics* and the adventure *Exciting Comics*. From there, they expanded into other genres with comics like *Tales of Horror*, most of which never caught on. Benton, *Comic Book in America*, 96, 148.

92. Benton, 90.

93. Edward Norworth, "Slump in Comics: The Industry Needs More than a Publishing Code," *Barron's National Business and Financial Weekly*, January 17, 1955.

94. Subcom. to Investigate Juvenile Delinquency, Interim Report.

95. Benton, *Comic Book in America*, 53.

96. Russell Porter, "Press Is Warned on Rivalry of TV," *New York Times*, April 22, 1954.

97. Parsons, "Batman and His Audience," 71–73. Jean-Paul Gabilliet supports this claim by arguing—against the majority of historians—that comic book sales actually hit their peak in 1952 (two years earlier than the estimates of others) and had already begun to fall by 1953, well before the Senate hearings. It is difficult to know if Gabilliet is correct about sales. He argues that there were three thousand titles in circulation at the market's peak while most other historians put the number at around six hundred fifty, a figure confirmed by the report issued by the Senate Subcommittee to Investigate Juvenile Delinquency. Nonetheless, Gabilliet's argument for an early decline is compelling. See Gabilliet, *Of Comics and Men*, 46–49.

98. Peter Bart, "Advertising: Superman Faces New Hurdles," *New York Times*, September 23, 1962; Peterson, *Magazines in the Twentieth Century*, 360.

99. Norworth, "Slump in Comics."

100. Timothy Havens and Amanda Lotz, *Understanding Media Industries* (New York: Oxford University Press, 2012), 155.

101. Du Bois, "Superman, Batman and Ivanhoe."

102. *Juvenile Delinquency (Comic Books)* hearings, testimony of Benjamin Freedman (June 4, 1954), 215–18.

103. Four Star Comics Corp v. Kable News Company, 224 F. Supp. 108 (US Southern District of New York 1963); Norworth, "Slump in Comics."

104. *Juvenile Delinquency (Comic Books)* hearings, testimony of Harold Chamberlain (June 4, 1954), 231–32.

105. Gaines interview, in von Bernewitz and Geissman, *Tales of Terror!*, 183.

106. Parsons, "Batman and His Audience," 75.

107. *Juvenile Delinquency (Comic Books)* hearings, testimonies of Helen Meyer and Matthew Murphy (April 22, 1954), 197.

108. Richard Maltby, "The Production Code and the Hays Office," in *Grand Design: Hollywood as a Modern Business Enterprise, 1930–1939,* ed. Tino Balio, vol. 5, History of the American Cinema (New York: Scribner, 1993), 47, 67.

109. *Juvenile Delinquency (Comic Books)* hearings, testimonies of William Richter (April 22, 1954), 183–89; Monroe Froehlich, Jr. (April 22, 1954), 167–83; Benjamin Freedman (June 4, 1954), 215–22; Harold Chamberlain (June 4, 1954), 222–33; and George B. Davis (June 4, 1954), 236–47.

110. Norworth, "Slump in Comics."

111. Feldstein interview, in von Bernewitz and Geissman, *Tales of Terror!,* 87–88.

112. As quoted in Diehl, *Tales from the Crypt,* 96.

113. As quoted in Nyberg, *Seal of Approval,* 112, 116; Beaty, *Fredric Wertham,* 162.

114. Daniels, *DC Comics,* 114–15.

115. Gabilliet, *Of Comics and Men,* 237.

116. Brown, "Comic Book Fandom and Cultural Capital"; Rhoades, *Complete History of American Comic Books;* Kaltenbach, "Comic Book Kingdom"; Judge, "Holy Censorship, Batman!"; "Comic Books Profit by Rush to Legitimacy."

117. Du Bois, "Superman, Batman and Ivanhoe."

118. For more on the rise of licensing, see the introduction and chapter 3. The importance of licensing became clear in the mid-1960s after DC Comics and Marvel were both bought out by emerging multimedia conglomerates interested in their licensing potential. This was particularly true of DC, which had already spun this end of the business off into the Licensing Corporation of America (LCA), one of the most profitable media businesses in America in the 1960s. Charlton and Harvey had also moved into licensing and IP library building by the mid-1960s, strategies that helped them to survive into the 1980s and 1990s respectively. For more on corporate strategy, see Kinney National Service, Inc., *Annual Report,* 1971, 1967; Warner Communications, Inc., *Annual Report,* 1986, 1971.

119. Du Bois, "Superman, Batman and Ivanhoe."

120. Press Release from Bill Gaines, September 14, 1954, and Gaines interview, in von Bernewitz and Geissman, *Tales of Terror!,* 28–29, 94, 181–84.

121. Havens and Lotz, *Understanding Media Industries,* 155.

122. Norworth, "Slump in Comics."

123. These comics were: *Adventures into the Unknown* and *Forbidden Worlds* from American Comics and *Black Magic* from Prize. *Juvenile Delinquency (Comic Books)* hearings, testimony of Harold Chamberlain (June 4, 1954), 222–33; Benton, *Comic Book in America,* 92, 142.

124. Du Bois, "Superman, Batman and Ivanhoe."

125. Duncan and Smith, *Power of Comics,* 44; Wright, *Comic Book Nation,* 201.

126. Du Bois, "Superman, Batman and Ivanhoe."

127. Benton, *Comic Book in America*, 98.

128. To further differentiate his product, Kanter also increased his prices and used painted covers and even a heavier paper stock. Martin Barker, *The Lasting of the Mohicans: History of an American Myth* (Jackson: University Press of Mississippi, 1995), 150; Michael Sawyer, "Albert Lewis Kanter and the Classics: The Man behind the Gilberton Company," *Journal of Popular Culture* 20, no. 4 (Spring 1987): 8.

129. *Interborough News Co.,* 127 F. Supp. 286.

130. Sawyer, "Albert Lewis Kanter," 14–16.

131. "Business Records: Bankruptcy Proceedings," *New York Times,* March 9, 1956, Business & Finance; "Michael Estrow," *New York Times,* April 15, 1956, Obituaries.

132. Gaines interview, in von Bernewitz and Geissman, *Tales of Terror!,* 183.

133. "Newsstand Giant Shrinks Away."

134. National Comics Publications v. Fawcett Publications, 191 F.2d 594 (2nd Cir. 1951); Benton, *Comic Book in America,* 51.

135. Benton, 95–96; John William Kitson, "Profile of a Growth Industry: American Book Publishing at Mid-Century, with an Emphasis on the Integration and Consolidation Activity Between 1959 and 1965" (PhD diss., University of Illinois at Urbana-Champaign, 1968); Recorded Conversation in the EC Offices (December 28–30 1955), in von Bernewitz and Geissman, *Tales of Terror!,* 271.

136. The head of Publishers Distributing Irving Manheimer was, at the time, involved in a corporate takeover of Macfadden Publications. Shanon Fitzpatrick, "Pulp Empire: Macfadden Publications, Transnational America, and the Global Popular" (PhD diss., University of California, Irvine, 2013).

137. *Juvenile Delinquency (Comic Books)* hearings, "An Evaluation of Comic Books," Exhibit 6B (July 1953), 40–45; Hadju, *Ten-Cent Plague,* 64–68; Gerard Jones, *Men of Tomorrow,* 194, 237.

138. Benton, *Comic Book in America,* 91; Eleanor Blum, "Paperbound Books in the United States in 1955: A Survey of Content" (PhD diss., University of Illinois, 1955); "ARA, Others Are Sued on Antitrust Charges by News Distributors," *Wall Street Journal,* January 2, 1976.

139. "History," Corporate Website, Kable Media Services, Inc., accessed January 11, 2014, www.kable.com/about/history.aspx.

140. *Four Star Comics Corp.,* 224 F. Supp.

141. Nyberg, *Seal of Approval,* 125; Duncan and Smith, *Power of Comics,* 44; Wright, *Comic Book Nation,* 181.

142. Peterson, *Magazines in the Twentieth Century,* 91–92.

143. Subcom. to Investigate Juvenile Delinquency, Interim Report.

144. "American News Gain in Late '54 Continues Into '55, Holders Told," *Wall Street Journal,* March 31, 1955.

145. "S.M. News Will Handle Newsstand Distribution of Time's Publications," *Wall Street Journal,* June 15, 1955.

146. Peterson, *Magazines in the Twentieth Century,* 70–72.

147. The losses were *Look, Vogue, Glamour,* and *Home & Garden.* "Strike Halts Deliveries by American News to New York Area Stands," *Wall Street Journal,* August 12, 1955.

148. "Antitrust Suit against American News, Union News Co. Is Settled," *Wall Street Journal,* September 2, 1955.

149. Periodical Distributors v. American News Co., Union News Co., Pacific News Co., and Manhattan News Co., 290 F. Supp. 896 (Southern District of New York 1968).

150. *Juvenile Delinquency (Comic Books)* hearings, testimony of William Eichhorn (June 4, 1954), 274–87.

151. Ashley, *Transformations,* 189–90.

152. "American News Co. Earnings Rose Nearly 400% in 1955 Despite Decline in Sales," *New York Times,* February 29, 1956, Business & Finance.

153. Warren Unna, "American, Union News Companies under Anti-Trust Inquiry by FBI," *Washington Post,* February 7, 1956, Sports.

154. "Newsstand Giant Shrinks Away," 59.

155. "American News Sees '59 Net Well Above '58," *Wall Street Journal,* May 27, 1959; "Newsstand Giant Shrinks Away," 60.

156. "Newsstand Giant Shrinks Away," 59–60.

157. "Newsstand Giant Shrinks Away," 59.

158. Ashley, *Transformations,* 189–90.

159. "Newsstand Giant Shrinks Away," 66.

160. Dell was not one of the companies that folded. Its business was so robust that its executives decided to follow in the path of other powerful magazine publishers, and start its own distribution business. And it was quite successful. By 1963, Dell was "perhaps the largest [company] concentrating on newsstand distribution." Peterson, *Magazines in the Twentieth Century,* 291. Archie Comics, the other comic book powerhouse distributed by ANC, also managed to find alternative distribution. Nyberg, "William Gaines," 126.

161. Peterson, *Magazines in the Twentieth Century,* 94.

162. Gaines interview, in von Bernewitz and Geissman, *Tales of Terror!,* 183.

163. Subcom. to Investigate Juvenile Delinquency, Interim Report, "Comic Books & Authority"; Ted Johnson, "Time Warner Cable Lawsuit: Another Attack on Channel Bundling," *Variety* (blog), June 19, 2003, http://variety .com/2013/tv/news/time-warner-cable-lawsuit-another-attack-on-channel-bundling-1200499130/.

164. In 1922, the ICC created Class B station licenses, reserved for quality live broadcasters who promised to establish control and order within the medium. In 1927, the FRC used General Order 40 to give the established general public service or commercial stations preference over propaganda or non-profit stations in a reordering of frequencies that hoped to improve the quality of the airwaves. Michele Hilmes, *Only Connect: A Cultural History of Broadcasting in the United States,* 2nd ed. (Belmont, CA: Cengage Learning, 2007), 42, 64.

165. David Morton, *Sound Recording: The Life Story of a Technology* (Baltimore: Johns Hopkins University Press, 2006), 89.

166. Hilmes, *Only Connect,* 75.

167. Chapter 4 covers the development of the direct market, another vivid example of the power of distribution.

3. SUPER ORIGINS

1. Arie Kaplan, *From Krakow to Krypton: Jews and Comic Books* (Philadelphia: Jewish Publication Society, 2008), 49.

2. *CBS Evening News,* December 23, 1975.

3. For the lead-up to the story, see Jennings Parrott, "Superman to Honor a Moral Obligation," November 25, 1975; Mary Breasted, "Superman's Creators, Nearly Destitute, Invoke His Spirit," *New York Times,* November 22, 1975. For its resolution, see David Vidal, "Superman's Creators Get Lifetime Pay," *New York Times,* December 24, 1975; "Superman Case Settled," *Chicago Tribune,* December 24, 1975; "It's a Bird, a Plane—a Happy Ending," *Washington Post,* December 27, 1975.

4. David Vidal, "Mild-Mannered Cartoonists Go to Aid of Superman's Creators," *New York Times,* December 10, 1975.

5. Samuel Frazer, "Superman to the Rescue," letter to the editor, *New York Times,* December 1, 1975.

6. Mary Breasted, "Superman's Creators, Nearly Destitute," *New York Times,* November 22, 1975; Parrott, "Superman to Honor a Moral Obligation."

7. Avi Santo, "Batman versus the Green Hornet: The Merchandisable TV Text and the Paradox of Licensing in the Classical Network Era," *Cinema Journal* 49, no. 2 (2010): 63–85.

8. Jerry Marsh, "Stealing 'Man of Steel,'" *Cleveland Jewish News,* March 17, 2000.

9. Siegel and Siegel v. Warner Bros., 542 F. Supp. 2d 1098 (C.D. Cal. 2008).

10. Detective Comics, Inc. v. Bruns Publications, Inc., 28 F. Supp. 399 (S.D. NY 1939), testimony from Max Gaines. According to Gaines, Siegel and Shuster's idea for Superman initially came to him in 1936. The pair had submitted it to Dell Publishing, for whom Gaines was printing two comic books. He wasn't interested at the time, but the following year, he wrote Siegel and Shuster and asked to see drawings. They sent him back a week's worth of strips. He ultimately decided he did not want them, but thought they might be useful to Jack Liebowitz and Vin Sullivan at DC Comics, and went ahead and forwarded the strips to them.

11. Erik Knutzen, "Man of Steel Splinters an American Dream," *Los Angeles Times,* February 25, 1979.

12. Les Daniels, *Superman: The Complete History* (San Francisco: Chronicle Books, 2004).

13. These workshops, depicted famously in Michael Chabon's *Kavalier and Clay,* were generally residential apartments or small rented spaces in which dozens of artists and writers would work long hours together to create individual stories or issues on a speculative and freelance basis. Most of them were defunct by the mid-1940s. For more, see Randy Duncan and Matthew J. Smith,

The Power of Comics: History, Form and Culture (New York: Continuum, 2009), 110–14; Gerard Jones, *Men of Tomorrow: Geeks, Gangsters, and the Birth of the Comic Book* (New York: Basic Books, 2005), 134–56; Jean-Paul Gabilliet, *Of Comics and Men: A Cultural History of American Comic Books*, trans. Bart Beaty and Nick Nguyen (Jackson: University Press of Mississippi, 2009), 111–16.

14. Gabilliet, *Of Comics and Men*, 118. These paid artists included Wayne Boring, Paul Cassidy, John Sikela, Ed Dobrotka, Ira Yarbrough, and Leo Nowak. Gabilliet notes that Siegel and Shuster "benefitted from exceptional conditions in comparison with other writers and artists." By 1941, they were earning $35 per page, which would have brought in $75,000 annually between the two men. By the late 1940s, they were earning $800 per week from the comic strip alone.

15. Daniels, *Superman*, 44–63.

16. Filed in 1947 and decided in favor of National in 1948, the suit challenged the release form that Detective Comics had asked Siegel and Shuster to sign upon publication of *Action Comics* #1. Jones, *Men of Tomorrow*, 247–49; *Siegel and Siegel*, 542 F. Supp. 2d 1098.

17. Gaines had believed that Siegel and Shuster benefited from a "relatively lush position" until "a couple of sharp lawyers got a hold" of them "and got them malcontented." Fred von Bernewitz and Grant Geissman, *Tales of Terror! The EC Companion* (Seattle: Fantagraphics Books, 2000), Recorded Conversation in the EC Offices (December 30, 1955), 273; Ted White, "The Spawn of M. C. Gaines," in *All in Color for a Dime*, ed. Dick Lupoff and Don Thompson (New York: Ace Books, 1970), 22.

18. Ron Goulart, "Golden Age Sweatshops," *The Comics Journal*, no. 249 (2002): 72–83; Bradford W. Wright, *Comic Book Nation: The Transformation of Youth Culture in America* (Baltimore: Johns Hopkins University Press, 2003), 6–7; Gabilliet, *Of Comics and Men*, 116.

19. Bart Beaty, *Comics versus Art* (Toronto: University of Toronto Press, 2012), 113.

20. *Detective Comics, Inc.*, 28 F. Supp. 399, testimony of William Eisner.

21. Dwight MacDonald, "A Theory of Mass Culture," in *Mass Culture: The Popular Arts in America*, ed. Bernard Rosenberg (Glencoe, IL: Free Press, 1957), 65.

22. Patricia Aufderheide and Peter Jaszi, *Reclaiming Fair Use: How to Put Balance Back in Copyright* (University Of Chicago Press, 2011), 20.

23. Martha Woodmansee and Peter Jaszi have noted that "the court wants a living breathing author" and will reward neither time and effort on its own nor more collective enterprises. Martha Woodmansee and Peter Jaszi, "Introduction," in *The Construction of Authorship: Textual Appropriation in Law and Literature*, ed. Martha Woodmansee and Peter Jaszi (Durham, NC: Duke University Press, 1994), 10–11.

24. Aufderheide and Jaszi, *Reclaiming Fair Use*, 23.

25. In the courtroom, DC's lawyers proved to be far more competent than their competitors, as did company heads Jack Liebowitz and Harry Donenfeld upon taking the stand. Unlike their counterparts at Bruns, these were men who had

experience with the American legal system, and they were at a place in their careers where they were ready to use the law to their advantage instead of being victimized by it. *Detective Comics, Inc.*, 28 F. Supp. 399, testimony from Harry Donenfeld.

26. The first notable example of this came in 1954 when the comic book industry faced a public controversy that targeted some of National's most popular characters, Superman included. Nonetheless, the Senate investigation that followed exonerated the publisher from blame, allowing it to lead a PR campaign and create a regulatory structure that positioned the company at the top of the market. Well into the future, National would wield considerable power over other publishers in the market. Chapter 2 examines the controversy and its resolution in detail.

27. *Detective Comics, Inc.*, 28 F. Supp. 399, testimonies from Jack Liebowitz and Jerry Siegel.

28. *Detective Comics, Inc.*, 28 F. Supp. 399, testimony from Jack Liebowitz.

29. *Detective Comics, Inc.*, 28 F. Supp. 399, testimony from Jerry Siegel.

30. *Detective Comics, Inc.*, 28 F. Supp. 399, testimony from Jerry Siegel.

31. Detective Comics, Inc. v. Bruns Publications, Inc., 111 F. 2d 432 (2nd Cir. 1940).

32. National Comics Publications v. Fawcett Publications, 191 F. 2d 594 (2nd Cir. 1951).

33. Reports have made this claim in a variety of ways: the single "sleepless night" appears in Breasted, "Superman's Creators, Nearly Destitute, Invoke His Spirit," November 22, 1975; Jerry Siegel Obituary, *Economist,* February 17, 1996; Marsh, "Stealing 'Man of Steel.'" For Superman appearing to Siegel "whole one night," see Harmetz Aljean, "The Life and Exceedingly Hard Times of Superman," *New York Times,* June 14, 1981. Andrew Veitch offers a depiction of Siegel figuratively giving "birth to a character" in "How Superartist Won the Dough," *The Guardian,* June 16, 1979.

34. *Siegel and Siegel,* 542 F. Supp. 2d 1098.

35. Starting in 1939, Siegel took the lead on both legal action and employment and rights negotiations for both himself and Shuster, and continued to throughout the course of their lives. Why Shuster did not take a more active role is unclear, but it seems likely that it was quite simply a matter of personality; Gerard Jones and Bill Gaines describe Siegel as angry and self-righteous and consequently more of a "troublemaker," while Shuster was quiet and milder in temperament. It is also possible that as the "author" or creator of the Superman story and dialogue (as opposed to the images), Siegel felt more entitled to recognition and financial reward. After all, it was Siegel, and not Shuster, who was called to the stand to testify to Superman's originality. Jones, *Men of Tomorrow,* 26–27, 35, 72, 186, 216, 269; Fred von Bernewitz and Grant Geissman, *Tales of Terror!,* Recorded Conversation in the EC Offices (December 30, 1955), 273.

36. White, "Spawn of M. C. Gaines," 22, 31.

37. Peter Coogan, *Superhero: The Secret Origin of a Genre* (Austin, TX: Monkey Brain, 2006).

38. Mark Rose, *Authors and Owners: The Invention of Copyright* (Cambridge, MA: Harvard University Press, 1995), 8.

39. Jane Gaines, *Contested Culture: The Image, the Voice, and the Law* (Chapel Hill: University of North Carolina Press, 1991), 209.

40. Paul Goldstein, *Copyright's Highway: From Gutenberg to the Celestial Jukebox* (Stanford, CA: Stanford Law and Politics, 2003), 4.

41. Woodmansee and Jaszi, "Introduction," 6–7.

42. Rose, *Authors and Owners*, 5.

43. Catherine L. Fisk, *Working Knowledge: Employee Innovation and the Rise of Corporate Intellectual Property, 1800–1930* (Chapel Hill: University of North Carolina Press, 2009), 8, 63, 74, 61.

44. Rose, *Authors and Owners*, 1–2, 7.

45. English literature scholar Jack Stillinger has argued that even in the Romantic Era—when the persona of the individual author-genius became solidified—joint, composite, and collaborative literary production was "an extremely common phenomenon" and indeed proved to be one of "the routine ways of producing literature all along." Jack Stillinger, *Multiple Authorship and the Myth of Solitary Genius* (New York: Oxford University Press, 1991), v, 202.

46. Thomas Streeter, "Broadcast Copyright and the Bureaucratization of Property," in *The Construction of Authorship*, ed. Martha Woodmansee and Peter Jaszi (Durham, NC: Duke University Press, 1994), 305–06.

47. Fisk, *Working Knowledge*, 219–26.

48. Over the course of the nineteenth century, Romantic literature and its discourse of original genius flowed into Britain from Germany. There, it blended readily with the liberal discourse of intellectual property first established by this law. The concept of authorship, as well as its obligatory association with originality, is thus "a relatively recent formation—the result of a quite radical reconceptualization of the creative process that culminated less than 200 years ago." Woodmansee and Jaszi, "Introduction," 3.

49. In the 1879 case *MacKaye v. Mallory*, for example, the press rallied behind an author for hire who believed he received too little profit after his play became very successful. The theater community was angered that this talented man was being treated like factory labor and robbed of proper credit. They argued that his "creativity entitled him to his own innovations." Legally speaking, however, they were quite wrong, since by this time only a contract could entitle him to such rights; accordingly, the court sided with the theater and the harsh deal it had struck with the playwright in writing, awarding the theater all financial and artistic rights to the work. Fisk, *Working Knowledge*, 156–57.

50. Cultural historian Michael Denning has noted that in the late nineteenth century, the economic structure of the dime novel business, which functioned as a "fully equipped literary factory," reinforced the medium's maligned reputation. So the public took little interest in the fate of its authors, who lost creative authority over their own work, saw their narrative voices disappear, and had to hold day jobs in other professions to sustain themselves. Michael Denning, *Mechanic Accents: Dime Novels and Working Class Culture in America* (London: Verso, 1998), 17–18, 20–21.

51. Fisk, *Working Knowledge*, 236–37.

52. Bill Schelly, *Founders of Comic Fandom* (Jefferson, NC: McFarland, 2010), 66–93, 189–97; Digby Diehl, *Tales from the Crypt: The Official Archives* (New York: St. Martin's Press, 1996), 145.

53. The fad initially peaked in 1944, with 40 different titles. By 1952, the only superheroes left were Superman, Batman, and Wonder Woman, all published by DC. Notably, though, these titles were not entirely "superhero" comics, in that editors utilized the characters to star in other genres like sci-fi, romance, and teen humor. The results were mixed. While Superman continued selling more than one million copies per issue, Wonder Woman sales were barely a third of that. Accordingly, the actual sales numbers were likely less important than the fact of keeping these characters in print. Gabilliet, *Of Comics and Men,* 34; John Jackson Miller, "Title Spotlights," *Comichron: The Comics Chronicles* (blog), June 8, 2014, www.comichron.com/titlespotlights.html.

54. Schelly, *Founders of Comic Fandom,* 202.

55. Schelly, 21–22.

56. For the most thoughtful account of the simultaneous development of fandom and comic book auteurism, see Will Brooker, *Batman Unmasked: Analyzing a Cultural Icon* (New York: Continuum, 2001), 250–58. For additional accounts, see Duncan and Smith, *Power of Comics,* 175–85; Matthew J. Pustz, *Comic Book Culture: Fanboys and True Believers* (Jackson: University Press of Mississippi, 2000), 43–47, and the collected works of fan historian Bill Schelly.

57. Brooker, *Batman Unmasked,* 254.

58. Jenkins noted this tendency early on in internet culture, on a message board dedicated to David Lynch's series *Twin Peaks.* In this case, the aura of directors also functioned as a kind of justification for their activities, providing a "high-culture rationale for their preoccupation" with what was still perceived by many as a lowbrow cultural form. Henry Jenkins, *Fans, Bloggers, and Gamers: Exploring Participatory Culture* (New York: NYU Press, 2006), 127.

59. Up through this time, it was standard to suppress information about creators even when the texts were enormously popular, so long as they were still a part of lowbrow forms. Miranda Banks, for example, has written about how the head writer and executive producer of *I Love Lucy* (1951–1957, CBS), Jess Oppenheimer, despite his enormous role in creating and shaping the role, was completely unknown to the public and even the object of some amount of disrespect within the television industry. Miranda Banks, "I Love Lucy: The Writer-Producer," in *How to Watch Television,* ed. Ethan Thompson and Jason Mittell (New York: NYU Press, 2013), 244–52.

60. Duncan and Smith, *Power of Comics,* 175–81.

61. Beaty, *Comics versus Art,* 113.

62. Erin Hanna, "Comic-Con 2013: The Fan Convention as Industry Space," *Antenna* (blog), July 19, 2013, http://blog.commarts.wisc.edu/2013/07/19/comic-con-2013-the-fan-convention-as-industry-space/.

63. Andrew Sarris, "Notes on the Auteur Theory in 1962," in *Film Theory and Criticism,* ed. Leo Braudy and Marshall Cohen, 6th ed. (New York: Oxford University Press, 2004), 561–64.

64. Pauline Kael, "Circles and Squares," *Film Quarterly* 16, no. 3 (1963): 677, 675, 679.

65. Kael, 674–75.

66. Leo Braudy and Marshall Cohen, eds., *Film Theory and Criticism*, 6th ed. (New York: Oxford University Press, 2004), 556.

67. Sarris, "Notes on the Auteur Theory in 1962," 563.

68. Other examples include Jim Steranko, *History of Comics* (Reading, PA: Supergraphics, 1970); George Perry and Alan Aldridge, *The Penguin Book of Comics* (New York: Penguin, 1971); Les Daniels, *Comix: A History of Comic Books in America* (London: Wildwood House, 1973); and Maurice Horn, *The World Encyclopedia of Comics* (New York: Chelsea House, 1976).

69. Peter Wollen, "The Auteur Theory" (1969), in *Signs and Meaning in the Cinema* (Bloomington: Indiana University Press, 1972), 104.

70. Mike Benton, *The Comic Book in America: An Illustrated History* (Dallas: Taylor, 1993), 74–82; "Comic Books Profit by Rush to Legitimacy," *Los Angeles Times*, November 28, 1974. According to Gabilliet, sales did peak around 1966, but they were in decline by 1968 and had leveled off again by 1970. Gabilliet, *Of Comics and Men*, 56.

71. N.R. Kleinfield, "Superheroes' Creators Wrangle," *New York Times*, October 13, 1979.

72. "National Periodical Says It Plans to Acquire Licensing Corp. for Stock," *Wall Street Journal*, May 17, 1966.

73. Santo, "Batman vs. Green Hornet," 69.

74. The company's name change did not come until 1971. Kinney National Service, Inc., *Annual Report, 1967–1971*.

75. Sales began to decline in 1967, the year Kinney decided to purchase NPP. Former industry leader Dell closed shop in 1973, and sales remained unsteady for the next decade. Benton, *Comic Book in America*, 71, 107.

76. Wright, *Comic Book Nation*, 255. Wright explains that the economic structures had remained essentially unchanged since the 1940s, and the publishers had retained many of the original staff.

77. A few examples from the 1960s and early 1970s: Warner Bros. bought Reprise Records, Random House bought Pantheon (and then RCA bought Random House), CBS bought the animation studio Terrytoons, Inc. and later Fawcett Publications (which had once sold comic books but now ran publications like *Woman's Day*), and Polygram bought Verve Records.

78. Describing the transition at Random House, editor Jason Epstein explains that his workplace had been "an unusually happy, second family" and functioned as a "second home for authors." In later years, though, authors came to depend on their agents instead of on their publishers. Jason Epstein, *Book Business: Publishing Past, Present, and Future* (New York: W.W. Norton, 2002), 5–6.

79. Andre Schiffrin of Pantheon explains that when media mogul S.I. Newhouse took over, he was known for saying "there is no person here who cannot be replaced by a ten-dollar-a-week clerk." Andre Schiffrin, *The Business of Books: How the International Conglomerates Took Over Publishing and Changed the Way We Read* (London: Verso, 2001), 88–89.

80. This perspective is reflected in the corporation's annual reports from National's purchase in 1967 through 1986, when Warner Communications

merged with Time Inc. Kinney National Service, Inc., *Annual Report,* 1967–1971; Warner Communications, Inc., *Annual Report,* 1971–1986.

81. Duncan and Smith, *Power of Comics,* 59.

82. Describing the story of eventual Marvel and DC freelancer Richard Buckler, fan historian Bill Schelly writes that "it took moving to New York City, and a period of near-starvation while staying week-to-week at the 34th St. YMCA in Manhattan, for [him] to make a realistic attempt to break into the industry," a not uncommon tale at the time. Schelly, *Founders of Comic Fandom,* 140. So-called successes like Buckler were thrilled to share tiny living quarters with other artists and rejoiced in even a limited amount of freelance work from Marvel or DC, hardly the kind of employment that could sustain the company's former creative staff, most of whom had been supporting families on their comic book salaries. Meanwhile, an untold number of failures—fans lured by writing contests and short-term promises of employment from publishers—moved their entire lives to New York only to find themselves returning back home empty-handed shortly after. Schelly, *Founders of Comic Fandom,* 129.

83. Wright, *Comic Book Nation,* 256.

84. DC Comics and Marvel were the only major players left. Archie Comics was still bringing in some profit. That company went public in the 1970s and, like DC and Marvel, relied on licensing to survive the decade. The other three remaining publishers, Charlton (specializing in fad genres), Gold Key (specializing in licensed characters, many of which they purchased when Dell closed its doors in 1974), and Harvey (specializing in titles for young children), barely managed to stay alive through the 1970s, and all had to close shop in the early 1980s. Benton, *Comic Book in America,* 77–78.

85. Warner Communications, Inc., *Annual Report,* 1975, 5, 41–42.

86. Paul Levitz, author's interview, Skype, July 13, 2017.

87. Wright, *Comic Book Nation,* 259.

88. Benton, *Comic Book in America,* 80.

89. Jordan Raphael and Tom Spurgeon, *Stan Lee and the Rise and Fall of the American Comic Book* (Chicago: Chicago Review Press, 2003), 204–05.

90. Kleinfield, "Superheroes' Creators Wrangle."

91. This time, the lawsuit revolved around DC's renewal rights, which Siegel challenged and tried to claim for himself and Shuster. Siegel v. National Periodical Publications, Inc., 364 F. Supp 1032 (Southern District of New York 1973).

92. Mary Murphy, "Superman Film Set for Leap Year," *Los Angeles Times,* August 9, 1975.

93. Jones, *Men of Tomorrow,* 316.

94. David Colton, "The Crime That Created Superman," *USA Today,* August 26, 2008.

95. When Siegel and Shuster settled their 1948 case, they had made a similar deal, relinquishing all future rights to Superman in exchange for a modest sum of money, $94,000. When the pair sued in the 1960s, trying to claim that renewal rights belonged to them and not to DC, it was that 1948 agreement that undid them, because it strengthened the original 1938 contract. And indeed, when Siegel's heirs tried to terminate the 1938 contract and take back

their rights, the concession for all rights that they made in the 1975 contract came under question. Ultimately, the judge ruled that because DC's annual stipend to them was "voluntary," the contract could not invalidate Siegel and Shuster's termination rights. However, the pair could not have known that the outcome would favor them (the law that instituted termination rights was not written until 1976) and must have realized that again reaffirming DC's rights in a contract was a risk. *Siegel and Siegel,* 542 F. Supp. 2d 1098.

96. Legal scholar Catherine Fisk explains that, in the early twentieth century, as firms were establishing the notion of corporate authorship in courtrooms (typically based on the argument that a single human author was unnecessary and impracticable in collaborative work settings), they had to make the idea acceptable internally as well. Most companies "managed to substitute non–legally binding norms of internal attribution of creativity to individuals for the old practice of copyright ownership" and still maintained employee loyalty. As a result, employees increasingly "sought recognition as much as financial reward," and attribution "began to substitute for intellectual property (and the legal status of being the inventor or author) as the currency that would enable employees to advance their careers." Fisk, *Working Knowledge,* 220, 210.

97. David Vidal, "Superman's Creators Get Lifetime Pay," *New York Times,* December 24, 1975.

98. Andrew Veitch, "How Superartist Won the Dough," *The Guardian,* June 16, 1979.

99. Bradford W. Wright, *Comic Book Nation: The Transformation of Youth Culture in America* (Baltimore: Johns Hopkins University Press, 2003), 257–58.

100. Raphael and Spurgeon, *Stan Lee,* 203.

101. Phillip Gutis, "Turning Superheroes into Super Sales," *New York Times,* January 6, 1985. The article, a puff piece on Kahn, lauds these strategies.

102. Michael Z. Hobson to Marvel Creators, "The New Incentive Payment Plan," Memo, December 22, 1981, *jimshooter.com,* http://jimshooter.com/2011/12/surprising-sinnott-and-items-of.html/.

103. The 5 percent of the sixty-cent cover price was split among contributing creators so that, for example, the letterer would earn .5 percent, the writer 1.5 percent, the inker 1 percent, etc. Hobson to Marvel Creators, "New Incentive Plan."

104. Levitz, author's interview.

105. Warner Communications, Inc., *Annual Report,* 1981, 35, 97.

106. Gutis, "Turning Superheroes into Super Sales."

107. Hobson to Marvel Creators, "New Incentive Plan."

108. Levitz, author's interview.

109. Bill Seiter and Ellen Seiter, *The Creative Artist's Legal Guide: Copyright, Trademark and Contracts in Film and Digital Media Production* (New Haven, CT: Yale University Press, 2012), 55.

110. Goldstein, *Copyright's Highway,* 136–157.

111. Ian Gordon, "Comics, Creators, and Copyright: On the Ownership of Serial Narratives by Multiple Authors," in *A Companion to Media Authorship,* ed. Jonathan Gray and Derek Johnson (Malden, MA: Wiley-Blackwell, 2013), 224.

112. Les Daniels, *Superman,* 103. Daniels tells the long history of Superman's evolution and all those involved. It was Weisinger who feared that Superman would become a fad.

113. Catherine L. Fisk, "Knowledge Work: New Metaphors for the New Economy," *Chicago Kent Law Review* 80 (2005): 864–65.

114. Aufderheide and Jaszi, *Reclaiming Fair Use,* 35–36.

115. Seiter and Seiter, *The Creative Artist's Legal Guide,* 30–31.

116. *Siegel and Siegel,* 542 F. Supp. 2d 1098.

117. *Siegel and Siegel.*

118. Michael Cieply and Brooke Barnes, "Warner Brothers Sues Superman Lawyer," *New York Times,* May 15, 2010.

119. DC Comics v. Pacific Pictures, CV 10–3633 ODW (C.D. Cal. West. Div. 2012).

120. *Siegel and Siegel,* 542 F. Supp. 2d 1098. The publisher's aggressive and careful maintenance of the character's many trademarks, which, unlike a copyright, are based more on use than on origin, also guarantees certain facets of Superman to DC, not Siegel and Shuster.

121. As of 2018, the legal battle might be at an end. The heirs of both Siegel and Shuster had separately, prior to the 2008 victory, decided to sell back to DC all of their rights to Superman and all related characters for undisclosed, but presumably large, sums of money. In the case of Shuster's claims, a 1992 deal between his surviving sister and DC had closed the matter, and in the case of Siegel's heirs, a 2001 deal struck by their lawyer had relinquished, finally, any remaining claims to the character. In the years that followed, individual family members unhappy with the terms they had struck had brought the matters back to court, resulting in the temporary return of Superman to the Siegel family. Nonetheless, subsequent decisions made in 2012 and 2013 reversed that victory and reinforced the earlier sale agreements, conceivably (but by no means definitively putting an end to the sixty-five-year legal fight. Laura Siegel Larson v. Warner Bros. Entertainment, No. 2013 US. Dist. LEXIS 55949 (Central District of California, April 18, 2013); *DC Comics,* CV 10–3633 ODW; Brooks Barnes, "Warner Brothers Wins in Superman Case," *New York Times,* January 12, 2013; "Judge: Superboy Flies for DC Comics," *Variety,* April 16, 2013.

122. Ted Johnson, "Caped Fear: Will Copyright Crunch Put Squeeze on Hollywood Franchises?," *Variety,* July 12, 2010.

123. Raphael and Spurgeon, *Stan Lee,* 214–16.

124. Marvel Worldwide Inc. v. Kirby, 777 F. Supp. 2d 720 (2nd Cir. 2011); Michael Hill, "The Marvel Method According to Jack Kirby," Jack Kirby Museum, *The Kirby Effect* (blog), July 25, 2015, http://kirbymuseum.org/blogs /effect/2015/07/25/according-to-kirby-1/.

125. An initial decision was made in July of 2011, and it was upheld on appeal on August 8, 2013. At first, Kirby's heirs had promised to continue the appeal process and bring the case to the Supreme Court, but in September 2014, they withdrew their petition. As of 2018, no further action has been taken. Marvel Worldwide Inc. v. Kirby, 777 F. Supp. 2d 720 (2nd Cir. 2011); Chad Bray, "Galactic Battle: Marvel Wins Legal Decision against Artist's Children," *Wall Street Journal,* August 9, 2013.

126. For examples, see Geoff Boucher, "Hero Complex: A Credit to His Name," *Los Angeles Times,* September 27, 2009, Calendar; Kevin Melrose, "Stan Lee Questioned on Lack of Jack Kirby Credit on Avengers Film," *CBR.com,* April 25, 2012, www.cbr.com/stan-lee-questioned-on-lack-of-jack-kirby-credit-on-avengers-film/; Jason McAnelly, "Jack Kirby 'Avengers' Credit Controversy Finally Over?," *Nerd Bastards,* April 25, 2012, http://nerdbastards.com/2012/04/25/jack-kirby-avengers-credit-controversy-finally-over/; David Brothers, "The Ethical Rot Behind 'Before Watchmen' & 'The Avengers,'" *Comics Alliance* (web magazine), April 18, 2012, www.comicsalliance.com/2012/04/18/creator-rights-before-watchmen-avengers-moore-kirby/.

127. Ryan Faughnder, "Comic Book Artist's Heirs Settle Marvel Dispute," *Los Angeles Times,* September 27, 2014, Business.

128. Seiter and Seiter, *Creative Artist's Legal Guide,* 6.

129. For an excellent example, see Christopher Sharrett, "Batman and the Twilight of the Idols: An Interview with Frank Miller," in *The Many Lives of the Batman: Critical Approaches to a Superhero and His Media,* ed. Roberta Pearson and William Uricchio (New York: Routledge, 1991).

130. Charles Hatfield, *Alternative Comics: An Emerging Literature* (Jackson: University Press of Mississippi, 2005), 26.

131. Benton, *Comic Book in America,* 86.

132. Jay Allen Sanford, "Two Men and Their Comic Books: The Birth of Pacific Comics," *San Diego Reader,* August 19, 2004, www.sandiegoreader.com/news/2004/aug/19/two-men-and-their-comic-books/.

133. Notable publishers that have folded include Eclipse, Pacific, Capital City, and Star*Reach. Companies like Fantagraphics and Top Shelf have a history of financial trouble, while others like Valiant, Kitchen Sink, and Mirage struggled until they were bought out by larger companies.

134. Duncan and Smith, *Power of Comics,* 121.

135. Marvel launched the creator-owned imprint Epic in 1982 and kept it running through 1996. DC did the same with Piranha from 1989 to 1994, and Dark Horse had Legend from 1994 to 1998. DC had more success with Vertigo, which it launched under Karen Berger a year after Image started, and with Jim Lee's Wildstorm (previously part of Image). Marvel has been using the Icon imprint since 2004 for its creator-owned titles, and in 2017, Dark Horse launched another creator-owned imprint, Berger Books, also under Karen Berger.

136. Raphael and Spurgeon, *Stan Lee,* 238; Matthew McAllister, "Ownership Concentration in the US Comic Book Industry," in *Comics and Ideology,* ed. Matthew McAllister, Edward Sewell, and Ian Gordon (New York: Peter Lang, 2001), 22–23.

137. Ray Mescallado, "Fanboi Politik: Creator's Rights in the Mainstream," *Comics Journal,* August 1999.

138. Tom DiChristopher, "Comic Book Publishers Thrive in the Industry," *CNBC,* January 24, 2016, www.cnbc.com/2016/01/24/comic-book-publishers-thrive-in-the-industry.html; Gregory Schmidt, "Indie Comic Book Publishers Make Moves toward TV and Film," *New York Times,* October 4, 2015, Media.

139. McAllister, "Ownership Concentration in the US Comic Book Industry," 22–23; Mescallado, "Fanboi Politik."

140. Henry Jenkins, "The Guiding Spirit and the Powers That Be: A Response to Suzanne Scott," in *The Participatory Cultures Handbook,* ed. Aaron Delwiche and Jennifer Jacobs Henderson (New York: Routledge, 2013), 53–58.

141. John Caldwell, *Production Culture: Industrial Reflexivity and Critical Practice in Film and Television* (Durham, NC: Duke University Press, 2008), 234.

142. Michel Foucault, "What Is an Author?," in *The Foucault Reader,* ed. Paul Rabinow (New York: Pantheon Books, 1984), 101–20.

143. Henry Jenkins, Sam Ford, and Joshua Green, *Spreadable Media: Creating Value and Meaning in a Networked Culture* (New York: NYU Press, 2018), chap. 4.

144. Jonathan Gray, *Show Sold Separately: Promos, Spoilers, and Other Media Paratexts* (New York: NYU Press, 2010), 82.

145. Eric Hoyt, "Writer in the Hole: *Desny v. Wilder,* Copyright Law, and the Battle over Ideas," *Cinema Journal* 50, no. 2 (2011): 39.

146. Jaszi, "On the Author Effect," 38.

147. Jyotsna Kapur, "New Economy / Old Labor: Creativity, Flatness, and Other Neo-Liberal Myths," in *Knowledge Workers in the Information Society,* ed. Catherine McKercher and Vincent Mosco (Lanham, MD: Rowman and Littlefield, 2007), 164.

148. Fisk, "Knowledge Work," 867.

149. Fisk, 844.

150. Caldwell, *Production Culture,* 58.

4. TALES OF THE COMIC BOOK CULT

1. Ann Hornaday, "Everywhere You Look, Crypt and More Crypt," *New York Times,* September 4, 1994, Arts.

2. Tom Shales, "Chills and Chuckles: HBO's New Season of 'Crypt' Creeps," *Washington Post,* June 19, 1991.

3. Bill Carter, "HBO Finds Hits the Networks Miss," *New York Times,* July 15, 1991, Media Business; Jack Mathews, "'Crypt' Disinterred for HBO," *Los Angeles Times,* June 8, 1989.

4. Hornaday, "Everywhere You Look."

5. Grant Geissmann, *Foul Play! The Art and Artists of the 1950s EC Comics* (New York: Harper Design International, 2005), 16–17.

6. Digby Diehl, *Tales from the Crypt: The Official Archives* (New York: St. Martin's Press, 1996), 145.

7. Mike Benton, *The Comic Book in America: An Illustrated History* (Dallas: Taylor, 1993), 167–69, 181–83.

8. Trina Robbins, *From Girls to Grrrlz: A History of Female Comics from Teens to Zines* (San Francisco: Chronicle Books, 1999), 67–70.

9. In 1962, Dell, the industry's largest publisher, ended its relationship with Western Printing, which had been publishing its comics for more than twenty years and also controlled the licenses for many of Dell's most popular titles, including *Walt Disney Comics* and *Bugs Bunny.* Western subsequently decided to publish these titles under its own new imprint, Gold Key, which instantly became a major industry player. Benton, *Comic Book in America,* 110, 125–26.

10. John Jackson Miller, "Comic Book Sales Figures for 1969," Comichron, accessed June 23, 2018, www.comichron.com/yearlycomicssales/postaldata/1969 .html.

11. Jean-Paul Gabilliet, *Of Comics and Men: A Cultural History of American Comic Books,* trans. Bart Beaty and Nick Nguyen (Jackson: University Press of Mississippi, 2009), 73; Paul Lopes, *Demanding Respect: The Evolution of the American Comic Book* (Philadelphia: Temple University Press, 2009), 72; Randy Duncan and Matthew J. Smith, *The Power of Comics: History, Form and Culture* (New York: Continuum, 2009), 93.

12. J. Howard Rutledge and Peter Bart, "Comic Books: Slight Sales Recovery Leaves Volume below Pre-Clean-Up Days," *Wall Street Journal,* October 5, 1955; Peter Bart, "Some Comic Book Men Pine for Sin, Sex as Their Sales Skid," *Wall Street Journal,* February 25, 1959.

13. Four Star Comics Corp v. Kable News Company, 224 F. Supp. 108 (US Southern District of New York 1963).

14. Gabilliet, *Of Comics and Men,* 76, 141; Lopes, *Demanding Respect,* 72; Duncan and Smith, *Power of Comics,* 93.

15. Roger Sabin, *Adult Comics: An Introduction* (New York: Routledge, 1993), 172; John B. Wood, "Old Comic Book Store Is No Laughing Matter," *Boston Globe,* October 26, 1975.

16. Gabilliet, *Of Comics and Men,* 636.

17. Lopes, *Demanding Respect,* 80.

18. Charles Hatfield, *Alternative Comics: An Emerging Literature* (Jackson: University Press of Mississippi, 2005), ix.

19. Lopes, *Demanding Respect,* 75.

20. Hatfield, *Alternative Comics,* ix, 8.

21. Jonas Mekas, "A Call for a New Generation of Film-Makers," in *Film Culture Reader,* ed. P. Adams Sitney (New York: Praeger, 1970), 74; Jonas Mekas, "Notes on the New American Cinema 1962," in *Film Culture Reader,* ed. P. Adams Sitney (New York: Praeger, 1970), 102.

22. Hatfield, *Alternative Comics,* 18–20.

23. Robbins, *From Girls to Grrrlz,* 85.

24. Gabilliet, *Of Comics and Men,* 82; Sabin, *Adult Comics,* 174.

25. Bill Schelly, *Founders of Comic Fandom* (Jefferson, NC: McFarland, 2010), 41–48.

26. Duncan and Smith, *Power of Comics,* 68–69.

27. Hatfield, *Alternative Comics,* 26.

28. In a desperate attempt to compete and recapture shelf space, DC and Marvel brought back one of the most disastrous practices of the fifties: overproduction. For three years, they saturated the market, only to reverse direction in 1978 and cancel nearly a third of their titles in what became known as the "DC Implosion." The following year, Marvel finally entered the direct market. Meanwhile, legal action against Seuling opened his new method of distribution up to more companies, creating a boom in comic book shops, which grew in number from approximately seven hundred to three thousand in just three years. See Benton, *Comic Book in America,* 79–80; N. R. Kleinfield, "Superhe-

roes' Creators Wrangle," *New York Times*, October 13, 1979; Gabilliet, *Of Comics and Men*, 87; Lopes, *Demanding Respect*, 100.

29. Bradford W. Wright, *Comic Book Nation: The Transformation of Youth Culture in America* (Baltimore: Johns Hopkins University Press, 2003), 262; Benton, *Comic Book in America*, 85; Patrick Parsons, "Batman and His Audience: The Dialectic of Culture," in *The Many Lives of the Batman: Critical Approaches to a Superhero and His Media*, ed. Roberta Pearson and William Uricchio (New York: Routledge, 1991), 76.

30. By the end of the eighties, their combined unit sales accounted for approximately three-quarters of the direct market. Twenty-five years later, the situation has not changed a great deal. DC and Marvel account for approximately 65–70 percent of market share in specialty shops. Three minor publishers account for another 15–20 percent: Image, a creator-oriented publisher that has nonetheless benefited immensely from the transmedia success of its breakout title *The Walking Dead*, and Dark Horse and IDW, both of which specialize in licensed titles. See Patrick Reilly, "Superheroes Battle It Out in Comic Book Resurgence," *Crain's New York Business*, June 3, 1986; John Jackson Miller, "1991 Comic Book Sales Figures," *Comichron: The Comics Chronicles* (blog), accessed June 7, 2018, www.comichron.com/monthlycomicssales/1991.html; "Publisher Market Shares: August 2018," Industry Statistics, *Diamond Comic Distributors, Inc.*, accessed September 19, 2018, www.diamondcomics.com/Home/1/1/3/237.

31. Reilly, "Superheroes Battle It Out."

32. Chuck Rozanski, "The Vicious Downward Spiral of the 1990's," Tales from the Database (blog), *Mile High Comics*, 2002, www.milehighcomics.com /tales/cbg36.html; Parsons, "Batman and His Audience," 77.

33. Lopes, *Demanding Respect*, 110; Benton, *Comic Book in America*, 90.

34. Rozanski, "Vicious Downward Spiral"; Benton, *Comic Book in America*, 86; Duncan and Smith, *Power of Comics*, 76–77, 95.

35. Reilly, "Superheroes Battle It Out."

36. Paul Levitz, author's interview, Skype, July 13, 2017.

37. Parsons, "Batman and His Audience," 77.

38. Will Brooker, *Batman Unmasked: Analyzing a Cultural Icon* (Continuum, 2001), 260.

39. Mark Jancovich, "A Real Shocker: Authenticity, Genre, and the Struggle for Cultural Distinction," *Continuum* 14, no. 1 (April 2000): 33.

40. Decades later, this exclusion continued to be a problem. Suzanne Scott has noted that shops are "reminiscent of a secret clubhouse with policed social barriers of entry" for female readers in particular. Suzanne Scott, "Fangirls in Refrigerators: The Politics of (In)visibility in Comic Book Culture," *Transformative Works and Cultures* 13 (2013), https://doi.org/10.3983/twc.v13i0 .460; Robbins, *From Girls to Grrrlz*, 7.

41. According to Trina Robbins, in 1974, there were just two female artists left in mainstream comics. Trina Robbins, *The Great Women Cartoonists* (New York: Watson-Guptill Publications, 2001), 102.

42. Barbara Saltzman, "Superman: From Phone Booth to Sound Booth," *Los Angeles Times*, January 26, 1975.

43. Robert Zintl, "Pow! Bam! Sock! Superwomen Muscle On In," *Chicago Tribune*, February 26, 1978.

44. For general thoughts on this topic, see Joan Hilty, "Wonder Girl's Head-Sized Breasts Illustrate the Sexism Problem in Comics," *The Guardian*, May 3, 2014, www.theguardian.com/commentisfree/2014/may/03/wonder-girl-breasts-sexism-comics; Nick Hanover, "A Chorus of Silence: On the Impossibility of Reporting on Chronic Abusers in Comics," *Loser City*, September 8, 2015, http://loser-city.com/features/a-chorus-of-silence-on-the-impossibility-of-reporting-on-chronic-abusers-in-comics. After Schwartz's death, *The Comics Journal* published claims from three named women. The piece has since been scrubbed from the internet. Katherine Keller, "It's Not Love. It's Not Flirting. It's Not Flattering.," *Sequential Tart*, February 2006, www.sequentialtart.com/archive/feb06/art_0206_6.shtml; Heidi MacDonald, "How a Toxic History of Harassment Has Damaged the Comics Industry," *The Beat*, October 1, 2015, www.comicsbeat.com/how-a-toxic-history-of-harassment-has-damaged-the-comics-industry/. Over the last decade, a spate of sexual harassment allegations have been made, and in response to a handful of these, men have come forward to apologize. For a thorough accounting, see Aria Baci, "A Brief Timeline of Harassment and Sexual Assault in the Comics Industry," *The Mary Sue*, November 29, 2017, www.themarysue.com/comics-assault-timeline/. Notably, it took until the 2017 Harvey Weinstein scandal and the #MeToo Movement for DC Comics to fire editor Eddie Berganza in response to the *many* formal and public allegations against him. Jessica Testa and Tyler Kingkade, "DC Comics Fires Longtime Editor Following Sexual Harassment Claims," *BuzzFeed News*, November 11, 2017, www.buzzfeed.com/tylerkingkade/dc-comics-suspends-editor-following-buzzfeed-news-report.

45. Darla Miller, "Heroines of the New Comics Have Character," *Chicago Tribune*, April 22, 1979.

46. Angela McRobbie and Jenny Garber, "Girls and Subculture," in Angela McRobbie, *Feminism and Youth Culture* (Boston: Unwin Hyman, 1991), 1–8.

47. Joanne Hollows, "The Masculinity of Cult," in *Defining Cult Movies: The Cultural Politics of Oppositional Tastes* (Manchester, UK: Manchester University, 2003), 35; Dick Hebdige, *Subculture: The Meaning of Style* (London: Routledge, 1979).

48. Hollows, "Masculinity of Cult," 36.

49. Angela McRobbie, "Settling Accounts with Subcultures: A Feminist Critique," *Screen Education* 39 (Spring 1980): 20.

50. McRobbie and Garber, "Girls and Subculture," 3.

51. Scott, "Fangirls in Refrigerators," sec. 1.4.

52. See, for example, the still-running webzine *Sequential Tart*, www.sequentialtart.com/; the defunct *Friends of Lulu*, https://friendsoflulu.wordpress.com/about/; and the kick-starter publication *My So-Called Secret Identity*, www.mysocalledsecretidentity.com/backstory.

53. Shawna Kidman, "Women and Superheroes, by the Numbers," In *Media Res*, November 16, 2015, http://mediacommons.futureofthebook.org/imr/2015/11/16/women-and-superheroes-numbers.

54. DC became the object of much anger in 2011, after launching its "New 52" line with *fewer* female creators. Alison Flood, "DC Comics Promises to Hire More Women after Reader Backlash," *The Guardian*, August 1, 2011, Books, www.theguardian.com/books/2011/aug/01/dc-comics-women-writers-creators. In 2017, female representation within the industry's ranks and in the pages of comics remained dismal. Rich Johnston, "Gendercrunching February 2017: At DC and Marvel, Women Predominantly Write Female Characters," *Bleeding Cool*, May 2, 2017, www.bleedingcool.com/2017/05/02/gendercrunching-february-2017-at-dc-and-marvel-women-predominantly-write-female-characters/. Negative online chatter, whether or not it is representative of a majority of comic book fans, can sometimes make progress seem further away than ever. Adam White, "Female Marvel Comics Editor Harassed Online for Milkshake Selfie," *The Telegraph*, July 31, 2017, www.telegraph.co.uk/books/news/female-marvel-comics-editor-harassed-online-milkshake-selfie/.

55. Roberta Pearson and William Uricchio, "Notes from the Batcave: An Interview with Dennis O'Neil," in Pearson and Uricchio, eds., *Many Lives of the Batman*, 29; Wright, *Comic Book Nation*, 280.

56. Paul Levitz of DC, quoted in Wright, *Comic Book Nation*, 261.

57. Peter Bart, "Advertising: Superman Faces New Hurdles," *New York Times*, September 23, 1962.

58. Both of these developments date back to around 1970, the year of the first San Diego–hosted Comic-Con and the first edition of Bob Overstreet's price guide.

59. Duncan and Smith, *Power of Comics*, 19.

60. Hatfield, *Alternative Comics*, 24.

61. Pierre Bourdieu, *Distinction: A Social Critique of the Judgment of Taste*, trans. Richard Nice (Cambridge, MA: Harvard University Press, 1984), 56, 7.

62. Jason Mittell, *Complex TV: The Poetics of Contemporary Television Storytelling* (New York: NYU Press, 2015), 6–8.

63. Barbara Maltby, "What Do Movie Producers Do?," *American Scholar* 65, no. 1 (Winter 1996): 31–43; Douglas Gomery, "The New Hollywood: 1981–1999," in *Producing*, ed. Jon Lewis (New Brunswick, NJ: Rutgers University Press, 2016); Mary Reinholz, "Where the Boys Are," *Broadcasting & Cable* 130, no. 42 (October 9, 2000): 72–76; Alec Foege, "All the Young Dudes," *Mediaweek* 15, no. 31 (September 5, 2005): 16–20; Simon Houpt, "He Earns Little Money . . . So Why Do Advertisers Love Him?," *The Globe and Mail*, March 9, 2002.

64. Henry Allen, "Horror Comics from the '50s Are Alive!," *Washington Post*, September 24, 1972, Film; Chris Kaltenbach, "A Comic Book Kingdom: 'Up, Up and AWAYYYY,'" *The Sun*, December 4, 1983.

65. Anita Gold, "Pow! Awk! Shazam! Superman Flies Once Again," *Chicago Tribune*, February 25, 1973.

66. This reporting played a considerable role in the rise and fall of the speculator market in the early nineties. Gold, "Pow! Awk! Shazam!"; Wood, "Old Comic Book Store Is No Laughing Matter"; Kaltenbach, "Comic Book Kingdom"; Knight News Wire, "Comic Book Popularity Growing by Leaps and

Bounds!," *Hartford Courant,* December 10, 1978; Andrew Kreig, "Craving for Comics a Funny Business," *Hartford Courant,* September 22, 1975.

67. A comment like this one was typical: "Trivia is what the whole comic book boom is based on." Barbara Carlson, "To Him, the Comics Aren't Mickeymouse," *Hartford Courant,* February 17, 1973.

68. "Comic Books Profit by Rush to Legitimacy," *Los Angeles Times,* November 28, 1974. A similar assertion is made in Cynthia Dagnal, "A Socially Relevant Superman?," *Los Angeles Times,* September 3, 1976.

69. "Comic Books Profit by Rush to Legitimacy." A similar claim is made in Mark Gauvreau Judge, "Holy Censorship, Batman! Guess Who's Banning Comic Books," *Washington Post,* June 9, 1996.

70. "Comic Books Profit by Rush to Legitimacy"; Dagnal, "Socially Relevant Superman?" For others with a similar assessment of the social relevance strategy, see Wright, *Comic Book Nation,* 231–33; Lopes, *Demanding Respect,* 69–70; Gabilliet, *Of Comics and Men,* 75.

71. Bart Beaty, *Comics versus Art* (Toronto: University of Toronto Press, 2012), 128.

72. Beaty, 118–25. For examples of the mainstream press commenting on the sophistication of *Maus,* see Judge, "Holy Censorship, Batman!"; Desson Howe, "Comic Strips Bad Image Off," *Washington Post,* August 18, 1989.

73. Hatfield, *Alternative Comics,* xi.

74. Critics and historians have defined the "graphic novel" in a number of different ways, with some rejecting the term entirely. But for the purposes of this study, with its emphasis on distribution practices, this definition remains the most useful. Examples of graphic novels include Will Eisner's *A Contract with God* (1978), published by Baronet Books and considered by some to be the very first graphic novel, and also publications like *Arkham Asylum* (1989) by Grant Morrison and Dave McKean, published by DC. Since it was first published within floppy comics, *Maus* was technically a trade paperback. Similarly, Frank Miller's *Dark Knight Returns* (1986), which was initially published by DC in four floppy issues and later collected into a single bound volume, could also be considered a trade paperback. Also included in this latter category are many recent popular comic book arcs, like Ta-Nehisi Coates's 2016 run on *Black Panther,* collected into three bound volumes titled *A Nation under Our Feet* and released in 2016 and 2017.

75. Reilly, "Superheroes Battle It Out."

76. Diehl, *Tales from the Crypt,* 145.

77. Some of the more prominent fans include Bhob Stewart, Larry Stark, Larry Ivie, Ron Parker, Mike Vosburg, Jerry Weist, Roger Hill, Fred von Bernewitz, Grant Geissman, Russ Cochran, and Ian Ballantine. Schelly, *Founders of Comic Fandom,* 26, 36, 66, 83–86, 93, 125–26, 142, 148.

78. Beaty, *Comics versus Art.* Beaty points out the fandom's theoretical contributions (112–13) and notes that Spiegelman has written about EC often (117).

79. Diehl, *Tales from the Crypt,* 1996, 145; Beaty, *Comics versus Art,* 113.

80. John F. Brodsen, "Tempo: It's Alive! Comic Terror Is Back from the Crypt," *Chicago Tribune,* February 15, 1984, 5; Wood, "Old Comic Book Store Is No Laughing Matter"; Allen, "Horror Comics from the '50s Are Alive!"

81. Diehl, *Tales from the Crypt,* 166; Hornaday, "Everywhere You Look," *New York Times,* September 4, 1994, Arts.

82. Diehl, *Tales from the Crypt,* 166.

83. The project began with prolific director/producer Walter Hill and his partner David Giler, who got Joel Silver on board. Silver got the rights from publisher Bill Gaines for "very little" and soon brought on Richard Donner (who directed *Superman,* the first modern superhero film) and Zemeckis (right off his *Back to the Future* success). Hornaday, "Everywhere You Look"; Diehl, *Tales from the Crypt,* 161–65.

84. Jack Mathews, "'Crypt' Disinterred for HBO," *Los Angeles Times,* June 8, 1989.

85. Paul DiMaggio, "Cultural Entrepreneurship in Nineteenth-Century Boston," *Media, Culture & Society* 4, no. 1 (1982): 33–50.

86. Maltby, "What Do Movie Producers Do?," 34.

87. Known as "the boy wonder" in the 1930s, Irving Thalberg began overseeing production at Universal when he was just 20 years old. When he joined MGM as the head of production in 1925, he was only 26. Darryl Zanuck quit as production chief at Warner Bros. to found 20th Century Pictures in 1933, when he was only 31. Just two years later, a 31-year-old David Selznick, having had a string of successes at RKO, struck out on his own with Selznick International Pictures. Even Lew Wasserman, the last of the early moguls, was still in his early 30s when MCA first became a major player in Hollywood deal-making of the mid-1940s. If anything, rising Hollywood power producers of the 1980s were *older* than many of their predecessors.

88. Throughout the 1970s and 1980s, the Financial Interest and Syndication (Fin-Syn) Rules prevented broadcast networks from owning an interest in their own prime-time programming or from collecting revenue from syndication. This further exaggerated a need for massive first-run ratings. In the 1980s, the growth of cable led to a decline in audiences, and a more lax antitrust approach from the Department of Justice led to an increasing number of media mergers. Both of these developments, along with the final elimination of the Fin-Syn rules in 1993, contributed to a shift toward niche audiences.

89. Michael Newman and Elana Levine, *Legitimating Television: Media Convergence and Cultural Status* (New York: Routledge, 2012), 29.

90. Newman and Levine, 29.

91. Michael Curtin and Jane Shattuc, *The American Television Industry* (New York: British Film Institute, 2009), 38; Michele Hilmes, *Only Connect: A Cultural History of Broadcasting in the United States,* 2nd ed. (Belmont, CA: Cengage Learning, 2007), 204; Lynn Spigel, *Welcome to the Dreamhouse* (Durham, NC: Duke University Press, 2001), 35.

92. Avi Santo, "Para-Television and Discourses of Distinction: The Culture of Production at HBO," in *It's Not TV: Watching HBO in the Post-Television Era,* ed. Marc Leverette, Brian Ott, and Cara Louise Buckley (New York: Routledge, 2008), 33.

93. Mark Alvey, "Too Many Kids and Old Ladies: Quality Demographics and 1960s US Television," in *Television: The Critical View,* ed. Horace Newcomb, 7th ed. (New York: Oxford University Press, 2007), 18.

94. Houpt, "He Earns Little Money . . . So Why Do Advertisers Love Him?";
Stuart Miller, "Television: Buyers Give TV Numbers a Different Face," *Variety*,
July 8, 1991.

95. See for example: Fred Rothenberg, "Soap Sponsors: Long in the Tooth,"
Los Angeles Times, June 18, 1982, Part VI; "ABC-TV Demos Appear Improving despite Household Ratings Slump," *Variety*, October 22, 1986, Radio-Television; Stuart Miller, "Television: Buyers Give TV Numbers a Different Face,"
Variety, July 8, 1991.

96. Morrie Gelman, "Radio-Television: Meters & VCRs Shaping P'time
Ploys," *Variety*, May 20, 1987.

97. Terry Lefton, "Ups and Downs: 18–49 Men," *Brandweek* 40, no. 19
(May 10, 1999): S12–14; Kipp Cheng, "Setting Their Sites on Generation 'Y,'"
Adweek, August 9, 1999. In response to the shift, networks like ESPN, Fox,
UPN, and Comedy Central moved more and more aggressively into a wider
variety of young male-targeted formats. Reinholz, "Where the Boys Are," 76;
Foege, "All the Young Dudes."

98. Carol Vinzant, "Some Couch Potatoes Are More Equal Than Others:
The Dollars and Nonsense of TV Advertising," *On the Issues* 6, no. 3 (July 31,
1997): 32; Houpt, "He Earns Little Money"; Reinholz, "Where the Boys Are."

99. Jennifer Holt, *Empires of Entertainment: Media Industries and the Politics of Deregulation, 1980–1996* (New Brunswick, NJ: Rutgers University
Press, 2011), 46.

100. Holt, 2. The FCC began regulating cable in the late sixties, restricting
content on new networks like HBO. There was, for example, a 1972 ruling, advocated for by the National Association of Broadcasters, which prevented cable
from showing sports events that had aired on commercial television. For more,
see George Mair, *Inside HBO: The Billion Dollar War Between HBO, Hollywood, and the Home Video Revolution* (New York: Dodd, Mead, 1988), 15–28;
William Kunz, *Culture Conglomerates: Consolidation in the Motion Picture and
Television Industries* (Lanham, MD: Rowman and Littlefield, 2007), 168.

101. Holt, *Empires of Entertainment*, 41, 67.

102. Home Box Office, Inc. v. FCC, 567 F.2d 9 (D.C. Cir. 1977); Deborah
Jaramillo, "The Family Racket: AOL Time Warner, HBO, The Sopranos, and
the Construction of a Quality Brand," *Journal of Communication Inquiry* 26,
no. 1 (January 2002): 59–75; Holt, *Empires of Entertainment*, 22–27.

103. In 1979, the Department of Justice (DOJ) refused to investigate HBO
for monopolistic practices and instead, in a 1981 decision, prevented Paramount, Universal, Fox, and Columbia from developing their own movie channel Premiere. This ruling was based on the notion that HBO should benefit from
its bold entrepreneurship, and that the studios would be introducing complete
vertical integration into an industry that did not currently have it. Of course,
Warner Communications Inc. was already fully integrated, as was Time. In
1983, the DOJ again used antitrust law to limit studio involvement in a proposed merger between Showtime and The Movie Channel. Holt, *Empires of
Entertainment*, 26–43; Mair, *Inside HBO*, 47–49.

104. The films also received outside financing from Wall Street and benefited
from very deep corporate pockets, including those of Coca-Cola, which

owned Columbia. Mair, *Inside HBO,* 44–73; Holt, *Empires of Entertainment,* 47–53.

105. The quote comes from MPAA president Jack Valenti. Mair, *Inside HBO,* 13, 79; Penny Pagano, "Cable TV Official Sees 1987 as Watershed Year," *Los Angeles Times,* January 20, 1987; Jane Hall, "HBO Chief Fuchs Sees Diversity as Key to the Future Cable," *Los Angeles Times,* November 4, 1992, Calendar.

106. Albert Scardino, "Problems Beset Time-Warner Talks," *New York Times,* March 6, 1989.

107. John McMurria, "Long-Format TV: Globalization and Network Branding in a Multi-Channel Era," in *Quality Popular Television,* ed. Mark Jancovich and James Lyons (London: BFI, 2003), 65–87; Patrick Parsons and Robert Frieden, *The Cable and Satellite Television Industries* (Boston: Allyn and Bacon, 1998), 196–98.

108. In fact, overall domestic household ratings at HBO declined in the five years leading up to the merger and would continue to do so over the next two decades. It was a problem that seemed not to hamper growth in the slightest. Instead, HBO could rely not only on subscription rates (which did not necessarily parallel ratings), but also on film production, ancillary revenue, and international growth. Bill Gorman, "Where Did Primetime Broadcast Audiences Go?," Entertainment, *TV by the Numbers* (blog), April 12, 2010, http://tvbythenumbers .zap2it.com/2010/04/12/where-did-the-primetime-broadcast-tv-audience-go /47976/.

109. Ann Hornaday, "Programming for Reputation. And Profits.," *New York Times,* November 7, 1993, Arts & Leisure; Hall, "HBO Chief Fuchs." In the long term, a more aggressive pursuit of original programming also helped domestic subscriber growth. By the early 2000s, numbers had reached a plateau of around twenty-eight million (up from twenty million a decade prior), and that is, more or less, where it remains in 2018. Gary Edgerton and Jeffrey P. Jones, "HBO's Ongoing Legacy," in *The Essential HBO Reader,* ed. Gary Edgerton and Jeffrey P. Jones (Lexington: University Press of Kentucky, 2008), 317.

110. Christopher Anderson, "Drama Overview: Producing the Aristocracy of Culture in American Television," in *The Essential HBO Reader,* ed. Gary Edgerton and Jeffrey P. Jones (Lexington: University Press of Kentucky, 2008), 30–33; Gary Edgerton, "Introduction: A Brief History of HBO," in *Essential HBO Reader,* ed. Edgerton and Jones, 1–20; RB, "Cable Special Report: Original Cable Programming—HBO," *Broadcasting & Cable,* February 19, 1996.

111. For financial success, see Justin Bachman, "HBO Finally Reveals Profit Numbers. Take That, Netflix," *Bloomberg Business Week,* February 5, 2014. For critical praise, see Janet McCabe and Kim Akass, "It's Not TV, It's HBO's Original Programming: Producing Quality TV," in *It's Not TV: Watching HBO in the Post-Television Era,* ed. Marc Leverette, Brian Ott, and Cara Louise Buckley (New York: Routledge, 2008), 92; Anderson, "Drama Overview," 24.

112. Hall, "HBO Chief Fuchs."

113. Scott Williams, "HBO's Horror Anthology Keeps Its Macabre Tone," *Washington Post,* July 21, 1991.

114. Mathews, "'Crypt' Disinterred for HBO."

115. Tom Shales, "TV Preview: Hauntingly Familiar HBO's New 'Crypt,'" *Washington Post,* June 10, 1989, Style; Chris Willman, "Another Batch of 'Tales from the Crypt' on HBO," *Los Angeles Times,* April 21, 1990, TV Reviews; Williams, "HBO's Horror Anthology."

116. Shales, "TV Preview"; Chris Willman, "Crypt Tales Subtle as a Sledgehammer," *Los Angeles Times,* June 10, 1989; Rick Kogan, "Frightless: HBO's Tales from the Crypt' Are More Stereotyped Than Scary," *Chicago Tribune,* June 9, 1989.

117. Willman, "Another Batch of 'Tales from the Crypt' on HBO"; Willman, "Crypt Tales Subtle as a Sledgehammer."

118. Bill Carter, "HBO Finds Hits the Networks Miss," *New York Times,* July 15, 1991, Media Business.

119. Jeffrey Sconce has described similar reading practices in relation to trash cinema, where a "calculated negation and refusal" of more sophisticated fare suggests that the politics of taste and social hierarchies are "more complex than a simple high-brow/low-brow split." Jeffrey Sconce, "Trashing the Academy: Taste, Excess, and an Emerging Politics of Cinematic Style," *Screen* 36, no. 4 (1995): 372.

120. Sarah Cardwell, "Is Quality Television Any Good? Generic Distinctions, Evaluations and the Troubling Matter of Critical Judgment," in *Quality TV: Contemporary American Television and Beyond,* ed. Janet McCabe and Kim Akass (London: I. B. Tauris, 2007), 25–26.

121. John J. O'Connor, "A Summer Cycle of Horror Shows on HBO," *New York Times,* June 15, 1989; Kogan, "Frightless."

122. Diehl, *Tales from the Crypt,* 169, 180.

123. Diehl, 176.

124. Diehl, 180.

125. Daniel Cerone, "Nightmarish 'Tales' Turns Into a Director's Dream," *Los Angeles Times,* June 3, 1990, Home edition, Television; Daniel Cerone, "Toned-Down 'Tales from Crypt' Starts on Fox Tonight:," *Los Angeles Times,* January 22, 1994, Calendar; Mathews, "'Crypt' Disinterred for HBO"; Hornaday, "Everywhere You Look."

126. Willman, "Crypt Tales Subtle as a Sledgehammer"; Shales, "TV Preview"; Kogan, "Frightless."

127. Willman, "Another Batch of 'Tales from the Crypt' on HBO"; Williams, "HBO's Horror Anthology"; John J. O'Connor, "Winning His Heart, Not to Mention His Gallbladder," *New York Times,* June 26, 1992, Late edition; Van Gordon Sauter, "Tales from the Crypt," *Variety,* June 22, 1992.

128. Howard Rosenberg, author's interview, July 3, 2013.

129. Anderson, "Drama Overview," 28.

130. Rosenberg, author's interview.

131. Anderson, "Drama Overview," 38.

132. Rosenberg, author's interview.

133. Nancy Mills, "Cable Beckons the A-Team Box-Office Giants," *Los Angeles Times,* May 26, 1991, Home edition, Calendar.

134. Anderson, "Drama Overview," 34–38.

135. Willman, "Another Batch of 'Tales from the Crypt' on HBO."

136. O'Connor, "Winning His Heart"; Sauter, "Tales from the Crypt."

137. Tone, "Tales from the Crypt," *Variety,* June 17, 1991, 72.

138. Williams, "HBO's Horror Anthology."

139. Sauter, "Tales from the Crypt"; Tom Shales, "Chills and Chuckles: HBO's New Season of 'Crypt' Creeps," *Washington Post,* June 19, 1991.

140. Matt Roush, "Contrasting HBO Offerings Showcase Beau Bridges," *USA Today,* June 14, 1991, Life, 3D; Matt Roush, "Crypt Opens with Trademark Creaks and Chills," *USA Today,* September 30, 1993, Life, 3D.

141. McCabe and Akass, "It's Not TV."

142. Jaramillo, "Family Racket," 585.

143. Angela McRobbie, "Settling Accounts with Subcultures: A Feminist Critique," *Screen Education* 39 (Spring 1980): 37–49; Joanne Hollows, "The Masculinity of Cult."

144. Bambi Haggins and Amanda Lotz, "Comedy Overview: At Home on the Cutting Edge," in *The Essential HBO Reader,* ed. Gary Edgerton and Jeffrey P. Jones (Lexington: University Press of Kentucky, 2008), 163.

145. See for example, Michael Sragow, "The Great Migration," *Film Comment,* May 2012.

146. Alvey, "Too Many Kids," 31.

147. Mark Jancovich and Nathan Hunt, "The Mainstream, Distinction, and Cult TV," in *Cult Television,* ed. Sara Gwenllian-Jones and Roberta E. Pearson (Minneapolis: University of Minnesota Press, 2004), 28.

148. Hollows, "The Masculinity of Cult," 49.

149. From the earliest days of comic book criticism in the late 1950s, writers like Larry Stark and Bhob Stewart were determined to show that comics were "a valid art form" deserving of "ongoing critical discussion." This impulse remained strong for decades, as foundational comics scholars like Scott McCloud, Thomas Inge, and Will Eisner worked to establish the medium's artistic pedigree by tracing its history through ancient and medieval Western artistic traditions, associating it with artists like Max Ernst and Monet, and criticizing the lack of "serious intellectual review" around it. See Fred von Bernewitz and Grant Geissman, *Tales of Terror! The EC Companion* (Seattle: Fantagraphics Books, 2000); Scott McCloud, *Understanding Comics: The Invisible Art* (New York: William Morrow, 1994), 18–20; M. Thomas Inge, *Comics as Culture* (Jackson: University Press of Mississippi, 1990); Will Eisner, *Comics and Sequential Art: Principles and Practices from the Legendary Cartoonist* (New York: W. W. Norton, 2008), xi. This desire for status has been so prevalent that more recently, scholars who nonetheless lament comics' continued status as a "devalued popular object" within academia recommend that we stop working so hard to legitimize it. Greg Smith, "It Ain't Easy Studying Comics," *Cinema Journal,* In Focus: Comics Studies Fifty Years after Film Studies, 50, no. 3 (Spring 2011): 111; Greg Smith, "Surveying the World of Contemporary Comics Scholarship: A Conversation," *Cinema Journal* 50, no. 3 (Spring 2011): 139; Angela Ndalianis, "Why Study Comics," *Cinema Journal* 50, no. 3 (Spring 2011): 114.

150. Jeffrey A. Brown, "Comic Book Fandom and Cultural Capital," *Journal of Popular Culture* 30, no. 4 (1997): 28–29.

151. See, for example, Shawn O'Rourke, "A Brief Historiography of the Age of Marginalization," in *Ages of Heroes, Eras of Men: Superheroes and the American Experience,* ed. Julian C. Chambliss, William Svitavsky, and Thomas Donaldson (Newcastle, UK: Cambridge Scholars Publishing, 2013), 241–48.

152. John Tulloch, "'We're Only a Speck in the Ocean': The Fans as Powerless Elite," in *Science Fiction Audiences: Watching Star Trek and Doctor Who,* ed. John Tulloch and Henry Jenkins (London: Routledge, 1995), 143–67; Beaty, *Comics versus Art,* 102.

153. Dwight MacDonald, "A Theory of Mass Culture," in *Mass Culture: The Popular Arts in America,* ed. Bernard Rosenberg and David Manning White (Glencoe, IL: Free Press, 1957), 70.

154. Clement Greenberg, "Avant-Garde and Kitsch," *Partisan Review* 6, no. 5 (1939). Republished in *Mass Culture: The Popular Arts in America,* Bernard Rosenberg and David Manning White (Glencoe, IL: Free Press, 1957), 106.

155. Clement Greenberg, "Steig's Cartoon," *The Nation,* March 3, 1945. Republished in Jeet Heer and Kent Worcester, eds., *Arguing Comics: Literary Masters on a Popular Medium* (Jackson: University Press of Mississippi, 2004), 40.

156. Fredric Jameson, "Postmodernism, or the Cultural Logic of Late Capitalism," *New Left Review* 1, no. 146 (August 1984): 65.

157. Lynn Spigel, *TV by Design: Modern Art and the Rise of Network Television* (Chicago: University of Chicago Press, 2008), 174, 8.

158. Henry Jenkins, *Convergence Culture: Where Old and New Media Collide* (New York: NYU Press, 2008), 23, 258.

159. Benton, *Comic Book in America,* 90.

160. John Jackson Miller, "Title Spotlights," Research Resource, *Comichron: The Comics Chronicles* (blog), accessed June 8, 2014, www.comichron .com/titlespotlights.html; Reilly, "Superheroes Battle It Out."

161. Anderson, "Drama Overview," 35.

162. Lawrence Levine, *Highbrow/Lowbrow: The Emergence of Cultural Hierarchy in America* (Cambridge, MA: Harvard University Press, 1988), 234.

163. Liam Burke, *The Comic Book Film Adaptation: Exploring Modern Hollywood's Leading Genre* (Jackson: University Press of Mississippi, 2015), 82–83; Glenn Gaslin, "The Disappearing Comic Book," *Los Angeles Times,* July 17, 2001, sec. E.

164. Geoff Boucher, "Spider-Man on Top," *Los Angeles Times,* March 25, 2001, Magazine edition.

165. Patrick Goldstein, "A Cause for Marvel: Rise of Films Based on Comic Books," *Los Angeles Times,* July 10, 2001, sec. F.

166. Gaslin, "Disappearing Comic Book."

5. MUTANT RISK

1. Joe Brown, "DC Comics: Kraang! Krakoom! Kraakk!," *Washington Post,* June 11, 1993; Michael Flagg, "No One Is Laughing Now," *Los Angeles Times,* April 12, 1993.

2. Tim Jones, "Secret of Superheroes' Vulnerability: Competition," *Chicago Tribune*, August 21, 1994.

3. Chuck Rozanski, "Perelman's Team Nearly Destroyed the Entire World of Comics" and "The Vicious Downward Spiral of the 1990's," Tales from the Database (blog), *Mile High Comics*, 2002, www.milehighcomics.com/tales; John Jackson Miller, "1994 Comic Book Sales Figures," *Comichron: The Comics Chronicles* (blog), www.comichron.com/monthlycomicssales/1994.html.

4. This *Wall Street Journal* article, written a year into the crash, provides a full assessment of Marvel's health, "still very bright," but does not mention publishing until the last paragraph. It notes, "In addition to trading cards, Marvel is also a publisher of comic books, a business that has also declined since the early 1990s. . . . The fall-off in sales, however, has been largely offset by an increase in related merchandising and licensing businesses." Jeffrey Trachtenberg, "Marvel Says Net in '94 to Be Lower Than Expected," *Wall Street Journal*, December 21, 1994.

5. Paul Levitz, author's interview, Skype, July 13, 2017.

6. Claudia Eller and James Bates, "Spider-Man Raises Bar for New Films," *Los Angeles Times*, May 7, 2002, sec. C.

7. Geoff Boucher, "Spider-Man on Top," *Los Angeles Times*, March 25, 2001, Magazine.

8. David Bloom, "Comic Capers Captivate Studios," *Variety*, June 24, 2002, Film.

9. "Movie Franchises and Brands Index," *Box Office Mojo*, accessed January 13, 2018, www.boxofficemojo.com/franchises/.

10. Newsarama Staff, "Upcoming Marvel and DC Movies: 2018–2022," *Newsarama*, April 23, 2018, www.newsarama.com/21815-the-new-full-comic-book-superhero-movie-schedule.html.

11. Liam Burke, *The Comic Book Film Adaptation: Exploring Modern Hollywood's Leading Genre* (Jackson: University Press of Mississippi, 2015), 78.

12. Jonathan Bing, "Showbiz Develops Deja View: Hollywood Raids Its Vaults," *Variety*, March 4, 2002; David Thompson, "The Spider Stratagem," *Sight and Sound*, April 2002, 24–26. See also Bloom, "Comic Capers Captivate Studios"; John Horn, "A Daredevil Leap for Minor Superhero," *Los Angeles Times*, February 10, 2003, sec. E; Patrick Goldstein, "The Big Picture: In Box-Office Game, It's All About the Franchise Players," *Los Angeles Times*, November 20, 2001, sec. F.

13. Bloom, "Comic Capers Captivate Studios"; Patrick Goldstein, "A Cause for Marvel: Rise of Films Based on Comic Books," *Los Angeles Times*, July 10, 2001, F. See also Boucher, "Spider-Man on Top"; Michael Hiltzik, "The Next Runaway Industry," *Los Angeles Times*, November 22, 2004, sec. C; Jonathan Bing, "F/X Turn New Page for Comic Books: Hollywood Looks to X-Men as Gauge of Future Adaptations," *Variety*, June 12, 2000, Film.

14. Thomas Schatz, "The New Hollywood," in *Film Theory Goes to the Movies*, ed. Jim Collins, Hilary Radner, and Ava Preacher Collins (New York: Routledge, 1993), 8–36; Giuseppe Richeri, "Global Film Market, Regional Problems," *Global Media and China* 1, no. 4 (December 1, 2016): 312–30.

15. Robert Welkos, "A Few New Tricks to the Hollywood Trade," *Los Angeles Times*, August 8, 1999; Bill Grantham and Toby Miller, "The Modern Entertainment Marketplace: 2000–Present," in *Producing*, ed. Jon Lewis (New Brunswick, NJ: Rutgers University Press, 2016); Levitz, author's interview.

16. Burke, *Comic Book Film Adaptation*, 34–46.

17. Critics have suggested that more complicated heroes like Batman were also an antidote to the anxieties of the time. Thompson, "Spider Stratagem"; Geoff Boucher, "Undressed for Success?," *Los Angeles Times*, August 28, 2001.

18. Sony had to pull a teaser that featured Spider-Man's web hanging precariously between the World Trade Center towers.

19. Chapter 1 provides a more detailed explanation of how and why comic books suited this moment of convergence in Hollywood.

20. "Film Reviews: Howard the Duck," *Variety*, August 6, 1986. Also see Gene Siskel's comments in "Flick of Week: 'Vagabond' One of Finest Films in Years," *Chicago Tribune*, August 8, 1986.

21. Janet Maslin, "Excess Baggage and the Movies," *New York Times*, June 7, 1987, sec. A; Vincent Canby, "The Stories behind the Oscars," *New York Times*, April 5, 1987, A; Aljean Harmetz, "That's Hollywood: The Strike That Never Was," *New York Times*, August 9, 1987, sec. A.

22. Lawrence Cohn, "Big-Budget Pics Bat .400 in 1986," *Variety*, January 15, 1987.

23. Michael Fleming, "Turtles, 'Toons and Toys 'R' In," *Variety*, April 18, 1990.

24. Sean Howe, "Avengers Assemble!," *Slate*, September 28, 2012, www .slate.com/articles/business/the_pivot/2012/09/marvel_comics_and_the_ movies_the_business_story_behind_the_avengers_.html; Devin Leonard, "Calling All Superheroes," *CNN Money*, May 23, 2007, https://money.cnn.com/ magazines/fortune/fortune_archive/2007/05/28/100034246/index.htm.

25. The quote comes from Uslan himself, who has told the story often in the press. Thom Sciacca, "Batman: The Comic Connection," *Variety*, June 28, 1989.

26. Geoff Boucher, "X-Men's Secret Power: Respect for the Marvel Comic's Serious Themes," *Los Angeles Times*, July 24, 2000.

27. Phillip Napoli, "Media Economics and the Study of Media Industries," in *Media Industries: History, Theory, and Method*, ed. Jennifer Holt and Alisa Perren (Malden, MA: Wiley-Blackwell, 2009), 167.

28. Todd Gitlin, *Inside Prime Time* (New York: Pantheon Books, 1985), 23.

29. Timothy Havens, *Black Television Travels* (New York: NYU Press, 2013), 79.

30. John Caldwell, *Production Culture: Industrial Reflexivity and Critical Practice in Film and Television* (Durham, NC: Duke University Press, 2008).

31. Havens, *Black Television Travels*, 4.

32. Havens, 172.

33. Jennifer Holt notes that 414 deals were struck, worth a combined total of $42 billion. They include the Time Warner merger for $9.1 billion and the Sony-Columbia-Tristar deal for $4.8 billion. Jennifer Holt, *Empires of Entertainment: Media Industries and the Politics of Deregulation, 1980–1996* (New

Brunswick, NJ: Rutgers University Press, 2011), 18; Thomas Schatz, "The Studio System and Conglomerate Hollywood," in *The Contemporary Hollywood Film Industry,* ed. Paul McDonald and Janet Wasko (Malden, MA: Blackwell Publishing, 2008), 26.

34. Quotes from Hilary de Vries, "Batman Battles for Big Money," *New York Times,* February 5, 1989, Film; Jack Mathews, "Batman, the Gamble," *Los Angeles Times,* June 18, 1989; Brian Alexander, "Comic Artists Grin as Hollywood Turns Kids' Stuff Green," *Los Angeles Times,* May 16, 1989. A Marvel writer/artist adds: "Keep your fingers crossed. A bunch of bad movies could come out and kill off [the trend] for the next 20 years." Pat Broeske, "Those Mean Guys from the Comics," *Los Angeles Times,* December 11, 1988.

35. Anne Thompson, "Field of Dreams: 15th Annual Grosses Gloss," *Film Comment* 26, no. 2 (March 1990): 59; "Batman," *Box Office Mojo,* www.boxofficemojo.com/movies/?page=main&id=batman.htm.

36. Holt, *Empires of Entertainment,* 122. Studio head Terry Semel noted that "it was the first time we utilized the whole machine of the company. The marketing, the tie-ins, the merchandising, the international." Quoted in Schatz, "Studio System and Conglomerate Hollywood," 28.

37. Richard Woodward, "Comics as Inspiration: Are We Having Fun Yet?," *New York Times,* April 23, 1989, sec. H.

38. Alexander, "Comic Artists Grin"; Fleming, "Turtles, 'Toons and Toys 'R' In."

39. Janet Maslin, "Comics' Heroes Are Dwarfed by Movies," *New York Times,* July 1, 1990, sec. A.

40. Jack Mathews, "The Class of '90: Handicapping Hollywood," *Los Angeles Times,* May 27, 1990.

41. Thompson, "Field of Dreams," 64.

42. Mathews, "Class of '90."

43. Anne Thompson, "Flatliners: The 16th Annual Grosses Gloss," *Film Comment* 27, no. 2 (March 1991): 30; Michael Fleming, "Gumshoe on Trail of Caped Crusader," *Variety,* June 13, 1990, Spotlight: Marketing.

44. Patrick Goldstein, "Jeffrey Katzenberg's Notorious Memo: How Does It Hold Up 20 Years Later?," *Los Angeles Times, The Big Picture* (blog), February 10, 2011, http://latimesblogs.latimes.com/the_big_picture/2011/02/jeffrey-katzenbergs-notorious-memo-how-does-it-hold-up-20-years-later.html.

45. Jeffrey Katzenberg, "The World Is Changing: Some Thoughts on Our Business," Memo, January 11, 1991, www.lettersofnote.com/2011/11/some-thoughts-on-our-business.html.

46. The quote is from Mike Medavoy, chairman of TriStar. Bernard Weintraub, "The Talk of Hollywood: Though a Year Old, Disney Memo Still Provokes Gossip," *New York Times,* February 11, 1992.

47. Disney's next two dismal quarterly earnings reports would reveal Katzenberg's folly whether he admitted to it preemptively or not. Jeanie Kasindorf, "Mickey Mouse Me at Disney," *New York Magazine,* October 7, 1991. Blockbusters had performed poorly across the board while more modest films like *Home Alone* had proved huge hits; Katzenberg vowed to learn from this mistake. Disney's own *Pretty Woman* had greatly exceeded expectations, so while

Katzenberg seemed more preoccupied with his failures than his successes, he was sure to point to that winning film as a model for future projects. For the overall performance of blockbusters, see Edward Silver, "The Highs and Lows of Future Special Effects Movies," *Los Angeles Times,* March 25, 1991.

48. Katzenberg, "Katzenberg Memo."

49. Kasindorf, "Mickey Mouse Me at Disney."

50. Katzenberg's boss at Disney said it was "a kind of map" for the company's future, and Bob Daly at Warner Bros. claimed that everyone had "more or less" come "to the same conclusion." Weintraub, "Talk of Hollywood."

51. Paul Richter, "Struggle for Independents," *Los Angeles Times,* March 4, 1990; Silver, "Highs and Lows of Future Special Effects Movies"; Richard Stevenson, "Taming Hollywood's Spending Monster," *New York Times,* April 14, 1991, sec. A; Alan Citron, "Blockbusters Lose Box Office Grip," *Los Angeles Times,* July 19, 1991, Business.

52. Among the films that came out of the deal were *True Lies* (1994), *Titanic* (1997), and *Avatar* (2009). David Fox, "Fox Signs Cameron to $500 Million Deal," *Los Angeles Times,* April 22, 1992.

53. Harold Vogel, *Entertainment Industry Economics: A Guide for Financial Analysis,* 9th ed. (Cambridge, UK: Cambridge University Press, 2015), 132–34.

54. Alongside its motivational calls to action, Katzenberg's 1991 manifesto had also made strong recommendations along these very lines. Advocating films that promised "considerable upside potential with minimal downside risk," Katzenberg was asking his fellow executives to pursue deals that were not just leaner, but smarter. Other studios were pursuing a similar strategy. At Paramount, CEO Sumner Redstone began requiring that at least 25 percent of a film's financing come from outside sources. Edward Epstein, *The Big Picture: Money and Power in Hollywood* (New York: Random House, 2005), 112.

55. Bill Todman, Jr., author's interview, phone, March 6, 2018.

56. Edward Epstein, *The Hollywood Economist: The Hidden Financial Reality behind the Movies,* 2nd ed. (Brooklyn: Melville House, 2012), 114.

57. Robert Marich, "Cannon Ran, Stumbled, Wouldn't Call It Quits . . . ," *Variety,* October 5, 1988.

58. Richter, "Struggle for Independents."

59. The near collapse of Carolco, after its huge success with *T2* (TriStar Pictures, 1991), for example, added to Katzenberg's memo in scaring off Hollywood insiders from big budgets. Weintraub, "Talk of Hollywood."

60. Marich, "Cannon Ran, Stumbled . . . "

61. Jim Sulski, "Heroes on the Cheap," *Chicago Tribune,* May 11, 1993.

62. The company used a tax haven in the Dutch Antilles and an amortization scheme that made every film, even the flops, look like an asset. These efforts achieved for Cannon a staggeringly low 2 percent tax rate in 1984 and attracted $300 million in three years of debt offerings from eager Wall Street investors. Marich, "Cannon Ran, Stumbled . . . "

63. Michael MacCambridge, "Cannon Suffers More Losses in Quarter as Net Worth Sinks," *Variety,* September 2, 1987.

64. Marich, "Cannon Ran, Stumbled . . . "

65. Michael Hiltzik, "A Tangled Web of Deal Making," *Los Angeles Times,* August 29, 1998, Saturday Journal edition; Shawn Levy, "Distribution Profile: The View from Golan's Heights," *Boxoffice,* February 1, 1990.

66. Jordan Raphael and Tom Spurgeon, *Stan Lee and the Rise and Fall of the American Comic Book* (Chicago: Chicago Review Press, 2003), 239; Sulski, "Heroes on the Cheap."

67. Robert Ito, "Fantastic Faux!," *Los Angeles Magazine,* March 2005.

68. Richard Klein, "New World Buys Marvel Comics, Becomes Prominent in Animation," *Variety,* November 26, 1986.

69. Howe tells a story describing how New World's president Bob Rehme thought he had just bought Superman instead of Spider-Man, and was rather disappointed by the mistake. Sean Howe, *Marvel Comics: The Untold Story* (New York: HarperCollins, 2012), 295.

70. Kathryn Harris, "Real Cliffhanger: Will New World Be the Next Financial Horror in Hollywood?," *Los Angeles Times,* March 6, 1988; Richard Stevenson, "New World's New Order," *New York Times,* May 15, 1988.

71. Amy Dawes, "It's a New Future for New World Pictures," *Variety,* December 28, 1988.

72. In October, a month before the sale, New World had been aggressively pitching comic book projects for television, prompting the *New York Times* to run a piece on the probable rise of superheroes in Hollywood. It seems likely that, for Sloan and Kupin, this article appearing in the press was more important than the actual projects it covered. Aljean Harmetz, "Superheroes' Battleground: Prime Time," *New York Times,* October 11, 1988, Arts.

73. Kathleen Hughes, "Perelman, Outbidding Parretti, Agrees to Acquire New World for $145 Million," *Wall Street Journal,* April 11, 1989, B.

74. Lawrence Cohn, "Film Industry's Course in 1988 Was More an Amble Than a March," *Variety,* January 11, 1989.

75. Kevin Goldman, "New Line Cinema Finds Itself a Survivor—Company Builds Success with Low-Budget Movies," *Wall Street Journal,* July 31, 1990; Geraldine Fabrikant, "Finding Success in Movie Niches," *New York Times,* April 4, 1990.

76. Steve Fore, "Golden Harvest Films and the Hong Kong Movie Industry in the Realm of Globalization," *Velvet Light Trap* 34 (Fall 1994): 40–58; John Hazelton, "New Line Turns Turtle," *Screen International,* August 12, 1989.

77. Schatz, "Studio System and Conglomerate Hollywood," 29.

78. Thompson, "Flatliners," 30.

79. Many anecdotes confirm Perelman's lack of knowledge about comic books and likely motivation in purchasing the company. Howe, *Marvel Comics;* Raphael and Spurgeon, *Stan Lee;* Dan Raviv, *Comic Wars: How Two Tycoons Battled Over the Marvel Comics Empire—and Both Lost* (New York: Broadway Books, 2002). For Perelman's history with Revlon, see Tina Grant, ed., "History of Revlon Inc.," in *International Directory of Company Histories* (Chicago: St. James Press, 2004).

80. Paul Noglows, "Comic Book Heroes Flex Megapic Muscle," *Variety,* November 30, 1992, Weekly edition; Richard Harrington, "Stan Lee: Caught in Spidey's Web," *Washington Post,* February 4, 1992; Richard Turner,

"MCA's Theme-Park Division Licenses Marvel Comic Book and TV Characters," *Wall Street Journal*, June 20, 1994; Nancy Haas, "Marvel Superheroes Take Aim at Hollywood," *New York Times*, July 28, 1996, Investing.

81. Haas, "Superheroes Take Aim."

82. Paul Noglows, "Marvel Taps Toy Tsar to Cash In on Comic Craze," *Variety*, April 26, 1993, Finance; Alexandra Peers, "Perelman Scoops Up Marvel's Depressed Shares," *Wall Street Journal*, August 17, 1994.

83. Noglows, "Marvel Taps Toy Tsar."

84. Noglows, "Comic Book Heroes"; Colin Brown, "Disney, Time Warner in Line to Save Marvel," *Screen International*, November 22, 1996.

85. Diane Goldner, "Sassa the Survivor in Marvelous Morass," *Variety*, June 16, 1997, Weekly edition, Film.

86. Adam Bryant, "Pow! The Punches That Left Marvel Reeling," *New York Times*, May 24, 1998.

87. Raviv, *Comic Wars*, 39–41.

88. Raphael and Spurgeon, *Stan Lee*, 243; John Jackson Miller, "1995 Comic Book Sales to Comics Shops," Comichron, accessed March 29, 2018, www.comichron.com/monthlycomicssales/1995.html; Chuck Rozanski, "The Comics World Is Dictated by the Success of Marvel Comics," Tales from the Database (blog), *Mile High Comics*, 2002, www.milehighcomics.com/tales /cbg39.html.

89. Howe, *Marvel Comics*, 367–70.

90. Noglows, "Comic Book Heroes."

91. Some profits were earmarked to go directly to Perelman's holding company Andrews Group, which had borrowed more than $70 million to buy Marvel at the outset. Other funds went directly to banks that had loaned Marvel money for its expansion into trading cards, stickers, and toys. Bryant, "Punches That Left Marvel."

92. Haas, "Superheroes Take Aim"; Goldner, "Sassa the Survivor."

93. Standard & Poors relabeled the stock as "highly vulnerable to nonpayment." John Lippman, "Perelman's Andrews Group Restructures Bid for Toy Biz amid Trouble at Marvel," *Wall Street Journal*, November 21, 1996, Marketing & Media.

94. Bryant, "Punches That Left Marvel Reeling."

95. Bryant, "Punches That Left Marvel Reeling."

96. Many observers have assumed, perhaps wrongly, that Perelman's goal was empire-building and concluded that because he failed in this aspiration, he failed generally—despite the significant financial gains. Goldner, "Sassa the Survivor"; Bryant, "Punches That Left Marvel Reeling"; Raphael and Spurgeon, *Stan Lee*; Raviv, *Comic Wars*.

97. Perelman's Andrews Group was a holding company, and not a private equity fund. The latter typically invests other people's wealth and functions on a shorter time horizon. However, the brief eight years that Andrews Group ultimately owned Marvel resembles that shorter time horizon.

98. Andrew deWaard, "Derivative Media: The Financialization of Film, Television, and Popular Music, 2004–2016" (UCLA, 2017), 76, 150.

99. Brown, "Disney, Time Warner in Line to Save Marvel"; Goldner, "Sassa the Survivor."

100. Goldner, "Sassa the Survivor."

101. Goldner; Noglows, "Comic Book Heroes"; Peers, "Perelman Scoops Up."

102. Bryant, "Punches That Left Marvel"; "Marvel Plan to Merge With Toy Biz Passes Muster With Icahn," *Wall Street Journal*, July 31, 1998.

103. Rozanski, "How Could We Possibly Make a Bid for Marvel?" Tales from the Database (blog), *Mile High Comics*, www.milehighcomics.com/tales /cbg40.html.

104. Hiltzik, "Tangled Web of Deal Making."

105. Todman, author's interview.

106. Noglows, "Comic Book Heroes."

107. Goldner, "Sassa the Survivor."

108. Rozanski, "How Could We Possibly Make a Bid for Marvel?"

109. Goldner, "Sassa the Survivor."

110. Pat Broeske, "From the Comics to a Screen near You," *New York Times*, October 18, 1992, Film; Noglows, "Comic Book Heroes"; Michael Fleming, "Too Marvel-Ous For Words," *Variety*, April 14, 1997, Weekly edition, Inside Moves; David Seidman, "Blam! Comic-Book Agents Hit the Scene Entertainment," *Los Angeles Times*, November 29, 1994.

111. Andy Marx, "A Look inside Hollywood and the Movies: See You in the Comics," *Los Angeles Times*, March 1, 1992; Broeske, "From the Comics to a Screen near You"; Noglows, "Comic Book Heroes."

112. Barbara Maltby, "What Do Movie Producers Do?," *American Scholar* 65, no. 1 (Winter 1996): 34–39; Epstein, *Big Picture*, 133–38.

113. Gitlin, *Inside Prime Time*, 26; Douglas Gomery, "The New Hollywood: 1981–1999," in *Producing*, ed. Jon Lewis (New Brunswick, NJ: Rutgers University Press, 2016), 111.

114. Howe, "Avengers Assemble!"

115. Todman, author's interview.

116. Warner Bros. passed the request on to Paul Levitz at DC, who never learned exactly how or why the request originated. Levitz, author's interview.

117. Maltby, "What Do Movie Producers Do?," 37–38.

118. Fleming, "Turtles, 'Toons and Toys 'R' In." In 1992, momentum seems to have picked up with multiple announcements in the trades. See Harrington, "Stan Lee"; Broeske, "From the Comics to a Screen near You"; Noglows, "Comic Book Heroes."

119. Hiltzik, "Tangled Web of Deal Making"; Michael Hiltzik, "Studio Rights to Spider-Man Are Untangled," *Los Angeles Times*, March 2, 1999, Company Town.

120. Anita Busch, "Spider-Man Project Caught in Web of Lawsuits," *Variety*, August 8, 1994, Weekly edition; Janet Sphrintz, "Spider-Man Spins Legal Web," *Variety*, August 17, 1998, Weekly edition; Michael Hiltzik, "The Writers: Untangling the Web," *Los Angeles Times*, March 24, 2002, Magazine.

121. Hiltzik, "Tangled Web of Deal Making."

122. Peers, "Perelman Scoops Up"; Noglows, "Comic Book Heroes."

123. Busch, "Spider-Man Project Caught in Web of Lawsuits"; Sphrintz, "Spider-Man Spins Legal Web"; Hiltzik, "Tangled Web of Deal Making."

124. Hiltzik, "Tangled Web of Deal Making"; Hiltzik, "Writers."

125. Bloom, "Comic Capers Captivate Studios."

126. Levitz recalled the stacks of scripts. Levitz, author's interview. Jay Epstein confirms his memory, noting that the studio commissioned six writers for a Superman film between 1993 and 2003. Epstein, *Big Picture*, 136. As an assistant and creative executive at DC Comics between 2004 and 2006, I came across and read many different scripts for characters that had been stuck in development the prior ten or so years. At this time, the absence of bidding wars, or any competition at all, still created a serious obstacle for potential projects.

127. Judy Brennan, "*Mask* Makes Dark Horse Into Sure Bet," *Los Angeles Times,* July 31, 1994; Seidman, "Blam!"; Marx, "A Look inside Hollywood."

128. "History," Company Website, Dark Horse, 2016, accessed September 20, 2018, www.darkhorse.com/Company/History/.

129. *The Rocketeer,* interestingly, had played a prominent role in Katzenberg's memo. Although the executive disparaged other comic book films, he strongly supported this upcoming movie, budgeted at $35 million. With no big stars or participation deals, "all the money will be on the screen," he noted excitedly, encouraging Disney to find more mid-range films with breakout potential just like it. Proving Katzenberg's miscalculation, this film bombed, giving mid-range films a bad rap, including those based on comic books. Katzenberg, "Katzenberg Memo"; Peter Bart, "Katzenberg Manifesto Revisited," *Variety,* September 9, 1996, Columns.

130. Martin Barker and Kate Brooks, "Waiting for Dredd," *Sight and Sound,* August 1, 1995; Ealine Dutka, "Give This Guy $20 Million," *Los Angeles Times,* May 14, 1995.

131. Haas, "Superheroes Take Aim"; John Canemaker, "Slipsliding Between Animation and Reality," *New York Times,* November 24, 1996, Film; Janet Maslin, "Holy Iceberg! Dynamic Duo vs. Mr. Freeze," *New York Times,* June 20, 1997.

132. Paul Iorio, "The Next Wave: After the Successful Adaptation of 'Men in Black,' Producers Are Looking to Other Comic Books," *Los Angeles Times,* January 10, 1998.

133. Tom Russo, "Putting the X-Men to the Test," *Los Angeles Times,* July 2, 2000, Movies; Levitz, author's interview. *Men in Black* had come from a story published by Malibu Comics, one of the companies swept up by Marvel during Perelman's spending spree. But Malibu had optioned the property to Columbia before being bought by Marvel. It was also allowed to maintain its licensing operation independently, a factor that likely helped get the film out of development and into production. John Brodie, "A Marvel-Ous Acquisition," *Variety,* November 7, 1994, Weekly edition, Film; John Lippman, "Men in Black Puts Sony in the Green," *Wall Street Journal,* July 7, 1997.

134. Haas, "Superheroes Take Aim."

135. Noglows, "Comic Book Heroes"; Broeske, "From the Comics to a Screen near You"; Brown, "Disney, Time Warner in Line to Save Marvel";

Ryan Parker and Aaron Couch, "Wesley Snipes Reveals Untold Story behind His Black Panther Film," *Hollywood Reporter, Heat Vision* (blog), January 30, 2018, www.hollywoodreporter.com/heat-vision/black-panther-wesley-snipes-reveals-untold-story-behind-90s-film-1078868.

136. Robert Levine, "Does Whatever a Spider (and a CEO) Can," *New York Times,* June 27, 2004.

137. According to reports, budgets were up 500 percent in just fifteen years, and were ballooning out of control without necessarily achieving better results. Costly stars failed to deliver and expensive sequels were not attracting bigger audiences. Haas, "Superheroes Take Aim"; Leonard Klady, "Budgets in the Hot Zone: The Sum Also Rises," *Variety,* March 16, 1998, Weekly edition; Sharon Waxman, "Blockbuster or Endangered Species?," *Washington Post,* May 19, 1998; Lisa Bannon, "A Tough Summer for Big-Budget Movies," *Wall Street Journal,* September 4, 1998.

138. Bart, "Katzenberg Manifesto Revisited."

139. Leonard Klady, "Why Mega Flicks Click," *Variety,* November 25, 1996.

140. Klady, "Why Mega Flicks Click."

141. Chris Petrikin, "20th Climbs out of Fox Hole," *Variety,* September 7, 1998, Weekly edition. Around this time, Disney, for example, tried paying below-the-line workers on massive films like *Pearl Harbor* through deferments and was proudly and publicly rejecting any financing partners that reduced the studio's potential upside. Charles Lyons, "Blockbuster or Ball-Buster?," *Variety,* March 20, 2000.

142. In 1995, there were twenty-seven thousand screens in the United States. By 2001, there were thirty-eight thousand. At this point, a typical movie in wide release debuted on thirty-five hundred screens. Rick Lyman, "Even Blockbusters Find Fame Fleeting in a Multiplex Age," *New York Times,* August 13, 2001. With so many theaters with so many screens so close to each other, distributors had to abandon theatrical tiering, when films screened at cheaper second-run theaters several weeks after their initial release. James Bates, "Films' Big Openings Fade Fast, But Studios Cash In," *Los Angeles Times,* August 12, 2001; Vogel, *Entertainment Industry Economics,* 146.

143. By 2001, more and more of the industry's revenue was being earned in a shorter and shorter time frame. In the fallout of this shift, theater chains began declaring bankruptcy, filing claims with the SEC, and complaining publicly about their loss of leverage in negotiations with the big studios. Bates, "Films' Big Openings Fade Fast"; Lyman, "Even Blockbusters Find Fame Fleeting"; Vogel, *Entertainment Industry Economics,* 141–44.

144. Don Groves, "Hollywood Biggies Rule Overseas," *Variety,* January 6, 2003, Weekly edition, Film.

145. Levitz, author's interview; A. O. Scott, "Resigned to Another Blockbuster," *New York Times,* May 19, 2002; Jedidiah Leland, "More Is Less: Hollywood's Sequel Addiction Explained," *Film Comment,* February 2004; Eller and Bates, "Spider-Man Raises Bar for New Films."

146. The occasional breakout success inspired big studios to acquire or start their own "indie" units to handle this special category of film. Miramax (owned

by Disney), Sony Classics, Fox Searchlight and other similar distributors took over the handling of artistic, intelligent, low-budget films. Schatz, "System and Conglomerate Hollywood," 29–30.

147. Alisa Perren, *Indie, Inc.: Miramax and the Transformation of Hollywood in the 1990s* (Austin: University of Texas Press, 2012); Klady, "Why Mega Flicks Click"; Claudia Puig, "In Hollywood, Ever Bigger Is Better," *Los Angeles Times,* June 2, 1997, sec. F; Groves, "Hollywood Biggies Rule Overseas."

148. Katzenberg, "Katzenberg Memo."

149. Waxman, "Blockbuster or Endangered Species?"; Bannon, "A Tough Summer for Big-Budget Movies."

150. "Yearly Box Office," *Box Office Mojo,* accessed November 30, 2017, www.boxofficemojo.com/yearly/?view2 = ytdcompare; Scott Mendelson, "15 Years Ago, 'Godzilla' Was a Flop. By Today's Standards, It Would Be a Hit.," Forbes, May 20, 2013, www.forbes.com/sites/scottmendelson/2013/05/20/15-years-ago-godzilla-was-a-flop-by-todays-standards-it-would-be-a-hit/#31e61cb813f6.

151. Schatz, "Studio System and Conglomerate Hollywood," 35.

152. Sergio Sparviero, "Hollywood Creative Accounting: The Success Rate of Major Motion Pictures," *Media Industries* 2, no. 1 (2015): 31–32; Epstein, *Hollywood Economist,* 92.

153. Epstein, *Hollywood Economist,* 85.

154. Vogel, *Entertainment Industry Economics,* 128.

155. Many such formulas have been offered up over the years. See Anne Thompson, "The 12th Annual Grosses Gloss," *Film Comment* 23, no. 2 (April 1987): 68; Maltby, "What Do Movie Producers Do?"; Bannon, "Tough Summer for Big-Budget Movies."

156. Epstein, *Big Picture,* 107–25.

157. Sparviero, "Hollywood Creative Accounting."

158. Epstein, *Big Picture,* 120–22.

159. Sparviero, "Hollywood Creative Accounting," 27.

160. Howe, *Marvel Comics,* 398.

161. Michael Fleming, "Marvel Takes Cues from Its Superheroes," *Variety,* July 13, 1999.

162. Janet Sphrintz, "Inside Moves: Spider-Man Breaks Free of Legal Web," *Variety,* March 8, 1999; Kim Masters, "Marvel Studios' Origin Secrets Revealed by Mysterious Founder: History Was 'Rewritten,'" *Hollywood Reporter,* May 5, 2016, www.hollywoodreporter.com/features/marvel-studios-origin-secrets-revealed-889795.

163. John Lippman, "Sony, Marvel Look to a Different Web for Success: One Spun by Spider-Man," *Wall Street Journal,* March 2, 1999.

164. Leonard, "Calling All Superheroes."

165. Howe, "Avengers Assemble!"

166. Goldstein, "Cause for Marvel."

167. Levitz, author's interview.

168. Susanna Hamner, "Marvel Comics Leaps into Movie-Making," *CNN Money,* June 1, 2006, http://money.cnn.com/magazines/business2/business2_archive/2006/05/01/8375925/index.htm.

169. Masters, "Marvel Studios' Origin Secrets"; Boucher, "Spider-Man on Top."

170. Noglows, "Comic Book Heroes"; Fleming, "Too Marvel-Ous For Words"; Iorio, "Next Wave."

171. Bing, "F/X Turn New Page."

172. Bing, "F/X Turn New Page."

173. Todman, author's interview.

174. Marc Graser and Chris Petrikin, "Geek Gab Freaks Film Biz," *Variety,* October 18, 1999, Weekly edition.

175. Russo, "Putting the X-Men to the Test."

176. Russo; Bing, "F/X Turn New Page"; Todman, author's interview. In this regard, Fox was keeping with its reputation for cost-cutting. Their films' average budget was half the industry standard, and studio boss Bill Mechanic was proud of the accomplishment. Don Groves, "Fox's Mechanic Guards the Money House," *Variety,* November 15, 1999, Weekly edition, Inside Moves.

177. Patrick Goldstein, "In Box-Office Game, It's All About the Franchise Players," *Los Angeles Times,* November 20, 2001.

178. Jeff Jensen, "X-Men," *Entertainment Weekly,* July 21, 2000, http://ew.com/article/2000/07/21/x-men-0/.

179. Russo, "Putting the X-Men to the Test"; Bing, "F/X Turn New Page"; Jensen, "X-Men."

180. Richard Natale, "X-Men Help to Rescue Summer," *Los Angeles Times,* July 17, 2000.

181. Levine, "Does Whatever a Spider (and a CEO) Can."

182. Elvis Mitchell, "They Oughta Be in Pictures: Comic Book Heroes Are Naturals, but Too Often Films Fail Them," *New York Times,* July 25, 2000; Boucher, "Spider-Man on Top."

183. Goldstein, "Cause for Marvel."

184. Goldstein, "Box-Office Game," November 20, 2001.

185. Glenn Gaslin, "The Disappearing Comic Book," *Los Angeles Times,* July 17, 2001; Michael Mallory, "Comics Fans Live a Film Fantasy," *Los Angeles Times,* July 24, 2001; Tony Perry, "The Cannes of Comics: A San Diego Gathering for Makers and Consumers," *Los Angeles Times,* August 5, 2002, sec. F.

186. Jonathan Bing, "A Tangled Web: Spidey Suitors Evaded Snare of Rights Snafu," *Variety,* May 20–26, 2002, Weekly edition, Inside Moves; Laura Holson, "With Spider-Man and Others, Sony Seeks to Revive Fortunes," *New York Times,* May 6, 2002; Hiltzik, "Studio Rights to Spider-Man Are Untangled."

187. Sufiya Abdur-Rahman, "Spider-Man Comic Fans Say He Passes Screen Test," *Los Angeles Times,* May 6, 2002.

188. Eller and Bates, "Spider-Man Raises Bar for New Films."

189. Horn, "Daredevil Leap."

190. Vogel, *Entertainment Industry Economics,* 134.

191. Sharon Swart, "Pic Biz Surfs Next Wave: Private Equity Steps Up as Germans, Brits Shift Schemes," *Variety,* May 9, 2005; Lindsay Chaney, "Studios Tap Equity: Fund Biz Suddenly Hot on Hollywood," *Variety,* August 8, 2005.

192. Because equity fund managers lacked insider knowledge about how the film business operates, they "made perfect civilian recruits for Hollywood" as it pursued its dream of risk-free filmmaking. Epstein, *Hollywood Economist*, 92–94.

193. Laura Holson, "Warner Venture with Investors," *New York Times*, June 22, 2005; Jill Goldsmith, "Studios in a Dash for Cash," *Variety*, November 21, 2005.

194. Jeffrey Ulin, *The Business of Media Distribution: Monetizing Film, TV, and Video Content*, 2nd ed. (New York: Focal Press, 2014), 27–28.

195. Chaney, "Studios Tap Equity"; Goldsmith, "Studios in a Dash for Cash."

196. DeWaard, "Derivative Media," 162. Also see Vogel, *Entertainment Industry Economics*, 166.

197. Ulin, *Business of Media Distribution*, 111.

198. In 2002, with the release of *Spider-Man*, merchandising revenue was indeed up, with sales reaching $300 million. Leonard, "Calling All Superheroes."

199. The deal was for a dozen films at a mid-range budget. Artisan agreed to fully finance and distribute the movies, taking a fee off the top, but splitting all revenue. These were far better terms than Marvel had been getting as a licensor, reflecting both the company's growing clout and the industry-wide shift in financing. The deal ultimately produced just two films (*The Punisher* in 2004 and *Man Thing* in 2005). Michael Fleming, "Artisan Deal a Real Marvel," *Variety*, May 16, 2000, http://variety.com/2000/film/news/artisan-deal-a-real-marvel-1117781709/; Bing, "F/X Turn New Page"; Masters, "Marvel Studios' Origin Secrets."

200. Masters, "Marvel Studios' Origin Secrets"; Howe, "Avengers Assemble!"

201. Hamner, "Marvel Comics Leaps into Movie-Making"; Merissa Marr, "In New Film Venture, Marvel Hopes to Be Its Own Superhero," *Wall Street Journal*, April 28, 2005.

202. Leonard, "Calling All Superheroes"; Masters, "Marvel Studios' Origin Secrets."

203. Masters, "Marvel Studios' Origin Secrets"; Marr, "In New Film Venture, Marvel Hopes to Be Its Own Superhero." Contemporaneous reports of the deal were far less laudatory. See Sharon Waxman, "Marvel Wants to Flex Its Own Heroic Muscles as a Moviemaker," *The New York Times*, June 18, 2007, Media, www.nytimes.com/2007/06/18/business/media/18marvel.html.

204. David Goldman, "Disney Buys Marvel Entertainment for $4 Billion," CNN Money, August 31, 2009, http://money.cnn.com/2009/08/31/news/companies/disney_marvel/; Masters, "Marvel Studios' Origin Secrets."

205. For a fairly typical analysis along these lines, see Martin Flanagan, Andrew Livingstone, and Mike McKenny, *The Marvel Studios Phenomenon: Inside a Transmedia Universe* (New York: Bloomsbury, 2016).

206. Bloom, "Comic Capers Captivate Studios."

207. Notably, when Katzenberg left Disney in 1994 to form Dreamworks, he pursued not the modest films for which he advocated in 1991, but massive animated features just like the ones that brought him success at Disney.

208. Horn, "Daredevil Leap."

209. Mitchell, "They Oughta Be in Pictures"; Boucher, "X-Men's Secret Power"; Gaslin, "Disappearing Comic Book"; Thompson, "Spider Stratagem"; Horn, "Daredevil Leap."

210. Holson, "With Spider-Man and Others."

211. Heidi MacDonald, "Hollywood Mystery: Someone Is Trying to Take Kevin Feige Down a Notch or Two," *The Beat: The News Blog of Comics Culture,* June 6, 2016, www.comicsbeat.com/hollywood-mystery-someone-is-trying-to-take-kevin-feige-down-a-notch-or-two/.

212. Hamner, "Marvel Comics Leaps into Movie-Making."

213. Fleming, "Marvel Takes Cues from Its Superheroes"; Goldstein, "Cause for Marvel"; Raviv, *Comic War;* Levine, "Does Whatever a Spider (and a CEO) Can"; Leonard, "Calling All Superheroes."

214. Leonard, "Calling All Superheroes."

215. N. R. Kleinfield, "Superheroes' Creators Wrangle," *New York Times,* October 13, 1979.

216. Broeske, "Those Mean Guys from the Comics."

217. Howe, *Marvel Comics,* 356.

218. Haas, "Superheroes Take Aim"; Boucher, "Spider-Man on Top."

219. Derek Johnson, "Cinematic Destiny: Marvel Studios and the Trade Stories of Industrial Convergence," *Cinema Journal* 52, no. 1 (Fall 2012): 1–24.

220. DeWaard, "Derivative Media," 2, 5.

EPILOGUE

1. See, for example, Alison Flood, "DC Comics Promises to Hire More Women after Reader Backlash," *The Guardian,* August 1, 2011, Books, www .theguardian.com/books/2011/aug/01/dc-comics-women-writers-creators; Olivia Waxman, "Chris Evans, Jeremy Renner Call Black Widow a 'Slut' and 'Whore,'" *Time,* April 23, 2015, http://time.com/3832841/chris-evans-jeremy-renner-scarlett-johansson-black-widow/; Kelly Lawler, "Whitewashing Controversy Still Haunts Doctor Strange," *USA Today,* November 7, 2016, www .usatoday.com/story/life/entertainthis/2016/11/07/doctor-strange-whitewash-ing-ancient-one-tilda-swinton-fan-critical-reaction/93416130/; Kieran Shiach, "DC's New Age of Heroes Suffers from an Old-School Lack of Diversity," *CBR.com,* December 6, 2017, www.cbr.com/dc-new-age-of-heroes-suffers-from-lack-of-diversity/; Kelly Kanayama, "Marvel Is Wrong about Diversity Killing Its Comics," *Nerdist,* April 3, 2017, https://nerdist.com/marvel-diversity-comics-david-gabriel-wrong/.

2. For some insight into this power and how Disney uses it, see Ricardo Lopez, "Disney vs. Netflix: Can Bob Iger Challenge the Streaming Giant?," *Variety,* August 11, 2017, https://variety.com/2017/film/news/disney-vs-netflix-bob-iger-challenge-streaming-giant-1202524308/; Erich Schwartzel, "Disney Lays Down the Law for Theaters on 'Star Wars: The Last Jedi,'" *Wall Street Journal,* November 1, 2017, Business; Tom Brueggemann, "How Disney Is Changing Hollywood Rules," IndieWire, November 11, 2017, www.indiewire .com/2017/11/disney-star-wars-the-last-jedi-hollywood-rules-exhibitors-theater-owners-1201894552/.

3. There have been a number of high-profile firings and removals in the wake of #MeToo, including John Lasseter (Disney/Pixar), Brett Ratner (on *Wonder Woman*), and Eddie Berganza (DC Comics), alongside an effort to bring in more female leaders. New policies and other changes within the major guilds and internally at both Disney and Time Warner seem promising. See Erich Schwartzel, "Disney Names Directors of 'Up' and 'Frozen' to Head Animation Units," *Wall Street Journal,* June 19, 2018; Sissi Cao, "#MeToo Movement Impels Companies to Rethink Sexual Harassment Policies," *Observer,* January 18, 2018, http://observer.com/2018/01/metoo-movement-companies-rethink-sexual-harassment-policies/; "Pirates and #MeToo," *Economist,* March 15, 2018, www.economist.com/united-states/2018/03/15/pirates-and-metoo; Danette Chavez, "Wonder Woman 2 Will Be 1st Film to Adopt New PGA Anti-Harassment Guidelines," *The AV Club,* January 23, 2018, www.avclub.com/wonder-woman-2-will-be-1st-film-to-adopt-new-pga-anti-h-1822353232.

4. There has been no shortage of writing on the significance of both *Wonder Woman* and *Black Panther,* and the nuanced ways in which they communicated their messages. For example, see Carrie Wittmer, "Why 'Wonder Woman' Matters to Women—and Is Already Changing the Movies We Watch," *Business Insider,* June 3, 2017, www.businessinsider.com/wonder-woman-matters-to-women-movies-2017–6; Alan Jenkins, "Black Panther, Wonder Woman and the Power of Representation," *Ebony,* July 18, 2017, www.ebony.com/life/black-panther-wonder-woman-representation; Tre Johnson, "Black Superheroes Matter: Why a 'Black Panther' Movie Is Revolutionary," *Rolling Stone,* February 16, 2018, www.rollingstone.com/movies/news/black-superheroes-matter-why-black-panther-is-revolutionary-w509105.

5. For a visual of this merger activity, as it stood in the summer of 2018, see Edmund Lee and Peter Kafka, "Here's Why Comcast Says It Should Own Fox's Business," *Recode,* May 23, 2018, www.recode.net/2018/5/23/17385214/comcast-versus-disney-fox-hulu.

6. Andrew Wallenstein, "Shonda Rhimes, Ryan Murphy Megadeals Left Producers Money Hungry, TV Execs Say," *Variety,* March 23, 2018, https://variety.com/2018/tv/news/shonda-rhimes-ryan-murphy-megadeals-left-producers-money-hungry-tv-execs-say-1202735524/; Nellie Andreeva, "Oprah Winfrey Partners with Apple for Original Content," *Deadline,* June 15, 2018, https://deadline.com/2018/06/oprah-winfrey-content-partnership-apple-for-original-programming-1202411370/; Ted Johnson, "AT&T-Time Warner Trial: Turner CEO Highlights Threat of Google, Facebook to Ad Business," *Variety,* March 28, 2018, https://variety.com/2018/politics/news/tat-time-warner-antitrust-turner-john-marti-1202738772/; Lisa Richwine, "AT&T Promises Fewer Ads, Tailored Programing After Merger," *Reuters,* June 18, 2018, www.reuters.com/article/us-at-t-stankey/att-executive-promises-fewer-ads-on-newly-acquired-time-warner-networks-idUSKBN1JE2NO; Bloomberg, "Netflix Is Selling $1.9 Billion of Junk Bonds to Fund More Shows," *Los Angeles Times,* April 23, 2018, www.latimes.com/business/hollywood/la-fi-ct-netflix-debt-20180423-story.html.

Index

Page numbers in italic refer to illustrations.

juvenile delinquency. *See* Senate
Subcommittee Hearings on Juvenile
Delinquency

Kable News Co., 80, 83, 141
Kael, Pauline, 110
Kahn, Jenette, 115–16, 119–20
Kanter, Al, 81
Kapur, Jyotsna, 133
Katzenberg, Jeffrey, 194–96, 211–14, 224,
292n54
Kefauver, Estes, 46, 48, 53, 59–60, 64
King, Nadine French, *140*
Kinney National Services, 34, 113–15,
264n118. *See also* Warner
Communications Inc.
Kirby, Jack, 6, 32, 108, 126–28
Krigstein, Bernie, 96
Kupin, Larry, 199–200, 293n72
Kurtz, Leslie, 21
Kurtzman, Harvey, 55, *158*

labor practices, 119–21. *See also* working
conditions
Larkin, Brian, 10–11
Leader News Co., 80, 81–82, 86
Lee, Jim, 129, 276n135
Lee, Stan, 32; audience strategy, 108, 155;
creative labor, 114, 126; creator rights,
119; industry lore, 218, 224, 226;
selling film rights, 116, 190, 200, 205;
women, 148–49. *See also* Marvel
Comics
Legendary Pictures, 221–24
legislation against comic books, 48, 67
legitimation of comic books, 109–12,
137–38, 153–61, 173–77, 230–31
Lev Gleason Publications, 54–55, 80, 83
Levine, Elana, 161
Levine, Lawrence, 177
Levitz, Paul, 120, 124, 146, 181, 209. *See
also* DC Comics
licensing, 2–4, 6–7, 20–24, 45, 137;
corporate media conglomerates, 90,
92–94, 100, 105, 112–16, 119–20,
129–30, 264n118; creator rights,
119–20, 125, 126; crisis and experimentation era, 31–39, 77, 81, 112–14, 116;
establishing era, 24–30; film financing,
205, 215–18; financial speculation, 182,
199–204, 219, 222; institutionalization
era, 39–43; periodization of comic book
history, 14, 15, 18–20; transmedia, 12,
153–54

Licensing Corporation of America (LCA),
33–34, 113, 264n118. *See also*
Superman
Liebowitz, Jack, 22–23, 25, 33–35, 53, 68,
77, 79, 98, 113–14. *See also* National
Comics
LL Cool J, 210
Lois & Clark (1993–1997 TV series), 40,
137
Lois Lane, 148
Lone Ranger, 29
Lopes, Paul, 48
Lotz, Amanda, 78
lowbrow media, 30–39, 93, 97, 104–5, 108,
110–11, 130
low-budget films, 213
lurid comics, 54–56

MacDonald, Dwight, 96–97, 174–75
Mad Magazine, 82, 86, 115, 157
magazine distribution, 72, 74–75, 78, 79,
82–83, 87
Magazine Enterprises, 85–86
Magazine Management Co. *See* Marvel
Comics
Maisel, David, 222–23, 223, 225–27
Maltby, Barbara, 160
manga, 41–42
Marvel Cinematic Universe, 2, 42–43, 130,
131, 168–69, 185, 223–24
Marvel Comics: audience strategy, 108,
140, 151, 177; bankruptcy, 41, 202–4,
216–17; comic book crisis, 68, 79, 81,
86; comic book sales, 176, 181, 279n30;
creator rights, 105, 119, 129–30; crisis
and experimentation era, 32; development hell, 204–208, 210–11, 219; as
Disney subsidiary, 42–43, 168–69,
224–26, 232–34; distribution, 79, 81,
146, 233–34; establishing era, 25, 32;
film financing, 196, 197–201, 204–6,
209, 215–17, 222–24, 227; industry
lore, 224–27; Jack Kirby lawsuit,
126–28; licensing, 35–36, 112, 200,
205, 216–17; media conglomeration,
34–35, 114, 200, 204; rise of comic
book film, 38, 179, 185, 227; Ron
Perelman, 41, 181, 200–204; social
relevance, 154–55; women, 140,
148–49; working conditions, 114,
116, 126
Marvel Enterprises, 204
Marvel Entertainment, 199
Marvel Incentive Plan, 119